LITIGATING WOMEN

This edited collection, written by both established and new researchers, reveals the experiences of litigating women across premodern Europe and captures the current state of research in this ever-growing field.

Individually, the chapters offer an insight into the motivations and strategies of women who engaged in legal action in a wide range of courts, from local rural and urban courts, to ecclesiastical courts and the highest jurisdictions of crown and parliament. Collectively, the focus on individual women litigants – rather than how women were defined by legal systems – highlights continuities in their experiences of justice, while also demonstrating the unique and intersecting factors that influenced each woman's negotiation of the courts. Spanning a broad chronology and a wide range of contexts, these studies also offer a valuable insight into the practices and priorities of the many courts under discussion that goes beyond our focus on women litigants.

Drawing on archival research from England, Scotland, Ireland, France, the Low Countries, Central and Eastern Europe, and Scandinavia, *Litigating Women* is the perfect resource for students and scholars interested in legal studies and gender in medieval and early modern Europe.

Teresa Phipps is a social historian of late medieval England and Wales, interested in women, law, and urban society. Publications include a monograph on women and justice in late medieval English towns (2020), a volume on medieval town courts (2019) and articles on coverture, trespass, and credit.

Deborah Youngs is a Professor of History at Swansea University, UK, with research interests in the social, legal and cultural histories of late medieval England and Wales. She is currently researching and publishing on women's litigation in the English court of Star Chamber.

LITIGATING WOMEN

Gender and Justice in
Europe, c.1300–c.1800

Edited by
Teresa Phipps and Deborah Youngs

LONDON AND NEW YORK

Cover credit: F.39r Conjugal Law, an adulterous wife appearing in court, from 'Justiniani in Fortiatum' (vellum) © Biblioteca Monasterio del Escorial, Madrid, Spain/Bridgeman Images

First published 2022
by Routledge
2 Park Square, Milton Park, Abingdon, Oxon OX14 4RN

and by Routledge
605 Third Avenue, New York, NY 10158

Routledge is an imprint of the Taylor & Francis Group, an informa business

© 2022 selection and editorial matter, Teresa Phipps and Deborah Youngs; individual chapters, the contributors

The right of Teresa Phipps and Deborah Youngs to be identified as the authors of the editorial material, and of the authors for their individual chapters, has been asserted in accordance with sections 77 and 78 of the Copyright, Designs and Patents Act 1988.

All rights reserved. No part of this book may be reprinted or reproduced or utilised in any form or by any electronic, mechanical, or other means, now known or hereafter invented, including photocopying and recording, or in any information storage or retrieval system, without permission in writing from the publishers.

Trademark notice: Product or corporate names may be trademarks or registered trademarks, and are used only for identification and explanation without intent to infringe.

British Library Cataloguing-in-Publication Data
A catalogue record for this book is available from the British Library

Library of Congress Cataloging-in-Publication Data
A catalog record has been requested for this book

ISBN: 978-0-367-23030-2 (hbk)
ISBN: 978-0-367-23028-9 (pbk)
ISBN: 978-0-429-27803-7 (ebk)

DOI: 10.4324/9780429278037

Typeset in Bembo
by codeMantra

CONTENTS

List of figures vii
List of tables ix
Acknowledgements xi
List of contributors xiii

    Introduction: Teresa Phipps and Deborah Youngs   1

1 Mothers and daughters and sons, in the law: Family conflict, legal stories, and women's litigation in late medieval Marseille   14
  Susan McDonough

2 Consent and coercion: Women's use of marital consent laws as legal defence in late medieval Paris   32
  Kristi DiClemente

3 Shades of consent: Abduction for marriage and women's agency in the late medieval Low Countries   48
  Chanelle Delameillieure

4 Female litigants in secular and ecclesiastical courts in the lands of the Bohemian Crown, c.1300–c.1500   63
  Michaela Antonín Malaníková

vi Contents

5 **Widowhood and attainder in medieval Ireland: the case of Margaret Nugent**   81
 Sparky Booker

6 **Choosing Chancery? Women's petitions to the late medieval court of Chancery**   99
 Cordelia Beattie

7 **Gendered roles and female litigants in north-eastern England, 1300–1530**   116
 Peter L. Larson

8 **Property over patriarchy? Remarried widows as litigants in the records of Glasgow's commissary court, 1615–1694**   133
 Rebecca Mason

9 **Women negotiating wealth: gender, law and arbitration in early modern southern Tyrol**   152
 Margareth Lanzinger and Janine Maegraith

10 **A litigating widow and wife in early modern Sweden: Lady Elin Johansdotter [Månesköld] and her family circle**   173
 Mia Korpiola

11 **Women litigants in early eighteenth-century Ireland**   193
 Mary O'Dowd

12 **Hidden in plain sight: female litigators, reproductive lives, archival practices and early modern French historiography**   209
 Julie Hardwick

Combined bibliography   223
Index   247

FIGURES

10.1 Simplified Family Tree of Lady Elin Johansdotter [Månesköld]   175

TABLES

4.1	Typology of lawsuits of marital disputes in the Judicial Act Books of the vicar general's court, years 1421–1424	69
4.2	Typology of lawsuits of marital disputes in the Judicial Act Books of the vicar general's court, years 1427–1437 (based on *Zittauer Urkundenbuch*)	70
7.1	Manors and sources of north-eastern England examined	118
8.1	Types of court cases dealt with by Glasgow's Commissary Court, 1615–1645 and 1658–1694	140
8.2	Sex of pursuers in litigation in Glasgow's Commissary Court, 1615–1645 and 1658–1694	141
8.3	Sex of defenders in litigation in Glasgow's Commissary Court, 1615–1645 and 1658–1694	141
8.4	Marital and relational status of female litigants in Glasgow's Commissary Court, 1615–1645 and 1658–1694	142

ACKNOWLEDGEMENTS

This volume originated in the AHRC project 'Women negotiating the boundaries of justice' (Ref: AH/L013568/1) which was based at Swansea University (from 2014 to 2018), in collaboration with colleagues at the universities of Cardiff and Glasgow. Such an opportunity comes around rarely, and we are grateful to the AHRC for providing us not only with the means to finance research activities but to work alongside a stimulating and supportive group of researchers. We would like to thank Alex Shepard, Garthine Walker, Sparky Booker, Emma Cavell, Rebecca Mason and Elizabeth Howard for many thought-provoking conversations and their excellent company.

In a world of ongoing restrictions due to the Covid-19 pandemic, we now feel even luckier that we were able to travel freely to conferences and organise various events for the project, because it was these occasions that prompted this volume and connected us with many of the contributors. They include those who participated in our two-day symposium in Swansea (2017), and in our sessions at the International Medieval Congress, Leeds (2018). We also benefited from stimulating discussions in panels/workshops organised by the project team at the Berkshire Conference (Hofstra, 2017), the Economic History Society's Women's Committee (Swansea, 2017) and the Social History Society Conference (Keele, 2018). Particular thanks are due to Trish Skinner and Tim Stretton for the considerable support they have given both to the project and to us as individuals. We are also indebted to the readers of the proposal for comments that helped to broaden the scope of the volume. Support for the project – intellectual, practical and personal – also came from kind colleagues at Swansea University, with our especial thanks to John Spurr, Sam Blaxland, Catherine Rozier and Charlie Rozier. Finally, we are very grateful to the editors at Routledge for their encouragement and flexibility as we worked to bring the volume together at the height of the Covid pandemic, and to all the contributors for their excellent chapters and commitment to the volume at an extremely challenging time, both personally and professionally.

CONTRIBUTORS

Cordelia Beattie is senior lecturer in medieval history at the University of Edinburgh, Scotland. She has published widely on medieval women and gender, and is the author of *Medieval Single Women* (2007) and editor of the four-volume *Women in the Medieval World* (2017).

Sparky Booker is assistant professor of history at Dublin City University, Ireland. She specialises in the social history of late medieval Ireland. Her publications in the area include articles on medieval sumptuary law (*Speculum*, 2021) and the Irish clergy (*IHS*, 2014) and an award-winning monograph, *Cultural Exchange and Identity in Late Medieval Ireland* (2018).

Chanelle Delameillieure is a postdoctoral researcher at KU Leuven, Belgium. Her research concerns medieval gender and family history, with a focus on marriage making and intergenerational family relations. She has published in *Journal of Family History* (2017) and co-edited a book (in Dutch) on medieval women (2019).

Kristi DiClemente is associate professor at Mississippi University for Women, USA, where she teaches ancient and medieval history. Her research examines marriage disputes in the Parisian archdeacon's court to uncover the married lives of medieval women, and their access to justice in fourteenth- and fifteenth-century Paris.

Julie Hardwick is John E. Green Regents Professor of history and a Distinguished Teaching Professor at the University of Texas-Austin, USA. Her most recent book is *Sex in an Old Regime City: young workers and intimacy in France, 1660–1789* (Oxford, University Press, 2020). For full details of her current and past work, see https://liberalarts.utexas.edu/history/faculty/jholwell.

Mia Korpiola is professor of legal history at the University of Turku, Finland (Faculty of Law). Her most important publications include *Between Betrothal and Bedding* (2009), *Regional Variations in Matrimonial Law and Custom in Europe, 1150–1600* (ed., 2011) and *Legal Literacy in Premodern European Societies* (ed., 2019).

Margareth Lanzinger is professor of economic and social history at the University of Vienna, Austria. Her work focusses on kinship, family and marriage, property, inheritance practices and marital property regimes, including co-edited volumes on the domestic sphere (*The Routledge History of the Domestic Sphere in Europe*, 2020) and on negotiations of gender and property (*Negotiations of Gender and Property through Legal Regimes*, 2021).

Peter L. Larson is associate professor of history at the University of Central Florida, USA. His research focusses on late medieval and early modern northeastern England, and he is author of the forthcoming *Reconsidering the Great Transition: Community and Economic Growth in County Durham, 1349–1660*.

Janine Maegraith is research associate at the Department of Economic and Social History, University of Vienna, Austria, and works on the project "The Role of Wealth in Defining and Constituting Kinship Spaces". Her research focusses on early modern social and economic European history, specifically Tyrol and Upper Swabia. She has recently published on property transfer, exchange and inheritance in early modern Southern Tyrol in *The History of the Family* (2021).

Michaela Antonín Malaníková is assistant professor of medieval history at Palacký University Olomouc, Czech Republic. She has published articles and book chapters dedicated to, for example, medieval identity, or female engagement in urban economy. In her latest research project, she focusses on structures and functioning of late medieval urban families.

Rebecca Mason is an Economic and Social Research Council postdoctoral fellow at the University of Glasgow, Scotland. She holds a PhD in history from the University of Glasgow. Her current research focusses on women's access to justice in early modern Scotland. She has published on women's legal status and property rights in seventeenth-century Glasgow.

Susan McDonough is associate professor of history at the University of Maryland, Baltimore County, USA. She studies women, gender and sexuality in the medieval Mediterranean, especially sex workers and single women. She published *Witnesses, Neighbors, and Community in Late Medieval Marseille* (2013) and co-edited *Boundaries in the Medieval and Wider World: Essays in Honor of Paul Freedman* (2018).

Mary O'Dowd is professor emeritus of gender history in Queen's University Belfast, Northern Ireland. Her research focusses on the history of women and gender in Ireland. Her most recent publication is *Marriage in Ireland, 1660–1925* (2020), co-authored with Maria Luddy.

INTRODUCTION

Teresa Phipps and Deborah Youngs

At Michaelmas, 1401, in the town court of Caernarfon (North Wales) Margaret Stanmere brought several cases against different townsmen: Matto ap Conyn for trespass, Jankyn ap Dafydd ap Gwion for debt, and Richard Newhall for a debt of 4s for malted oats.[1] While the nature of the trespass complaint is unknown, the debts likely arose from Margaret's business in the town, possibly relating to brewing, and the legal actions reveal her links with local trade networks that included both English and Welsh, men and women. The very mundanity and typicality of these cases remind us that litigation in premodern Europe was a normal part of life, and something in which women regularly engaged. It is also through such legal records that we are able to glimpse the lives of ordinary women and men, often otherwise undocumented, not only in terms of their engagement with the legal process but broader aspects of their everyday activities and relationships. As such, they provide unparalleled sources for understanding the experiences and identities of premodern women.

We know little else about Margaret Stanmere as an individual, but since the turn of the twenty-first century increasing attention on women's engagement with the law in premodern Europe means we now know far more about the ways women like her negotiated legal institutions and disputes. As a result, we are increasingly aware of the multiple arenas in which they sought and accessed justice and the wide range of legal issues that they managed. A growing collection of studies, based on original court material and other official legal documentation, show women contesting property disputes, economic and commercial obligations, marital contracts, defamation, violence, and wrongdoing, among many other issues, and they did so both independently and in alliance with others, including family members. They used courts that were local to them, but also travelled long distances to access justice at the highest level, or petition those in positions of power. Legal recourse was not only limited to elite

DOI: 10.4324/9780429278037-1

women but was part of the lives of women at almost all levels of society, from courts in rural manors and towns to central courts presided over by monarchs or their highest representatives, as well as ecclesiastical courts. Furthermore, as the example of Margaret Stanmere shows, much of women's (and men's) legal action arose from their everyday lives: their commercial activities, their familial and interpersonal relationships, and the cycles of marriage, death, and inheritance that punctuated life (in different ways) for premodern women and men. Legal action did not necessarily represent crisis; more often, it related to quotidian issues or disputes, though, of course, there are moments of rupture recorded in the legal records too.

This diversity of legal experience lies at the heart of this volume, which explores women as active participants in the legal process across a wide range of contexts, all rooted in original archival research. We approach the idea of 'litigating women' in the broadest sense, to encompass the taking of legal action by women in various forms and jurisdictions, which Julie Hardwick describes here as their 'mobilising' of the legal process. This could take many forms, not limited to the combative interpersonal lawsuits or criminal prosecutions that the term 'litigating' can sometimes conjure up. Women were active (sometimes proactive, sometimes reactive) participants in a wide range of legal processes and actions, as both plaintiffs and defendants, initiating complaints and responding to the grievances of others. They petitioned officials, governments, and the church; testified about their experiences; instigated or challenged contracts; and were party to arbitrations. Several of the chapters use case studies to illuminate the intricacies of individual experience, the factors that may have promoted or limited their ability to negotiate justice, allowing for comparison across different contexts. Collectively, the chapters present a familiar picture of women as a minority of litigants, ranging from around 10% to 25% in any given context, figures that correspond to findings elsewhere.[2] But this does not mean that the presence or experiences of women litigants were exceptional or insignificant, both in their own time or to the historical study of the law.[3] Taken together, the chapters demonstrate that women were regularly present in the courts, and some were able to tell their own stories in their own right. Furthermore, the presence of (or lack of) women as litigants reveals much about the way the law worked, and how justice systems understood the status of those over whom they governed. This volume is therefore as much about law in action as it is about women.

In exploring women's individual experiences, the authors foreground women's choices, strategy, personality, and the individual circumstances of their lives. They illustrate the major shift that has taken place in the historiography of women and the law over the last forty years. Early studies of premodern women in Europe had largely based their views on law codes, legal treatises, commentaries, and statutes.[4] This led historians to overly pessimistic analyses as they emphasised the restrictions on women's legal rights and capacity, with only a hint at possible departures from the letter of the law.[5] The assumption was that the law was something created by men and dominated by male litigants, meaning, by implication, that there was little point in searching for women in court records as they would not be found.[6] Hence, rather than exploring the experience of women as litigants, the focus tended to be on what women could not do. Married women were said to be particularly lacking in legal rights, due to various legal principles that placed wives and their property under the legal authority of their husbands, the most well-discussed example being the English common law principle of coverture.[7] For these reasons the earliest studies of women's legal status and experiences often focussed on singlewomen, and particularly widows, with works analysing inheritance practices and disputes relating to dower. Discussion of married women tended to focus on either the making of marriage or the limitations of married women in relation to their husbands, rather than their capacity to act.[8]

However, the chapters presented here demonstrate how much has changed in the research on premodern women and law. As the lengthy bibliography that accompanies this volume testifies, the systematic sifting of court records by a growing group of scholars has not only broadened our perspective on women's engagement with the law, challenging notions of women's widespread legal disabilities or invisibility, but added considerable layers of complexity. The law has been shown not as something 'done to' women, or a system of rules imposed on them, but as a process that women engaged in as both individuals and collectively with others of shared interests. Women are not viewed simply as victims of a situation or always in opposition to the law, but active participants in its development.[9] Challenges have also come to the presumed legal incapacity or invisibility of married women, with suggestions that this has been overplayed.[10] Studies of both early modern France and Portugal, among others, have noted the potential for married women to be involved in a range of legal contracts, and their ability to circumvent theoretical norms that supposedly incapacitated them in order to bring charges against their husbands if they mismanaged marital assets.[11] What has yet to be fully interrogated, however, are the husbands themselves as gendered subjects of litigation, again reflecting the assumptions about the maleness of the law.

The growing body of research has also revealed the jurisdictional, spatial, temporal, and several personal variables that impacted on women litigants' motives, strategies, and successes. For this reason we have not commissioned specific studies, or tried to cover every jurisdiction, country, or social class: no single volume could achieve such a comprehensive coverage. Nevertheless, we have tried to ensure a breadth of law, locality, chronology, and issues, while offering a cluster of themes that aid comparison. Some of the chapters here have emerged from well-established historiographies, such as those in England where, since the 1980s, historians have examined women's legal actions (often alongside their work and economic status) in an array of courts and jurisdictions.[12] Other areas, like neighbouring Scotland and Ireland, have received less attention, but this volume shows the richness of the records for further studies in these areas. Various aspects of women's legal status have also been explored in other parts of western Europe, including France, the Low Countries, Germany, Italy, Spain, and Scandinavia in both single-authored studies and collected essays.[13] The historiography has developed at different rates in different areas, and is discussed in the various relevant chapters here. The emerging interest in women's legal status and actions in eastern and central Europe is reflected in the inclusion of Michaela Antonín Malaníková's study of marital cases in Bohemia, which have been rarely explored. This can be situated alongside other recent studies such as Tomasz Wiślicz's work on marriage in rural early modern Poland, informed by an array of legal records, or a collection of essays on 'other' women in central and eastern Europe, demonstrating the potential for further research on the opportunities and barriers that women faced when engaging with the law.[14]

In drawing these studies together, several important themes are highlighted in the way we approach the study of women as litigants and in their collective experience. One notable feature is the plurality of legal systems operating across Europe in this period, a reminder that there was no single legal discourse governing women's legal status or rights.[15] While there is evidence to show a reduction in the number of courts in some areas during the early modern period (as Margareth Lanzinger and Janine Maegraith note in their chapter here), the rate of change differed across Europe; indeed, it has been calculated that by the eighteenth century the kingdom of France had more than 200 autonomous legal systems.[16] Chapters in this volume reflect this diversity by drawing on women's litigation in central or royal courts, ecclesiastical jurisdictions, as well those of individual towns and rural communities. In some cases women's experience focussed on one particular court, but other chapters reveal women's capacity for pursuing cases in more than one jurisdiction. These might overlap as they did on issues of marriage (as chapters by Sparky Booker, Chanelle Delameillieure, and Antonín Malaníková show here), illustrating how disputes could cut across boundaries.[17] Litigants sometimes sought out the benefits of a specific jurisdiction, or moved a suit from one to another, as Cordelia Beattie argues in her chapter. This may have been borne of necessity, but also of persistence or strategy. Those facing formidable or well-connected opponents over many years or in multiple disputes might seek alternative jurisdictions in the hope of achieving success. This is particularly evident in Mary O'Dowd's study where, after making the initial choice to bring complaints against their husbands, both Elizabeth Fitzmaurice and Catherine Cunningham had to negotiate multiple courts and jurisdictions in Ireland and England, with their own particular rules, requirements, and practices.

All these courts would have generated a range of written material, but these chapters highlight the uneven survival of these records through the ages. In some instances, we are reliant on sole survivors of a once rich archive, while in others one needs to sift through thousands of cases. There is considerable variation in the type of record, from narrative sources to curial summaries, and we all have to engage with how they have been subsequently archived (as Hardwick's chapter demonstrates). In determining ways to read and interpret the sources, our contributors remind us of the challenges inherent in attempting to recover women's voices (or any voices) in legal records and why we need to continually question their reliability.[18] Chapters reveal how the documents we read and the suits they record were shaped by their specific context and by the interests of litigants, their counsels or guardians, as well as curial and scribal conventions, or idiosyncrasies. As we explore below, litigants and their supporters could weave fictional discourses into the bare facts of cases in order to achieve success. Observable patterns may well relate to scribal practice and personal preferences of clerks: what we are seeing is what clerks thought mattered (as seen in the chapters by Peter Larson and Rebecca Mason).

Such considerations also impinge on any analysis of women's motivations for engaging in litigation. Formulaic and laconic records inevitably confound attempts to reconstruct the details of exactly why and how women litigants pursued particular directions, or the precise degree of their involvement, particularly in contexts such as early modern Tyrol where women were required to use 'gender guardians'. Nevertheless, this volume demonstrates how a careful reading of legal sources can allow us to recover women's concerns and to proffer views on their motivations, strategies, and tactics. These actions are sometimes interpreted as evidence of 'agency' through which women sought to determine their own lives in the context of a patriarchal legal system that governed them.[19] This search for agency has, in part, reflected the feminist origins of much of the scholarship on premodern women and the law, which originally attempted to recover the lives of women, their actions and power to push back against the idea of women's disabilities or their status as victims of patriarchy. However, the term can be problematic, as Gwen Seabourne has recently argued: agency has various definitions and the temptation to class action as agency can lead to the complexities and 'reality' of women's engagement with the law being obscured.[20] In their analyses of women litigants, both Marie Kelleher and Dana Wessell Lightfoot have argued that the term can suggest a resistance to dominant structures, which, in the context of patriarchal premodern societies, implies an overly simplistic binary of male dominance and female resistance.[21] For many women, going to court was also not necessarily positive, but rather a sign of how regularly women's rights were denied and they were effectively coerced into legal action in order to secure these rights.[22] This issue is also raised by Beattie and O'Dowd in their studies in this volume, the latter questioning whether the two Irishwomen at the heart of her study would have felt that their efforts were worthwhile.

Nevertheless, scholars such as Lightfoot, Martha Howell, and, notably, Allyson Poska have argued that the overarching patriarchal framework that underpinned premodern (and modern) societies gave scope – or, indeed, prompted – women to act with agency if their actions fitted within dominant gender norms.[23] Rather than patriarchy and female agency being opposing factors, women were able to manoeuvre within patriarchal structures to their own advantage, and it is this strategic positioning that we see repeatedly within the studies that make up this volume.[24] Indeed, the strategies deployed by women, their legal advisors or representatives, and their wider supporters, often saw them 'buy into' different patriarchal norms in order to construct an acceptable legal narrative – something that male litigants and witnesses also attempted.[25] Here, Booker suggests that women might position themselves as passive, such as emphasising their lack of power over husbands, where it might aid their case. Lanzinger and Maegraith note how women in southern Tyrol could exploit patriarchal norms, claiming poverty or deferring to male relatives in order to avoid paying taxes or debts, while at other times they might subvert those same gender norms, for example, by asserting their capability in contrast to their husband's incompetency. Susan McDonough's study of family conflict in late medieval Marseille highlights the gendered positioning used by female litigants who sought to appeal to contemporary patriarchal ideals relating to women's roles as mothers and grandmothers, carers and household managers, in the hope of achieving success in court. Elsewhere, other legal narratives drew on the common trope of the poor (female) petitioner seeking judicial protection from a powerful and malicious (male) opponent, such as the Chancery bill of Elizabeth Thornton described in Beattie's chapter. While this was a less overtly gendered narrative that was also employed by male plaintiffs, it, nevertheless, reflected the patriarchal power structures of premodern societies and the role of law in providing protection for the weak and poor, thereby fitting within what Poska has termed 'agentic gender expectations' of society. These expectations meant that women had the opportunity 'to act independently, achieve success, and exert power and authority in many aspects of their lives'.[26] These strategies were not always successful; sometimes the same gendered norms that women employed in making their cases could also be used against them in discrediting women's characters, as O'Dowd's study demonstrates.

For some women, [re]positioning their legal status meant appropriating their marital or family status, those very aspects that have often been seen to limit a woman's capacity, in order to aid their legal claims. The multiple lawsuits fought by the Swedish noblewoman Elin Johansdotter, the subject of Mia Korpiola's chapter, exemplify how one woman deployed her changing marital status according to the demands of different suits, sometimes taking the role of the 'invisible' wife, and at other times insisting she represent herself, despite calls for her husband to act on her behalf. Far from exemplifying limitations on her legal capacity, Johansdotter used marriage as a means of sharing the burden of litigation, tapping into her husbands' social and political networks when it suited her. Booker's study of widowhood and attainder in late medieval Ireland also reveals the strategic way that women inhabited their familial and marital identity to their advantage. The Irish widow Margaret Nugent simultaneously claimed the status of the vulnerable widow to gain parliament's support in pursuing her dower land, while also highlighting her separation from her husband, rejecting her marital ties in favour of her natal ties in order to demonstrate political loyalty. The careful positioning of women like Margaret Nugent and Elin Johansdotter was likely a reflection of their own legal aptitude, but also that of their legal advisers, family members, and wider social networks, all of which were a benefit of their privileged status.

What these explorations also raise is women's legal knowledge of the law, that of their advisers, and how they are reflected in the choices they made about how or where to pursue or defend cases. This knowledge was part of the 'legal consciousness', discussed by Anthony Musson and others for late medieval England, which evolved as people from all sections of society, including women, assimilated concepts of law. The significant increase in litigation during the sixteenth and seventeenth centuries has also been seen as educating more women about legal opportunities.[27] Women's choices regarding litigation were informed by their understandings of the probable biases of different courts and officials, and their ability to apply this to their own particular circumstances. Beattie's chapter on Chancery highlights women's navigation of multiple English jurisdictions and the options they faced, including the specific type of writ to bring and how to frame the suit with the hope of achieving the desired outcome.

Women may have gained legal knowledge personally through direct experience, or accessed it via friends, family, attorneys, or wider social networks. These factors are illustrated particularly well in the chapters here focussing on litigation relating to marriage. In Delameillieure's chapter on abduction in the medieval Low Countries, we gain an insight into the choices that litigants and their legal representatives made in devising narratives that sought to prove or refute abduction. Women's knowledge of the law is evident both in the stories that they constructed (often with the help of attorneys) to argue their cases, but more importantly in the actions and choices that were taken outside the court to demonstrate their consent or lack thereof. These issues are also central to Kristi DiClemente's study of consent in late medieval Paris, where women successfully argued against attempted coerced marriage, sometimes without legal counsel. In Paris, as has been suggested elsewhere, legal knowledge circulated within communities and social networks, evidenced in the language used by witnesses in their testimony. This also informed the tactics and narratives used by women in court, as Antonín Malaníková's study of litigation relating to marriage in late medieval Bohemia reveals. This includes the defence that women had only agreed to a marriage 'in jest' as a means of distinguishing between flirting and a serious promise of marriage. None of these tactics were accidental, but speak to women's intentional choices, sometimes informed by legal advisors, as to what approach would be most likely to bring success in court.

The decision to engage in legal action was often a necessity as women sought access to the resources they believed they were entitled in order to support themselves or their families. As discussed above, this was not 'agency' as resistance, but simply an essential part of the negotiation of everyday life. The so-called 'pregnancy declarations' that are the subject of Hardwick's chapter were a direct result of the informed decisions made by young women following illegitimate pregnancy, and also reflected the necessity of providing for the resulting child. Hardwick argues for a new interpretation of these documents, not as evidence of the state regulation of young women's sexuality, but as paternity suits which offered young women a means by which to manage their reproductive lives, restore their honour, and seek financial support for their children. Women constructed their pleas in order to conform to contemporary understandings of acceptable relationships, as this was a prerequisite for successful litigation, once again exemplifying a way in which women's legal narratives adhered to the patriarchal and heteronormative expectations of premodern society.

Similarly, women used both litigation and arbitration as tools to claim or secure the goods or property that were frequently redistributed as marriages and deaths repeatedly reshaped family structures. Mason's study of the litigation of remarried widows in seventeenth-century Glasgow highlights the active role that many women took (often with the support of their new husband) in claiming property that they were owed following the death of a husband or seeking payments required for the maintenance of children, both of which could mean initiating litigation against close family members. For remarried widows, the cases recorded in the commissary court offer an insight into the multiple ways in which women's changing or blended marital statuses required complex negotiations of the patriarchal rules of the early modern household, often requiring legal intervention to settle the conflicting demands and tactics of different parties. Lanzinger and Maegraith show how disputes among family members in early modern Tyrol were dealt with by both arbitration and litigation as women of middling status sought access to shared wealth. Individual women's unique family histories and ties, such as the number of siblings, the timing of parental death, and the nature of prior inheritances, all played their part and combined to inform the ways in which each woman sought to manage their property rights.

What these life cycle and familial variables also show is that if we simply focus on the gender of a litigant, many complexities are obscured. This volume's focus on women as a group of litigants does not mean that all women shared common characteristics or a universal 'female' experience, any more than there was a single 'male' experience; they should not be essentialised as a monolithic group. Context is everything. For example, in Larson's examination of various local courts of late medieval north-eastern England, we see the courts' varying practices, customs, and biases, undermining any assumption of a 'typical' women's experience across courts of a similar 'type'. In these courts, the sex of litigants was not the only factor that determined their access to justice; rather, Larson suggests, far more attention was paid to their tenant status. The individual stories revealed in other, more detailed court records also demonstrate that gender was just one of many intersecting factors that formed each woman's identity and contributed to their experience of the law. These women lived lives which were mediated by multiple networks and hierarchies – marital, familial, political, religious, ethnic, community, economic – none of which were constant, but all of which informed the position of any individual litigant (female or male) as they presented themselves before a court, and as they were perceived by that court. We see evidence of these networks and varying statuses, some more clearly than others, through the witnesses women used to support them in court, the family members they chose to plead with, or the political allies that intervened on their behalf.

Among these variables, the importance of marital status, as noted above, cannot be underestimated, although as research over the last decade or so has made clear, this did not operate in accordance with a neat tripartite model of singlewoman/wife/widow.[28] In many places throughout this volume, we see the varying and often complex influence of a woman's current marital status alongside the legacy of previous marriages and their connections within wide family networks, as well as women's ability to push against the apparent restraints that their marital status imposed on them. In the local courts of late medieval Durham, Larson notes the inconsistency in recording women's marital status, arguing that coverture was not a rigidly prescribed rule, but rather was invoked when it was needed. Mason's focus on the status of the remarried widow as litigant in seventeenth-century Glasgow exemplifies the way in which women's multiple familial and marital ties, often changing multiple times over the course of their life, lay at the heart of their legal actions. The influence of women's individual marital histories is also demonstrated in unique ways in Korpiola's study of Swedish noblewoman Elin Johansdotter, whose status changed from wife to widow multiple times over the course of her various cases at the Court of Appeal.

Women's familial wealth and connections were also intrinsic to their experience as a litigant. We see this in Booker's study of Irish widow Margaret Nugent, whose husband's Lancastrian political allegiance was at the root of why she needed to petition parliament for her dower land. But the way that this claim proceeded was a product of her ties to her natal family, particularly her father, with whom she sought to align herself in order to demonstrate her loyalty to the Yorkist side. Korpiola's study of Elin Johansdotter also repeatedly demonstrates the importance of familial and social connections at the top of Swedish society and beyond, and the way in which these influenced her litigation. Family networks could also impact on women's litigation in negative ways, especially when those of one's opponents attempted to interfere. This could be particularly obstructive when there was a significant difference in the social standing of a female litigant and her opponent, as outlined in O'Dowd's chapter. The Irishwomen Elizabeth Leeson and Catherine Cunningham faced multiple challenges from their well-connected husbands and their wider families. The fact that these women were eventually successful in their repeated claims and appeals suggests, however, that while family connections may have made a case more expensive and protracted, this did not necessarily make a case insurmountable.

Each individual chapter must therefore be viewed as a unique exploration of its specific context and the women who engaged with the law within this setting. Yet taken together, the chapters point to some commonalities and suggest a continuity of women's experiences as litigants across time and place, even if the variability of individual choices and experience lies at the core of this continuity. Judith Bennett has famously argued in relation to women's work and economic status that there was an enduring 'patriarchal equilibrium' that extended from the middle ages to the industrial period and beyond, with 'much change in European women's experiences as workers over the last millennium, but little transformation in their work status in relation to that of men'.[29] The picture of women's experiences as litigants can also be understood in a similar way, with long-term continuity sitting alongside the less tangible influences of individual circumstance, personality, and strategy. For this reason, the experiences of a woman like Caernarfon's Margaret Stanmere, with whom we opened this introduction, would not look too alien to women at an equivalent court several hundred years later, whether in Wales or elsewhere in Europe.

In bringing together these studies, we also demonstrate the value of legal records (of all jurisdictions, periods, and places) in offering crucial insights into the lives of the individuals that came into contact with the different courts, and of the structures and norms that underpinned the way those legal systems operated. We are far from the early days of women's legal history and the assumptions about the invisibility or incapability of women as litigants, or the stereotypes that still exist in the popular imagination in relation to premodern women and law. The concerted efforts of historians over recent decades have 'excavated' the stories of ever-growing numbers of women of all statuses who actively engaged with the law as part of the management of their business or working lives, property, familial and interpersonal relationships, and socio-political networks, to which this volume continues to add. Nevertheless, as Gwen Seabourne has most recently noted, in the broader context of ('classical') legal history, 'at times women are quite spectacularly absent'.[30] The richness of the premodern legal record means that there will always be more research to be done and more stories to be told. The legal status of Jewish, Muslim, and heretical women within Europe is not examined here, but requires ongoing attention and comparison across diverse cultural and religious contexts.[31] There is also considerable scope for further study of central and eastern Europe, as well as transnational approaches, particularly given the influence of European legal systems in imperial contexts across large parts of the world after c.1450, where colonial and native laws and gender norms intersected to impact both women and men.[32] The twelve chapters in this volume therefore form part of an important, broader initiative to recover the infinite variety of different women's experiences in negotiating the boundaries of justice.

Notes

1 G. P. Owen and Hugh Owen (eds.), *Caernarvon Court Rolls, 1361–1402* (Caernarvon, 1951), p. 166.
2 For example, for England: Penny Tucker, *Law Courts and Lawyers in the City of London, 1300–1550* (Cambridge, 2007), pp. 234–235, 238; Emma Hawkes, "'She Will … Protect and Defend Her Rights Boldly by Law and Reason ….': Women's Knowledge of Common Law and Equity Courts in Late-Medieval England," in Noel James Menuge (ed.), *Medieval Women and the Law* (Woodbridge, 2000), p. 151; Timothy S. Haskett, 'The Medieval English Court of Chancery', *Law and History Review*, 14

(1996), pp. 286–287; Teresa Phipps, *Medieval Women and Urban Justice* (Manchester, 2020), pp. 53, 59, 62.
3. Garthine Walker, *Crime, Gender and Social Order in Early Modern England* (Cambridge, 2003), p. 4. See too Cordelia Beattie's cautionary comments on counting women in this volume.
4. Janet Senderowitz Loengard, 'Legal History and the Medieval Englishwoman: A Fragmented View', *Law and History* Review, 4 (1986), pp. 162–163.
5. As illustrated in the landmark studies by Eileen Power, *Medieval Women*, ed. Michael M. Postan (Cambridge, 1975), p. 2 and Shulamith Shahar, *The Fourth Estate: A History of Women in the Middle Ages*, second edn, trans. Chaya Galai (London, 2003), pp. 13–16.
6. R. A. Houston, 'Women in the Economy and Society of Scotland', in R. A. Houston and I. D. Whyte (eds.), *Scottish Society 1500–1800* (Cambridge, 1989), pp. 118–147, at p. 118.
7. The English doctrine of 'coverture' is set out in the legal treatise known as Bracton: see *Bracton on the Laws and Customs of England*, trans. Samuel E. Thorne, vol. 4 (Cambridge, MA, 1977), p. 287. Caroline Barron, 'The 'Golden Age' of Women in Medieval London', *Reading Medieval Studies*, 2 (1989), pp. 35–37. For a more detailed overview see Cordelia Beattie and Matthew Frank Stevens, 'Introduction: Uncovering Married Women', in Beattie and Stevens (eds.), *Married Women and the Law in Premodern Northwest Europe* (Woodbridge, 2013), pp. 1–10.
8. For example, Sue Sheridan Walker (ed.), *Wife and Widow in Medieval England* (Ann Arbor, 1993), p. 4; Loengard, 'Legal History', pp. 168–171; Inger Dübeck, 'Legal Status of Widows in Denmark 1500–1900', *Scandinavian Journal of History*, 29 (2004), pp. 209–223; Judith M. Bennett and Amy Froide (eds.), *Singlewomen in the European Past, 1250–1800* (Philadelphia, 1999).
9. Marie A. Kelleher, *The Measure of Women: Law and Family Identity in the Crown of Aragon* (Philadelphia, 2011), pp. 145–146.
10. For example, Beattie and Stevens, 'Uncovering Married Women', p. 10.
11. Darlene Abreu-Ferreira, 'Women, Law and Legal Intervention in Early Modern Portugal', *Continuity and Change*, 33 (2018), pp. 297–298; Sarah Hanley, 'Social Sites of Political Practice in France: Lawsuits, Civil Rights, and the Separation of Powers in Domestic and State Government, 1500–1800', *American Historical Review*, 102 (1997), p. 31.
12. This includes various works by Barbara Hanawalt, Maryanne Kowaleski, Judith M. Bennett, Tim Stretton, Cordelia Beattie, Garthine Walker, Sara Butler, Amy Erickson, and Alex Shepard, and expanding beyond England to the 'common law world': see Lindsay R. Moore, *Women Before the Court: Law and Patriarchy in the Anglo-American World, 1600–1800* (Manchester, 2019); Tim Stretton and Krista Kesselring (eds.), *Married Women and the Law: Coverture in England and the Common Law World* (Montreal, 2013). See this volume's bibliography for specific references.
13. For example, Sara McDougall, Julie Hardwick, and Suzannah Lipscomb on France; Maria Agren and Mia Korpiola on Sweden; Shennan Hutton on Ghent; Sheilagh Ogilvie on Germany; Dana Wessell Lightfoot and Marie Kelleher on Spain; Carol Lansing, Trevor Dean, and Patricia Skinner on Italy; with a wide range of studies on women in the Mediterranean brought together in Jutta Gisela Sperling and Shona Kelly Wray (eds.), *Across the Religious Divide: Women, Property and Law in the Wider Mediterranean (ca. 1300–1800)* (London, 2010).
14. Tomasz Wiślicz, *Love in the Fields: Relationships and Marriage in Rural Poland in the Early Modern Age: Social Imagery and Personal Experience*, trans. George Szenderowicz (Warsaw, 2018); Christopher Mielke and Andrea-Bianka Znorovsky (eds.), *Same Bodies, Different Women: 'Other' Women in the Middle Ages and the Early Modern Period* (Budapest, 2019).
15. Kelleher, *The Measure of Woman*, p. 146.

16 Janine M. Lanza, *From Wives to Widows in Early Modern Paris* (Aldershot, 2007), p. 23. For a recent discussion on these multiple jurisdictions in medieval England see Tom Johnson, *Law in Common: Legal Cultures in Late-Medieval England* (Oxford, 2020).
17 Explorations into ways in which disputes cut across jurisdictional boundaries, or how custom, local law and canon law interacted, can be found in, for example: Anthony Musson (ed.), *Boundaries of the Law: Geography, Gender and Jurisdiction in Medieval and Early Modern Europe* (Aldershot, 2005); Mia Korpiola (ed.), *Regional Variations in Matrimonial Law and Custom in Europe 1150–1600* (Leiden, 2011).
18 For a recent analysis on different approaches see Tim Stretton, 'Women, Legal Records and the Problem of the Lawyer's Hand', *Journal of British Studies*, 58 (2019), pp. 684–700.
19 Merry Wiesner-Hanks discusses the issues associated with 'agency' as argument or conclusion in the introduction to *Challenging Women's Agency and Activism in Early Modernity* (Amsterdam, 2021), pp. 11–12. On patriarchy and the governing of premodern households/families see Julie Hardwick, *The Practice of Patriarchy* (Philadelphia, 2010).
20 Gwen Seabourne, *Women in the Medieval Common Law c.1200–1500* (Palgrave, 2021), p. 91. See also Alexandra Shepard and Tim Stretton, 'Women Negotiating the Boundaries of Justice in Britain, 1300–1700: An Introduction', *Journal of British Studies*, 58 (2019), p. 680; Bronach Kane and Fiona Williamson, *Women, Agency and the Law, 1300–1700* (London, 2013).
21 Kelleher, *The Measure of Women*, pp. 146–147; Dana Wessell Lightfoot, *Women, Dowries and Agency: Marriage in Fifteenth-Century Valencia* (Manchester, 2016), pp. 7–8.
22 Seabourne, *Women in the Medieval Common Law*, p. 91.
23 Martha Howell, 'The Problem of Women's Agency in Late Medieval and Early Modern Europe', in Sarah Joan Moran and Amanda C. Pipkin (eds.), *Women and Gender in the Early Modern Low Countries, 1500–1750* (Leiden, 2019), pp. 21–31; Allyson Poska, 'The Case for Agentic Gender Norms for Women in Early Modern Europe', *Gender and History*, 30 (2018), p. 355.
24 Lightfoot, *Women, Dowries and Agency*, pp. 7–8. Jamie Smith, 'Women as Legal Agents in Late Medieval Genoa', in Charlotte Newman Goldy and Amy Livingstone (eds.), *Writing Medieval Women's Lives* (Basingstoke, 2012), p. 114.
25 Bronach Kane's study of witness testimony in late medieval church courts is one of the few studies to acknowledge the impact of patriarchy in men's engagement with the law, and to examine men as gendered subjects: Bronach C. Kane, *Popular Memory and Gender in Medieval England: Men, Women and Testimony in the Church Courts, c.1200–1500* (Woodbridge, 2019). Poska has also argued that patriarchy served as a means for men to control other men. Poska, 'Agentic Gender Norms', p. 356.
26 Poska, 'Agentic Gender Norms', p. 355.
27 Musson, *Medieval Law in Context*, pp. 8–9. Cynthia J. Neville, 'Common Knowledge of the Common Law in Later Medieval England', *Canadian Journal of History/Annales Canadiennes d'Histoire* (1994), p. 464. Tim Stretton, *Women Waging Law in Elizabethan England* (Cambridge, 1998).
28 See for example Beattie and Stevens, *Married Women and the Law*; Rebecca Mason, 'Women, Marital Status and Law: The Marital Spectrum in Seventeenth-Century Glasgow', *Journal of British Studies*, 58 (2019), pp. 787–804; Shennan Hutton, *Women and Economic Activities in Late Medieval Ghent* (New York, 2011), pp. 47–57; Jennifer McNabb, '"She Is But a Girl": Perceptions of Young Women as Daughters, Wives, and Mothers in the English Courts, 1550–1650', in Elizabeth S. Cohen and Margaret Reeves (eds.), *The Youth of Early Modern Women* (Amsterdam, 2018), pp. 77–96.
29 Judith M. Bennett, *History Matters: Patriarchy and the Challenge of Feminism* (Philadelphia, 2006), pp. 61–62.
30 Seabourne, *Women in the Medieval Common Law*, p. 1.
31 For example, Emma Cavell, 'The Measure of Her Actions: A Quantitative Assessment of Anglo-Jewish Women's Litigation at the Exchequer of the Jews, 1219–81', *Law and History Review*, 39 (2021), pp. 135–172; Cordelia Beattie and Kirsten Fenton

(eds.), *Intersections of Gender, Religion and Ethnicity in the Middle Ages* (London, 2011); Anna Rich Abad, 'Able and Available: Jewish Women in Medieval Barcelona and Their Economic Activities', *Journal of Medieval Iberian Studies*, 6 (2014), pp. 71–86.

32 For example, Indrani Chatterjee, 'Women, Monastic Commerce and Coverture in Eastern India circa 1600–1800 CE', *Modern Asian Studies*, 50 (2016), pp. 175–216; Susanah Shaw Romney, '"With & Alongside His Housewife": Claiming Ground in New Netherland and the Early Modern Dutch Empire', *The William and Mary Quarterly*, 73 (2016), pp. 187–224; Lindsay R. Moore, *Women Before the Court*; Aske Laursen Brock and Misha Ewen, 'Women's Public Lives: Navigating the East India Company, Parliament and Courts in Early Modern England', *Gender & History*, 33 (2021), pp. 3–23.

1

MOTHERS AND DAUGHTERS AND SONS, IN THE LAW

Family conflict, legal stories, and women's litigation in late medieval Marseille

Susan McDonough

Luiseta Bariesse lived a relatively ordinary life, for a while. Like many women from well-off urban families in fourteenth-century Marseille, she married and had children. In preparation for her marriage, Luiseta's family negotiated a dowry, which her betrothed husband recognized.[1] But the life she expected ended with her husband's death. At this moment, Luiseta's life became a matter of the historical record, when she brought a series of cases before the judge of Marseille's Palace Court, its court of first instance. Before the market tables in front of the doors of Notre Dame des Accoules, Luiseta asked the judge to prioritize her needs before the many claimants on her husband's estate and to authorize the return of her dowry.[2] Her story unfolded in the paper folia of the court's register. Her youngest daughter, still nursing at the time of her father's death, was ill and Luiseta had no resources to nourish or get medical care for her children. Worse, she contended that the guardian chosen to administer her daughters' inheritance had fudged their father's post-mortem inventory and cheated them by over two hundred livres. To make the latter case, Luiseta litigated with enforcements. She joined with her mother Alegreta to petition the court to change her daughters' guardian because of his malfeasance.

This chapter's close reading of cases like Luiseta's will demonstrate how women in late medieval Marseille used the civil courts not only to protect their property but also to argue publicly for the righteousness of their claims of the soundness of their judgement, and of their communal good standing. That good standing rested on arguments about how well women cared for their relatives in maternal, uxorial, or filial roles, navigating the potentially conflicting demands on them as mothers, wives, widows, and property owners. What strategies did women deploy as part of the extra-legal cases they built within their legal arguments? Deliberate choices undergirded how women narrated their claims, accused their opponents, and selected their co-litigants.

DOI: 10.4324/9780429278037-2

Working with lawsuits as sources requires the maintenance of a delicate balance. Scholars must be attentive to the requirements of the law and how that shaped the form of the sources.[3] However, medieval litigants, both men and women, had some leeway to frame and broadcast their legal woes. For a compelling story, litigants peppered the formulaic documentary record with personal details, perhaps chosen in collaboration with legal advisors who suggested which version of their story had the best chance of winning a favourable judgement. Historians have long been attentive to these legal stories. Natalie Zemon Davis famously argued that early modern pardon petitions to the king of France were evidence of how ordinary people shaped and told stories, rather than faithful recreations of something that had really happened.[4] Lawsuits, like royal petitions, have a fictional quality to emphasize the righteousness of the litigants to the judges. Jeanette Fregulia has argued that lawsuits cannot show much about the interior lives of women, but they can show at least in public presentation a pride in their expertise and a certainty that the courts would back them up.[5] The art historian Marian Bleeke examined literary texts and sculptures to posit that 'medieval women in general should be understood as active makers of the meanings of their own lives'.[6] In this chapter focussing on a set of cases involving women who brought their family members to court, I will argue that as litigants, women made meaning of their lives through the stories they told in Marseille's courts. When they contested control over dowries, asserted their right to land, or claimed rights to an inheritance, women, as they made a case based in Roman and statutory law, also told stories emphasising their worthiness of the judge's favourable ruling.

Going to court was about more than simply winning a case. As Daniel Smail has maintained, medieval people brought lawsuits to pursue their hatreds and to harass their opponents as much as they did to recover their property.[7] Women brought cases to the court, a public forum, to right a legal wrong and to stake out their identities as authorities and worthy beneficiaries of the court's favour within their family constellations. The three case studies (involving five discreet cases) analysed here suggest women's certainty that they should be compensated for the emotional and physical care they offered as wives, mothers, and grandmothers.[8] The dowered female litigants were also mothers, whose dotal retrocession cases had the potential to disadvantage their own children. Litigating women, then, navigated competing loyalties among legal and social pressures that often appealed to or relied on principles that existed in parallel to the law itself. The legal strategies the women deployed teach us about interfamilial care and responsibilities and how both were gendered in the late Middle Ages.

The legal structure

Like many jurisdictions in Mediterranean Europe, late medieval Marseille boasted a robust legal system. In addition to criminal and ecclesiastical courts, judges heard civil cases in the palace court or two other courts designated the *curiae alterium iudicium* or 'other courts'. Litigants could transfer cases from the 'other court' to the palace court by challenging the original presiding judge; these cases are called *causae suspicionis* or 'cases of suspicion' and they are quite common in the palace court registers. No clear rules governed the court where litigants would initiate their civil cases, but there were some differences. Judges of the 'other courts' were citizens of Marseille and appointed by the city's municipal council, whereas palace court judges were required to be strangers to the city, who presided over the court for a one-year term.[9] Above the palace court and the criminal court were two courts of appeals. After losing a case in the court of first instance, litigants could appeal their cases twice, within thirty days of the adverse judgement. Litigants built their civil cases on a mix of statutory law and Romano-canonical law, as was typical throughout the northern Mediterranean region after the legal revolution of the twelfth century.[10]

Presenting to the judge of the palace court, litigants worked with their procurators, their legal stand-in who may or may not have had any legal training, or other legal advisors to craft a libel (*libellum*), which laid out their legal claims, and a list of titles (*tenor titulorum*), which enumerated the various points that the litigant intended to prove. These points were the result of some collective action; litigants might have a procurator or a lawyer, and all of the documents were written up by a notary paid for his service. It is hard to parse who contributed each aspect of the legal strategy, but in Marseille, the women who chose to air their familial grievances in court were actively involved in shaping the documents presented on their behalf and framing the details of the stories they wanted told. Their legal opponents had the same opportunity to present their own cases.[11] Cases in the palace and appellate courts relied on witness testimony and on documentary proof, often copies of notarized agreements, last wills and testaments, or bills of sale. Copies of all of these might be included in the official record, along with any procedural motions the hostile parties might make.

It was not unusual for women to use the courts to protect their rights in late medieval Marseille. Between 1323 and 1416, years for which we have the uninterrupted records of the palace court, women were the principal litigants in 22% of cases, and they participated in additional 5% of cases as part of a married couple.[12] Technically married women needed their husband's permission before opening a court case, and occasionally a notarial casebook will contain an example of such permission.[13] I've noted elsewhere that these notarial acts are uncommon and women's presence as both litigant and witness in Marseille's courts was unremarkable to their opponents or onlookers.[14] Women litigants in Marseille, who were as likely to represent themselves as being represented by a procurator, illustrate what Thomas Kuehn has called women's legal personhood.[15]

Though Marseille's archives are rich, in a quirk of archival fate, very few of the judgements produced by Marseille's judges have survived. While scholars have access to cases from a court of first instance, a court of first appeals, and a court of secondary appeals, they cannot always know how the judges ruled on the cases before them and cannot know how effective the women's stories were in persuading the judge to rule in their favour.[16] Many of the litigants, including the women whose names appear in this article, pled their cases before Marseille's judges but did not leave other traces in the archive, so scholars can only make inferences about their age, economic status, or community connections. A further challenge is the language of the court, Latin, although Marseille's denizens spoke a vernacular Provençal. Only very occasionally are snippets of the vernacular recorded, usually insults or bits of conversation.[17] The formal Latin of the official record is only an imperfect replica of what litigants or their witnesses might actually have said during the proceedings.

However, scholars interested in the medieval quotidian can find in the archive a broad cross section of people, as men and women, citizens and foreigners, urban oligarchs and poor artisans all used Marseille's courts to make their cases and to tell their stories. Those stories and the cultural scripts they draw from and rely on were common currency among ordinary people, not only those learned in the law.

The palace court judge ruled according to statutory and Romano-canonical law, but extra-legal storytelling had an effect as occasional hints in the extant court records show. Judges held deeply engrained ideas about mothers and children and articulated expectations for them in the court records. In 1396, the widow Berengaria Lymosine sued her sons Antoni and Isnard Bonhomi for the return of her dowry.[18] Her sons protested, saying she had agreed to give them a seven-year grace period to settle their debts, using proceeds from her dowry, and argued before the judge that she was reneging on this. In the margins of this dotal retrocession case the judge, however, was having none of it. 'Lawsuits between mothers and sons are odious,' he ordered, and referred both mother and sons to arbitration.[19]

This intriguing hint of a judge's personal opinions on familial relations is relatively rare, though it indicates that the efforts women made to craft stories could be effective. The judge was not the litigants' only audience. Women also crafted the narratives contained in their libel and list of titles to address their local community. Rather than the closed courtrooms in dedicated buildings of modern judicial dramas, until 1424, the courts in Marseille met in the open markets next to the parish church Notre Dame des Accoules. All of the discussions, heated or calm, were performed for the benefit of those who chose to come to the court, or even those customers of the market. Perhaps, sometimes, the market goers who served as the audience for the court even interjected, signalling their support of one side over another. If they did, the court notaries chose not to make a record of it. But the litigants would have been aware of their multiple audiences. Beyond the important goal of persuading a judge on the legal merits of their cases, women used the court to broadcast their characters and make public their opponents' weaknesses. Women could positively shape their reputations as mothers, businesswomen, and managers of their households and their property in the court's public forum.

The case studies

Here, let us return to the story that opened this chapter. The lengthiest dispute I will discuss, Luiseta Bariesse's family affair, was narrated over the course of three separate litigations. Her brother-in-law was her legal adversary and sometimes her mother was her co-litigant. At issue was control over Luiseta's dowry as well as the support for and guardianship of her minor children. Represented by her *curator*, Pons Antrasi, on 18 December 1395, she requested that Antoni de Bayono, the judge of the palace court enforce an agreement she had made with her brother-in-law Antoni Germani, who was the guardian of her daughters.[20] There were two different sums of money at stake.[21] The first was the restitution of Luiseta's dowry, the very large sum of seven hundred livres. For comparison's sake, the average dowry for a fourteenth-century woman in Marseille was about two hundred livres.[22] Luiseta was concerned the dowry reverted to her control, standard practice in medieval Southern Europe, when a husband's death ended a marriage.[23] The second sum was for *alimenta*, or the cost of food and shelter for Luiseta and her daughters.[24] In Luiseta's plea for *alimenta*, her personalized narrative emerged. Despite what her husband's will should have provided for her,

> from the time of her husband's death until now, which is approximately three months, neither Luiseta nor her nursing daughter Hugueta have received anything for their *alimenta* ... although [Hugueta] has been ill since the feast of All Saints, on account of which she required healing. Thus, her *curator*, named above, asks that the judge compel the said Antoni expeditiously to give Luiseta the *alimenta*, which he received both from his mother and his sisters and from many other people in the sum of twelve pounds.[25]

In this emotional appeal we learn facets of Luiseta's personal life she deemed important to her case: she was a nursing mother of a sick child at the mercy of a man cruelly withholding the funds she needed to sustain her child's very life. Luiseta's argument before the palace court in late fourteenth-century Marseille finds later echoes in England's Chancery court, where Capern has traced litigants employing 'language of maternity' that emphasised litigating mothers' 'weakness and vulnerability'.[26] This trope invited the court's intervention on behalf of women both in early modern English law and the *ius commune* of the medieval Mediterranean. That this language was accessible to litigating women across time and legal systems suggests that the rhetoric surrounding motherhood and its legal application remained remarkably stable across the late medieval and early modern period.

The story of Luiseta's maternal vulnerability hinged on specific elements. Her daughter Hugueta, probably under two, was nursing at the time of the trial.[27] That Luiseta was a nursing mother added moral valence to her legal claims. As Rebecca Winer has argued for medieval Western Europe, 'powerful messages- lay devotional manuals, medical advice, ecclesiastical pronouncements and artwork in churches- linked maternal breastfeeding to a moral and caring ideal of motherhood'.[28] The portrait of the nursing Luiseta emphasized Hugueta's youth and vulnerability and thus justified the need for the *alimenta*. Morally deserving of recompense, with a sick toddler, Luiseta turned to the court to force her brother-in-law, her daughters' guardian, to fulfil his legal and ethical responsibility towards a widow legally entitled to the *alimenta*.

This gendered positioning as a recent widow and a nursing mother was not a strategy unique to Luiseta's case. Rather, she was one of many women who narrated themselves as responsible parents and involved the needs of their children in their legal arguments. On 26 July 1396, in another such example, the widow Silona Filhone went to court to protect her children, whose guardian she was, against the collection of a seven-florin debt that her dead husband had owed to his friend Bernat. She reminded the court that it was 'in the judicial interest to make sure that wards and orphans and widows are taken care of, rather than unduly oppressed'.[29] Marie Kelleher has reconstructed the delicate balancing act medieval widows had to maintain when asking for the court's intervention. Although widows were entitled to special protection because they fell into the legal category of 'poor and miserable persons,' in order to act as head of a newly constituted household, widows had to renounce that very protection and be able to prove their economic self-sufficiency.[30] Strategically, then, Luiseta embraced that first category, a woman in need of the court's action without her husband's protection.

That strategy worked. The court agreed quickly that Luiseta's story was compelling and that she was in need of and entitled to immediate financial assistance. Two short days after Luiseta presented her case, the judge ordered each side to choose 'two upright, worthy, and suitable men' (*duos probos valentes et ydoneos viros*) to calculate the *alimenta* due to Luiseta from the time of her husband's death until the present day, 'according to the condition and quantity of goods of the deceased Bertran, and in consideration of the status of their persons'.[31]

Although the court ruled in her favour, the restitution of Luiseta's dowry was not as quick; winning a case and gaining resolution were not the same thing. Antoni Germani delayed repaying Luiseta Bariesse's dowry. He neglected to show up for court, and when he did, he asked the court for a copy of all of the documents thus far, 'since he hadn't been present in the court proceedings for a long time'.[32] These moves were common. While one risked a fine for contumacy, many litigants stretched the court's time and patience either to force their opponents to continue investing their time and money or to scramble for other options.[33] One month later, on 24 January 1396, the judge ordered Antoni to repay Luiseta's dowry in full. He agreed to do so the following day.[34]

That was not the end of the legal contest between Luiseta and Antoni. In a second related case six months later, Antoni was the plaintiff. On 15 June 1396, he appeared before the judge Antoni Riqueti to ask, on behalf of his nieces Johaneta (whose name was never mentioned in the first legal contest) and Hugueta, that he could halt payment on the remaining 107 pounds of Luiseta's dowry. His story rivalled Luiseta's plea for *alimenta* in its pathos. He was asking for the court's intervention, 'first, because the *bona* and [economic] abilities of the aforementioned girls are so modest and diminished that if the dowry is repaid in full, the girls' condition will devolve into extreme poverty, and in the future, without a great deal of money, they will not be able to be sustained'.[35]

On behalf of the girls, Antoni, their guardian, made a powerful argument that invoked cultural expectations and fears: first, that children deserved to be protected[36] and second, that poverty was a state best avoided. Antoni alluded to a hungry present and also a dire future for his nieces should their mother's dowry be repaid in full.[37] He was trying to frighten the court with the spectre of girls reliant on the charity of others, unable to marry, and thus at risk to all of the dangers to which poor, single women might fall prey.[38] Trying to halt the full repayment of Luiseta Bariesse's dowry, Antoni Germani wanted to make the court and the larger community aware of the stakes for his nieces.[39]

He was also attacking his sister-in-law, painting her as a selfish mother willing to sacrifice her daughters' wellbeing, a direct challenge to Luiseta's carefully crafted image from the earlier case, that of grieving and caring *mater lactans*. His argument was straightforward: repaying Luiseta's dowry in full would make it impossible to provide a dowry and a future for her own children. Here, Antoni was making a case for his role as protector of the girls who were at risk of poverty. Antoni's petition to the court troubled and undermined Luiseta's claim that she, their mother, was the best person to act in the girls' best interest. When he anchored his legal counterarguments in an ethos of care for the girls, he also reminded the court that care for children was not uniquely a maternal instinct, but one shared by a broader community of caregivers. While mothers should be carers, in Marseille's narratives, not all carers were mothers.

Luiseta responded perhaps knowing she had an advantage since the judge had already ordered the restoration of her dowry. She and her curator focussed on a measured response and they decided to focus on the legitimacy of the petition itself, rather than the story it told.[40] After a series of appearances before the judge requesting that Antoni be ordered to pay Luiseta's court costs, Pons Antrasi asked the judge one final time to order Antoni to pay up. He asked this, he said, in light of the fact that the 'petition against Luiseta was incompetently drawn up and [because] she had been heedlessly harassed in this matter'.[41] This focus on the petition worked. The judge ordered Antoni to auction off a vineyard to complete the repayment of Luiseta's dowry and to pay her legal expenses.[42]

The legal contest between Luiseta and Antoni continued on 8 July 1396, only weeks later. In a new case, Luiseta and her mother Alegreta joined forces to petition the court to remove Antoni Germani as their daughters' and granddaughters' guardian.[43] This pairing of a mother and a grandmother was part of the strategy. It was an unusual legal team in Marseille. Grandmothers were frequent litigators, especially when they were the guardians of their grandchildren.[44] Mothers and daughters were occasional adversaries in the palace court.[45]

The decision to present two-generation united maternal front signalled that Luiseta acted with the full support of her natal family. Even through the dry, legal prose, it is not difficult to discern the fury behind Luiseta and Alegreta's joint words: 'At the time the said Antoni took up the guardianship of the two girls, he promised and swore that he would administer and take care of them and their goods well and faithfully,' which included procuring dowries for them and making a detailed inventory of their inheritance from their father.[46] The women's libel argued forcefully that Antoni had not kept those vital promises. Rather, he 'administered the girls' *bona* negligently, guiltily, and even deceitfully'.[47] Anchoring their accusation of deceit was their claim that Antoni had fraudulently omitted two hundred pounds, the price of a sale of a home Bertran had sold to the blacksmith Guilhem Blancardi, from the post-mortem inventory of Bertran's estate that he submitted to the court.[48] Even worse (*deterius*), they claimed, Antoni had installed his own mother Rixendis in the house, 'claiming rights in the house on behalf of the girls,' even though he knew the house had been sold.[49] Added to this preferential treatment for his mother was the accusation that Antoni let Rixendis claim a number of things, including three wine casks from Bertran's house that were rightfully the girls'. They also accused him of neglecting the harvest vineyards that the girls had inherited so that they were no longer fertile.[50] Their charges ended with a long list of small bits of land, a white donkey, and household goods that the girls inherited and that Antoni sold but which he had neglected to account for in the inventory of the girls' inheritance. Item by sold-but-not-inventoried item, they built a case for his malfeasance, and ended with a plea to the judge to remove Antoni as the girls' guardian.

For this third and final appearance before judge Antoni Riqueti, Luiseta built on her first legal story, that of the grieving mother worthy of the court's protection. This case presented Luiseta as a mother intervening on her children's behalf when the person meant to be fulfilling that role, their uncle and guardian, had failed. Because of her decision to co-litigate with her own mother, Luiseta explicitly brought before the court tensions between her natal family and the family she had married into. Luiseta's decision to enlist her mother's allegiance to challenge Antoni Germani's guardianship was a critique of the choice her husband had made to make his brother the guardians of their children. With the alliance of Luiseta the mother and Alegreta the maternal grandmother against the paternal uncle, these cases permitted a public performance that emphasized the matriline. Typically, in medieval Southern France, mothers did have guardianship of their children after their father's death, and the record is silent on why Luiseta was not so designated.[51] Perhaps Luiseta chose the mechanism of the courts to try to bring this expected, or even correct, order into their lives.

Luiseta's decision to make a public claim that the paternally aligned guardian of her children was not acting in good faith is a reminder of the tension that could exist between women's natal families and their marital families. As soon as Luiseta decided to use the courts to enforce the return of her dowry, she entered into an adversarial position not only with her dead husband's estate but with his patrimony. Since selling land was one way of raising the money to make Luiseta's dowry whole, that put her at odds with her husband's brother, who had a vested interest in maintaining that land as part of his family's holdings.[52] We do not know how the judge ruled in the final case between Luiseta and Alegreta on the one hand and Antoni Germani on the other. Harder to access through the documents, but surely very present for the litigants is the emotional tangle they all found themselves in. Suing a brother-in-law, who had legal voice for her own children, in the wake of her husband's death could not have been easy, even when the judges ruled in Luiseta's favour.

The case exemplifies conflict between natal families and marital families. Thomas Kuehn has suggested that the marriage of a dowered woman led to the end of her 'daily involvement' with her father, without any mention of continuing connections between women and her female relations.[53] Yet Luiseta and Alegreta's joint case against Antoni on behalf of their female descendants and Tovah Bender's more recent work have shown that, in fact, women remained deeply intertwined with their natal families even after marriage.[54] Married women maintained both affective ties and quotidian contact with their natal families, and when death intervened, women like Luiseta looked to their mothers to support them in the next phase of life.

The mother-daughter pair used their role as litigants to make an argument for the matriline over the patriline.[55] The women's story painted Antoni Germani as a cheat trying to benefit himself and his natal family. His mother was living in a house that had been sold and she was appropriating things that ought to have been either kept or sold for her grandchildren. Luiseta and her mother appeared as competent and clear headed, mindful of the details even in moments of terrible grief. In their version of events, they were paying attention to the girls' inheritance, noting when things went missing or when sales weren't being recorded. Their narrative drew on cultural scripts emphasizing women, mothers and wives, as responsible for the goings-on in their household.[56] Bringing Antoni's neglectful management of the girl's estate to the court's attention, they also let the court know that they had been watching and, when needed, they had intervened on behalf of the girls to make sure that they had the inheritance and dowry to which they were entitled. Though the language isn't used directly, the women emerge as adept managers, as, in other words, heads of households. They made the case that they were the ideal guardians of the two girls as well as managers of their inheritance and their own goods. It flips the logic of the first case between Luiseta and Antoni on its head and provides a path for Luiseta, perhaps buoyed by the success of her first two cases, to move away from needing the court's protection towards self-sufficiency.

The cultural scripts designating worthy women were deeply held and deployed, as the second case study under discussion here illustrates. Legal story telling that emphasized women's capabilities within their families and as managers of their property was so powerful its use was not confined to women. Male litigants wrote scripts emphasizing women's maternal care and piety when it was to their legal advantage, hoping for a spill over benefit to themselves in the form of a judge's favourable ruling. On 28 March, 1384, for example, a dispute over a donation of an estate to the diocese of Marseille opened. The chaplain of the city's cathedral told a moving story of a grandmother Silona Guasqui's devotion to her ill daughter and her grandson Berengar, who was contesting his pious grandmother's donation. Silona was not herself a litigant in the case, yet the chaplain mobilized her careful stewardship of the land and her familial devotion to argue that the land was hers to dispose of as she wished, despite her grandson's claims that the land had been his deceased mother's dotal land, and thus his by inheritance. The long and complicated case referenced arbitration and auctions; it relied on a broad spectrum of proofs from witness testimony to copies of notarized sales of slaves. In a mixture of Latin and Provençal, the chaplain and Berengar did battle over the right to donate land and claims of maternal affection, filial devotion, and grandmotherly pride.[57]

The chaplain's rhetorical argument rested on Silona's deep piety, her role as a mother to her motherless grandson, her role as a nurse for her infirm daughter, and her role managing her property well and soberly. This was his narrative: As a result of 'the pure and sincere love' (*purum amorem et sincerum*) that she had for the Church, after the death of her husband, the *domina* Silona Guasqui made a *donatio inter vivos* to the church, of an estate and the fruits of its lands over which she had presided 'peacefully and quietly and as the true lady and possessor' for the previous twenty years.[58] During this time, her grandson Berengar had lived with her, because, as witnesses would confirm, his mother Sanxia was an invalid who could not discharge her responsibilities either as a mother or as a manager of the property her son inherited after her husband and his father's death. Thus Silona took over the management of that property, in addition to her own.[59] It was Silona who paid her daughter's debts, and, when she died, sold some of her own *bona* to pay for her daughter's funeral and to purchase mourning clothes for herself and for Berengar.[60]

The chaplain defended the Church's right to Silona's estate with a story that cast Silona as the consummately caring mother and grandmother, as well as a long-standing manager of her own property and her grandson's. The legal goal was to prove the land was Silona's to dispose of as she wanted and to halt Berengar's attempt to claim the estate. Drawing on a cultural script of the pious and competent woman, the chaplain hoped to assure the judge of the rightness of the Church's claim. While we don't know the outcome of the case, this dispute demonstrates that the power of narratives about women's competency was such that they were mobilized in litigation, even when women themselves were not the litigants.

The cases so far have shown that when women litigated, they crafted legal personae for themselves that often sat at the crossroads of multiple identities.[61] Luiseta, across three separate cases, emphasized both her maternal need to provide for her young, ill children and her uxorial understanding: she knew what her husband's inventory should have contained and did not hesitate to bring her brother-in-law's malfeasance to the court.

In the final example, dating to 7 August 1385, Marita Bariole rolled out her multiple identities in one dotal retrocession case brought against her minor daughter Bartolomea and Bartolomea's tutors. In its opening clauses, Marita was identified as her labourer father's dowered daughter and her husband's widow, and a few paragraphs later, as the mother of Bartolomea.[62] This was complicated territory because her daughter was her legal adversary. Marita had to balance a claim to property that was legally hers against the perception that she was potentially disadvantaging her young daughter in order to set herself up in her next marriage. While Antoni Germani had tried to make the case that Luiseta Bariesse was endangering her daughters' financial well-being, neither he nor Luiseta had introduced the possibility of a remarriage. Perhaps Luiseta had no interest in or prospects for remarriage, despite the cultural norm. Women had to decide whether marriage or widowhood was more financially and socially advantageous.[63] Marita made a different calculation and remarried.

Marita's procurator Johan de Ysia presented her list of titles to the court. They went to great lengths to establish the normalcy of her dotal contract and the logical, legal conclusion that she was owed her dowry's return. They are paraphrased and condensed here:

> [Marita] asserts ... that after the marriage was contracted and was consummated by carnal copulation between Marita and Bartolmieu, the said Marita in October 1350 gave as her dowry to her father-in-law Peire de Barioli, the father of the said Bartolomieu, as the father and legitimate administrator of Bartolomieu, the following items, which included a *hospitium* [an urban dwelling of significant size] and substantial vineyards in the city's suburbs, as well as all the other goods which came to her from her father and her mother, which she inherited from her sister Laureta, the wife of Pons Bochardi. Also, before Bartolomieu died, he wrote a will that designated his daughter Bartolomea and his wife Marita as his universal heirs and in this same will he recognized Marita's dowry. [The libel contained a copy of the section of the will that listed the land and goods constituting Marita's dowry] Item, at the time of his death and before it, Bartolomieu had, held, and possessed Marita's dowry. Item, Peire de Bariole, Bartolomieu's father admitted to receiving Marita's paraphernal goods, in the amount of fifty *livres*, which he promised to use to purchase vines adjacent to those of Arnulfi Broche and Raynaut Bohery and the public street. Item, Bartolomieu had and received 58 *livres* for the sale of some of Marita's dotal vineyards, which he promised to restore to her dowry. Item, Bartolomieu, in his last will and testament left to Marita all of her clothes, furniture, and jewellery, to recognize the marital goods and services that she spent on behalf of her husband. On account of all of this, Marita's procurator acts against Bartolomea, the daughter and heir of Bartolomieu and against her

guardians, the noble Jacme Atulphe and the labourer Hugo Isnard, and asks that the judge rule that all of the particulars be returned to Marita and that they be responsible for her legal fees.[64]

Buried in this list of dotal assigns is the clause referencing Bartolomieu's will, which is worth reflecting on. It is a formula, acknowledging a husband's legal right to recognize his wife as one of his beneficiaries. Francine Michaud has shown that husbands in Marseille frequently left their wives legacies of cash, jewellery, and sometimes property in their wills, so this would not have made Bartolomieu unusual.[65] Leaving jewellery and furniture to Marita was a tangible recognition of Marita's service as Bartolomieu's wife, services that she was willing to litigate to obtain. It made explicit the bargain that medieval women entered into when they married: in exchange for acting as a wife, for providing sexual relations and maintaining a household, there would be financial recompense. At the very least, this payment should be the proper return of their dowries, but often, this included some additional legacy from their husbands. I have written elsewhere about the idea of an 'economy of care' in which medieval people participated, the notion that 'medieval people recognized that the labour of caring for someone had a quantitative value and the courts were the forums for assuring that recognition'.[66] Litigating to make sure she received the legacy from her husband was about the past. Marita made public her husband's recognition that she had been a worthy wife. It was also about her future- her ability to transform a legacy into a solid financial foundation.

When Marita's legal opponents, the guardians for her daughter Bartolomea, asserted that her husband Bartolomieu had, in fact, 'revoked and annulled the entire legacy to Marita, and did not wish Marita to have it at all,' they were attacking her future financial wellbeing, and publicly questioning whether her husband had recognized her as a wife worthy of post-mortem thought and care.[67] In the record's margin next to all but one of the guardian's five titles is the stark 'Non credit,' or 'She does not believe this,' which was a signal to the court that the litigant would contest the claim with witness testimony or other documentary proof.[68]

The only one of the guardians' titles that Marita conceded was this: 'The said Marita contracted with Hugo Rogeri and decided that the said Bartolomea contracted with words in the present tense with Monet Rogeri, the brother of the said Hugo'.[69] Put differently, Bartolomea's guardians claimed that Marita had arranged the marriage of her nine-year-old daughter to the brother of her own second husband.

Marita did not contest this title. As noted above, it would not have been unusual for Marita, a widow, to remarry. Nor would it have been unusual for a widowed mother to be involved in planning a marriage for the daughter of her first marriage. Michaud has shown that family members other than their fathers frequently dowered women in Marseille, so again, Marita's actions were perfectly within the mainstream.[70] Two details make this unusual, however. While it was not uncommon for two sisters to marry two brothers, I could find no other example of a mother and daughter marrying two brothers.[71] Further, by the fourteenth century, while women in Mediterranean Europe could be married by their late teens, nine-year-old girls were not considered nubile.[72] And the language of the title, suggesting Marita approved the exchange of words 'in the present tense' certainly suggested that this was a marriage, not a long-lasting betrothal. Canon law of the Middle Ages distinguished between present (I take you as my husband/wife) and future consent (I will take you as my husband/wife) to a marriage, where the former was a betrothal and the latter an actual marriage.[73]

Marita's own procurator brought his concerns about this to the court. In a standard rebuttal to the titles brought by the opposing litigants, he listed reasons why each title was 'impertinens' or legally irrelevant. When he arrived at the fourth title, which was the one about the mother-daughter marriage plan, he had this to say: 'In the fourth title, where it says that Marita and Bartolomea her daughter had contracted [marriage] with two brothers, it is certain that the said Bartolomea hasn't reached an age where she can be married, since she is but nine years old, as is clear from her appearance and her body'.[74]

Why was Marita's own procurator undermining the legality of an event she had conceded had happened? The first and perhaps simplest explanation is scribal error. Perhaps the court notary was moving too quickly and wrote 'credit,' rather than *non credit ut ponitur* (she doesn't believe it as it is stated) or *non credit* as he had next to the other four titles. We cannot know, but this may be evidence of a legal disagreement between Marita and her procurator. Perhaps Marita wanted the court to know she had arranged for her daughter to marry her own betrothed's brother. As a strategy, this point positioned Marita as a woman in command of her future, who made plans on behalf of her daughter as well. Sara McDougall has argued that late medieval people made many choices about marriage partners not in line with the strictest interpretation of canon law. Perhaps Marita assumed there would be no repercussions for this unusual marital pairing.[75] From Marita's perspective, marrying two brothers would intensify her legal and social connections with her daughter and pull her daughter further into a network of familial connections that she controlled, away from the family of her deceased husband.

I am speculating, of course. Yet the conflict between Marita's agreement with the title about her marriage plans and her procurator's legal challenge to it stands as an important reminder that despite all of the strategizing that went into litigation, there were many opportunities for the unexpected to appear. In those moments, the carefully crafted legal stories women told to the judge and their broader community risked unravelling.

While the record is silent on the outcome of Bartolomea's potential marriage, it reveals that Marita did, in fact, remarry. On 10 May 1396, Marita was identified as 'the widow of the deceased Bartolomieu Bariole, now the wife of Hugo Rogeri'.[76] She was still claiming that lands purchased with funds from her dowry had not been returned to her and arguing that her opponents were liable for her legal expenses. The record of the case ended two folia later, with no indication of a resolution or hint of how the judge might have ruled. Not having access to the judgements is one of the frustrations of working with these civil court records, as rich as they are.

Conclusion

So, where does this leave us? Women in Marseille who litigated could not come to court and tell just any story they wanted. But the court's location outdoors in the marketplace meant that their legal opponent and the judge were not their only audiences. The notaries who recorded the court's business made no note of the passersby or their possible interjections, but the women knew their arguments could make their way back to family and neighbours, to friend and to foe. Women litigants, in collaboration with notaries and sometimes procurators or lawyers, built their cases within a legal framework and a set of cultural scripts that emphasized their rootedness in their families, as Luiseta and Alegreta's joint appearance signified. The women also signalled their competence, when they noted each and every one of the items missing from Antoni Germani's inventory. Luiseta further positioned herself as a widow in need of protection when she asked the court to intervene on her behalf and on behalf of her small children. Rather than contradictory, these different positionings show Luiseta, her mother, Marita, and the other women litigating in Marseille as attentive to strategies that would bolster their community standing and give them the best shot at a favourable judgement. At moments of crisis, impending poverty, loss of a partner, women came to court to tell their stories. Litigating gave women an opportunity to make public a version of themselves as mothers, managers, mourners, and more that would quite literally be written into history.

Notes

1 For an overview of the dotal regime in Marseille, see Daniel Lord Smail, 'Démanteler le patrimoine: les femmes et les biens dans la Marseille mediévale', *Annales. Histoire, Sciences Sociales* 52:2 (1997) pp. 343–368.
2 Luiseta Bariesse's first case against her husband's estate is found in Archives Départmentales des Bouches-du-Rhône (hereafter ABDR) 3 B 124; the case began on fol. 278r on 12 December 1395. She is later involved in two litigations with her daughters' representative, found in ABDR 3 B 126; the first case began on fol. 140r on 15 June 1396 and the second on 171v on 8 July 1396.
3 Scholars have been attentive to the limitations of what we can learn from medieval and early modern litigation. Lu Ann Homza has recently summarized these concerns in 'When Witches Litigate: New Sources from Early Modern Navarre', *Journal of Modern History* 19 (June 2019), p. 250.
4 Natalie Zemon Davis, *Fiction in the Archives: Pardon Tales and Their Tellers in Sixteenth-Century France* (Stanford, 1987).
5 Jeanette M. Fregulia, 'Stories Worth Telling: Women as Business Owners and Investors in Early Modern Milan', *Early Modern Women*, 10:1 (Fall, 2015), p. 130.
6 Marian Bleeke, *Motherhood and Meaning in Medieval Sculpture: Representations from France* (Woodbridge, 2017), p. 8.

7 Daniel Lord Smail, *The Consumption of Justice: Emotions, Publicity and Legal Culture in Marseille, 1264–1423*, (Ithaca, 2003).
8 I have made this argument elsewhere. See my *Witnesses, Neighbors, and Community in Late Medieval Marseille* (New York, 2013), esp. pp. 68–70.
9 Régine Pernoud, *Les statutes municipaux de Marseille* (Paris and Monaco, 1949), p. xxvi.
10 Manlio Bellomo, *The Common Legal Past of Europe, 1000–1800* (Washington, D.C., 1995).
11 All of these procedures were laid out in legal manuals like Guillaume Durand, *Speculum clarissimi viri Guilelmi Durandi, una cum Iohanni Andreae ac Baldi doctorum in utraque iurium* (Lyon, 1547).
12 Smail, *The Consumption of Justice*, p. 44.
13 One such example in the notarial casebook of Johan de Scalis is an acta dated 7 March 1424, which records the Spaniard Anfos de Portugalli granting permission to his wife Maria to appoint procurators to represent her in court. See ADBR 355E88, fol. 7v.
14 McDonough, *Witnesses, Neighbors, and Community*, p. 40.
15 Thomas Kuehn, 'Person and Gender in the Laws', in Judith Brown and Robert C. Davis (eds.), *Gender and Society in Renaissance Italy* (New York, 1998), pp. 87–106. For the legal requirement of a husband's permission to litigate, see McDonough, *Witnesses, Neighbors, and Community*, p. 40. For more on women as litigants, see Smail, *Consumption of Justice*, p. 44, and as witnesses, see McDonough, *Witnesses, Neighbors, and Community*, pp. 5–6, 32–34.
16 There are sometimes clues that indicate how a judge was leaning, which a reading of the marginal notes on individual cases can reveal. In the case to establish the priority of creditors from the estate of Jacme Reynaut, which his daughter Batrona the wife of Johan d'Aix brought to the court, the judge's marginal notations make clear that Batrona's claim on her dowry was the first priority. See ADBR 3 B 119, fol. 74r. The case began on 22 April 1392 on fol. 67v.
17 The case to establish the priority of creditors of the estate of Laurens Bernart is one such example. The witness testimony contains transcriptions in Provençal of conversations between some of the women claiming their right to be repaid. See ADBR 3 B 119; case began on 22 April, 1392 on fol. 67v; the witness testimony began on 83r.
18 ADBR 3 B 127; case began on 8 March 1396 on fol. 34r.
19 ADBR 3 B 127 fol. 44r: 'quia lis est odiosa inter mater et filios vivito amicabiliter debet terminari'. For more on the arbitration process and the frequency with which civil cases ended in arbitration, see Thomas Kuehn, *Law, Family, and Women: Towards a Legal Anthropology of Renaissance Italy* (Chicago, 1991), esp. pp. 19–74.
20 We can glean some information about Luiseta's age because she litigates with a *curator*. This was a legal requirement for women under the age of twenty-five, who wished to claim their dowries. See Francine Michaud, *Un signe des temps: Accroissements des cries familiales autor du patrimoine à Marseille à la fin du XIIIe siècle*, (Toronto, 1994), p. 148.
21 ADBR 3 B 126; case began on fol. 278r. The clause recounting the agreement to sell land is on fol. 281r.
22 Smail, 'Démanteler le patrimoine', p. 343.
23 Kathryn Reyerson, *Mothers and Sons, Inc. Martha de Cabanis in Medieval Marseille* (Philadelphia, 2018), p. 32.
24 Thomas Kuehn, *Emancipation in Late Medieval Florence* (New Brunswick, 1982), p. 21.
25 ADBR 3 B 126 fol. 279r: Ipsaque Ludoviceta neque pro se neque pro Huguneta eius filia quam lactat, usque nunc a tempore mortis defuncti, quod est trium mensus cum dimido vel circa a dicto tutore pro alimentis nichil habuit propterquam xxii grossis, licet dicta filia fuerit infirma a festo omnium sanctorum cura, eapropter requirit dictus curator curatorio nomine quo supra, per vos dictum dominum iudicem compelli et cogi dictum Antonium ad tradendum et expediendum ipso Ludovicete alimenta praeterita quo mutuo recepit tam a matre et sorore suis quam etiam a diversis aliis personis quam finam ascendere xii librarum.

26 Amanda Capern, 'Maternity and Justice in the Early Modern English Courts of Chancery', *Journal of British Studies*, 58 (October 2019), p. 705.
27 Rebecca Winer, 'Conscripting the Breast: Lactation, Slavery, and Salvation in the Realms of Aragon and Kingdom of Majorca', *Journal of Medieval History*, 34 (2008), p. 177.
28 Winer, 'Conscripting the Breast', p. 166.
29 ADBR 3 B 126 fol. 212r; the case between Silona Filhone and the sailor Bernart Valencia began on 22 July 1396 on fol. 179r: Et quia iudicis interest pupillos et orfanos et viduas succerrere ne indebite oprimantur.
30 Marie Kelleher, *Measure of Women: Law and Female Identity in the Crown of Aragon* (Philadelphia, 2010), pp. 62–65.
31 ADBR 3 B 124 fol. 281. The text reads: Et alias donec et quosque eidem Ludovicete satisfactum fuerit de dote supra per eam postulatam et etiam taxare habeant alimentam dictarum pupillaram, iuxta facultatem et quantitatem bonorum dicti Bertrandi considerate condicione personarum.
32 ADBR 3 B 124 fol. 282r: cum a longe tempore circa in presenti causa non fuerit processum.
33 On delaying tactics, see Smail, *Consumption of Justice*, pp. 47–48.
34 ADBR 3 B 124 fol. 283r.
35 ADBR 3 B 126 fol. 140r-v.: Primo quia bona et facultates pupillarum predictarum sunt ita modice et ad eo extenuate quod si predicta dos integraliter solveretur, ipse pupille ad extremam pauperitate totaliter devenuerunt e futuris temporibus non possent sine magna pecunia substentari.
36 Danièle Alexandre-Bidon and Didier Lett, *Les enfants au Moyen Age Ve-XVe siècles* (Paris, 1997), pp. 99–108.
37 Lucie Laumonier has shown that poverty was not necessarily an impediment for young women receiving dowries, as charitable institutions and extended family members would often provide the funds. That said, a dowry-less future was likely the threat Antoni Germani was holding out to the court. See her 'Meanings of Fatherhood in late Medieval Montpellier: Love, Care, and the Exercise of *Patria potestas*', in Raffaella Sarti (ed.), Men at Home, Special Issue of *Gender & History*, 27:3 (November 2015), pp. 559–660.
38 Sharon Farmer, *Surviving Poverty in Medieval Paris: Gender, Ideology, and the Daily Lives of the Poor* (Ithaca, 2005), p. 126.
39 Sally Mayall Brasher, *Hospitals and Charity: Religious Culture and Civic Life in Medieval Northern Italy*, (Manchester, 2017), pp. 20–23.
40 ADBR 3 B 126 fol. 142r.
41 ADBR 3 B 126 fol. 143r: … et quia inepte facta dicta peticio contra dictam Ludovicetam et ipsam in hoc fuerat temere vexata.
42 ADBR 3 B 126 fol. 143r.
43 ADBR 3 B 126; the case began on fol. 171v.
44 An example of such a case is that of Rostanga Anglici, a widow and guardian of her grandchildren. The merchant Peire Olivari brought her to court over an outstanding debt the grandchildren's father owed him. The case is found ADBR 3 B 125 and began on 6 July 1395 on fol. 105r.
45 Hugueta Lanrigue and her mother Mathea Guille must have had quite a contentious relationship, as a pair of suit and countersuit from 1391 suggest. They battled over an unpaid rent and a lien that Matthea Guille imposed on her daughter. The cases are both in ADBR 3 B 845; the first began on 8 May 1381 on fol. 116r and the second on 10 May 1391 on fol. 170r.
46 ADBR 3 B 126 fol. 172r. [Q]uod licet dictus Antoni tempore sibi decretis tutele dictarum pupillarum promisisset et iurasset dictas pupillas et earum bona bene et fideliter regere et gubernare earum dotalia procurando et inutilia pro posse evitando.
47 ADBR 3 B 126 fol. 172v. [T]am negligenter quam culpabiliter seu etiam dolose bona ipsarum pupillarum administravit.

48 For more on post mortem inventories, see Daniel Lord Smail, *Legal Plunder: Household and Debt Collection in Late Medieval Europe* (Cambridge, 2016), pp. 24–25, 61–62. Luiseta and Alegreta were not unique in suing over fudged inventories. For a comparative case see ABDR 3 B 126: Johan de Xies accused his sister-in-law of omitting important things from her husband's post-mortem inventory. The case began on 26 May 1396 on fol. 129r.
49 ADBR 3 B 126 fol. 173r: [E]t quod deterius est cum Rixendis mater ipsius Antoni Germani de facto anno proximo lapso de mense septembris … ipsarum pupillarum predictum hospitium occupavit se ius in eo habere pretendendo.
50 ADBR 3 B 126 fol. 173r-v.
51 On mothers as guardians of their children see Kelleher, *Measure of Woman*, p. 71 and Reyerson, *Mother and Sons, Inc.*, p. 80. For an example in Marseille, see *acta* in which Garcendis de Jotis, as mother and tutor of her son, recognized the payment of a debt owed to her deceased husband's estate; ADBR 351 E 37, notarial casebook of Johan Georgi, fol. 34v.
52 For more on difficult dotal retrocessions, see Michaud, *Un signe des temps*, pp. 143–144.
53 Thomas Kuehn, *Heirs, Kin, and Creditors in Renaissance Florence* (New York, 2008), p. 66.
54 Tovah Bender, 'Their Father's Daughters: Women's Social Identities in Fifteenth-Century Florence', *Journal of Family History*, 38:4 (2013), pp. 371–386.
55 Andrée Courtemanche, *La richesse des femmes: Patrimoines et gestion à Manosque au XIVe siècle* (Montreal, 1993), p. 15.
56 This is a point made over and over again in conduct literature. The narrator of the *Menagier de Paris* consoles his wife that he will pay for household help, yet her responsibility within the household is 'the command, the supervision, and the conscientiousness to have things done right'. See *The Good Wife's Guide: Le Ménagier de Paris, a Medieval Household Book*, trans. Gina L. Greco and Christine M. Rose (Ithaca, 2009), p. 181.
57 ABDR 3 B 122; case began on fol. 89r.
58 ADBR 3 B 122 fol. 96v-98r. A *donatio inter vivos*, is s gift made during the donor's lifetime. The act certifying this gift is found in the notarial casebook of Guilem Barbani, ADBR 351 E 92, fol. 18v-19v.
59 Guilhem de Massilia's testimony was clear on this point. See ADBR 3 B 122 fol. 146r-v.
60 ADBR 3 B 122 fol. 155v.
61 Kelleher, *Measure of Woman*, p. 12.
62 Marita Bariole's case is in ADBR 3 B 105; the case began on fol. 118v on 7 August 1385.
63 For a recent resume of the debate over widows' agency, see Ellen Kittel and Kurt Queller, 'Wives and Widows in Medieval Flanders', *Social History* 41:4 (2016), pp. 436–454.
64 ADBR 3 B 105 fol. 119r-121r. The clause in italics was: quod bonis maritis et serviciis per eam impensis dicto marito suo et renumerationem eorundem.
65 Michaud, *Un signe des temps*, pp. 59–61.
66 McDonough, *Witnesses, Neighbors, and Community*, p. 69.
67 ABDR 3 B 105 fol. 125r.
68 For more on this procedure, see McDonough, *Witnesses, Neighbors, and Community*, p. 40.
69 ADBR 3 B 105 fol. 125v: Item ponnunt dicti tutorum et si negatum fuerit intendunt quod dicta Marita contraxit cum Hugone Rogeri et fecit quod dicta Bartolomea contraxit pro verba de presenti cum Moneto Rogeri fratre dicte Hugonis.
70 Michaud, *Un signe des temps*, p. 92.
71 Such a marriage, between a mother/daughter pair and two brothers would likely have run afoul of the canon law prohibitions against incest, broadly drawn even after the Fourth Lateran Council of 1215. See James A. Brundage, *Law Sex, and Christian Society in Medieval Europe* (Chicago, 1987), pp. 355–357. That doesn't mean those prohibitions were followed.

72 For a discussion of women's age of marriage in the medieval Mediterranean, see Reyerson, *Mother and Sons, Inc.*, p. 35 and Rebecca Winer, *Women, Wealth, and Community in Perpignan, 1250–1300: Christians, Jews, and Enslaved Muslims in a Medieval Mediterranean Town* (Aldershot, 2006), pp. 25–26.
73 Brundage, *Law, Sex, and Christian Society*, pp. 264–265.
74 ADBR 3 B 105 fol. 126v: Quarta position que dicit quod Marita et Bartolomea filia sua contraxerunt cum duobus fratribus. Et tamen est certo certius quod dicta Bartolomea non parvenit ad annum nubiliem cum non sit etatis nonem annorum ut prout ex aspectu seu corporis apparere.
75 See Sara McDougall, *Bigamy and Christian Identity in Late Medieval Champagne* (Philadelphia, 2012), pp. 11–12.
76 ADBR 3 B 105 fol. 150r: '... dicte Marite relicte condam Bartolomei de Bariole nunc uxore Hugonis Rogerio'.

2
CONSENT AND COERCION

Women's use of marital consent laws as legal defence in late medieval Paris

Kristi DiClemente

When Jeanne, daughter of Jehan de Sartrouville, entered the court of the archdeacon of Paris in February 1385, her goal was to convince the court that she was not engaged. The plaintiff, Guy Kaerauroez, claimed that Jeanne had consented to be his wife and had thus created a legally binding marriage contract. Jeanne argued that her consent was forced and that she had no intention of marrying him. Indeed, she told a harrowing story of being attacked by a group of Guy's friends while walking through a neighbouring village, and that she consented only 'for fear', *pro terrore*, of those friends who had drawn blades and pushed her to the ground.[1] To further prove the coercion, she claimed that she 'immediately retracted' her words of consent, *statim hic reclamavit*, and so the contract was invalid.[2] When asked about Jeanne's version of the story, Guy agreed that it was the truth and the court ruled that there was no consent and therefore no marriage contract.[3]

Although not always true in practice, free consent of both parties was legally required to create a marriage contract in fourteenth-century France. This consent could not be coerced through physical violence, threats, trickery, imprisonment, kidnapping, or any other means. Jeanne's story above contains obvious coercion through violence, and the violence alone should have negated the agreement that Jeanne made under duress. What is significant about this case for the current study is not the violence, but that Jeanne's understanding of marriage law, and consent included the need for a verbal denial of the suit. Sartrouville v. Kaerauroez is the sole case in this study that involves obvious physical violence as a means of coercion, but Jeanne's insistence on her immediate verbal dissent shows an understanding of the importance of the words of consent and the intention behind those words. Evidence from the Officialité of Paris indicates that female litigants protested against the validity of marriage contracts in court by focussing on the intent behind consent rather than solely on the words

DOI: 10.4324/9780429278037-3

and actions of the event. This focus on both words and intention indicates that litigants understood the requirements for consent and therefore knew how to use them to argue against marriage contracts.

Marriage disputes are an excellent way to see how medieval women navigated the legal system because they participated in these cases to a higher degree than most other types of cases and acted in a variety of roles. Women often brought marriage cases to court or they personally defended themselves from unwanted marriages, and through these activities we can begin to hear their voices in the text, although imperfectly. Despite having access to the legal system, women like Jeanne were still vulnerable to coercion through violence and social pressure from partners and family, and were often taken to court to defend against accusations of marriage consent. Legal cases arising from coerced marital consent can tell us how women as defendants participated in the legal process, their understanding of intention and consent, and their access to justice and the legal system in fourteenth-century France more broadly.

Evidence for this study comes from marriage contract disputes from the 1384 to 1387 register of the Officialité of Paris, which is the only surviving fourteenth-century register from the Archidiaconal court of Paris.[4] The examination of this register allows us a view of ordinary women and the ways they used the law and the court to argue their cases. The focus of this chapter is on the general understanding of marital consent as indicated by specific examples of female defendants who used this understanding against attempted coerced marriages in court. These women were called to court because they denied alleged marriage contracts, and I argue that they understood the value of the intention behind their verbal consent under the law and used that knowledge to shape their performances and testimony within the court. In addition, the court recognised verbal dissent as an effective defence against attempted coercion and ruled accordingly.

The court

The Officialité was located on the Île de la Cité in the heart of Paris, and its jurisdiction covered the majority of northern Île de France and parts of Picardy. In total it 'encompassed two deaneries and approximately 180 rural and urban parishes'.[5] The majority of the litigants and witnesses for whom we have locations came from either within the city limits or the area that today forms the Parisian suburbs, but in the fourteenth century were independent villages. Additionally, while information about most litigants' occupations and social status are not readily available, when present it indicates that most litigants, both male and female, had steady employment in a trade or craft. Some occupations of litigants represented in this register were maid, butcher, rope maker, hatter, seamstress, and locksmith. There are several entries that include knightly titles, *domina/dominus*, but they are rare. Additionally, the social status of litigants is suggested by the fact that they were required to pay court fees, fees for legal representation, and fines for disobeying the court's ruling. Court fees could range from a few *derniers* to several *livres*, whereas fines sometimes reached 100 *livres*, a princely sum, which would have been unavailable to the poor.

The Officialité heard both civil and criminal complaints about issues that involved the Church but were deemed not sufficiently important to go to the Bishop's court. According to James Brundage, much of the court's business enforced the 'church's disciplinary rules concerning sexual misbehaviour, drunkenness, marital disputes, infractions of the church's prohibition on Sundays and feast days, and the like'.[6] The court was particularly concerned with issues of morality and personal conduct, and within the Officialité's register are a variety of cases concerning injury (both physical and verbal assaults), debt, ecclesiastical concerns (e.g. the election of church wardens and transfers of church property), testamentary issues (e.g. the appointment of tutors for orphans), and matrimonial cases (e.g. contract disputes and separation cases).[7] This register contains 376 marriage cases, roughly 25% of the total cases recorded. Ninety one of these cases were requests for marital separations based on complaints of cruelty, neglect, profligacy, and adultery. The remaining 285 cases were contract disputes in which litigants contested the validity or even the existence of marriage contracts.

Marriage contract disputes are an effective way to uncover the role women played as litigants in the court. Due to the nature of these complaints, each case involved a woman as either plaintiff (41.5%), or defendant (58.5%), and although the cases are short and do not include extensive depositions or testimony, the number of women involved in this court allows us to draw some conclusions about women's experiences within the legal system. This study examines thirty-five of these contract cases in which female defendants hinged their defences on their verbal lack of intention to marry, *nec intentio*, or displeasure/disagreement with the alleged marriage, *non placere*. Their understanding of verbal consent and the intention behind the words in the creation of legal marriage contracts is most evident in these cases.

Despite the number of women in the cases, the use of court cases has its limits for the study of daily life due to its extraordinary nature, and there are several issues with the production of court registers that are important to remember throughout this discussion. First, the probability of litigants and witnesses bending the truth—or outright lying—about the events in question is a timeless problem for judges. In order to work around this problem, I will be analysing the cases as a kind of performance that was interpreted by the court officials, which can then tell us how the women and their communities understood the consent laws and used them in court. We cannot assume that the events in question occurred exactly as recorded, but the way the women focussed on their intentions can shed light on their understanding of the legal process of marriage.

The second issue is that litigants in the Parisian Officialité had the opportunity to hire legal counsel to advice their cases, and some cases under consideration here contain evidence of their presence. The main group of officials who worked with litigants in the Officialité were the *procuratores*, who could represent the litigants as a proxy, advise them about the law, and draw up legal documents on behalf of the court.[8] In some cases, they also instructed their clients in appropriate court behaviour to improve their chance of success.[9] Daniel Lord Smail argues that legal counsellors in medieval Marseille shaped the testimony of witnesses to create a homogenous story for the court forming 'a sequence of depositions designed to build up an image of an aesthetic of truth'.[10] Although it was not necessary for litigants to hire *procuratores*, if the case was complex there was a good chance one was involved, and their presence and name were noted in the legal record. Professionals could therefore shift the litigants' understanding of consent laws and push the focus of their defence towards their intentions behind consent and away from the specific words and rituals.

A third limit to the reliability of court cases as a direct representation of events was the mediation of a notary. This issue is twofold as it involved a third party writing down an abbreviated series of events while also translating the testimony from vernacular speech into legal Latin formulae.[11] Unlike court records from the English consistory court, which contain lengthy depositions in vernacular English, the Parisian register contains only four cases with short, incomplete depositions, all of which were recorded in Latin. These two difficulties can raise questions about the exact phrases litigants used and the stories they told to the court, but it does not render the registers unusable. Instead, this mediated language indicates the official reception of the court performance and translates it into legal formulae. Therefore, historians can view the registers through the lens of contemporary society, which casts light on societal norms. According to Smail, 'Disputants can't choose how they engage in disputes. Instead, local culture provides them with a limited number of scripts that they, as actors, must follow'.[12] Thus, what we learn from specific cases and arguments is more about what the court and society expected than the specific details of the particular case under review. For cases of disputed marriage contracts, the court expected some form of free verbal consent, and when it was absent, they deemed the contract invalid.

In late medieval Europe, free consent of the couple was the only legal requirement to form an indissoluble marriage in the eyes of the Church; the dowry, bans, church, priest, and other ritual trappings were merely incidentals. They were important incidentals for creating a licit union and for cementing the social aspects of marriage, but they were not necessary to the creation of the marriage sacrament itself. By the fourteenth century, there were two options for verbal consent to marry: future and present consent. Words of future consent, *verba de futuro*, initiated the marriage contract and created a union that was legally binding but was not fully realised until consummation. Words of present consent, *verba de praesenti*, initiated the contract and finalised the marriage sacrament at once, without the need for consummation. Both forms of consent were used to varying degrees in the Middle Ages to create a marriage, but present consent was indissoluble whereas contracts created with future consent but without consummation could be dissolved by the ecclesiastical court. The Officialité of Paris heard both types of cases; however, within the fourteenth-century register only two cases involved *verba de praesenti* and the remainder were *verba de futuro*, with and without later consummation.[13]

The 283 contract cases with *verba de futuro* fall into three broad categories for analysis that can help clarify the ways women used the court system: 19% of plaintiffs explicitly claimed consent with consumption, 59% of plaintiffs claimed consent without consummation, and in 22% of cases consummation is unclear. Although it is not exact, often the type of case correlated with the role women played within it: in cases with consummation, 86% of the plaintiffs were women, and these women lost all of the seventeen cases for which we have the conclusion; only one consummation case ended in a valid marriage and the plaintiff was male.[14] Alternately, in cases of future consent without consummation, only 27% of the plaintiffs were women and of the twenty six known outcomes, only one ended in a marriage contract; similarly, a single male plaintiff was successful out of the fifty four known outcomes. What these numbers show is that, in general, defendants were successful in arguing their cases against marriage contracts regardless of gender, and that the majority of these successful defendants were women. One reason for the success rate of defendants in cases without consummation was their knowledge of consent, and the way they denied the marriage contracts in court. This knowledge was especially obvious in the cases where others were attempting to coerce or manipulate them into these contracts.

Consent and coercion

Although not formally trained in the intricacies of present and future consent, there is evidence that the litigants understood that free consent involved more than simply saying the correct words. Marriage requirements such as public banns show that general knowledge of legal requirements was widespread in medieval communities; without understanding the purpose behind these actions, they were meaningless. In a broader discussion of legal understanding within the community, Tiffany Vann Sprecher argues that in the fifteenth- and sixteenth-centuries the Parisian parishes regulated the behaviours, including illicit marriages, of their clergy within the court system.[15] It is not such a leap to accept that women who policed others' marriages would understand the legalities surrounding their own. Similarly, Bronach C. Kane, in her book *Popular Memory and Gender in Medieval England*, states, 'In the church-court testimony, men and women demonstrated detailed knowledge of the workings of the law. Witnesses relied on language that suggests the dissemination of legal expertise in everyday conversations and through social networks'.[16] Litigants' use of consent laws within the Parisian marriage contract cases shows a similar widespread understanding of the court system and marriage laws in fourteenth-century Paris. Regardless of whether women received their legal education from their communities or their legal counsel, they clearly came into court with that knowledge and successfully used that knowledge to avoid coerced marriages.

Unfortunately, the register itself provides few details of the events leading up to a suit; these cases do not contain direct testimony from the litigants, rather they list names of the parties involved in the case and provide basic summaries of the arguments. The notaries relied on standard formulae to record the process in court; therefore, many aspects of the cases are similar. In general they were 'he said/she said' arguments where the plaintiff claimed a marriage contract with the defendant using *verba de futuro*, and the defendant denied contracting the union. The case of Jehan le Museur and Jeanne la Riche Femme represents the simplest form of spousal contracts without consummation within the register.[17] Jehan took Jeanne to court to enforce a marriage contract of *verba de futuro*. Jeanne denied the marriage, swearing that she had never contracted the marriage, nor had she promised to marry him. The plaintiff, having no witnesses, deferred to her oath, and the court absolved Jeanne of the petition, allowing both to freely marry someone else later.[18] This basic formula is common throughout the register, and while the cases are repetitive there are slight differences that can speak to the ways litigants performed their cases in the court.

One of these minor shifts in the formula is when notaries used *nec intentio* (no intention) and *non placere* (displeasure) to describe defendants' verbal denial of *verba de futuro* marriage contracts. *Nec intentio* appears in the register thirteen times: it is used to describe women's lack of consent eight times, men's three times, and on the remaining two occasions, the notary used the phrase to indicate a mutual denial of the contract. Defendants used a form of *non placere* in twenty-seven cases, usually to indicate a conditional contract that hinged on a family member's agreement to the match. In three of these cases, female defendants used this phrase to indicate their own displeasure with a match and in the two entries of this type for which we have the result, the female defendant was successful. Only once did a man use this phrase for his own defence, and he was also successful. Agnes de Maubeuge, discussed below, was the only defendant who used both phrases to signal her lack of consent to a marriage contract. Indeed, in each case for which the court's decision exists, defendants who argued *nec intentio* and *non placere* were absolved of the petitions. The addition of these phrases to the standard legal formula suggest that the majority female defendants understood that consent was more than merely the *verba*, focussed on their lack of free consent, and were successful in court including in the face of significant pressure from family and friends.

The first case in which *nec intentio* appears within the register was the April 18, 1385 case of Philip de Baillon c. Adelina, widow of Jehan Asse.[19] Philip insisted that he had created a contract with Adelina using *verba de futuro*, which she denied. She swore that she 'never contracted the espousal with the aforementioned plaintiff, nor promised to take him in marriage, nor at any time was it her intention to take him as her husband'.[20] The court absolved Adelina of Philip's petition, and the court denied the contract. Similarly, in February 1386 Jehan Galteri took Jeanne la Goupill to court to enforce a marriage contract through *verba de futuro*. Jeanne swore that she 'never contracted marriage with Jehan nor had she any intention to take him in matrimony'.[21] This case was also dismissed, and Jeanne was absolved of Jehan's petition.[22] In both cases the defendants used their intention and verbal lack of consent as the basis of their arguments against marriage contracts, indicating that these women understood the importance of free consent and used that knowledge in court. Unfortunately, there is no direct testimony from the litigants, but the recording of *nec intentio* sets the defence within the bounds of a cultural script that Smail saw in Marseille. In addition, there is no evidence of legal counsel in either case and the notary recorded that the defendant swore to the dissent, both indicating that the women knew the importance of intention and consent in the marriage creation process when they entered the court.

In some cases, there is evidence of manipulation or trickery to coerce the women to agree to marriages. Through the use of physical rituals plaintiffs argued that the women had consented, and in these cases the intentions behind the verbal consent and ritual were critical to the defendants' arguments. In a case that revolved around a ritual exchange of food the importance of intention is starkly evident.[23] In August 1386, Étienne Derot took Laurencia Chippon to court to enforce a marriage contract that he claimed they had made through an unwitnessed *verba de futuro*, which Laurencia denied. She replied that they had walked to her godmother's house together, and Laurencia had given Étienne a *gastellus* (a small cake, or loaf of bread) from which they exchanged pieces similar to a modern wedding cake ritual.[24] Étienne insisted that this exchange of food, for which he had witnesses, indicated a marriage contract, whereas Laurencia claimed that it did not, and she had no intention of marrying him.[25] In this case, Étienne performed an exchange of bites of a *gastellus* before a witness to reinforce the alleged unwitnessed *verba de futuro,* and signified his intention to marry Laurencia. Public espousals often included an exchange of gifts as visual representations of the promises made; thus, his insistence that this exchange represented marriage was not unheard of. In the register, Laurencia's lack of intention appears directly after Étienne's statement about the purpose of the food exchange, 'afterwards the same plaintiff said that he gave the piece of bread to the defendant in the name of marriage (*nomine matrimonii*), and the same defendant said that it was never her intention (*nunquam fuit intentionis sue*) to take the plaintiff himself in marriage'.[26] As with Jeanne de Sartrouville, Laurencia's immediate denial of the contract shows that she knew it was her intention to consent, and the verbal denial of that consent, that was important in court.

Although unusual within this register, in general, a gift of food could be interpreted as a gift of espousal, similar to a coin, ring, or gloves.[27] In addition, despite the legality of the words of consent, according to Diana O'Hara, 'the gifts were themselves crucial foci of investigation when the validity of a marriage was debated'.[28] The marriage feast, especially, was a symbol of the Eucharist and signified the sacramental nature of marriage.[29] More than just a gift then, the exchange of food was often evidence of a marital relationship as Vann Sprecher found in her research on priests and their sexual partners: 'Theoretical links among sex, eating, and drinking associated all three with marital life ... eating with a man was one aspect of a spousal relationship'.[30] April Harper especially sees this connection in many medieval fabliaux, particularly with illicit sex.[31] 'Not only are food and sex often paired activities, they are occasionally viewed as being comparable and interchangeable'.[32] Étienne clearly intended the witnessed ritual to reinforce the unwitnessed *verba de futuro*, and Laurencia needed to refute the meaning of the ritual if she was going to succeed in her defence; it is in this sense that the importance of Laurencia's intention was critical. Laurencia denied having said the unwitnessed words of consent and focussed her defence on the meaning of the witnessed food exchange by arguing against its symbolic nature and focussing on her intention. Étienne may have viewed the food exchange as a symbolic consummation of the union: in effect, making the espousal more complete and indicating a conjugal relationship. Perhaps this was the reason Laurencia verbalised the intention behind ritual in her defence against the espousal, fearing the symbolic consummation would cement the union.

When confronted with a case of two men vying for the same woman, one with agreed on *verba de futuro*, and the other with a hand-clasping ritual, the court similarly upheld the verbal agreement over the ritual. Laurence de Blagi brought Jehan Odin and Alice Thiefre to court in October 1386 claiming a contract with Alice based on a hand-clasping ritual witnessed by Alice's godfather. In the register the notary used the word *cepit* (seize, grasp, or capture) to describe what happened to her hand indicating that her godfather put it unwillingly into Laurence's hand.[33] In addition to the forced ritual, Alice claimed an unwitnessed *verba de futuro*, with Jehan two weeks earlier.[34] The court upheld this earlier unwitnessed contract between Alice and Jehan, ruling that it had been contracted first, thus giving Laurence the license to marry elsewhere, whether he wanted to be released or not. In this case, Jehan had two things going for him: First, his *verba de futuro* occurred over two weeks before the hand clasping happened (September 1 vs. September 19). Second, Alice acknowledged the consent behind those words but denied consent with the second ritual. For the court, it was the intention behind the verbal consent and the timing of those words that removed the symbolic meaning from the hand-clasp ritual.

In general, legal canonists agreed that ritual without words did not constitute a marriage, even if both parties had intended these rituals to do so.[35] In a case such as Étienne and Laurencia's where there was disagreement about the meaning of the food exchange, Laurencia's understanding of consent and her lack of intention removed the contractual meaning from both the contested words and the ritual. As with Jeanne de Sartrouville, Laurencia's immediate denial of the contract shows that she knew it was her lack of intention to marry Étienne that would free her, not the ritual of the food exchange itself or the alleged words of consent. In the end, the court absolved Laurencia of Étienne's petition and denied the contract. Although rituals were an important part of licit marriages, what these cases show is that even when events contained movements that in a different context would constitute a marriage ritual, without the intent to consent the contract did not exist.[36] Defendants' successful use of *nec intentio* during their arguments against marriage contracts suggests that litigants understood the laws of free consent in the marriage making process, and they used that knowledge to successful conclusions.

Nec intentio was not the only way women showed their lack of consent to the court officials. Some women used pleasure (*placere*) and displeasure to show their dissent, with which they invoked personal and familial authority to avoid unwanted marriage contracts. Forms of *placere* were most commonly used in the register to indicate a conditional contract between the litigants. Generally, a female defendant stated in court that she had agreed to marry the plaintiff on the condition that her father, guardians, or friends agreed to the match. Invariably these relations did not agree to the marriage, and they often appeared in court stating that the marriage did not please them, *non placuit nec placet*. The first case in the register that hinged on the agreement of a female defendant's father was Thomas Domont c. Pierrette la Cousine who appeared in court in January and February 1385.[37] In their first appearance on January 2, Thomas claimed a marriage contract with *verba de futuro*. Pierrette agreed that Thomas had requested her hand in marriage, and she had responded that she would do nothing unless her father agreed (*nisi placeret patri suo*).[38] Pierrette's father, who was not named, 'presented himself to the court and claimed that he did not agree nor was it pleasing to him'.[39] The first entry is the only one in this case for which the notary recorded any details about the dispute; the remainder of the entries were continuances and acknowledgement of witnesses without any details, and other information about court processes. The conclusion to the case is not present in the register, but in each case with this formula for which we have the result, the court official ruled against the marriage contract.

The presence of these conditional marriage contracts shows that women understood the nuances of marital consent and used societal expectations of family hierarchy and obedience to manipulate that nuance and win their cases. In the case above, the words for Pierrette's conditional case, while technically a conditional agreement, do not include any sense of positive feeling, which was not as clear in all cases of this kind. There is no evidence that Pierrette's father attended court after the first appearance; however, there were multiple witnesses and the presence of legal counsel. The absence of her father suggests that Pierrette chose to use her role as a dependent to refuse the marriage contract rather than being forced to refuse by her father, and the witnesses show the community support for this decision. The idea of women actively choosing to use displeasure to indicate lack of consent is supported by the women who used this paternal language to describe their own displeasure with a match and successfully defend against family wishes.

One example of a woman performing her own displeasure in this way was when the widow Agnes de Maubeuge denied the suit of Guillaume de Lyons-la-Foret in July 1387. Guillaume claimed that he and Agnes had exchanged words of future consent and were betrothed.[40] Agnes disagreed and said that her brother, a master of Theology, had told her on numerous occasions that Guillaume wished to marry her, but she refused. Her refusal is very clear in the text, she states 'that she had always responded that it was not pleasing to her, nor did she ever agree'.[41] As with Alice above, on one occasion Agnes's brother took her hand and placed it in Guillaume's hand against her will presumably to strengthen the desired marriage contract. In the end Guillaume deferred to Agnes's oath that she had never contracted a marriage with him, and the court absolved Agnes of Guillaume's petition for her hand, allowing both to marry elsewhere.[42]

Perhaps due to her widowed status, Agnes was able to defy her brother's marriage choice based on her own displeasure rather than that of a male guardian. The physical placement of Agnes's hand in Guillaume's indicates some level of coercion, although not to the level of violence that appeared in Jeanne de Sartrouville's or even Alice Thiefre's cases. The refusal of the coerced marriage itself is important to this case because her brother's status as a scholar implies an education with possible legal knowledge. We do not have a record of Agnes's exact words or actions while in the court, but she successfully performed her lack of consent, and the official recognised Agnes's authority over her choice of marriage partner. There is no evidence within the text of legal counsel for either party reinforcing the idea that Agnes understood the laws of consent prior to entering the court. Similar to the case of Alice Thiefre above, Agnes's unnamed brother attempted to force a hand-clasping ritual to further cement the marriage contract. Unlike Alice, however, Agnes did not dispute the meaning of the hand clasping and instead focussed her defence on her own displeasure and lack of intent, recorded as both *non placere* and *nec intentio* in the entry. This argument could indicate different levels of legal understanding among the laity, but in both cases the defendants clearly understood the importance of free consent and denied they had given it.

Although somewhat less clear, the October 1385 case of Henri Rouet and Agnes, daughter of the late Simon de Longuerue, also illustrates the importance of consent in a disagreement about a family member's choice of marriage partner.[43] According to Henri, Agnes's late father and her mother, who was still alive at the time of the case, had promised her hand to Henri by means of a written contract. Agnes denied this contract and claimed that if her parents had made this agreement with Henri, it did not please her (*non sibi placet*) nor was she of a legal age to contract a marriage at the time of the contract, and at the time of the trial she verbally denied the match.[44] In addition, she argued that if she had known about this agreement at the time it was made, she would have vehemently protested the union.[45] This litany of protest covered nearly every possible way a person could legally contest a marriage contract. The court postponed its ruling for two days and warned Agnes's mother and her guardians against forcing a stronger union between Agnes and Henri before they could make a decision, on penalty of excommunication and a forty *livres* fine.

The parties returned to court two days later and, perhaps because of Agnes's vehement denials, this time Henri brought six witnesses—five women and one man—to testify on his behalf, and a written contract that recorded Simon de Longuerue's agreement to the union between Henri and Agnes. Agnes again protested the union in the court (*hodie rea reclamavit*).[46] The couple were to return the following day for further questioning, but unfortunately that appearance was not recorded in the register, and the couple disappeared from the record. Without a ruling on the case, it is difficult to draw conclusions about the court's decision on this matter, or to know if Agnes had succumbed to pressure and agreed to marry Henri. Regardless of the outcome, the injunction against Agnes's mother and guardians in their first appearance suggests that the court took Agnes's defence seriously. What is evident form the case, however, is that Agnes argued against the contract with Henri despite family pressure, the presence of witnesses, and a written contract.[47] The notary's use of *reclamare* indicates a vocal refusal of the match in court, although he did not record the actual words of refusal. In addition to the refusal itself, Agnes also claimed that the match did not please her/she did not agree to it (*non sibi placet*) as in the case of Agnes de Maubeuge. Again, the female defendant fought in court against the wishes of her family in order to assert control over her marriage. This case, taken in conjunction with other female defendants in the register, indicates that lay women understood the importance of the intention behind verbal consent in the formation of marriage contracts, even when this set them against the wishes and agreements of their family members. Female defendants' successful use of verbal dissent throughout the register shows that women were privy to a certain level of legal knowledge that circulated in their communities, and with this knowledge they successfully navigated the legal system.

Throughout their daily lives, women had numerous opportunities to converse with friends and acquaintances from the neighbourhood. Alexandra Verini, in her comparison of female friendship systems in the work of Christine de Pizan and Margery Kempe, states that 'late medieval women often operated within networks of female friends and relatives, circulating books as well as public and private concerns'.[48] In her discussion of female networks in Westminster, Katherine French argues that for single women in particular, friends 'guided young women through the intricacies of courtship and marriage', and while she is discussing guidance for choosing marriage partners, these conversations must have also dealt with the legalities of contracting marriage.[49] In his examination of the York Cause papers, Frederik Pedersen argues that the laity in fourteenth-century York had a rudimentary knowledge of marital canon law which they brought to court.[50] He states, 'The knowledge of the canon law rules for marriage permeated every level of society from the highest to the low'.[51] He presents three possible ways that the laity could have gained this knowledge considering their relative illiteracy: instruction about marriage requirements from local priests,[52] confession, and from the court itself.[53] Indeed, the system of contracting marriage itself required that the laity have basic knowledge of the law or the announcement of banns would be worthless for identifying impediments to marriage.[54] The purpose of the banns was to ferret out any impediments to a marriage, and for this to be effective those who were listening had to understand how marriage contracts worked. Although it was not a perfect system, church authorities understood the ease of contracting clandestine marriages and wanted to avoid further complications due to these impediments. As with the York Cause Papers, in the cases within the Parisian archidiaconal register, the litigants knew that specific words uttered with intention could create marriage contracts, and while actions could reinforce those words they could not replace them; therefore, they focussed on words that indicated lack of free consent when defending their cases in court.[55] If, as Pedersen states, litigants learned about the legal system through being a part of it they would certainly pass that information along to their communities.

Despite the paucity of detail in the Parisian court cases, evidence shows that women also had the support of their families, friends, and other members of their community in court, most clearly in the conditional cases mention above. More broadly, female defendants were twice as likely to have witnesses as male defendants: thirty-two cases for women versus sixteen for men. Similarly, female defendants had more witnesses per case with an average of 1.5 witnesses, whereas male defendants had an average of 1.1 witnesses. In general, plaintiffs had more witnesses than defendants, but women still averaged 2.7 witnesses to men's 2. Of the 175 witnesses referenced in these contract cases, 49 were women; thus, while female witnesses were a minority, they were not insignificant. Their presence in these cases was unsurprising as in her discussion of gender and testimony in medieval England, Kane argues that women were viewed as experts in marital issues, and there is no evidence to indicate that the Parisian women's testimony was less valuable than men's in these cases.[56] The presence of witnesses throughout the register shows community support for the litigants, and women drew from this support network more often than men did. From this community, women learned the importance of verbal consent and entered the court prepared to argue against marriage contracts to which they did not consent.

For the courts, the intention to marry was the critical aspect of marriage consent, and this focus allowed defendants to argue, often successfully, against marriage contracts. In two cases of *verba de futuro* followed by consummation, the differing intentions of the plaintiff and defendant gave each a different outcome. In August 1386, Agnes la Bigote brought Gilles de Vaupoterel to court claiming a consummated marriage. Gilles agreed to the sex but denied the rest and the official absolved him of Agnes's petition. The striking aspect of this decision was that the court gave Gilles, the defendant, permission to marry, *dantes reo licentiam contrahendi*, without mention of the plaintiff.[57] Similarly, a year later Jeannette la Picanone took Philip Bourdon to court and the case proceeded as the previous case had with the same result that the defendant could marry.[58] In these two cases the court's decision revolved around the intention of the litigants, and although they judged that the marriages had not taken place, the court recognised that Agnes and Jeanette intended marriage and therefore the ruling specified only the defendants' freedom. This does not mean that the plaintiffs could not marry, rather the court recognised that they believed themselves to be married and that they might consider another marriage as bigamy. As Donahue points out 'the largest barrier to the now-plaintiff's contracting elsewhere is likely to have been her conscience and whatever advice she received from her confessor'.[59] In these cases and those discussed above, litigants understood that without intention the alleged *verba de futuro* were meaningless. Evidence throughout the register indicates that women took knowledge of free consent from their communities and their legal counsel and were able to navigate the legal system with some success. Even in cases where the women were not successful, they still used this knowledge of free consent to argue against the marriage contracts.

Conclusion

Session twenty-four of the Council of Trent in November, 1563 began with the question of marriage and touched on many aspects from its sacramental nature to concubinage to coercion. The one major change made to marriage occurred in the first of the canons, commonly called *Tametsi*. It was here the council decreed that consent alone no longer made a valid or indissoluble marriage: 'The holy synod now renders incapable of marriage any who may attempt to contract marriage otherwise than in the presence of the parish priest or another priest, with the permission of the parish priest or the ordinary, and two or three witnesses; and it decrees that such contracts are null and invalid and renders them so by this decree.'[60] This decree required an officiant to perform the marriage ceremony and removed the problem of unintended and secret words of consent.[61] John W. O'Malley, in his examination of the negotiations before and during the council, argues that '[n]o single provision of the entire council affected the Catholic laity more directly than *Tametsi*'.[62] Although the council stated bigamy as their reason for the decree, this change was equally significant to the legal understanding of consent, and upended the centuries of community knowledge shown in the Parisian register, indeed, none of the cases examined in this paper could have existed in the same form after *Tametsi*.

Marriage was a central institution of daily life, and the evidence from the fourteenth-century register shows that litigants understood the laws of free consent and how to contract a marriage, including how to manipulate the ambiguities inherent in the contract; *Tametsi* removed this ambiguity. The women in the Archidiaconal court acted within a specific cultural milieu, and their arguments represented the best way to win their court case at the time. The pre-*Tametsi* plaintiffs who claimed they exchanged words of consent with defendants, sometimes with rituals, understood the significance of the words and their limitations. They gained this knowledge from the community, their priests, or their legal counsel and used it successfully to centre the arguments of their defence. While the arguments in court against the creation of marriages and specific marriage partners may not reveal the lived experiences of the litigants, they can represent the community ideals for marriage creation, and the understanding of legal knowledge. Women, in particular, used this understanding to successfully argue lack of consent, and defended themselves against coerced marriage contracts. Despite the requirement of a priest and witnesses in *Tametsi*, the centrality of free consent remained constant. No longer would anyone think coerced words in the street created a valid marriage contract, and women like Johanna Sartrouville could avoid the court fees. *Tametsi* therefore marked the end of the medieval marriage contract, and the need for women to defend themselves against unwitnessed words of consent.

Notes

1 Archives Nationales de France (hereafter AN) Z1O 26 fol. 24r.
2 AN Z1O 26 fol. 24r.
3 AN Z1O 26 fol. 24r.
4 Cases in this register have been used to examine marriage in comparison to other courts, as in, Charles Donahue, *Law, Marriage, and Society in the Later Middle Ages: Arguments about Marriage in Five Courts* (Cambridge: Cambridge University Press, 2007), but as of the writing of this note, they have not been used to analyze women's role in the legal system. See also Ruth Mazo Karras, *Unmarriages: Women, Men, and Sexual Unions in the Middle Ages* (Philadelphia: University of Pennsylvania Press, 2012) for a discussion of later registers from this court.
5 Tiffany Vann Sprecher, 'Power in the Parish: Community Regulation of Priests in the Late Medieval Archdeaconry of Paris, 1483–1505' (PhD Diss., The University of Minnesota, 2013), p. 5.
6 James Brundage, *Medieval Canon Law* (London: Longman, 1995), p. 122.
7 Brundage, *Medieval Canon Law*, 122; Donahue, *Law, Marriage, and Society*, pp. 304–305.
8 Léon Pommeray, *L'Officialité Archidiaconale de Paris Aux XVe-XVIe Siècle: Sa Composition Et Sa Compétence Criminelle* (Paris: Librairie du Recuile Sirey, 1933), p. 140.
9 Pommeray, *L'Officialité Archidiaconale*, p. 144. See also, Daniel Lord Smail, *The Consumption of Justice: Emotions, Publicity, and Legal Culture in Marseille, 1264–1423* (Ithaca, NY: Cornell University Press, 2003), p. 45. See also Philippe de Beaumanoir, *The Coutumes de Beauvaisis of Phillippe de Beaumanoir*, trans. F.R.P. Akehurst (Philadelphia: University of Pennsylvania Press, 1992), pp. 57–59.
10 Daniel Lord Smail, 'Witness Programs in Medieval Marseilles,' *Voices from the Bench: The Narratives of Lesser Folk in Medieval Trials*, edited by Michael Goodich, pp. 227–250 (New York: Palgrave, 2006), p. 229.
11 Smail argues that the notaries in Marseille translated the testamentary notes after the fact based on the records' neat and orderly nature. The Parisian cases may have been similarly translated. Daniel Lord Smail, *The Consumption of Justice: Emotions, Publicity, and Legal Culture in Marseille, 1264–1423* (Ithaca, NY: Cornell University Press, 2003), p. 57.
12 Smail, *The Consumption of Justice*, p. 15.
13 See, Donahue, *Law, Marriage, and Society*, for a comparison of *verba de praesenti* and *verba de futuro* in Paris and England.
14 Thomas Voisin c. Oliveta la Rousse, January 19, 1387. AN Z^{1O} 26 fol. 250r.
15 Tiffany Vann Sprecher, 'Power in the Parish: Community Regulation of Priests in the Late Medieval Archdeaconry of Paris, 1483–1505' (PhD Diss., The University of Minnesota, 2013), p. 3.
16 Bronach C. Kane, *Popular Memory and Gender in Medieval England: Men, Women, and Testimony in the Church Courts, c. 1200–1500* (Woodbridge: Boydell Press, 2019), p. 21.
17 Donahue discusses the formulae of these cases in *Law, Marriage, and Society*, chapter 7.

18 '*actor proposuit sponsalia per verba de futuro, re integra; lite ex parte ree negative contestata, actor detulit juramentum ree, que juravit se nunquam contraxisse nec promissiones matrimoniales habuisse cum dicto actore; quo juramento attento ream ab impetitione actoris absolvimus, dantes etc.*,' AN Z^{1O} 26 Fol. 252r.
19 AN Z^{1O} 26 fol. 53r.
20 '*que juravit se nunquam contraxisse sponsalia cum dicto actore nec promissiones matrimoniales habuisse nec unquam fuisse intentionis sue ipsum actorem habere in maritum*,' AN Z^{1O} 26 fol. 53r.
21 '*nec intentionis que fuisse ipsum habere in maritum*,' AN Z^{1O} 26 fol. 152v.
22 AN Z^{1O} 26 fol. 152v.
23 This is the only case in the register that refers to a food or gift exchange. There are examples of gift exchange in the fifteenth-century registers, however. For more information on marriage rituals see D.L. D'Avray, *Medieval Marriage: Symbolism and Society* (Oxford: Oxford University Press, 2005), and Diana O'Hara, *Courtship and Constraint: Rethinking the Making of Marriage in Tudor England* (Manchester: Manchester University Press, 2000).
24 AN Z^{1O} 26 fol. 211r.
25 '*et dicit eadem rea quod nunquam fuit intencionis sue ipsum actorem habere in maritum, cetera negando*,' AN Z^{1O} 26 fol. 211r.
26 '*postea idem actor dixit quod nomine matrimonii tradiderat dictam peciam panis dicte ree, et dicit eadem rea quod nunquam fuit intentionis sue ipsum actorem habere in maritum*,' AN Z^{1O} 26 fol. 211r.
27 O'Hara, *Courtship and Constraint*, p. 69.
28 O'Hara, *Courtship and Constraint*, p. 63.
29 D.L. D'Avray, *Medieval Marriage: Symbolism and Society* (Oxford: Oxford University Press, 2005), p. 60.
30 Vann Sprecher, 'Power in the Parish,' pp. 148–149.
31 April Harper, '"The Food of Love:" Illicit Feasting, Food Imagery and Adultery in Old French Literature' in April Harper and Caroline Proctor (eds.) *Medieval Sexuality: A Casebook* (New York: Taylor and Francis, 2007), pp. 86–87.
32 Harper, 'The Food of Love,' p. 86.
33 AN Z^{1O} 26 fol. 221r.
34 AN Z^{1O} 26 fol. 221r.
35 Donahue, *Law, Marriage, and Society*, p. 366.
36 Donahue, in his brief discussion of this case, posits that Étienne may have been trying to trick her into the marriage. Donahue, *Law, Marriage, and Society*, p. 366.
37 AN Z^{1O} 26 fols. 8ter r, 13v, 16r, 19v, 22r, 26v, and 29r.
38 '*rea respondit quod nichil faceret nisi placeret patri suo*,' An Z^{1O} 26 fol. 8ter r.
39 '*qui pater coram nobis comparens nobis respondit quod non placuit nec placebat sibi*,' An Z^{1O} 26 fol. 8ter r.
40 AN Z^{1O} 26 fol. 304r.
41 *que semper respondit quod non placebat sibi nec unquam placuit*, AN Z^{1O} 26 fol. 304r.
42 It is possible that Guillaume was equally uninterested in this marriage considering how little he seemed to fight for it. AN Z^{1O} 26 fol. 304r.
43 AN Z^{1O} 26 fol. 122r.
44 '*rea negavit fideidationes, et si pater et mater ipsius aliquid promiserunt dicto actori, non sibi placet, nec pro tunc erat in etate et ex nunc reclamat*,' AN Z^{1O} 26 fol. 122r-122v.
45 '*si citius ipsum actorem potuisset reperire citius reclamasset, etc.*,' AN Z^{1O} 26 fol. 122v.
46 AN Z^{1O} 26 fol. 123r.
47 The presence of a written contract is very unusual in these cases and as far as I can tell, this is the only case in the register that includes one.
48 Alexandra Verini, 'Medieval Models of Female Friendship in Christine de Pizan's *The Book of the City of Ladies* and Margery Kempe's *The Book of Margery Kempe*.' *Feminist Studies* 42, no. 2 (2016), p. 379.

49 Katherine L. French, 'Loving Friends: Surviving Widowhood in Late Medieval Westminster,' *Gender and History* 22, no. 1 (April 2010), p. 22.
50 Frederik Pedersen, 'Did the Medieval Laity Know the Canon Law Rules on Marriage? Some Evidence from Fourteenth-Century York Cause Papers,' *Mediaeval Studies* 56 (1994), pp. 111–152.
51 Pedersen, 'Did the Medieval Laity Know,' p. 138.
52 Pedersen, 'Did the Medieval Laity Know,' p. 147.
53 Pedersen, 'Did the Medieval Laity Know,' p. 149.
54 Pedersen, 'Did the Medieval Laity Know,' p. 147.
55 Pedersen, 'Did the Medieval Laity Know,' p. 129.
56 Kane, *Popular Memory*, p. 59. See also, Elisabeth Van-Houts, *Medieval Memories: Men, Women, and the Past, 700–1300* (New York: Routledge, 2001), 8–11. Patrick Geary, *Phantoms of Remembrance: Memory and Oblivion at the End of the First Millennium* (Princeton, NJ: Princeton University Press, 1994).
57 AN Z^{1O} 26 fol. 205r.
58 '*quo juramento attento, reum ab impetitione absolvimus, dantes eidem reo licenciam etc.*' AN Z^{1O} 26 fol. 315r.
59 Donahue, *Law, Marriage, and Society*, pp. 348–349.
60 'Trent: 1545–1563,' *Decrees of the Ecumenical Councils, Volume Two: Trent to Vatican II*, edited by Norman P. Tanner S.J. (Washington, DC: Georgetown University Press, 1990), p. 756.
61 'Trent: 1545–1563,' p. 755. For an example of differing opinions, Sara McDougall sees bigamy as the main marriage issue in fifteenth-century Troyes the 'crisis of marriage,' whereas Charles Donahue found few bigamous unions in his study of courts in England and the Continent. Sara McDougall, *Bigamy and Christian Identity in Late Medieval Champagne* (Philadelphia: University of Pennsylvania Press, 2012), p. 2. Charles Donahue, *Law, Marriage, and Society in the Later Middle Ages: Arguments about Marriage in Five Courts* (Cambridge: Cambridge University Press, 2007).
62 John W. O'Malley, *Trent: What Happened at the Council* (Cambridge, MA: Harvard University Press, 2013), p. 227.

3
SHADES OF CONSENT

Abduction for marriage and women's agency in the late medieval Low Countries

Chanelle Delameillieure

> Kateline Vanderstraten, daughter of the late Goerd Vanderstraten, stood before the aldermen of Leuven and publicly acknowledged that she went with Janne Herdans the younger by choice without any coercion to marry the same Janne and take him as her husband before the Holy Church, and all things the aforementioned Janne had done to her has happened with her consent and will.[1]

This deed stems from the registers of the city governors or 'aldermen' (*schepenen*) of Leuven, a midsize city in the Duchy of Brabant. These officials promulgated ordinances, judged civil and criminal offenses and even fulfilled a notary function, meaning that in return for a small fee, citizens could address the aldermen for the registration of a contract, privately settle a conflict, or, as was the case here, make a formal statement. On 22 January 1458 Kateline made a declaration which the aldermen transcribed into a legally valid charter that she then took home with her. The aldermen always made a brief copy of each charter in their registers and while the charters have been lost, these registers have been preserved. They tell us about people like Kateline Vanderstraten. We learn how she went to the bench of the aldermen in Leuven's city hall to declare that she had gone with a man called Janne Herdans according to her own will, and that it was not a violent abduction or a coerced marriage. By making this statement, Kateline not only acknowledged her consensual elopement but also endorsed the validity of their marriage.

The agency of abducted women is a subject of much debate in current research. Some scholars believe that abductions could in fact have been elopements in disguise used by young people to circumvent parental control, while others consider this interpretation of consent as ahistorical or argue that the legal records do not allow us to ascertain the 'true' nature of the abduction cases presented within them.[2] In this chapter, I tackle these debates by examining legal narratives describing the

DOI: 10.4324/9780429278037-4

abductee's consent or lack thereof in a range of legal records from the medieval Low Countries. By combining records from the city of Leuven's secular authorities with the church court records of the diocese of Liège – to which Leuven belonged – I argue that although abducted women could act as legal agents, they had little room to manoeuvre after being abducted. This chapter begins with a contextual explanation of abductions in the Low Countries and the historiographical discussions surrounding them, before examining the reasons why women like Kateline made such declarations of consent. The second section studies consent narratives used by different parties in the legal courts, while the final section tries to ascertain the social reality behind these legal narratives and the impact this would have had on the abductee's ability to play an active role in her own abduction.

Abduction and consent

Today abduction refers to the act of taking a person somewhere against their will, however, abduction in the medieval Low Countries was only understood in relation to the making of a marriage. From the twelfth century until the Council of Trent, mutual consent formed the core element of a marriage. The exchange of words of present consent in itself, or the exchange of words of future consent followed by sexual intercourse, were the only ways to contract a valid marriage in medieval Christian Europe. Other additional requirements, like the presence of a priest and the calling of banns, had to be met in order to validate this legal contract, however. Marriages that did not meet those additional requirements were considered clandestine, and the couple in question could face punishment yet their marriage was nevertheless valid and thus unbreakable.[3] While clandestine marriages through words of present consent were common in England, they occurred only very rarely in the Low Countries where the vast majority of the clandestine marriages were contracted through words of future consent followed by sexual intercourse.[4]

A striking aspect of marriage law is the fact that the involvement of relatives was not required. By enabling clandestine marriages, canon law thus in theory granted individuals a free choice of spouse. Still, such clandestine unions were condemned and punished in church courts.[5] In the Low Countries, ecclesiastical judges mostly ordered these clandestinely married couples to pay a fine and to celebrate their wedding properly within forty days.[6] These ecclesiastical punishments offered little comfort to disgruntled families, because the marriage they contested did not cease to exist. Therefore, secular laws emerged as a counter-reaction to canon law. In the Low Countries, ducal and urban authorities targeted the abduction, whether violent or consensual, that preceded a clandestine marriage. By seizing a wealthy woman away from her domestic environment, trying to convince her to say, 'Yes, I do', a man could enforce a beneficial marriage. If it concerned a consensual 'abduction', sometimes referred to as elopement in disguise or seduction in Anglophone research, a couple ran away together to get married in secret, afterwards presenting their families with a fait accompli. By making such abductions and seductions punishable, authorities hoped to prevent fortune seekers from seizing away wealthy daughters, or to discourage widows and young people who were planning to bypass their families.

In secular legal texts and criminal records a distinction was made between forced and consensual abduction, two legal categories with different legal consequences. In Low Countries' law, the abduction of minors was always illegal regardless of the girl's consent. Custom determined that parents had the right to be involved in their offspring's marriage and set the age of majority at about twenty-five years old.[7] This was quite a few years later than the canonical age of marriage and granted parents control over their adolescent children. The abduction of adults, however, was only considered an offense if it happened with force and violence. In theory, adult women in the Low Countries were – in the eyes of the law – fully independent and could marry whoever they wanted. Many abducted women were in their twenties, as people usually got married relatively late in the Low Countries to a partner who was about the same age.[8] The absence or presence of the abductee's consent therefore legally marked the difference between violent abduction and consensual 'abduction'. Many historians believe elopement was a well-known phenomenon in the late Middle Ages used by individuals to choose their own spouse.[9] Others contend that the majority of the abduction cases were not elopements, but socio-economic strategies used by men to marry wealthy women in order to climb the social scale.[10] Both historiographical tendencies can easily lead to oversimplifying the historic reality.

First, the elopement argument view creates a dual image of abductions as conflicts between 'frustrated' children and 'authoritarian' parents.[11] However, such views stem from interpreting medieval notions of consent as a form of free choice and resistance against arranged marriages. Over the last twenty years, marriage historians have problematized the concept of consent, arguing that the gap between consent and coercion was sometimes blurry and that there existed a large grey zone between these opposite ends of the spectrum.[12] Second, in the other view of abductions, the women involved are often reduced to passive victims of either their family or their abductor.[13] Some historians have expressed their doubts about abduction as a means for women to determine their own marriage. However, the claim that 'elopement' was exceptional does not automatically imply female victimhood. Historians have shown that women had legal options and defended themselves in court denouncing their abduction,[14] or made use of canon law to fight against forced marriage or to choose a spouse.[15] Looking only at legal records produced shortly after the abduction – and transcribed by a male scribe – is not enough to make claims about female victimhood.

It is indeed problematic that research on women's consent has to be conducted on the basis of legal records created in a male legal system.[16] Although it is tempting to read the statement above as the words that were actually pronounced by Kateline, historians have repeatedly warned not to take these legal records at face value. On the one hand, the stories in these statements, and other legal records, served a purpose and were shaped in order to make the chance of achieving it as high as possible. On the other hand, we should ask ourselves whose declarations of consent these actually were. The record suggests that Kateline pronounced these words, but the highly standardized format of these declarations forces us to acknowledge that these statements probably represented not only Kateline's voice but many voices, of her relatives, her abductor, the aldermen and the scribes.[17]

In order to not fall prey to the challenges and particularities of one specific type of record, I am using a combination of fifteenth-century records from different bodies. In addition to the declarations of consent, I have included final sentences issued by the city aldermen, and the accounts of the bailiff, who represented the duke of Brabant in the city of Leuven. The bailiff in Leuven had multiple roles. First, his task was to bring cases to court, collect evidence and make sure that those convicted actually carried out their punishment. However, he also had the right to make out of court settlements by allowing suspects to buy off prosecution with a fine (called *compositie*) or he could decide to relieve individuals who had already been convicted by exchanging their sentence imposed by the aldermen with a fine.[18] Alongside these secular accounts, I include the Liège church court records. This diocese covered a part of the Duchy of Brabant, in which Leuven fell, the County of Loon and the prince-bishopric of Liège. For the fifteenth century, only one register on legal practice, dating from 1434 to 1435, has survived.[19] It contains five abductions, covered in seven separate deeds. Two of the five abductions include a final sentence by the court and corresponding records in which the case is presented in more detail; the other three abductions are known via records which contain accounts of the abduction as presented by the prosecutor, the plaintiff and, sometimes, also the defendant. Although these abductions did not concern people from Leuven itself, the inclusion of examples from other areas in the diocese offers a useful comparison, especially as they also include references to the declaration of consent by abductees. Moreover, combining secular and ecclesiastical records offers a more rounded view of the legal context in which abductions took place and of the legal 'world' which sought to control them.

Legal value of consent

All over the late medieval Low Countries, abducted women like Kateline declared their consent formally. This practice can be observed in cases heard by the church court of the diocese of Liège, but it was also regularly referred to in pardon letters granted to abductors all over the Burgundian Low Countries.[20] These records indirectly show how widespread this practice was, however, what the Leuven records contain are actual transcripts of these statements. The registers of the Leuven aldermen are formidably extensive. Thanks to an ongoing digitalisation and transcription project, they are partially searchable.[21] A search via this tool yields over eighty declarations, similar to the one made by Kateline, covering the years 1383 to 1461. This practice served two purposes, namely, to avoid charges of rape or violent abduction and to strengthen the claim that the marriage between abductor and abductee was valid.

Ideally, an abducted woman declared her consent directly after the abduction and right before the actual marriage. This is illustrated by the abduction story offered in the plea of abductor Rutger Bacheleur, who lived in Maastricht, to the church court in Liège. This case was initiated by a prosecutor of the Liège court at the request of Rutger Bacheleur against Yda Slickbaert, his alleged wife, and Arnout Meyer, her new husband.[22] Rutger claimed that he and Yda had gotten married after he had abducted her with her consent. Yda, however, argued that she was forcefully abducted and had married another man in the meantime. Like other abductors who came to Liège for the enforcement of their marriage, Rutger's plea elaborates on what had happened, placing Yda's consent at the centre. The plea states that Rutger had abducted Yda 'with her consent' (*consentientem animo*) and brought her to the house of a friend in the parish of Heerle. There, the plea continues, Yda declared her consent 'without the slightest coercion but, on the contrary, in complete freedom' (*minime coacta, quinymmo in sua plena existens libertate*). Rutger's plea states that Yda confirmed to the bailiff and the aldermen of the village, and in the presence of the priest, that she went to Heerle with the intention of marrying Rutger. Consequently, the plea states, the couple exchanged marital promises and had sexual intercourse several times. The presence of both local secular officials and a priest when Yda declared her consent, and the fact that this act is mentioned in a plea before a church court, reveals the importance of such declarations.

The final sentences promulgated by the city court of Leuven and the accounts of the bailiff show that consent could be considered a mitigating circumstance that, occasionally, even led to the abductor's acquittal. In his accounts, the bailiff regularly explained why he had allowed an out of court settlement by pointing to the abductee's consent. For example, when Laureys Moens abducted Lijsbet Vandamme with the help of his brother, the Leuven bailiff allowed them both to pay a *compositie* to settle things. The record states that the men were poor, a common motive in these accounts, and that it concerned a 'silly' offence (*onnoesel*) since the abductee had gone with the men by choice.[23] In another case from around 1410, Jan Uter Helcht and his accomplices abducted Elisabeth Leydens, who declared her consent before the aldermen of Leuven. Although the bailiff tried to overturn this declaration of consent by finding witnesses who had heard Elisabeth cry, an important element in proving a lack of consent, he did not succeed and was therefore urged by the town's aldermen to release the group of abductors.[24] In other cities too, there is evidence that consensual abductions, especially if they concerned adult women who were fully legally capable in the Low Countries, were not always punished.[25] These declarations could, therefore, make a difference in secular jurisdiction. The records do not contain any evidence that these people received any legal guidance at this early stage, which suggests that people were aware of the legal difference between violent abduction and seduction.

Although consent declarations were a phenomenon that especially impacted on secular jurisdiction, they were also included in the church court records, which Rutger Bacheleur's plea illustrates. In his legal narrative, the abduction and statement of consent which would allegedly have been made by Yda, served as contextualising elements or 'paralegal' details as McSheffrey and Pope, and Youngs have called them.[26]

They were not essential legal requirements but provided a context that helped to strengthen the abductor's main argument, namely, that marital consent had been exchanged by both parties. In church courts, judges were obviously concerned with marital consent. Canon law did not consider abduction an impediment to marriage as long as the abductee had consented to the marriage.[27] Still, some abductors and their attorneys included consent declarations made after the abduction in their argumentation before the church court of Liège, which indicates that they believed the judge might consider it important. A Ghent case study analysed by Monique Vleeschouwers-Van Melkebeek even shows that an abductor specifically asked the aldermen of Ghent for a written record of the abductee's consent declaration so he could present it as evidence to the church court of Tournai, which was investigating the alleged marital bond between him and the abductee.[28] The legal value of these declarations and people's awareness of them should thus not be underestimated.

But what do these consent declarations tell us about the abductee's agency? To understand Kateline's declaration with which this chapter started, a better understanding of how the consent of abductees was understood legally and socially in the Low Countries is necessary.

Consent in legal narratives: love and will

When describing abduction, the sources mostly use verbs like 'to lead away' (*wechleiden*) or 'to abduct' (*ontschaken*) which literally meant bringing someone from one place to another. Additional phrases were used to inform about the abductee's alleged consent. For example, the 1438 bailiff account states that Willem De Colven had abducted Trudeken Herwouts 'with her will and consent' (*met haers dancs ende willen*).[29] Two years later, a group of men was punished for abducting Metteken Lyens 'against her will and consent' (*tegen haeren wille ende teghen haeren danck*).[30] These records mostly do not offer any contextual information that allows us to find out what constituted consent or a lack thereof in these specific cases.

In addition to these concise explications, the sources contain more detailed consent descriptions which were more likely to reflect specific details in each case or at least how they were presented in court. Some records explicitly label the abduction as a case of seduction. Zanneken Marchant was seduced by Hennen Molenplas who had used 'courtly words' to get her to leave her guardian's house.[31] Other records embedded their narratives with the well-known cultural and literary topoi of the 'impossible marriage' which had met with parental resistance.[32] For example, on 19 June 1418, the aldermen of Leuven sentenced Hendrik Van Calsteren to undertake a pilgrimage to Cyprus for abducting Ydeke Roenvox, the daughter of Willem Roenvox. The final sentence describes the event as follows; Ydeke had left her father to go to Hendrik 'under the pretence of an abduction' (*onder den schijn van enen scake*). She was described as a minor, which indicates that this 'abduction' was a punishable offense. Ydeke's father, Willem, filed a complaint.[33] In another case, a female accomplice, Margriet van Breedsip, had helped a man perpetrate an abduction for marriage, and she defended herself when the Leuven bailiff examined the matter. She admitted her involvement, but stated that she did not know that the abduction was against the victim's will because 'she had a happy face' during her removal (*want sij bliedelic ghelaet hadde*).[34] Another act states that the abductor took a woman on his wagon and brought her to the next village. There, he stepped off and entered an inn. During the time he was away, the abductee 'stayed sitting on the wagon and did not step off the wagon to leave', which apparently implied her consent.[35] Many of the consent declarations in the Leuven aldermen registers equally describe this consent as an individual and positive choice. For example, love is twice included as a factor that motivated these women to follow their abductor. Margriete Pasteels went with Willem Vanderstraten freely, out of sincere love (*uut rechter liefde*), whereas Heilwige Vander Lynden went with Joes Eemond the younger, out of love to marry him before the Holy Church (*uut rechter liefden ende om den voirscreven joese na staet der heiliger kercken te truwene*).[36] Consent narratives in legal records thus tend to describe a consensual abduction as a very consensual act of love, individual choice and independence.[37]

Conversely, the sources describe non-consensual abductions as violent events including rape and abuse. Three elements are generally emphasized, namely the violent behaviour of the perpetrator, the resistance of the abductee, and her outcry, which was an essential legal requirement to prove a non-consensual abduction. Wouter Vliege had dragged his victim through hedges and bushes which caused injuries to her legs that she later showed to the bailiff when filing her complaint.[38] Willeken Paternoster abducted Baten Alsteens at night from the street. He spoke many 'indecent words' and beat her up because she acted recalcitrantly and refused to leave with him.[39] Around 1418, Janne Mijs violently abducted Lijsken Spapen. He reportedly grabbed her by her neck, beat her, and pulled her across a moat. The record states that Lijsken cried out loud for help and shouted, 'Where do you want to lead me?'[40] Ruelen Van Ijsere abducted widow Machteld Truydens violently in 1466. He brought her to a forest just out of Leuven. Ruelen allegedly raped her and forced her to take him as her husband, which she refused.[41] Whereas the records on consensual abduction describe the abduction as a tool for making love matches and circumventing parental approval, the records on violent abductions describe the abductors as ruthless criminals and the abductees as victims who fell prey to terrible violence.

While these descriptions of abductions as either acts of free choice or of brutal attacks could certainly correspond to the lived reality of these cases, the importance of strategy in litigation must not be overlooked. Garthine Walker noted that both the narratives of the abductee as a victim and active co-accomplice could come together in one and the same case.[42] The church court records of Liège contain a couple of cases in which the abductor's version of events is placed directly against the abductee's version of events. An exceptionally lengthy example is that of Joost Claeszoon, abductor, versus Katrien Huysman, abductee, and her new husband Jan Hambrouck. In 1434, Joost Claeszoon from Oudenbosch, a village located near Bergen-op-Zoom, a city north of Antwerp initiated a case before the Liège church court against Katrien Huysman, who lived in the same village. Katrien refused to acknowledge that she was Joost's wife and had even married another man, Jan Hambroeck. Joost's plea tells us in great detail what had happened between him and his alleged wife. Joost consistently highlighted the consent and free will of Katrien. Katrien, in contrast, invoked the impediment of force and fear and highlighted the abductor's violence and her resistance and passivity extensively.

According to the plea, Joost abducted Katrien a couple of days after they had planned their abduction and told each other how much they loved one another in the presence of many honourable witnesses. Katrien's defence, however, argued that a mob of men came to her mother's house with long knives, while she was milking the cows, and abducted her with threats and violence. She cried out loud and resisted as hard as she could. The abductors even had to lift Katrien from the ground by her arms as they covered her mouth to prevent her from crying. Both stories state that Joost took Katrien to the house of an unspecified relative of hers, Nicolaas Wijssen, in a nearby village. In Joost's plea, Katrien's relative asked her whether she had come there by choice, to which she responded affirmatively. Katrien's story does not include this consent declaration. Whereas the plea emphasizes Katrien's active involvement and how this was witnessed by many, the defence portrays Joost as a criminal, for example, by including that he carried weapons which was considered an aggravating factor in the eyes of the law, and Katrien as an honourable, obedient daughter who had not invoked any sexual violence, for example by including the fact that she was dutifully milking the cows.[43]

After these contradicting abduction accounts, both parties described the marriage, again highlighting consent versus force. First, marriage vows were exchanged in the presence of several witnesses. As found in ecclesiastical court records elsewhere in Europe, these vows are included in the vernacular, while the rest of the text is in Latin. The plea narrates how Joost and Katrien brought their right hands together in the house of Katrien's relative. Several 'honest and honourable' people could testify to the veracity of what had happened there. Joost said, '*Lijne*, I hereby give you my Christian faith which I received upon the baptismal font and I promise you upon that faith that I will take you and no one else as my lawful wife'.[44] Katrien answered, '*Joes*, I in return give you my Christian faith received upon the baptismal font, and I also promise you that I will take you and take you as my lawful husband'.[45] By putting Katrien's words of consent both in the future tense, which was the most common in the Low Countries, and in present tense, the plea puts forward the indisputable validity of the marriage. In Katrien's version of events, the exchanged words of consent were less intimate and emotional. She merely repeated what her abductors had told her to say. If she disobeyed, the men would 'bring her abroad to throw her in the water' or even murder her. After Joost had said, 'yes, I do', and Nicolaas had asked Katrien, 'And, Katelijne, do you also give your faith to Joost?', she replied, 'Yes, I give it too'.[46] A meal and a party followed the ceremony. The plea stated that Joost and Katrien spent about six hours together, during which they consummated the marriage twice. Katrien's defence, on the other hand, stated that she initially shared a room with Nicolaas Wijssen's daughter. Joost only joined her after this woman was called away unexpectedly. Although they were together in the room, for about one quarter of an hour, Joost did not push her to have sexual intercourse but instead promised her that he would leave her in peace. In the Low Countries, sexual intercourse was an important feature of marriage. The exchange of words of future consent accounted as the betrothal which had to be celebrated publicly in the Low Countries.[47] Afterwards, the marriage was celebrated, followed by a party and the consummation of marriage which perfected the union. This explains why one party emphasised the consummation of the marriage, while the other party denied that sexual intercourse had occurred between them.

We are presented with a typical 'he said/she said' narrative characterised by the juxtaposition of opposite stories interspersed with legal strategy. Joost used canon law to enforce a marriage which was – according to him – unwanted by some of Katrien's relatives, while Katrien appealed to the canonical impediment of force and fear. Based on the stories told by both litigants and their attorneys, this case could be interpreted as an elopement to escape parental involvement or as the defence of a woman who refused to marry her violent abductor. Plaintiffs, litigants and their attorneys shaped their narratives in court in order to obtain the best outcome. Their narratives therefore contain simplifications in which the parties concerned portrayed events and their own actions stereotypically as consensual or violent, and their own role as victim or accomplice.[48] These stories had to be plausible and recognizable and as a result, we are often presented with clichéd stories with little variation.

Abductees and consent

The examples above suggest that medieval people perceived consent as active, or that they at least knew the idea of free choice and attached it to the legal determinant of consent. The abductee could be a co-perpetrator in the minds of medieval people.[49] It is very tempting to interpret this recurrent language of love, free choice and individual will in several sources as evidence for elopements. Still, this link between consent, love and choice in litigation proceedings, statements and sentences does not per se represent a social reality. Gwen Seabourne has argued that the line between 'wholehearted' consent and coercion in elopement/abduction cases was often blurry. Still, cases within this grey zone also had to be categorised by the legal authorities as being either consensual or violent. Unfortunately, secular records do not specify the degree of consent sufficient for an abduction to be legally considered consensual. The only clue Low Countries law texts give us is the abductee's outcry as a yardstick for a lack of consent, which highly resembles the hue and cry in medieval England. They also distinguished between the abduction of adults and minors: in secular abduction laws, consent required being of age or needing one's parents' or guardians' permission. Nevertheless, these legal stipulations remain vague as to how consent was really gauged, which suggests it was open to interpretation and depended on each case, judge and situation.

Some cases are not described as clearly consensual or violent. Instead, the indicators offered in the record are mixed. A remarkable example is the abduction of Aleyde Vyssenaecks by Andries Hellinck, known to us because of her declaration of consent made before the Leuven aldermen on 16 October 1458; she went with Andries 'by choice and willingly to enter into matrimony with him'.[50] Everything Andries had done to her, the record states, had happened 'with her free and unprompted consent'. Directly after this declaration, however, a financial contract between Aleyde and Andries was registered by the aldermen. This contract determined that Andries had to pay Aleyde the sum of 100 *rijders*, a substantial amount of money, unless he and Aleyde got married. If the marriage between them did not take place, and if Andries was to blame for this, he had to pay her the agreed sum. Later records reveal that the marriage took place and that Andries therefore did not pay Aleyde.[51] The combination of these two records, a declaration of consent as individual choice on the one hand and a contract to force the abductor into marriage with the threat of a high monetary penalty on the other is striking and challenges the rosy image of an abduction used by two lovers to contract marriage secretly. This shows that what was considered consent by medieval law, did not have to correspond to social understandings of this concept that were put forward in the above-mentioned legal narratives. The legal category of consent could have applied to different shades of consent, some of which corresponded to free and active choice and others which corresponded to a more passive form of agreeing to, rather than willingly doing so.[52]

The occurrence of ambiguous abduction cases such as the one above should be understood against the background of two main factors. First, the abductee's decision to consent was often made at the encouragement or even under pressure from the abductor and relatives. This possibility is suggested by a record in the bailiff accounts that states that several men had abducted an anonymous woman and 'had made her proclaim' that the abduction had happened with her consent before the aldermen.[53] It is probable that the abductor regularly pressured the abductee to consent before local authorities since he would benefit from this declaration as it could save him from facing harsh penalties, which ranged from forced pilgrimage to decapitation. As well as the abductor, the woman's relatives could have pressured her to consent. Although many relatives were often involved, customary law determined that family consent only involved the parents rather than wider family members. If one parent passed away, however, the surviving parent had to consult the family of the deceased parent to discuss the choice of spouse for an underage girl. The Leuven records often state that a minor had to get married with the consent of relatives from both the mother's and father's side, sometimes even from all four grandparents' sides.[54] Disagreements often arose between the maternal and paternal relatives about the choice of spouse, one wanting a marriage that the other did not agree to. A declaration of consent and an 'abduction marriage' could thus have been wanted by one side of the abductee's relatives and contested by the other side.[55] In the Liège material, this becomes visible in the defence of another abductee, Heilwige Comans, who lived in the village of Bocholt. Her defence stated that she had only said that she went with her abductor by choice because she felt coerced to do so by the urgent requests of her aunt and some of her relatives.[56] The abovementioned Katrien was also brought to the house of another one of her relatives, which suggests that he may have been involved in the abduction and benefited from her marriage to Joost. Such cases therefore complicate the idea that these consent declarations were expressions of the abductee's free choice.

Second, mixed consent indicators can be understood better when viewing abduction as a process or chain of events with various choices on the part of the individual or opportunities for influence or persuasion by other parties. Between the planning of the abduction, the actual seizure of the woman, the marriage, the sexual intercourse and the legal settlement or reconciliation out of court, days or even weeks could go by during which the woman could change her mind, whether or not under the influence of others. On the one hand, it is possible that a woman went with her abductor by choice, but afterwards regretted her action and under pressure of family members claimed the opposite. This is how some abductor-plaintiffs in the Liège records, like Joost Claeszoon, explained the abductee's sudden refusal to acknowledge their marriage. On the other hand, however, the sources contain evidence that the opposite occurred frequently. Despite being abducted against their will, many women nevertheless agreed to marry their abductor. This reportedly happened to Lijsken Crieckmans who was led outside of the city of Leuven by Neelken van Ermeghem. The record states that although Lijsken had been abducted against her will, she kept going back to Neelken and was 'satisfied' (*tevreden*) with Neelken after a while.[57] The same happened to Kateline Zoert who was abducted by Marck van Cockelberge against her will but was then 'satisfied' after a while and married Marck. Colen Vander Varent abducted Heilwiich Toelen against her will but after a day, he already managed to change her mind and she was 'satisfied' with him and declared her consent before the aldermen of a village northeast of Leuven. This change of consent was probably mostly due to social expectations and cultural views regarding honour, sexuality and reputation that were deeply rooted in late medieval culture. As an event linked with marriage and sexual intercourse, the abduction in itself could impugn the honour of the abductee and her family, making a marriage to the perpetrator in these specific circumstances the best choice.[58]

Conclusion

Litigants, attorneys, and judges mostly explained consent stereotypically as extremely active and present, or as completely absent and passive. Although such descriptions could certainly have corresponded to what had happened, it is impossible to know or distinguish legal strategy from social reality. Therefore, accessing abductees' agency through these legal records is problematic and challenging. The dichotomy between abduction and elopement, although present in late medieval law and legal practice, has too often been adopted by historians who tend to label each case as medieval judges did. However, even medieval judges sometimes struggled with this as their verdicts show the abductees changing their mind and abductees being influenced or even pressured by relatives. Consent had different shades and for an abductee it was not constituted by a single event but by a chain of decisions she, the abductor, and her relatives made over a course of time. There was the consent to the initial removal, consent to stay with the abductor, and consent to marriage. At all of these stages, the abductee's consent might have been influenced by others as a certain degree of force was accepted by canon law, and secular law too considered familial involvement normal. Therefore, what was legally considered a consensual abduction in the late medieval Low Countries, might have in fact concerned a form of non-consensual consent, that is an abductee passively agreeing to marry an abductor that she had not wanted to go with initially and would not have wanted as her husband under normal circumstances. Finally, the legal narratives like the ones in the Liège records show that people who appeared before this court possessed an impressive knowledge of the law as all legal requirements for arguing a valid marriage were declared or vice versa were meticulously denied by abductors and abductees. However, the litigants had attorneys and were probably coached to say the right things. Therefore, their actions out of court are more trustworthy indicators of people's legal awareness and these indicate that people knew how to navigate both canon and secular law. Women pressed charges, shouted during their abduction, or searched for the aldermen to declare their consent directly after being abducted. Although they might have been pressured, it is nevertheless telling that so many declarations were made and taken into account by the judges. There is no evidence that at this point legal counsellors had yet been involved. Moreover, the Liège church court records include another interesting strategy used by women and their families to avoid a marriage to an abductor, namely, the contraction of another marriage to another man right after the abduction. It seems that a marriage could be a serious advantage when contesting to have a previous marriage declared invalid.[59] Further research into these strategies is needed, but for now they make clear that although it is difficult to access the abductee's agency through legal records, women were certainly not mere pawns.

Notes

1 *Item Katline Vanderstraten, dochter Goerds wilen Vanderstraten diemen hiet Goerds, in tegenwoirdicheit der scepenen van Loeven gestaen heeft openbairlic gekend en de gelijdt dat zij anderwile hoers dancks ende moetswillen sonder ennich bedwangt gegaen es met Janne Herdans den jongen om den selven Janne te trouwen ende te nemen tenen manne na staet der heiiigher kercken also zij oic gelijc sij seyde gedaen hadde en de dat zo wes de voirs creven Jan met of aen hoe re begaen mach hebben geschiet es hoers dancks en de goetwillen*, in: City Archives Leuven, Oud Archief, no. 7752, fol. 183v (22 January 1458) (Hereafter: CAL, 7752, 183v).
2 Gwen Seabourne, *Imprisoning Medieval Women: The Non-Judicial Confinement and Abduction of Women in England, ca. 1170–1509* (Farnham, 2011), pp. 145–161.

3 About canon law on marriage, see James Brundage, *Sex, Law and Marriage in the Middle Ages* (Aldershot, 1993); Philip L. Reynolds, *How Marriage Became One of the Sacraments: The Sacramental Theology of Marriage from It Medieval Origins to the Council of Trent* (Cambridge, 2016).
4 Charles Donahue, *Law, Marriage and Society in the later Middle Ages: Arguments about Marriage in Five Courts* (Cambridge, 2008), pp. 598–632, spec. 600, 601.
5 Richard Helmholz, *Marriage Litigation in Medieval England* (Cambridge, 1974).
6 Monique Vleeschouwers-Van Melkebeek, 'Aspects Du Lien Matrimonial Dans Le Liber Sentenciarum de Bruxelles (1448–1459)', *The Legal History Review*, 53 (1985), pp. 43–97.
7 Philippe Godding, *Le droit privé dans les Pays-Bas méridionaux du 12e au 18e siècle* (Gembloux, 1987), pp. 70–75.
8 According De Moor and Van Zanden, the medieval Low Countries formed the core region of the European Marriage Pattern, see Tine De Moor and Jan Luiten Van Zanden, 'Girl Power: The European Marriage Pattern and Labour Markets in the North Sea Region in the Late Medieval and Early Modern Period', *The Economic History Review*, 63 (2010), pp. 1–33.
9 Myriam Greilsammer, 'Rapts de séduction et rapts violents en Flandre et en Brabant à la fin du Moyen-Âge', *The Legal History Review*, 56 (1988), p. 50; Myriam Carlier, *Kinderen van de minne? Bastaarden in het vijftiende-eeuwse Vlaanderen* (Brussels, 2001), p. 3; Caroline Dunn, *Stolen Women in Medieval England: Rape, Abduction, and Adultery, 1100–1500* (Cambridge, 2013), p. 15; Julia Pope, 'Abduction: An Alternative Form of Courtship?' (IMC Kalamazoo, 2003), http://www.culpepperconnections.com/historical/abduction.htm; Fabrizio Titone, 'The Right to Consent and Disciplined Dissent: Betrothals and Marriages in the Diocese of Catania in the Later Medieval Period', in Fabrizio Titone (ed.), *Disciplined Dissent. Strategies of Non-Confrontational Protest in Europe from the Twelfth to the Early Sixteenth Century* (Rome, 2016), pp. 139–168.
10 Bert De Munck, 'Free Choice, Modern Love, and Dependence: Marriage of Minors and 'rapt de séduction' in the Austrian Netherlands', *Journal of Family History*, 29 (2004), p. 189; Seabourne, *Imprisoning Medieval Women*, p. 145; Sara M. Butler, '"I Will Never Consent to Be Wedded with You!": Coerced Marriage in the Courts of Medieval England', *Canadian Journal of History*, 39 (2004), pp. 247–270.
11 See for example Walter Prevenier, 'Courtship', in Margaret C. Schaus (ed.), *Women and Gender in Medieval Europe: An Encyclopedia* (New York, 2006), p. 179.
12 Butler, 'I Will Never Consent to Be Wedded with You!'; Seabourne, *Imprisoning Medieval Women*, pp. 152–153.
13 See for example De Munck, 'Free Choice, Modern Love, and Dependence', p. 199.
14 Deborah Youngs, '"She Hym Fresshely Folowed and Pursued": Women and Star Chamber in Early Tudor Wales', in Bronach Kane and Fiona Williamson (eds.), *Women, Agency and the Law, 1300–1700* (London, 2013), pp. 73–85.
15 C. Wieben, 'Unwilling Grooms in Fourteenth-Century Lucca', *Journal of Family History*, 40 (2015), pp. 263–276; Titone, 'The Right to Consent and Disciplined Dissent'.
16 For an overview of the methodological perks and challenges of studying women through legal records, see Tim Stretton, 'Women, Legal Records, and the Problem of the Lawyer's Hand', *Journal of British Studies*, 58 (2019), pp. 684–700.
17 Barbara A. Hanawalt, *'Of Good and Ill Repute': Gender and Social Control in Medieval England* (Oxford, 1998), pp. 125–141.
18 About the bailiff's right to make these financial settlements, see Guy Dupont, 'Le temps des compositions : pratiques judiciaires à Bruges et à Gand du XIVe au XVIe siècle (partie I)', Bernard Dauven and Xavier Rousseaux (eds.), *Préférent miséricorde à rigueur de justice: pratiques de la grâce (XIIIe-XVIIe siècles)* (Louvain-la-Neuve, 2012), pp. 53–95; Guy Dupont, 'Le temps des compositions: pratiques judiciaires à Bruges et à Gand du XIVe au XVIe siècle (partie II)', Marie-Amélie Bourguignon, Bernard Dauven and Xavier Rousseaux (eds.), *Amender, sanctionner et punir: Recherches sur l'histoire de la peine, du Moyen Âge au XXe siècle* (Louvain-la-Neuve, 2012), pp. 15–47.
19 The Liège church court has barely received any scholarly attention, see Sébastien Damoiseaux, 'L'officialité de Liège à la fin du Moyen Âge. Contribution à l'histoire

de la juridiction ecclésiastique de l'évêque de Liège (XIVe-XVIe siècles)', *Leodium*, 99 (2014), pp. 6–44 ; Emmanuël Falzone, 'Poena et Emenda. Les sanction pénale et non pénale dans le droit canonique médiéval et la pratique des officialités', Marie-Amélie, Bernard Dauven and Xavier Rousseaux (eds.), *Amender, sanctionner et punir: recherches sur l'histoire de la peine, du Moyen Âge au XXe siècle* (Louvain-La-Neuve, 2012), pp. 113–135.

20 For examples and edited pardon letters granted to abductors, see Peter Arnade and Walter Prevenier, *Honor, Vengeance, and Social Trouble: Pardon Letters in the Burgundian Low Countries* (Ithaca, 2015), pp. 138–172, spec. 165–172.

21 The project *Itinera Nova* started in 2009 and aims to digitalize the 1127 aldermen registers of Leuven from 1362 to 1795, see https://www.itineranova.be/in/home.

22 State Archives Liège, Archives of the diocese, no. 1, fol. 37rv, 131r (Hereafter SAL, 1, 37rv, 131r).

23 SAB, 12658, account from July to December 1472, 26v-27rv.

24 SAB, 12653, account from July to December 1410, 317rv.

25 Monique Vleeschouwers-Van Melkebeek found a similar case in Ghent, see Monique Vleeschouwers-Van Melkebeek, 'Mortificata Est: Het Onterven of Doodmaken van Het Geschaakte Meisje in Het Laatmiddeleeuws Gent', *Handelingen: Koninklijke Commissie Voor de Uitgave Der Oude Wetten En Verordeningen van België* 51–52 (2011), p. 364.

26 Shannon McSheffrey and Julia Pope, 'Ravishment, Legal Narratives, and Chivalric Culture in Fifteenth-Century England', *The Journal of British Studies*, 48 (2009), p. 827; Deborah Youngs, '"A Vice Common in Wales": Abduction, Prejudice and the Search for Justice in the Regional and Central Courts of Early Tudor Society', in Patricia Skinner (ed.), *The Welsh and the Medieval World: Travel, Migration and Exile* (Cardiff, 2018), 135.

27 Rachel Stone, 'The Invention of a Theology of Abduction: Hincmar of Rheims on Raptus', *The Journal of Ecclesiastical History*, 60 (2009), pp. 433–448; Sylvie Joye, *La femme ravie: le mariage par rapt dans les sociétés occidentales du Haut Moyen Âge* (Turnhout, 2012), pp. 405–434; Donahue, *Law, Marriage, and Society*, pp. 171, see n. 80 in particular.

28 Vleeschouwers-Van Melkebeek, 'Mortificata est', 370–371.

29 SAB, 12655, Account from July to December 1438, 325v-326r.

30 SAB, 12655, Account from July to December 1440, 366v.

31 SAB, 12656, Account from July to December 1455, 306v.

32 For further research into the marriage between lovers from different social backgrounds in late medieval Low Countries' literature, see Marc Boone, Thérèse de Hemptinne, and Walter Prevenier, *Fictie en historische realiteit: Colijn van Rijsseles De spiegel der minnen, ook een spiegel van sociale spanningen in de Nederlanden der late Middeleeuwen?* (Gent, 1985).

33 CAL, Oud archief, no. 584: *Dbedevaertboeck*, fol. 125r (19 June 1418) (Hereafter CAL, 584, 125r (19 June 1418); SAB, 12654, Account from July to September 1419, 209r, 251v.

34 SAB, 12653, Account from July to December 1404, 35r-36v, 37v.

35 *bleef dieselve Lijsbeth opten wagen sittende sonder vanden wagen te gaene oft erghers haer te willen vertrecken*, in SAB, 12658, Account from July to December 1472, 26v-28r.

36 CAL, 7764, 241r (7 April 1452); 7747, 8r (30 June 1430).

37 Goldberg has argued that love was linked with consent in late medieval England which explains why such references can be found in litigation narratives. They did not per se correspond to a reality but show that love was included to construct a credible consent story, see Jeremy Goldberg, 'Love and Lust in Later Medieval England: Exploring Powerful Emotions and Power Dynamics in Disputed Marriage Cases', Paper presented at *Emotions and Power c.400–1850*, conference (York, 2017).

38 SAB, 12654, Account from December 1418 to July 1419, 190v.

39 SAB, 12657, Account from December 1467 to July 1468, 306r, 307rv, 307v-308r.

40 SAB, 12654, Account from September to December 1418, 219rv.

41 SAB, 12658, Account from July to December 1473, 75rv.

42 Garthine Walker, '"Strange Kind of Stealing": Abduction in Early Modern Wales', in Michael Roberts and Simone Clarke (eds.), *Women and Gender in Early Modern Wales* (Cardiff, 2000), pp. 63–68.

43 Carrying weaponry was considered forbidden in many Low Countries' cities. By including the 'long knives', the defense portrays the abductor as an incorrigible criminal, see Raoul Van Caenegem, *Geschiedenis van het strafrecht in Vlaanderen van de XIe tot de XIVe eeuw* (Brussels, 1954), pp. 69–71; historians have noticed that women denouncing rape or abduction, offenses associated with their sexuality, stated that they were attending mass or doing all kinds of domestic activities during the assault in order to present themselves as honourable women who did not invoke the sexual violence in any way, see Miranda Chaytor, 'Husband(Ry): Narratives of Rape in the Seventeenth Century', *Gender & History* 7 (1995), pp. 378–407.
44 *Lijne, hier gheve ick u mijn kerstelijck trouwe die ick in der heyligher voenten ontfanghen hebbe ende ghelove u bij der selver dat ick u ende nyemant anders nemen en sal ende ick neeme u tot eenen witteghen wijve.*
45 *Joess, ick gheve u wederomme mijn kerstelijke trouwe die ick in der heyligher voenten ontfanghen hebbe ende bij der selve ghelove ic u dat ick u ende nyemant anders nemen en sal ende ick neeme u tot eenen witteghen manne.*
46 [...] *Joest, ghij gheeft hier Lijnken u trouwe*, dicto Judoco super hoc dicente quod ita, theutonice: *Ja ick.* [...] *Ende Lijnken, ghij gheeft hier oeck Joessen u trouwe.* Que Catharina [...] respondit in simili ydeomate in hunc modum: *Ja ick. Ick gheeffe hem weder.*
47 Donahue, *Law, Marriage and Society*, pp. 387–389.
48 Inneke Baatsen and Anke De Meyer, 'Forging or Reflecting Multiple Identities? Analyzing Processes of Identification in a Sample of Fifteenth-Century Letters of Remission from Bruges and Mechelen', in Violet Soen, Yves Junot, and Florian Mariage (eds.), *L'identité au pluriel: jeux et enjeux des appurtenances autour des Pays-Bas, 14e-18e siècles* (Villeneuve-d'ascq, 2014), pp. 28–34.
49 Noël James Menuge, 'Female Wards and Marriage in Romance and Law: A Question of Consent', in Katherine J. Lewis, Noël James Menuge, and Kim M. Phillips (eds.), *Young Medieval Women* (Sutton, 1999), pp. 154–155.
50 CAL, 7752, 79r.
51 A private contract from 1470 refers to Aleyde as Andries' widow, in CAL, 7363, 247v.
52 On the difference between consent and will, see Melanie Beres, 'Rethinking the Concept of Consent for Anti-Sexual Violence Activism and Education', *Feminism & Psychology*, 26 (2014), pp. 374–375.
53 *Ende huer doen verkoemen dat zij huers dancxs metter voirscreven Quinten hueren vrienden ontgaen was* SAB, 12656, Account from July to December 1458, 436r.
54 Leuven records sometimes stated that someone had to marry with the approval of two friends of the maternal family and two friends of the paternal family, thus representing the four grandparents' families, which is presumably how these 'four groups' of relatives here should be understood. See for example CAL, 7352, 212rv (15 March 1458).
55 Marianne Danneel, 'Orphanhood and Marriage in Fifteenth-Century Ghent', in Walter Prevenier (ed.), *Marriage and Social Mobility in the Late Middle Ages* (Gent, 1989), pp. 123–139.
56 SAL, 1, 83rv.
57 SAB, 12658, Account from December 1472 to July 1473, 50rv and Account from July to December 1473, 73rv.
58 Valentina Cesco, 'Female Abduction, Family Honor, and Women's Agency in Early Modern Venetian Istria', *Journal of Early Modern History*, 15 (2011), pp. 349–366.
59 Donahue also discusses a few cases in which this was the case, see Donahue, *Law, Marriage and Society*, p. 490.

4
FEMALE LITIGANTS IN SECULAR AND ECCLESIASTICAL COURTS IN THE LANDS OF THE BOHEMIAN CROWN, C.1300–C.1500[1]

Michaela Antonín Malaníková

In April 1424, a case was tried before the ecclesiastical court of the vicars general of the Prague Archdiocese (then located in Zittau)[2] in which Barbara, daughter of Mathias von Herwigsdorf,[3] made a request for the recognition of her marriage to Laurencius, the son of Hanuss of Benessaw, with whom, her account maintained, she had exchanged a vow of marriage. Laurencius was released from Barbara's claim, however, because she was unable to provide witnesses.[4] This brief entry raises many questions concerning the status and agency of female litigants, particularly because it offers two potentially different interpretations on the negotiating position and strategy of woman at court: was Barbara instigating a case where she was the victim of a broken marriage vow; or was she trying to obtain the recognition of a marriage, which in fact never took place? At a time when marriages were often contracted informally and without witnesses, both interpretations are equally likely. Such uncertainties have to be accepted as an integral part of reviewing medieval marital disputes, but these legal records remain an invaluable source for uncovering the strategies pursued by one or the other party. On a more general level, they also provide insights into contemporary perceptions and the functioning of medieval marriage as a legal institution. All of these perspectives will be applied when exploring female litigants as plaintiffs and defendants in the Czech lands.

The aforementioned dispute was recorded in Judicial Act Books of the Prague consistory, which, unlike most other such sources of church provenance in the Czech lands, survives to the present day.[5] Based on these records, this chapter will focus on marital disputes in order to analyse the involvement of women as litigants and their capacity for negotiation. As such, it is the first systematic study of Czech marital disputes that offers a detailed typology of these records and integrates the research results into a European context. It will consider the extent to which Barbara von Herwigsdorf represents a typical female litigant

DOI: 10.4324/9780429278037-5

of the period and examines whether female plaintiffs at this church court were more often inclined than their male counterparts to sue for alleged marriages. It will also consider other reasons that brought women to court, and the potential benefits a hearing of marital litigation at church court could bring them.

Throughout medieval Europe, marital disputes fell under the authority of ecclesiastical courts[6]; however, for urban populations, like the ones discussed here, municipal law also strongly influenced the creation and functioning of marriage because town courts dealt with many issues relating to a marital bond. For that reason, this chapter will begin by considering the legal options women had to negotiate marital disputes in a municipal court. It will focus on another urban centre within the Bohemian crown, Brno. This allows us to consider what type of marital issues were taken to the church courts, and what fell under the jurisdiction of the town courts, and how those same courts defined the status of a wife. Exploring these two case studies – one municipal and the other ecclesiastical – will enable a fuller analysis of the strategies female litigants applied, and the overall status of women in the medieval Czech lands.

Territorial context of the research and Brno's sources

The Czech lands experienced dynamic development during the fourteenth and fifteenth centuries. While the accession of the Luxembourg dynasty (1310) had ushered in a heyday for the Bohemian crown, notably during the reign of Charles IV (the Czech king and Roman emperor), by the end of the fourteenth century the lands were embroiled in religious dissent and political hostilities. The Hussite Wars (1420–1436) represented a significant rupture in the field of religious, political and cultural life in Central Europe.[7] Certain parts of the Kingdom remained under the influence of the catholic party, including, among others, Upper Lusatia, with one of its centres in Zittau, where the administration of the Prague diocese was transferred in 1421 from Hussite-occupied Prague.

The city of Brno has been chosen as a case study for various reasons. In the Middle Ages, it was a medium-sized royal city with a population of between 5,000 and 8,000. Like Zittau, Brno remained on the catholic side throughout the Hussite wars.[8] Brno town law was one of the most influential within the Lands of the Bohemian Crown. It is generally characterised by well-preserved medieval sources, primarily a document which has come to be known as 'The Book of Law of the Town of Brno from the mid-14th Century' (in Czech: *Právní kniha města Brna z poloviny 14. století / Kniha písaře Jana z poloviny 14. století*; in German: *Das Brünner Schöffenbuch*). This was in use not only in the town itself but in other rural and urban localities within the Czech lands, and also affected the municipal laws of the Old and the New Town of Prague.[9] The Book of Law is based on the privileges granted to the city of Brno as well as older legal verdicts made by members of the local municipal court; however, the influence of other laws, especially Roman and Canon, is also traceable here. To understand further the 'realities' of the marital union as captured by Brno municipal sources, the so-called Memorial Books are also used.[10] These books comprise miscellaneous cases of undisputed judiciary, and cover issues concerning acquisitions, heritage, testaments, neighbour and property litigations, purchases, sales, and debts, among other things. Hence the advantage of using Brno for analysis is that it has both a set of secular sources that allows us to analyse the position of married women through the prism of legal norms alongside the written agenda, and day-to-day practices of the town council and court as recorded in the Memorial Books.

Spousal relations and concept of marriage in the municipal law: medieval Brno

This section will discuss how the status of an urban wife was defined in Brno municipal law and highlight how this corresponded to the principles of Canonical marriage law. It also aims to determine key aspects of marital cohabitation according to the urban legislation. The Book of Law of the town of Brno addresses the formation of marriage primarily with regard to its legitimacy, focussing on the property and personal rights of spouses and children arising from a valid marriage.[11] As such, issues connected to marriage were mainly included in the division of the Book that concerned mechanisms of inheritance within the family.[12] Municipal law was in line with Canon law in most aspects.[13] While it acknowledged the secular form of entering into marriage, in accordance with the church norms, it insisted that it be a public act in order to prevent *matrimonium clandestinum* as a potential source of discord and uncertainty, especially in relation to property.[14] The secular marriage ceremony was supposed to take place in the presence of witnesses from a range of credible burghers, ideally town councillors.[15]

Based on the principles of Canon law, Brno municipal legislation understood marriage as an agreement between the two parties and therefore placed emphasis on the free consent of the future husband and, explicitly, the wife. Each woman, whether widow or a daughter, was supposed to be able to marry whomever she had chosen.[16] The Book of Law stated that if an orphan was prevented from marriage by a relative or by a tutor, they should confide in a town councillor, confessor or priest, and the intention to marry was to be announced publicly at the town council.[17] However, the freedom to marry was often illusory, and parents or relatives sometimes had the last word, even when they were no longer present.[18] In some last wills of Brno provenance both testators and testatrixes made their children's rights to inheritance conditional on the will and consent of their chosen executors, including their choice of a marriage partner. Mitzscho Bohemus in the mid-fourteenth century entrusted his executor with the tutelage of his two minor daughters, who were not to marry without first consulting him.[19] In late 1470s Katerina, widow of Andreas Swanczel from Brno, bequeathed her daughter Barbara a house with all its furnishings, but only if she obediently followed the advice of Katerina's executors and the town representatives in the choice of marriage partner. If she did not, she would lose her right to the inheritance.[20] It is significant that these provisions apply only to girls and although they do not prove forced marriage, they illustrate social and economic constraints used by families to secure their influence over their children's marriages.

In characterising the personal-legal relations of spouses in these urban sources, the guardianship of a husband was of primary importance. Guardianship took various forms in different legal systems and geographical areas. According to the Brno municipal law, the bond between the spouses was defined rather rigidly.[21] The wife was legally subordinate to her husband and the declaratory superiority of the man as 'the lord and administrator of the woman's body as well as of her property' can be found in several legal articles of The Book of Law.[22] A level of flexibility in gender roles within a marriage was, however, reflected in the fact that this same legal source defined several situations when it was possible for a wife to assume the administration of a family property.[23] A similar procedure was applied in cases when the husband was missing or out of town for long periods of time and the family was legally paralysed by his absence. Fridericus Rotsmid departed from Brno with the company (*cum clientibus*) of King Matthias and left his wife Ursula in the town. When later, in 1478, she wanted to sell their house she made an explicit indication that her husband had not returned and that it was not clear whether he was still alive.[24]

As is well known, after the Fourth Lateran Council the conditions introduced for the formation and termination of marriage became stricter; the latter being either through annulment (*divortium quoad vinculum*), or a separation from 'table and bed' (*divortium quoad thorum*). This Canon law concept influenced the termination of marriage as defined by The Book of Law of the Town of Brno, but so too did Roman law. This manifested itself most explicitly in connection with the reasoning for divorce on the part of both husband and wife, which corresponded almost exactly to Roman Novellae.[25] According to the Book of Law, legitimate reasons for the dissolution of marriage by both husband and wife alike were adultery, preparing an uprising, poisoning, murder, robbery, and beating. If separation was requested by the husband, the reasons also included if a wife was a swindler, committed sacrilege, or if she, without the knowledge her husband, spent time outside the house. If a wife wanted to be separated from her husband, she could use accusations of forgery, bribery and a dissolute lifestyle as legitimate reasons.[26] However, this passage in The Book of Law, which significantly expanded those reasons established by the Canon law, probably did not reflect actual legal practice, and it cannot be found in the legal compendium based on The Book of Law compiled in Brno only twenty years later.[27]

Physical violence was one of the reasons why married women brought spousal disputes to the church courts (as discussed later).[28] The municipal law of Brno did not question whether a husband could physically punish his wife, it only discussed the form and intensity of beating.[29] Excessive coercion against a wife is the reason given in the unique case where the separation of marriage was resolved by the municipal court, under the presidency of the Moravian Margrave, then lord of the city. This case seems to have attracted considerable attention as it is mentioned in both The Book of Law and the Memorial Book in relation to the year 1353.[30] The dispute concerned the wealthy burgher Georius Ferreus (or in the German version Georg Eisnen) who had systematically and cruelly tyrannised his young wife Katerina, barely at the age of majority and the daughter of town councilman Peter Smelclin. It was reported that he had pulled her by her hair around the house, stomped on her body and committed other 'unlawful and undignified' forms of punishment.[31] Katerina's parents and other councilmen tried to discourage him from this kind of behaviour and asked him to justify his actions. He answered that his wife had done nothing wrong, but he wanted to begin disciplining at an early age so she would fear him and not rebel against his orders. Once more, Katerina's parents and the town authorities attempted to mitigate the situation, but did not take any particular steps. The situation grew worse until, following an incident where she was almost strangled, Katerina managed to escape back to her parents. She, alongside her parents, sued her husband and achieved a dissolution of the marriage by the municipal court.[32] This lawsuit raises many questions, including why this case of spousal dispute, unique in Brno municipal sources, was dealt with by the secular and not by the ecclesiastical court. The likely explanation is that it concerned the highest stratum of urban society and it served an exemplary purpose. The detailed description of the case as well as the presence of the margrave at the court hearing supports this interpretation.[33]

The interaction between secular and ecclesiastical law is also addressed by The Book of Law in other verdicts concerning marriage. For example, it stated that the binding nature of an engagement vow (*verba de futuro*) should not be secured by any agreed fine; if that was to happen, its examination was to be dealt by the Canon law.[34] Similarly, it stipulated that if a wife was separated from her husband by the church court, she could not be denied the right to her dowry.[35] Hence, the municipal law explicitly incorporated the verdicts by ecclesiastical court and acknowledged its jurisdiction. Town law focussed on the consequences of marital issues for a couple and their children, primarily with regard to the hereditary rights. However, some of the offences were on the boundaries of both jurisdictions and authorities could overlap as manifested by the unique case of separation considered by the Brno municipal court.

Marital disputes in ecclesiastical sources: the court of the vicars general of Prague diocese

As we have seen, in order for the municipal courts to harmonise with the ecclesiastical view of marriage, it was necessary to establish a consensus on fundamental issues. While town councils and courts saw marriage primarily through the prism of property relations and, with rare exceptions, did not strictly resolve marital disputes, it was the ecclesiastical courts which dealt with the validity of marital unions and spousal relationships; their records therefore offer a more detailed view of individual bonds. Church courts were also, in general, more permissive than urban courts in providing a space for women's voices to be heard, regardless of marital status,[36] and hence will be key to our investigation of negotiating practices and strategies of female litigants.

The marital disputes studied here went to the church court of the administrator of the Prague diocese after 1421, when its leadership was relocated from Prague to Zittau. Here, two officials with the title of vicar general (*in spiritualibus et temporalibus*) performed the regular administrative agenda. In terms of territory, their activity was limited only to that part of Bohemia which remained Catholic. The function of the official merged at that time with the function of the administrator of the diocese. The agenda of spousal disputes was preserved in the Judicial Act Books of the vicars general[37] of the Prague diocese in Zittau in 1421–1424 and 1427–1437 and is one of the most comprehensive set of marital disputes available for the medieval Czech lands.

Matrimonialia comprise a significant part of all cases recorded. Out of c.640 entries enrolled for the period 1421–1424, seventy-one cases related to marriage, or almost 11%.[38] To extend and enrich the research sample, seventy-six cases of marital disputes heard in court between 1427 and 1437, which are available in the form of modern summaries, are also included. These summaries (accessible in the so-called *Zittauer Urkundenbuch*)[39] cover only those entries in the Judicial Act Books that are related to the territory and inhabitants of the Upper Lusatia, whose centre was the town of Zittau. This is justified not only because considerable number of matters discussed before the court of vicars general in Zittau concern the adjacent territory but also because these summaries are very detailed and reliable. Of the seventy-one marriage disputes in 1421–1424, forty-four are also included in *Zittauer Urkundenbuch* (62%) and they offer precise information: dates, names of litigants, their place of origin or other identifier, the nature of the dispute and its circumstances, records of alleged direct speech, testimony of witnesses, the course of the proceedings and the final judgement (if any; unfortunately this is missing in a considerable number of cases). As at the courts in Freising, York or Paris, the trials under analysis were conducted as instance litigations and not as ex officio causes, and, in the vast majority of cases, in the physical presence of both disputing parties, and, where possible, in front of witnesses.[40] Testimonies received in writing were also taken into account.

Given that a large percentage of the matrimonial agenda of the court of the vicars general consists of cases of alleged marriages, (see Tables 4.1 and 4.2 below) the court placed great emphasis on the exact wording and form of marital vows made, which were essential for determining a valid marriage.[41] The sources suggest that the commencement of marriage was often a secular act that took place outside the church and without the presence of its representatives. Ritual practices such as the joining of hands and exchanging gifts were often mentioned by litigants as evidence for their alleged marriages.[42] For some couples, the religious validation of marriage came through a church solemnisation only after their marriages had already taken place elsewhere, a situation also documented for medieval England.[43] Like the formation of a marriage, its termination could take place without the supervision of the church, and sources indicate that a significant percentage of couples informally ended unhappy or dysfunctional marriages; self-divorce was an inexpensive, less formal and probably more common alternative.[44] Therefore, it is reasonable to assume that cases where ecclesiastical courts investigated multiple (or bigamous) marriages represent only the tip of the iceberg of real marital practice. Within the Czech lands the influence of the Church on marital practices seems to remain limited as old habits and traditions continued to be strongly held.[45] Like elsewhere in Europe, the informal character of marriages had the potential to create uncertainty, tension and even conflict, and was the main reason that brought people to the ecclesiastical court.[46]

Female plaintiffs: alleged marriages and marital violence

Spousal disputes involved women in various life phases and marital statuses from all social strata except the nobility. Within the records we find girls on the threshold of adulthood who flirted with their peers[47]; mothers who attempted to confirm the validity of a marriage in order to provide social and economic stability for both themselves and their children; and women who, after many years of married life full of violence and quarrels, sought change. The youngest age explicitly mentioned in the Books is eleven years. Ursula, daughter of Nicolaus Tepfer living in Zittau, in 1437 requested an exemption from the claims of Hanussius Pachman, son of Andreas Dresler, who demanded recognition of marriage. Ursula denied it and argued that she was only eleven years old, so could not marry for at least another year. Hanussius mentioned he had given her two decorative cypress wood knives, which Ursula admitted, but said she had given them to her mother. The final verdict is missing.[48] At the other end of the age spectrum, Katherina Fewerin, a widow from Zittau, was accused in 1436 of breaking a marriage vow that was allegedly made thirty years previously. Nicolaus Kraczr claimed that she had told him 'If my brother agreed, I would marry you'; however, despite the brother's agreement, no marriage had taken place. Kraczr could not substantiate his claim by any testimony, and it was rejected by the court.[49] The typicality of these cases can be seen in Tables 4.1 and 4.2.

TABLE 4.1 Typology of lawsuits of marital disputes in the Judicial Act Books of the vicars general's court, years 1421–1424

Litigant	Type of action					
	Recognition of alleged marriage	Removal of impediment to a marriage	Investigation of bigamy	Investigation of abandonment of marriage	Other	Total number of litigants
Woman	20	2	3	3	1	29 (41%)
Man	17	9	1	1	4	32 (45%)
Couple	0	1	3	3	3	10 (14%)
Total number of cases	37 (52%)	12 (17%)	7 (10%)	7 (10%)	8 (11%)	71 (100%)

TABLE 4.2 Typology of lawsuits of marital disputes in the Judicial Act Books of the vicars general's court, years 1427–1437 (based on *Zittauer Urkundenbuch*)

Litigant	Type of action					
	Recognition of alleged marriage	Removal of impediment to a marriage	Investigation of bigamy	Investigation of abandonment of marriage	Other	Total number of litigants
Woman	15	4	2	2	4	27 (36%)
Man	21	7	3	0	1	32 (42%)
Couple	0	2	1	2	12	17 (22%)
Total number of cases	36 (47%)	13 (17%)	6 (8%)	4 (5%)	17 (22%)	76 (100%)

As these tables show, over half (52%) of the marital suits at the vicars general's court, 1421–1424, sought to enforce alleged marriages.[50] A comparable proportion, 47%, can also be seen in the cases brought by the inhabitants of Upper Lusatia, 1427–1437. In both samples, women slightly predominate as plaintiffs. In the source sample from 1421 to 1424 female plaintiffs form 54%, and for the later period 1427–1437 their proportion is higher at 58%. Yet female plaintiffs do not dominate as we might expect. In fact, the gender ratio in these cases seems exceptional in comparison with other contemporary European courts such as Freising or Regensburg where women dominated significantly.[51]

Among the female plaintiffs, the most vulnerable were pregnant women or those with children. In addition to emotional considerations, these women were led by practical concerns and wanted to protect their status as legal wives, as well as ensure the legitimacy of their children with its significant social and economic implications. Indeed, female plaintiffs with children comprise about a third of those applying for marriage recognition in both source samples. One plaintiff who found herself in this situation was Margaretha, daughter of Henyngi Jungeri from Newnstath. In 1422 she alleged a marriage *per verba de presenti* had been made with Hanuss son of Hanuss Pychner from Albersdorff, when she was still a virgin; he denied the claim. As she was pregnant, she therefore asked the court to make him pay compensation for her loss of virginity and to assist in raising their child.[52] Hanuss admitted having sex with her. While Margaretha could not substantiate her claim with witnesses, Hanuss, prompted by friends, finally (re-)established marriage with her.[53] This case reveals the motivations behind a pregnant woman or one with small children bringing a case to court and the strategies she could apply. It is likely that Margaretha was aware that, with no supporting testimony, her claim of alleged marriage had only a minimal chance of success.[54] However, she also knew that if the defendant admitted the intercourse (if not a marriage), she had a fair chance of gaining at least financial compensation for the loss of her virginity as well as, eventually, alimony for her child. Sometimes the mere fact that a woman made an accusation, together with social pressure, prompted a hesitant man to agree for marriage.[55] Bringing cases to court were a useful means by which women could have their relationships formalised, and their status and that of their children secured.

The reactions of the defendants were, quite naturally, diverse. Some of the alleged spouses refused to marry, but by admitting to sexual intercourse, they de facto committed themselves to financial penalties. Out of the ten cases examined in 1421–1424 where the defendant admitted sexual intercourse (and eventually also paternity) but refused to (or could not) enter into marriage, in five instances he was sentenced to pay the compensation for defloration and/or alimony for the child.[56] Where the defendant admitted paternity but refused marriage, the court could also force him to assume custody and the child's upbringing[57] after a certain period of time.[58] The Judicial Act Books record several such cases when an illegitimate child born either out of wedlock or from an adulterous relationship was entrusted to the custody of the father.[59] In August 1429, Dorothea the daughter of Hans from Swarow, sued for the recognition of her marriage with Mathias Grunner. She argued that she had given him money (a wedding gift) and that the marriage had been consummated. She could not prove her claim by testimony and therefore her request was rejected. The court, however, granted her financial compensation and, after three years, Mathias was required to assume the custody of their child (the sex of the child is not given).[60] Religious courts in other contemporary European localities similarly emphasised the shared responsibility of both parents, indicating a flexible approach to children conceived out of wedlock.[61] Even if the female plaintiff failed to prove the validity of marriage the court took into account the social and economic dimension of illegal cohabitation (or perhaps even one-off sexual intercourse) as well as its practical consequences on themselves and their families. However, if the defendant denied the sexual relationship, the court in Zittau was inclined to dismiss marriage claims by the female plaintiff,[62] in accordance with the Canon law principles that honoured the man's word over that of a woman.[63]

Naturally, women plaintiffs in alleged marriage cases had diverse motivations. Sometimes they could be led by desire for romance or wealth. In May 1435 Barbara, daughter of Martin Richter in Lichtinhan brought a claim of marriage against Zittau burgher Nicolaus Wagner.[64] She claimed they had exchanged marital vows two years previously, but Nicholas refused to marry her before the Church. Barbara wanted to fulfil her marital obligations and had talked about the marriage to other people, but stated that the defendant had offered her money so she would not force him to marry.[65] Nicolaus responded by claiming he had only promised her marriage if he recovered from his illness; his intention was simply to seduce her. He was, nevertheless, unsuccessful in his efforts because – in his own words – he was already sixty years old and had been ill for the last three years. Nicolaus confirmed he had gifted her money, but only with the intention of ensuring she take better care of him in his illness. Finally, he added that he offered her money not to leave him free, but to leave him alone. This detailed record provides two different perspectives of people living in intense coexistence.

Nicholas's motivation seems clear: he needed someone who would take care of him in his illness. Barbara, on the other hand, perhaps wanted to secure her status as a moneyed man's wife or indeed as a future widow.

Tables 4.1 and 4.2 also indicate the number of abandonment cases. In most of these, the reason was excessive violence by the husband, and they were initiated either by beaten wives or by men complaining that their wives had abandoned them. As already indicated in connection with the agenda of municipal courts, violence between spouses was investigated only if the beating escalated to the point that wife had reasons to fear for her life and ran away. Relevant, in this regard, is the hearing held in January 1435, in which Caspar Scheffer, a dyer from Zittau, and his wife Katherina Fridman met in court. Under penalty of excommunication, Katherina was ordered to return to her husband. She replied that she would rather die. As a consequence she was given three days to reflect and Caspar was ordered not to beat her.[66] In other cases the church court could take specific steps to prevent further violence against a wife, such as demanding the husband commit to a financial pledge to guarantee that his violent behaviour would not be repeated. In February 1423, Marziko, the son of Cubczonis from Wesczie, had to pledge such a guarantee before both the ecclesiastical court and the mayor and council of the city of Zittau as a security of his wife Anna's person and life.[67] Violence in marital cohabitation seems to be the point where the ecclesiastical and secular courts followed similar practices, and where urban jurisdiction strayed into an area otherwise covered by the Church. From the point of view of ecclesiastical authorities, it was to ensure that married couples continued living together and thus de facto preserve marriage as a sacrament. For municipal authorities, it was a matter of preventing a crime that would otherwise fall within their jurisdiction. In each case, both sides seem to be aware of a necessity for cooperation.

Female defendants: 'Joking' girls and wives leaving unsatisfactory marriages

In cases where individuals or couples tried to silence any opponents to their intended marriages (amounting to 17% of all cases) we find similar issues to those in alleged marriages because the issue cited was typically a claim of pre-contract. Women in these cases were usually trying to protect their marriages against male plaintiffs claiming to be their rightful husbands. The vast majority of suits aiming to remove impediment to a marriage resulted in the withdrawal of the opposition, which demonstrates the difficulties in thwarting someone's wedding plans. In a society where a considerable percentage of marriages remained private matters, a pre-contract was hard to prove.

In these cases, we see various strategies used by women to resist these impediments and have their favoured marriage recognised. They reveal the active participation of young girls in flirting and courtship and the strategies they used to resist the unsolicited obligations of marriage at church courts. In addition, there were wives who decided to leave problematic marriages and sought their happiness elsewhere, sometimes in another marriage. Such cases shed further light on female behaviour and space for action, and provide a counter view to the image of women as victims of family pressure and patriarchal society.

In 1430, Anna daughter of Hanussius Pelcz from Zittau asked the court to force Paul Rozemhayn, son of Paul Rozemhayn to withdraw his objection to her marriage with Martinus from Dieczin with whom she supposedly exchanged vows several weeks earlier and from whom she received a silver ring. Paul, however, believed he had already wed her the year before and described the situation as follows: he had helped her carry some wood and she said she had nothing to pay him, but with herself. He replied that he would take her and she agreed with laughter. Paul failed in his claim because Anna managed to persuade the court that she gave her approval only 'in jest'.[68] The situation where the defendant played the card of 'just a joke' or having done something just 'out of friendship' is not unique in the examined material, and is the equivalent of stating that certain flirtatious behaviour was not meant to be taken seriously. Altogether, the motif of (not) meaning something seriously played a role in seven of the studied seventy-one cases.[69] Women were defendants in six of them, which suggests that using 'joking' as an argument was a typical (and successful)[70] strategy of young women who wanted to decline an unwanted marriage.

On other occasions women might be defendants in cases of marital impediments that paradoxically allowed them to marry partners they really wanted. One example can be found in September 1431 where Nicolaus the son of Johannes Lessner objected to a marriage between Margaretha Scholcz and Petrus Trenkler that had taken place eight days previously, arguing a pre-contract. Margaretha supported Nicolaus's claim and said she had entered into a new marriage under the pressure of her stepmother. As a result the court pronounced the first marriage between Nicolaus and Margaretha valid, despite the fact they had been married by a monk outside their parish.[71] As this case suggests, the hearing at the ecclesiastical court may have been a tool to enforce the preferred personal choice of partner despite the wishes of the families. The emphasis of Canon law on mutual consent as the minimal standard level of marriage formation provided a sufficient argument to do so.

Just as some female defendants did not hesitate to oppose the demands of unwanted alleged husbands, others did not hesitate to leave dysfunctional marital relationships and enter new ones. Evidence from cases of bigamy tried in other Central European localities suggests this practice was probably more common than our tables might indicate.[72] Only cases where bigamy was proven have been included, though many engagement disputes and alleged marriage cases may also indicate bigamy.[73] In a sense, it was a natural result of the practice of clandestine marriages, examined by the church courts only when they were discovered and prosecuted. This underlines the considerable level of flexibility in medieval relations as well as tendency to assume unorthodox (from the perspective of the Church) solutions for marital difficulties. In 1421–1424 (see Table 4.1) there were seven cases (10%) relating to bigamy, with four where the wife was accused.[74] In the second sample (1427–1437) six such cases have been found (8%) and in two of these the bigamous partner was the wife.[75] In these situations it was crucial for the church court to verify which of the marriage commitments was older. Only in one case[76] did the court order a wife to continue living with the alleged second husband because it was not clear whether the first husband was still alive. In this particular instance, however, bigamy may well have been an excuse by the wife who did not want to live with her husband who was described as violent. This would explain not only the court's final verdict but also its explicit warning to the husband that he should not beat or injure his wife in any way, but behave to her kindly under the penalty of excommunication.[77]

Each of these bigamy trials is complex and allows us to glimpse the twists and turns of medieval married life. In October 1422 Hanussius Tyrffl from the Zittau suburbs and Katherina, daughter of Petrus Tyczko de Respnaw, met before the court. They stated they had been married before the Church for fifteen years.[78] After one year of cohabitation, however, Katherina left Hanussius because 'she did not like him'. Three years after she left Hanussius she married *in facie ecclesie* Nicolaus Pogner from Legnicz with whom she had six children, two of whom were still alive at the time of the trial. Her former husband did not ask the court to make her return, because he was (in his own words) 'a cripple, blind and poor'. He, however, asked her to pay the costs for the hospital where he lived at that time. Katherina agreed she would return to her mother and live in chastity (as would Hanussius) and would make her living honestly. This was, in effect, a de facto separation. Suits where annulment or separation were the main aim are rare in these sources, and only appear as potential solutions in cases of impotence or illicit degree of kinship, although judicial practice at individual medieval church courts could differ significantly in this respect.[79] What is interesting in this story is the possibility that Hanussius always knew about his wife's new life and it was only when he needed additional financial support did he make any formal objection. This case indicates that sometimes 'fading out' a marriage could have come from mutual agreement as an attempt to circumvent the obstacles imposed otherwise by the Church and to meet the individual needs of the spouses.

Conclusion

These two case studies, based on urban and religious legal sources in the Czech lands, demonstrate a consensus in approach to the formation and dissolution of a marriage bond. Both legal systems emphasised free mutual consent as well as the public nature of exchanging marriage vows. The ceremony could be secular, but it had to be recognised publicly: secret marriages were undesirable for both legal frameworks. Canon law recognised *matrimonium clandestinum* as valid in nature, but the recorded agenda of the court of vicars general of the Prague Archdiocese, 1421–1437, shows that informality in marriage formation was a major source of uncertainty and tension. Similarly, it is noticeable how claims of pre-contract often happened in private. From the point of view of the municipal authorities, the practice of secret marriages was dangerous because it had the potential to bring disharmony and confusion to urban society. Town representatives strove for clear and transparent relations between the original families and the families arising from marriage, as well as between spouses and children, especially regarding the smooth handover of inheritance and property rights. Although, on a normative level, both jurisdictions promoted free consent, the reality could be very different, whether because of economic pressure from the family or physical coercion of parents, as rarely evidenced in church sources. For ecclesiastical courts, however, free consent was the paramount from which it did not want to compromise. If there was a clash of interests, couples longing for marriage could potentially seek protection at church courts.

What this chapter has also shown is the typicality of Barbara von Herwigsdorf's legal action, whose claim of alleged marriage at the church court began this paper. The largest percentage of cases heard before the ecclesiastical court related to alleged marriages and in these cases, women most often acted as plaintiffs where they wished a purported marriage vow to be recognised. Within the alleged marriage cases, the most vulnerable plaintiffs were pregnant women or women with small children seeking marriage recognition. For them, bringing the suit to an ecclesiastical court could only be beneficial. Social restraints together with financial sanctions offered a means to have their relationships formalised and to secure their and their children's legal and social status. If the male defendant refused to enter into marriage, but recognised the child's paternity, mothers were entitled to financial compensation for defloration and alimony for the child. This indicates that church courts acknowledged the shared responsibility of parents and protected the position of a mother. In some cases, the court even transferred the custody of a child into the hands of its father.

At the same time, looking across all cases, women were slightly more likely to find themselves in the position of defendants. An interesting strategy was chosen by some women who came to the court to face the demands of suitors they did not want to marry: to claim they were joking or doing something just 'out of friendship' had the potential to rescue them from tricky situations. Men were more active as plaintiffs especially in situations when they sought to remove impediments to a marriage, typically a claim of alleged previous marriage. Women also found themselves at court in a number of other situations, such as lawsuits of multiple marriages. We learn that not only commencement of marriage but also its dissolution could happen in an informal way: contrary to what we might expect, women were often the party who left the marriage. While suits of separation or annulment of a marriage are rarely documented, where they do appear it suggests that violence in marital cohabitation, whose victims were women, often made the ecclesiastical and secular court representatives cooperate in their interests and those of the female plaintiffs.

Notes

1 The text was written with the support of the project: *Individuals – Families – Urban Society. Social structure of late medieval Moravian towns* by Czech Science Foundation (grant project registration number 19–19104S). I would like to thank the editors of the volume, Deborah and Teresa, for their valuable suggestions and comments on the chapter.
2 Zittau, one of the urban centres of Upper Lusatia and now part of the state of Saxony in Germany, belonged until the Thirty Years' War to the Lands of the Bohemian Crown.
3 All names are written in the form they appear in the edited sources this essay draws on.
4 *Soudní akta konzistoře pražské (Acta Iudiciaria Consistorii Pragensis)*, Tom. VII (1420–1424), ed. by Ferdinand Tadra, Prague 1901, p. 105, n. 9.
5 Practically all of the written agenda of the official from the first phase of the existence of the office were consumed by fire in the Lesser Town of Prague at the beginning of the Hussite uprisings in 1419. After the conversion of the Prague Archbishop to the Hussite party in April 1421, the leadership of the Prague archdiocese was transferred to the Prague Chapter, respectively in hands of the two officials with the title of vicar general. They continued with the regular administrative agenda outside of Prague, which was Hussite, specifically in Zittau, where part of the Chapter was situated, cf. Hledíková, Zděňka – Janák, Jan, *Dějiny správy v českých zemích*: Od počátků státu po současnost, Prague 2005, pp. 179–188.
6 On the institution of marriage within the framework of the agenda of the Fourth Lateran Council see David L. D'Avray, 'Lateran IV and Marriage. What Lateran IV Did Not Do about Marriage?', in Gert Melville and Johannes Helmrath (eds.), *The Fourth Lateran Council: Institutional Reform and Spiritual Renewal* (Didymos Verlag, 2017), pp. 137–142. For the situation in the Lands of the Bohemian Crown concerning the implementation of the regulations of that Council see Robert Antonín et al., *Čtvrtý lateránský koncil a české země ve 13. a 14. století*, (Prague, 2020); to marriage law here cf. Janiš, Dalibor, *Manželské právo*, pp. 226–242. I'd like to thank Dalibor Janiš for providing me with the text before publication.
7 For a historical overview of the Lands of Bohemian Crown during the middle ages see Mikuláš Teich (ed.), *Bohemia in History* (Cambridge, 1998), pp. 39–97. For Hussitism and the Hussite Wars, see Michael Van Dussen, Michael and Pavel Soukup (eds.), *A Companion to the Hussites* (Leiden, 2020).
8 For a recent account of Brno's medieval history see Jan Libor (ed.), *Dějiny Brna 2. Středověké město* (Brno, 2013).
9 The Book of Law was written by Jan, a notary of Brno, between 1342 and 1358. On his career in Brno see Miroslav Flodr, 'Cesta k právu a spravedlnosti. Jan, notář města Brna', in Libor Jan and Zdeněk Drahoš (eds.), *Osobnosti moravských dějin 1* (Brno, 2006), pp. 89–102. For the edition and commentary on The Book of Law of the Scribe see Miroslav Flodr (ed.), *Právní kniha města Brna z poloviny 14. století. I. Úvod a edice*, (Brno, 1990); Flodr (ed.), *Nálezy brněnského městského práva. Svazek I. (–1389)* (Brno, 2007). For publications analysing Brno municipal law in medieval period see Flodr, *Brněnské městské právo. Zakladatelské období (–1359)*, (Brno, 2001). On municipal laws in the Czech lands in broader context cf. František Hoffmann, *Středověké město v Čechách a na Moravě* (Prague, 2009), pp. 393–462.
10 Both Memorial books were edited, see Miroslav Flodr (ed.) *Pamětní kniha města Brna z let 1343–1376 (1379)* (Brno, 2005); Flodr (ed.) *Pamětní kniha města Brna z let 1391–1515* (Brno, 2010).
11 See Flodr, *Brněnské městské právo*, p. 267.
12 Flodr, *Právní kniha*, pp. 260–261, n. 345–347.
13 For example, in defining the minimum age for marriage, see Flodr, *Právní kniha*, p. 372, n. 650 c) or in the determination of the inadmissible degree of kinship, see Ibid.,

p. 261, n. 347. The main principles of Canon law with regard to marriage are summarised Sara McDougall, 'Women and Gender in Canon Law', in Judith M. Bennett and Ruth Mazo Karras (eds.), *Women and gender in Medieval Europe* (Oxford, 2013), pp. 163-178.
14 On the forms of marriage and its formation in the Czech lands in the Middle Ages see Jana Janišová and Dalibor Janiš, 'Manželství v historických souvislostech', in Renáta Šínová and Ondřej Šmíd et al. (eds.), *Manželství* (Prague, 2014), pp. 21-34; see also Martin Nodl, 'In facie ecclesiae', in Martin Nodl and Kras Paweł (eds.), *Manželství v pozdním středověku: rituály a obyčeje* (Prague, 2014), pp. 53-61.
15 Flodr, *Brněnské městské právo*, p. 269.
16 The marital law of Brno in a comparative perspective has been analysed in Gertrud Schubart-Fikentscher, *Das Eherecht in Brünner Schöffenbuch* (Stuttgart, 1935). On the proclamation of free consent in the Brno municipal law see Flodr, *Právní kniha*, p. 261, n. 350 and also on p. 317, n. 504 i). On the formation of marriage in Brno municipal law see Flodr, *Brněnské městské právo*, pp. 267-269.
17 Flodr, *Právní kniha*, p. 316, n. 504 e).
18 Flodr, *Brněnské městské právo*, pp. 267-269; Jan, *Dějiny Brna*, pp. 302-308; Janišová and Janiš, 'Manželství v historických souvislostech', pp. 33-34.
19 Flodr, *Právní kniha*, p. 391, n. 716, a).
20 The record is dated 21 February 1479, see *Pamětní kniha města Brna z let 1391-1515*, p. 397, n. 798.
21 For the issue of legal and social status of wife and property co-ownership between husbands in medieval Brno see Michaela Antonín Malaníková, 'Poručnictví, nebo partnerství? Status manželky a majetkové poměry manželů ve středověkém Brně', *Theatrum historiae*, 22 (2018), pp. 33-49. On the (property) relations between urban and aristocratic husbands in Late Medieval Bohemia see John Klassen, 'The Development of the Conjugal Bond in Late Medieval Bohemia', *Journal of Medieval History*, 13 (1987), pp. 161-178 and Idem, 'Household Composition in Medieval Bohemia', *Journal of Medieval History*, 16 (1990), pp. 55-75.
22 *Vir enim non solum corporis, immo bonorum uxoris dominus est et rector,* see Flodr, *Právní kniha*, p. 312, n. 495 a). On this issue also see Flodr, *Brněnské městské právo*, pp. 269-271.
23 Flodr, *Právní kniha*, p. 315, n. 503.
24 *Pamětní kniha města Brna z let 1391-1515*, p. 377, n. 773. Similar cases must have been quite common within urban society, as other entries in the Memorial Books testify: for example, *Pamětní kniha z let 1343-1376 (1379)*, p. 361, n. 994; pp. 706-707, n. 2153.
25 For a detailed analysis see Schubart-Fikentscher, *Das Eherecht*, pp. 195-196.
26 Flodr, *Právní kniha*, p. 314, n. 502.
27 Miroslav Flodr (ed.), *Příručka práva městského (Manipulus vel directorium iuris civilis)* (Brno, 2008).
28 On spousal disputes in the Lands of the Bohemian Crown see John Klassen, 'Marriage and Family in Medieval Bohemia', *East European Quarterly*, 19:3 (1985), pp. 257-274; Zdeňka Hledíková, 'Zápisy manželských sporů – nepovšimnutý pramen 15. Století', in Zdeněk Beneš, Eduard Maur and Jaroslav Pánek (eds.), *Pocta Josefu Petráňovi* (Prague, 1991), pp. 79-93; Božena Kopičková, 'Manželské spory žen pozdního středověku v protokolech ústředních církevních úřadů v Praze', *Documenta Pragensia*, 13 (1996), pp. 57-65.
29 Flodr, *Právní kniha*, p. 225, n. 237. This accords with the findings of Sara M. Butler where 'chastisement' as a form of physical discipline for wives was socially approved and internalised by both genders in medieval communities, see Sara M. Butler, 'The Law as a Weapon in Marital Disputes: Evidence from Late Medieval Court of Chancery, 1424-1529', *Journal of British Studies*, 43 (2004), p. 293. On marital violence see Butler, *The Language of Abuse. Marital Violence in Later Medieval England* (Leiden, 2007).

30 Flodr, *Právní kniha*, pp. 313–314, n. 502; *Pamětní kniha města Brna z let 1343–1376 (1379)*, pp. 320–321, n. 847.
31 Miroslav Flodr (ed.), *Flodr, Právní kniha*, p. 313.
32 Katerina was allowed to leave the house of a husband and return back to her parents, Georius had to pay her a *dos promissa* plus the *donationes antenuptiales* in a considerable amount.
33 Schubart-Fikentscher, *Das Eherecht*, p. 197.
34 Flodr, *Právní kniha*, p. 335, n. 540.
35 Ibid., p. 212, n. 187.
36 See Jeremy Goldberg, 'Gender and Matrimonial Litigation in the Church Courts in the Latter Middle Ages: The Evidence of the Court of York', *Gender & History*, 19 (2007), esp. pp. 52–55; Goldberg 'Echoes, Whispers, Ventriloquisms: On Recovering Women's Voices from the Court of York in Late Middle Ages', in Bronach C. Kane and Fiona Williamson (eds.), *Women, Agency and the Law, 1300–1700* (London, 2012), pp. 32–33.
37 The title suggested by Zdeňka Hledíková in 'Soudní akta generálních vikářů', *Sborník archivních prací* 1/XVI, 1966, pp. 157–171.
38 *Soudní akta*, passim. As for the total number of entries I rely on data provided by John M. Klassen, see Klassen, 'Marriage and Family', p. 257.
39 Joachim Prochno, *Zittauer Urkundenbuch I. (Regesten zur Geschichte der Stadt und des Landes Zittau 1234–1437)* (Görlitz, 1938), pp. 247–347. Records for the years 1425–1426 are missing.
40 Kirsi Salonen 'Marriage Disputes in the Consistorial Court of Freising in the Late Middle Ages', in Mia Korpiola (ed.), *Regional Variations in Matrimonial Law and Custom in Europe, 1150–1600* (Leiden, 2011), p. 190.
41 Charles Donahue, Jr., *Law, Marriage and Society in the Later Middle Ages. Arguments about Marriage in Five Courts* (Cambridge, 2007), pp. 16–18.
42 James A. Brundage, 'E pluribus unum: Custom, the Professionalization of Medieval Law, and Regional Variations in Marriage Formation', in Mia Korpiola (ed.), *Regional Variations*, p. 36.
43 This reversed procedure, that is, contract *per verba de presenti* followed by reading of the banns and finally marriage *in facie ecclesie* is testified in Ely, see Michael M. Sheehan, 'The Formation and Stability of Marriage in Fourteen-Century England: Evidence of an Ely Register', *Medieval Studies*, 33 (1971), pp. 238, 249.
44 Sara M. Butler, *Divorce in Medieval England. From One to Two Persons in Law* (London, 2013), p. 2.
45 On the slow penetration of canon law into the Czech environment see Martin Nodl, 'Pronikání kanonického práva do českého prostředí, jeho recepce nařízeními církve a rezistence laického prostředí vůči kanonickým předpisům', in Pavel Krafl (ed.), *Sacri canones servandi sunt. Ius canonicum et status ecclesiae saeculis XIII-XV* (Prague, 2008), pp. 650–658. See also Nodl, *In facie ecclesiae*. Similar conclusions apply also to neighbouring Poland, cf. Magdalena Biniaś-Szkopek, *Małżonkowie przed sądem biskupiego oficjała poznańskiego w pierwszej ćwierci XV wieku* (Poznań, 2018), pp. 102–110.
46 James A. Brundage, *Law, Sex, and Christian Society in Medieval Europe* (Chicago, 1987), pp. 189–191.
47 John Klasen has already pointed out the fact that the investigated sources document spontaneous pre-marital relations of both sexes: Klassen, 'Marriage and Family', p. 261.
48 Prochno, *Zittauer Urkundenbuch*, p. 340, n. 3.
49 Prochno, *Zittauer Urkundenbuch*, p. 338, n. 8.
50 John Klassen also emphasised the predominance of this type of disputes. In his typology of matrimonial disputes, he identified only two groups of lawsuits: alleged marriages and marriage impediments, see John M. Klassen, 'Marriage and Family', p. 258.

51 Salonen 'Marriage Disputes', p. 193.
52 See *Soudní akta*, p. 29, n. 55.
53 Ibid., p. 30.
54 Based on the analysed sources, alleged marriage lawsuits where the plaintiff (male or female) was not able to provide valuable testimony were rejected by the court. The same holds true for cases where plaintiffs were opting for removal of impediment to marriage, typically a claim of alleged previous marriage. If the party opposing a marriage was not able to support a pre-contract by credible testimony, his or her claims were dismissed. This finding is not surprising in the context of contemporary legal practice: Sheehan, 'Formation and Stability', p. 249.
55 Immediate recognition (or renewal) of the marriage vow and hence validation of a marriage by the church court was one of the possible outcomes of the trial; in this chapter's research sample three cases have been found. Compare Prochno, *Zittauer Urkundenbuch*, p. 296, n. 70; Ibid., p. 304, n. 42.
56 See *Soudní akta*, p. 34, n. 74; Ibid., pp. 56–57, n. 18; Ibid., pp. 78–79, n. 144; Ibid., pp. 102–103, n. 259; Ibid., p. 109, n. 20. Out of the remaining five cases, marriage was (re-)established in one case (Ibid., p. 29, n. 55, see case quoted in the footnote n. 48), but the outcome of the dispute is unknown in the remaining four cases.
57 In the only record where it was possible to work with the full text of the record (record of 1424), the taking into care is described as follows: ... *ipse Andreas puerum ad se reasumat et eundem amplius per se educat*, cf. Tadra p. 109, n. 20.
58 In one of the cases it is noted that the allocation of the child to its father was to happen after three years, but it is not clear how old the child was at that time: Prochno, *Zittauer Urkundenbuch*, p. 303, n. 38. In one of the two cases where the child was born from the adulterous relationship of a married woman it was decided by the court that the child's father would take him into his custody immediately after the birth so that his mother could return to her husband as soon as possible, see Prochno, *Zittauer Urkundenbuch*, p. 320, n. 18.
59 *Soudní akta*, p. 109, n. 20; Prochno, *Zittauer Urkundenbuch*, p. 283, n. 36; Ibid., p. 303, n. 35; Ibid., p. 303, n. 38; Ibid., p. 320, n. 18.
60 Prochno, *Zittauer Urkundenbuch*, p. 303, n. 38.
61 Salonen, 'Marriage Disputes', p. 196, 207.
62 The sources record only two such cases dated 1431 and 1432; in the latter, the woman was apparently a former prostitute, cf. Prochno, *Zittauer Urkundenbuch*, p. 314, n. 22; Ibid., p. 319, n. 15.
63 See McDougall, 'Women and Gender in Canon Law', p. 167.
64 Prochno, *Zittauer Urkundenbuch*, s. 333, n. 19.
65 Public knowledge (Latin term: *recognicione*) is often use by plaintiffs to support their argument for recognition of a marriage, see also Sheehan, 'Formation and Stability', p. 249.
66 Prochno, *Zittauer Urkundenbuch*, s. 331, n. 4.
67 *Soudní akta*, pp. 58–59, n. 26. For a similar case when a cruel husband had to pledge such a guarantee with the participation of guarantors from the citizens of Zittau see Ibid., pp. 12–13, n. 22.
68 Her reasoning, unfortunately, is not included, see Prochno, *Zittauer Urkundenbuch*, p. 308, n. 18.
69 In both samples together, see *Soudní akta*, pp. 26–27, n. 51; Ibid., pp. 37–38, n. 83; Ibid., p. 106, n. 11; Prochno, *Zittauer Urkundenbuch*, s. 308, n. 18; Ibid., s. 308, n. 19; Ibid., s. 328, n. 10; Ibid., s. 328, n. 8.
70 In three of the six cases the result is not recorded, in the remaining three the woman was exempted from the claims of the alleged groom.
71 Prochno, *Zittauer Urkundenbuch*, p. 315, n. 29.
72 The number of bigamy cases dealt with by a court of Poznań official in neighbouring Poland between 1404 and 1426 reaches 25% of all marital disputes, cf. Biniaś-Szkopek, *Małżonkowie przed sądem*, pp. 167–168.

73 Goldberg, 'Gender and Matrimonial Litigation', p. 48.
74 *Soudní akta*, p. 36, n. 78; Ibid., s. 51–52, n. 5; Ibid., pp. 63–64, n. 62; Ibid., p. 64, n. 63; Ibid., pp. 66–67, n. 69; Ibid., pp. 87–88, n. 184; Ibid., p. 99, n. 244. In three cases where married couples testified by making a joint statement together in court, bigamy concerned a woman.
75 Prochno, *Zittauer Urkundenbuch*, p. 287, n. 67; Ibid., p. 299, n. 6; Ibid., p. 303, n. 35; Ibid., p. 307, n. 8; Ibid., p. 320, n. 22; Ibid., p. 342, n. 13. This is comparable to similar localities: Biniaś-Szkopek, *Małżonkowie przed sądem*, pp. 168.
76 We know the verdict of seven cases out of a total number of thirteen in both samples.
77 *Soudní akta*, pp. 63–64, n. 62.
78 *Soudní akta*, p. 36, n. 78.
79 Pleas of annulment are infrequently attested in other ecclesiastical courts see Sheehan, 'Formation and Stability', p. 261. In rural areas of Yorkshire, on the other hand, suits for annulment were comparatively common, Jeremy Goldberg, *Women, Work and Life Cycle in a Medieval Economy: Women in York and Yorkshire c. 1300–1520* (Oxford, 1992), p. 251.

5
WIDOWHOOD AND ATTAINDER IN MEDIEVAL IRELAND

The case of Margaret Nugent[1]

Sparky Booker

In 1460[2] Margaret Nugent, a wealthy widow from the English colonial community in Ireland, came before the Irish parliament and requested that her dower lands be awarded to her. In bringing her petition before this body, she was availing herself of the judicial powers of parliament, an important but little studied aspect of its work in the later middle ages.[3] Most widows would not have had to mount such a case and could have sought their dower lands – the lands provided to them from their deceased husband's estate to support them in their widowhood – using a more straightforward administrative process.[4] Margaret's situation, however, was a complex one. Her deceased husband was William Butler, a Lancastrian adherent who was attainted in April 1455 by a parliament overseen by Thomas FitzGerald, Earl of Kildare and deputy to Richard Duke of York. In her petition, she had to argue that she should enjoy the profits of her dower lands despite her husband's attainder for failing to answer for felonies and the consequent seizure of his lands into crown hands. She also had to navigate complications relating to her marital status, since she had been separated from her husband before his attainder. She had to show that she remained legally his wife and thus entitled to dower. Her marital troubles had led to a case for separation in the bishop of Meath's consistory court, and these legal proceedings in an ecclesiastical court were discussed in her appeal to parliament. Her case thus sheds light on the interaction of ecclesiastical and parliamentary jurisdictions in English Ireland and provides a rare glimpse into the language and arguments that female litigants used in their cases before Irish parliaments, the primary equity jurisdiction available in the colony in the fifteenth century. This chapter will examine Nugent's petition of 1460 and related petitions she lodged in 1470 and her father made in 1458 and assess the extent to which her pleading strategies and experience at law were shaped by her gender.

DOI: 10.4324/9780429278037-6

Margaret was not the first or the last widow to face problems in accessing her dower after a husband's attainder but the problem was particularly common in periods of civil unrest.[5] In Ireland, as in England, the dynastic struggle for the crown between the houses of Lancaster and York, later called the Wars of the Roses, made widows of many wealthy women. Like any civil war, it also made traitors of those men who chose the losing side. Once they were attainted, the property of traitors was taken into the hands of the crown, leaving some widows bereft both of their husbands and their dower lands. The practice regarding the treatment of such widows was not consistent. The commons in the English Parliament had requested in the wake of the depositions of Edward II in 1327 and of Richard II in 1399 that a law be enacted to ensure that widows of traitors would automatically retain their rights to dower, but these requests were unsuccessful. Throughout the later middle ages and across the English polity the award of dower to the widows of traitors depended on a given monarch's grace in the matter. Their treatment by the crown depended on many factors, including their family connections and who they subsequently remarried (if they did so).[6] The crown was seen to have a 'moral obligation to support widows in need' and usually did not deny dower claims outright – though there were cases like that of Margaret Mortimer, mother of the Earl of March, whose dower lands remained in crown hands for over a decade until her death in 1334 – but the length of time that widows had to wait and the security of their claim from re-confiscation varied and depended on crown support.[7] In any case, to secure the return of their dower lands from forfeiture widows had to mount a successful petition to the crown, or in Margaret Nugent's case, to the king's deputy in Ireland via the prerogative court of Parliament. The notion that the crown had a duty to defend widows was well established by the fifteenth century and petitions relating to dower were among the most common type for female petitioners to the English parliament.[8] In this sense Margaret's choice to pursue her case in a parliamentary venue was not unusual, but we know relatively little about such petitions from Ireland given the fractured and incomplete nature of Irish medieval administrative records.[9] Additionally, the multiple petitions Margaret and her father submitted mean that we can flesh out the details of her case to a much greater extent than other female petitioners to the Irish parliament in this period.

Few scholars have examined in any depth the Wars of the Roses in Ireland, and none, to my knowledge, have looked at how the conflict affected those noble and gentry women who lost control of their property because of it.[10] The parliamentary material relevant to Margaret Nugent dates from the period 1455–1472 during which Irish parliaments were dominated by the Yorkist faction.[11] Pre-existing factional groups in the colony were mapped onto the English struggle with influential families in the colony choosing sides and bringing their extensive affinities along with them.[12] The house of Kildare and the wider Fitzgerald family aligned itself with York while the Butler earls of Ormond and their kin and allies supported the Lancastrians.[13] Lesser noble and gentry families in the colony therefore chose sides depending not only on their feelings about Henry VI and the Duke of York but also their relationships with Ormond and Kildare.[14] The colony as a whole was dominated by the Yorkists, and the leaders of that faction, the Geraldine earls of Kildare and Desmond, were the most powerful magnates in the colony for most of the 1450s and 1460s.[15] The popularity of the Duke of York in Ireland was furthered by his position as earl of Ulster but he also twice served as Henry VI's deputy. His time on the ground helped him to secure support in English Ireland for himself and his sons, one of whom, George duke of Clarence, was born in Dublin Castle in 1449.[16] Ireland became a refuge for York in 1459, as he fled England under a sentence of treason, and it was the launching pad for his bid for the crown in 1460 that culminated in his death at the battle of Wakefield.[17] Yorkist sympathies in the colony remained strong through the upheaval after Edward VI's death, through Richard III's reign and after the victory of Henry Tudor: two Yorkist pretenders were launched from the colony in the 1480s and 1490s.[18] As we will see, Margaret Nugent and her family fell into the Yorkist majority, but her husband William Butler was on the opposite side of the conflict and it is possible that this was a factor in the breakdown of their marriage.

Sources: Irish parliaments and private petitions

Given that relatively little work has been done on the Irish parliament as a legal, rather than as a legislative, venue it is necessary to briefly outline its procedures in this respect. The records that provide details of Margaret Nugent's petitions are the rolls of the Irish parliament, which heard these petitions in its capacity as the highest court in English Ireland and one that could, when appropriate, rule according to the principles of equity.[19] Irish parliaments and councils were the most popular equity jurisdiction available before 1494 in the English colony in Ireland which had a legal system and range of secular courts that were based on, though not identical to, those operating in England itself.[20] This legal system was first put in place in the decades after the English invasion of Ireland in the late 1160s, but continued to evolve in parallel with English courts and with a high level of influence from England. The law in Ireland was never applied in precisely the same way and with identical procedures as in England and the right of the 'land of Ireland' to preserve some distinct legal practices was asserted and accepted several times in the later middle ages.[21] Still, efforts were made to ensure that Irish courts did not stray too far from English models. These efforts came in many forms including legislative and royal directives from England, the education of students from Ireland at the Inns of Court and the deployment of English justices to Ireland.[22] The king's subjects in Ireland also had the right to go to his prerogative courts in England and they did so in small numbers, but the cost and difficulty of travel made the Irish parliament a more attractive option for most litigants.

In English Ireland by the mid-fifteenth century, parliament came to fill the role that had been served by the Irish privy council and acted as the highest court of appeal in the colony while also operating as an equity jurisdiction (like the court of chancery in England in this period).[23] Ellis argues that 'it began to supply the need for a court with the power to override the form of law in favour of justice'.[24] Two leading historians of Irish and English parliaments, H.G. Richardson and G.O. Sayles, argued that the language used in petitions to and the decisions of parliament in Ireland closely mirrored those of the English court of chancery.[25] The language and the arguments petitioners used in their original bills were shaped by the conventions of petitioning and by the advice of the legal advisors like those Margaret almost certainly employed, and cannot be treated as a representations of any petitioner's unmediated voice.[26] Moreover, the original bills or oral petitions made by petitioners in the fifteenth century are not preserved, but survive in a modified and probably abbreviated form in the acts that resulted from successful cases enrolled in the parliament rolls. These parliamentary records detail the background for each case and often echo the language used in petitions like Margaret's (as discussed below). Much is lost, however, since it is likely that petitions were delivered orally as they were before English parliaments, and may have included information that was not considered germane by the clerks tasked with enrollment.[27] There is no record of unsuccessful petitions, since these did not necessitate any action on the part of the council or the colonial administration more broadly and were therefore not recorded.[28] This makes it impossible to judge the overall success rates of petitioners, or investigate whether gender influenced success rates. The acts passed by parliament in response to the petitions of private petitioners were enrolled on the parliament rolls only after 1447 (generally in French) but other material from the colonial administration in the later fourteenth century can provide some hint of how widows and other female petitioners used these legal venues in the decades before Margaret's petition.[29]

The Irish parliament cooperated with the colony's other courts, and sometimes referred litigants to them. Conversely, some petitions were appeals from lower courts.[30] The parliamentary jurisdiction in Ireland, just as in England, was well integrated into the overall legal framework.[31] Petitioners (of whatever gender) had to justify their resort to parliament by explaining why they could not use the usual common law channels. Petitions to parliament were usually justified by one of the following arguments: (1) the poverty of the litigant, who might claim that common law methods of redress were too costly (2) the disproportionate influence and power of an adversary, which might make justices and juries in lower or local courts find in their favour; (3) the unavailability of 'justice' through common law channels; that is, if no appropriate writ existed to resolve their dispute.[32] Margaret cited the third of these justifications in her petition, noting that, in a common formulaic phrase, 'she can have no action by the common law to recover her reasonable dower'.

Who could petition in parliament? In theory, this venue was open to all subjects of the crown in Ireland – and the 1392–1393 parliamentary material demonstrates that this included a number of Irish people[33] – but in Ireland as in England, most petitioners were of middling or high-status.[34] In England this was even more the case by the fifteenth century than at the start of the fourteenth, as petitions of lower-status persons were increasingly siphoned off to other legal venues like the court of chancery.[35] It is difficult to determine from the small sample sizes whether this trend away from lower-status petitioners occurred in Ireland; since the Irish court of chancery seems to have done little business before the end of the fifteenth century it may not have and men described as millers, yeomen and husbandmen appeared as petitioners in the 1450s, though they were in the minority.[36] In practice, petitioners generally needed a supporter in parliament who was willing to introduce their bill and this may have ensured that most petitioners were of relatively high status.[37] Sometimes the relationship between a petitioner and a peer or member of parliament is clear. In Margaret Nugent's case, her father was baron of Delvin. Katherine Fleming, who petitioned in 1460 for the restoration of rents owed to her from her former husband after the dissolution of their marriage, also came from a family whose leading member sat in parliament as a peer. The Fleming barons of Slane were aligned with the Yorkist cause, and this may have been relevant in Katherine's decision to present her petition to parliament in this period and perhaps also to the favourable verdict she received.[38] Jenet, a widow who petitioned parliament in 1455, had been married to Christopher Plunkett, lord of Killeen, who was himself a peer and may have been the mother of his heir and successor as lord of Killeen.[39] There are other female petitioners for whom ties to the peerage are not immediately apparent, like Jenet Besbell who came before parliament in 1460.[40] Besbell seems to have been of lower status than most of the women who petitioned the Irish parliament between 1455 and 1460. Although she was a significant landowner, as is clear from her petition, neither she nor her deceased husband, John Whitacre, were members of leading gentry or noble families. There are no petitions from this period from women any further down the social scale – the female equivalent of the husbandman who petitioned in 1450 – but given the smaller number of female than male petitioners, it is difficult to know how significant this is.[41]

Women made up the minority of petitioners in Ireland, as they did in England.[42] In some 109 private petitions in the parliamentary records from 1455 to 1460, there were only thirteen named female petitioners in twelve petitions.[43] Of these, six women, including Margaret, petitioned singly (one in her capacity as an abbess), five alongside their husbands, one alongside male co-executors of her husband's will, and one, who lived in England, was represented by her male servants.[44] As in common law contexts, married women usually petitioned alongside their husbands rather than independently. Indeed, the petitions of married women to the English parliament were sometimes rejected summarily if they appeared without their husband as co-petitioner.[45] In rare cases, as when a woman's husband was in captivity or otherwise unavoidably absent, the English parliament allowed married women to petition without their husbands, and the Irish parliament may have permitted the same leeway, as common law courts in Ireland occasionally did.[46] In Ireland, again as in England, the majority of female petitioners were married or widowed, rather than unmarried.[47]

Margaret Nugent's struggle for her dower lands

Margaret Nugent fits well into the prevailing patterns for female petitioners to the Irish parliament in this period in that she was a widow, came from the 'four shires' region at the heart of the colony, submitted a petition about her dower lands and was of high status. Her family was, however, on the wealthier end of those represented in parliamentary petitions and her father was extremely well connected in the colonial administration. Richard Nugent was lord of Delvin and was not only a member of parliament but particularly influential in it. He was aligned to the Yorkist cause and had been the deputy of two chief governors of the colony: James Butler, fourth earl of Ormond, in 1444 and the Duke of York in 1449. He was a moderate, even conciliatory, figure during factional disputes between Sir John Talbot and the fourth earl of Ormond in the first half of the fifteenth century.[48] He was successful in navigating the fraught political environment of the mid-fifteenth century, as he served in local administrative roles in Meath throughout the 1450s and was granted exemptions from acts of resumption by the Irish parliament in 1460 and 1468. His political acumen is attested by the respect shown to him by the Irish as well as the English of Ireland. As a marcher lord whose lands in Meath (modern co. Westmeath) lay in the extensive borderlands with Gaelic areas, it may be no surprise that his death was noted in the Irish Annals of Ulster, but the praise they afforded him was unusually fulsome for one of the English of Ireland.[49] All in all, Delvin's apparent skill in gaining and keeping allies and his prominent position in the colonial administration and in colonial society may help to account for Margaret's eventual success before parliament. As discussed below, it is likely Margaret was well aware of his influence and emphasized her relationship to him in her petition.

As was typical of women of her status from the region at the core of the English colony, Margaret had married into another elite family of English descent, the Butlers, at whose head was the earl of Ormond. Indeed, the fourth earl and her father had brokered Margaret's marriage to William Butler, seventh baron of Dunboyne, sometime before the fourth earl's death in 1452.[50] The marriage helped to link these two families whose leading members cooperated politically in the 1440s. It also made sense territorially, since William was the head of a cadet branch of Butlers based in Meath with holdings to the south and east of Nugent lands. Nevertheless, the union was not a success. One of the issues between the couple may have been the fact that Butler was, like most of his immediate and extended family, a Lancastrian sympathizer. His pro-Lancastrian stance may have become increasingly unacceptable to his wife and her family as the 1450s progressed and the power struggle between the Duke of York and Henry VI devolved into open warfare.[51]

Butler was among a number of Lancastrians attainted in parliaments overseen by the Duke of York and by his deputies between 1455 and 1460. Butler was attainted and his lands seized in 1455 because he did not appear before the Irish court of King's Bench to answer for several crimes, among them stealing livestock and other goods and burning and pillaging in the company of other leading members of the Butler family and their Irish allies.[52] Seizure of land and the use of the language of attainder were routine for anyone who did not appear to answer serious charges in the courts of the colony, but the parliamentary record described Butler's actions as 'treasons' and other details of the charges against him suggest that they were seen in that light. The letter from the sovereign of Wexford town and the seneschal of the liberty of Wexford that precipitated his attainder alleged that he committed his crimes with Irish enemies of the king and many other Butlers – 'divers others of the said nation [i.e. the Butler family]' – and 'in the manner and guise of mortal war'.[53] It further alleged that Butler and his associates were 'people that will not obey the King's laws' and claimed that the Butler military force went riding with banners displayed over the county of Wexford. The phrase 'with banners displayed' signified open warfare and implied a 'treasonable usurpation' of the exclusive royal right to wage war.[54]

The accounts of Butler's crimes put before parliament in 1455 are not exceptional in the sense that other colonial lords throughout the fifteenth century were accused of similar actions – essentially of leading a raiding party with their Irish and English allies. It is nonetheless important to keep in mind the language of 'treason' used in the account and the context of Yorkist and Lancastrian factionalism. Whatever the truth of Butler's actions, allegations against him may have been pursued in part because of Kildare/Yorkist dominance of the Irish parliament in 1455.[55] This did not mean, however that there was no chance to reconcile with the colonial administration; in February 1458, several other leading members of the Butler family attainted alongside William Butler petitioned parliament and claimed that 'every one of them was so sick in his body, that none of them could appear before our said lord the King in his Chief Place' when they were called to do so.[56] Their claim was accepted, and their attainders lifted, provided that they were of good conduct in the future. William, apparently, made no such excuses and his attainder remained in force. His actions and attainder were, presumably, frowned on by his father in law, and, although we cannot know the exact causes of his marital breakdown, it is difficult to imagine that they did not strain his relationship with his wife (from whom he separated at some stage before 1458).

Sometime between February 1458 and the summer of 1460 (when Margaret made her petition) William died in battle fighting alongside 'O'Conghor, an enemy to our said sovereign lord the King''. This was most likely Conn O'Connor Faly, who was defeated by the earl of Kildare in 1459.[57] After his death, Margaret petitioned parliament to secure her dower.[58] The dower she requested was a third 'of the lands and tenements which were of the said William at any time during the said marriage had between him and the said Margaret'. This award of dower out of lands held at any time during the marriage, rather than the estate as it stood on the day of marriage, was common by the fifteenth century. However, both methods of defining the estate for the purposes of dower claims were accepted, and that Margaret specified the former may suggest that Butler's property grew after their marriage and she wanted to ensure that she got a third of his estate at its largest point.[59] Any strategic considerations about which type of dower to claim were irrelevant, however, if she could not overcome the issue of his attainder.

She did this by arguing that Butler's 'misconduct and offences' were 'much against [her] will', seeking to ensure that she was not tarred with the same brush as her husband. She further distanced herself from her him by alleging that he 'fell into great misconduct, as well against our sovereign lord the king, his people and his laws, and in avoiding his said wife and turning himself to the company of other women'. The disloyalty that William (allegedly) showed to his sovereign and fellow English of Ireland and that he showed to his wife were presented as two sides of the same coin.[60] This highlighted Margaret's position as a fellow victim of her husband's faithlessness. It also speaks to her innocence in his crimes and suggests that she was not in her husband's company when he committed criminal acts. The mention of William's sexual disloyalty and resort to other women is not legally relevant to the award of dower or his attainder, but petitions to parliament did not restrict themselves strictly to matters of direct legal import. Rather, they constructed versions of events that showed the petitioner as a victim of injustice, just as Margaret did.[61] Additionally, there may be further reasons, discussed below, that prompted Margaret to include accusations about William's adultery in her petition.

Margaret presented herself quite passively. While she asserted that Butler's actions were against her will, she did not claim to have done anything to prevent them or dissuade her husband. This position of passivity would not have been as believable or sympathetic in a male petitioner, given the widespread assumptions across medieval society about the power dynamics within marriage and other types of personal relationship between men and women.[62] The evidence we have for decisions made in common law courts in Ireland suggest that even wives or mistresses who committed crimes under their husband's direction were sometimes shown leniency, and the general assumption seems to have been that men exerted control over the women in their lives but not vice versa.[63] This assumption left space for wives or widows to distance themselves from their husbands' actions as Margaret did. Like Margaret, at least two widows making similar petitions to the crown in England in the 1320s emphasized their blamelessness and asserted that they had committed no crimes, even if their husbands had done so.[64]

The way that Margaret (and her legal advisors) initially described herself in her petition may also have been designed to put distance between herself and her deceased husband, while linking her more closely to her influential father. The parliamentary record begins with the introductory phrase, 'at the prayer of Margaret, daughter of Richard Nugent, knight, Baron of Delvin, formerly wife of William Botiller'. The identification of Margaret first as Nugent's daughter, rather than as Butler's wife, was unusual. Widows petitioning English and Irish parliaments about their dower in the mid-fifteenth century tended to identify themselves using their own name (sometimes just their first name and sometimes their first name and natal surname) followed by their deceased husband's name.[65] Examples from Irish parliaments in this period include 'Jenet, formerly the wife of Christopher Plunkett, knight, formerly lord of Killeen', 'Jenet Besbell, widow, formerly wife to John Whitacre', 'Alice Talbot, long since wife to Launcelot Fitz Richard esquire' and 'Parnell Bryan, formerly the wife of John Waryng'.[66] These opening clauses differ in their precise wording, as will be discussed further below, but these women all named their husbands directly after themselves, just as widowed petitioners in England usually did and they made no mention of their fathers or natal families (apart from the use of their natal surnames). It is likely that the structure of the opening clause of Margaret's petition, in departing from the usual pattern, was a deliberate attempt to imprint on the minds of her audience her close ties to her father and her alienation from her husband.

This argument relies on the assumption that the parliamentary rolls from Ireland are relatively faithful to the original petitions, since the original petitions do not survive. Slight variations in the way that the women are described – Besbell being called a widow, lately wife (*widdowe iaditz famme*) while Talbot was 'long since wife (*bien iaditz femme*)' for example – and personal touches in the narrative sections of petitions suggest a fairly faithful rather than a standardizing policy of the clerks who created these records. Moreover, the varying ways that these petitioning widows from Ireland are described on the parliament rolls echoes the different ways widows described themselves in original petitions to the English king, council and parliament that do survive. There is evidence from the English context of the same sort of flexibility and strategic thinking that Margaret displayed in how to frame one's name and identifying details at the start of a petition. The petition of Joan Asteley to Henry VI in 1455, for example, began with the phrase: 'Beseecheth meekly your humble oratrice, Joan Asteley, widow, sometime your nurse'. In a subsequent section of her petition relating to grants made to her former husband, she described herself as 'Joan Asteley, widow, late the wife of Thomas Asteley'.[67] In a single petition, Joan's way of describing herself shifted as was most relevant to the argument she was making and most likely to encourage a favourable response. Reminding Henry VI of her service as his nurse seemed the best option for Joan to begin her plea and rouse royal sympathy. In the same way, although it was not relevant from a legal perspective that Margaret was the daughter of the baron of Delvin, she clearly felt it might aid her petition to be seen primarily in that light rather than as the widow of her supposedly faithless traitor husband.

Margaret had to balance her argument carefully, however, and while she emphasised how distant her husband eventually became, she had to show that her marriage to him remained valid and that she was thus entitled to dower. Accordingly, her petition was careful to state that Butler 'took to wife the said Margaret' and lived with her as her husband for 'years and days' before his 'fall' into 'great misconduct'. Margaret's position as his wife was called into question by the fact that she and William were separated by 1458. We know of this separation because of a parliamentary petition made in 1458 by Richard Nugent. According to that petition, William had gone to a church court (probably that of the bishop of Meath), possessed by 'high malice', and had procured a separation from his wife by some unspecified 'method by him maliciously contrived'.[68] The separation seems to have been a separation *mensa et thoro* (from bed and board) rather than an annulment of the marriage, as a mention of a possible reconciliation confirms.[69] This meant that while Margaret and William could live separately, they remained married and could not marry anyone else. The usual way to procure a separation *mensa et thoro* was for the spouse seeking the separation to prove that the other spouse had committed adultery; other crimes, like cruelty, were often also alleged in requests for separations, but these were usually levelled by women at their husbands.[70] It is very likely therefore that William had accused Margaret of adultery and secured a separation on those grounds.

An accusation of adultery would explain Richard Nugent's assertion that the separation led to the 'slander and ruin of the said Margaret, which ruin of the said Margaret Richard would not wish for 500 marks'.[71] The reputational damage that such a claim could pose may provide a further explanation of why Margaret included accusations about William's infidelity in her petition two years later. It was another opportunity to counteract rumours arising from the case before the church courts that *she* had committed adultery and was therefore to blame for the separation. Clearing Margaret's name publicly may have been one motivation for Richard's 1458 petition, and he emphasized the validity of her marriage, asserting that William 'married in form of law the said Margaret and continued the wedlock with the said Margaret years and days'. His core purpose in the petition, however, was to request the return of a marital gift of £100 worth of money and horses which he had given to William to seal the wedding contract. Richard was successful in that parliament ordered that this sum be levied on Butler's lands and given to him. If the pair reconciled after the £100 was received, Nugent was to return the sum to his son-in-law.

That the marriage remained intact and was not annulled preserved Margaret's right to dower, provided that she had not committed adultery *and* lived with her lover. Under English law by the later thirteenth century, if a woman left her husband in order to live with her lover, she could be denied her dower rights when he died.[72] We do not know the particulars of the accusations that William made against Margaret, but it is possible that they endangered her dower claim. This was one more reason for both Margaret and her father to put the blame on William for the separation. This interplay between secular and ecclesiastical courts was a feature in many annulments and separations since only the ecclesiastical court could rule on the validity of marriage and grant separations, but secular courts were responsible for dealing with the division of property after marriages ended or, in this case, when accusations of adultery may have been relevant for a dower claim.[73]

Richard Nugent conducted other personal business successfully through private petitions in the parliament of 1458, as he sought and was granted discharge of debts and fines that he had incurred as sheriff of Meath. The reason given for parliament's decision to forgive these debts was that Nugent 'was in the service of our sovereign lord in the west part of Meath, resisting the malice of the Irish enemies of our said sovereign lord for many years now lately past'.[74] Martial service and especially service against 'Irish enemies' was commonly given as a justification for the forgiveness of debts, crimes, and other infractions by parliament.[75] Marcher lords, those that held lands in the borderlands at the edges of the colony, were particularly important in this respect, and many received a high degree of favour, like Nugent, and sometimes also much freedom of action because of their martial value to the colonial administration.[76]

Thus, Nugent's position in the colony was likely one of a number of factors that led the Irish parliament to allow Margaret possession of her dower lands. The work that she and her father did in their petitions to counteract any claims of her adultery and distance her from her husband's treason may also have helped to ensure that parliament looked on her request favourably. After granting Margaret 'for term of her life the third part of the manors aforesaid [William's manors of Dunboyne and Moymet in Meath]' and 'also the third part of all other lands, tenements, rents and services which the said William or any other to his use had and took any profit thereout during the said marriage', the parliamentary record laid out detailed administrative steps to make sure that Margaret would actually be able to take possession of these lands. Her dower claim was confirmed in a subsequent session of the 1460 parliament that awarded the remaining two-thirds of William's estate to his younger brother, Edmund Butler.[77] Parliamentary records show that Edmund Butler's lands were seized and restored to him during the 1460s, but Margaret's rights to dower were not mentioned in the records relating to the seizure of the Dunboyne estate.[78] When his lands were again seized in 1470 and restored in 1471–1472, however, Margaret's dower rights were reiterated with the phrase 'saving to Margaret, who was the wife of William Butler, her reasonable dower'.[79] The care taken in 1470 and after to mention her claim in any discussion of Butler's estate – and to therefore ensure that her tenure of the lands was not interrupted by Edmund's forfeiture of the estate of which they were part – followed yet another successful petition Margaret made to parliament in 1470. She alleged in her petition that 'Edmund Persson' (Edmund Butler) ousted her 'by force' from her dower lands.[80] In rehearsing Margaret's right to these lands, this later petition reiterated some of the arguments of ten years before asserting that 'the offences and trespasses which the said William committed were against the will of the said Dame Margaret' but also included new justifications. Although her petition admitted that it was 'by the Common law' that Margaret lost her dower due to William's attainder, it also asserted that 'Margaret has no other means to any extent by which she can live' and 'all manner of natural law wills that the wife should not be destitute after the death of her husband'. The record of the decision on Margaret's petition ended with the instruction that Margaret could 'have a writ directed to the sheriff of the county of Meath to put her into full possession of the said third part, to have and to hold for the term of her life, according to conscience and reason (*conscience et reisone*)'. The implied contrast in the record of Margaret's petition between common law on one hand and 'conscience and reason' or 'all manner of natural law (*toute manere ley naturale*)' on the other has been identified in other contemporary equity jurisdictions.[81] Parliament could operate with less rigid rules than lower common law courts and according to what its members saw as natural justice and right.[82] Thus, Margaret was again successful at parliament and its decisions helped her to enjoy her dower lands for much of the period between 1460 and 1471–1472. We can assume that she actually held the lands for most of this period given the fact that her father submitted several successful petitions to parliament over that period (in the parliaments of 1463 and 1465), and that he remained prominent in the Irish parliament throughout the 1460s. If she had been ousted from her lands long before her 1470 petition, she would presumably have made a petition earlier, in the parliaments of 1463, 1465, or 1467–1468 and with her father's backing.[83] After the 1471–1472 confirmation of her dower, she falls out of the parliamentary record and we do not know how long she lived or held her dower lands thereafter.[84]

Conclusion

We have examined above the details of Margaret's case and what we know about her life in the tumultuous period between about 1455 and 1471–1472. Like much of the nobility and gentry across Britain and English Ireland, the Wars of the Roses had an enormous impact on her life, her marriage and her ability to support herself. But how much and in what ways was that impact influenced by her gender? What can we learn from Margaret's case about the ways in which gender may have influenced her experiences at law specifically? Some important aspects of her experiences were not shaped to any great extent by the fact that she was a woman. Once she was a widow, Margaret was able to petition solely and, in that sense, just as a male petitioner might do. Her wealth and status meant that she was almost certainly able to employ legal counsel just as a male petitioner of her social milieu would have done. Any barriers to pleading in parliament seem to have been based not on gender but on status and whether a petitioner had access to the support of a peer or member of parliament.

However, the conundrums that prompted her petitions were created by her position as a widow, and a widow of a traitor at that. Taking and maintaining control of their dower lands in the face of confiscation, as in Margaret's case in 1460, or in the face of opposition from a husband's heir, with which she contended in 1470, were difficulties that widows often faced, while widowers usually did not. In general, those widowers who were so entitled rarely faced difficulties retaining their deceased wives' lands after they died, since they controlled these lands while their wives were alive and their tenure was uninterrupted by their deaths (and they retained control of their wives' full estate, not just a third, until they, in turn, died).[85] The retention by widowers of their wives' estates was known as the 'courtesy of England' and it was, as Seabourne notes, a 'rough parallel to the widow's dower', but widowers were not deprived of their right to courtesy for adultery.[86] The concerns that Margaret may have felt about her access to dower given her separation in the church court and accusations of adultery against her therefore would not have been an issue for a widower in a similar situation. The way that Margaret (and her legal advisors) crafted her petition did not obviously play on the common and gendered petitioning motif of the 'poor widow' but the assertion in her 1470 petition that 'all manner of natural law wills that the wife should not be destitute after the death of her husband' may have been used to remind her audience that parliament (in its role dispensing royal justice) had a duty to protect vulnerable widows. Furthermore, her 1460 petition positioned her in a passive way that may have only been available to her or effective for her because she was a woman and the justices did not expect her to control her husband. She was able therefore to navigate the difficulties posed by her deceased husband's attainder in a way that perhaps only a woman could do and turn widespread societal assumptions about women's lack of power within marriage to her advantage.

Margaret's gender also may have influenced and limited the ways in which she could garner support from the members of parliament. It dictated that she could not provide martial service or hold office; this may have been even more important in the frontier environment of the colony than elsewhere in the English polity. She had to rely on her father's service and the position he derived from it, while a man of her age and status would have had his own opportunities for military action and for office holding and the advancement and favour that both could bring. That is not to imply that male petitioners were not also dependent in many cases on family and social connections and similarly constrained by social status; the medieval world was one in which familial and social connections were at the core of the workings of governance and power. It is just that, perhaps especially in Ireland where martial service was so central to the way that political and social position and favour were afforded, women like Margaret were even more dependent on the support of their relatives than men.

In short, it was a complex picture. The way Margaret framed her petition, the nature of the problems she faced and the ways in which she could achieve a positive outcome were all influenced by her gender. It is likely, however, that what *most* influenced Margaret's experience was her social status and her family connections; it was almost certainly her father that provided her with access to parliament and support for her petitions in 1460 and 1470. Gendered expectations and assumptions permeated the legal system and provided both barriers and aids to Margaret's success but gender was just one facet of the many circumstances that shaped her experiences at law.

Notes

1 This research was conducted for the AHRC project 'Women Negotiating the Boundaries of Justice: Britain and Ireland, 1100–1750' (AH/L013568/1). Versions were delivered at the IMC in Leeds (2016) and the history seminars of the University of Limerick and University of Bristol; the author thanks the audiences and organisers. The author would also like to thank Coleman Dennehy for invaluable comments and advice on the paper and Caoimhe Whelan, Brian Coleman, Deborah Youngs and Teresa Phipps for their assistance with aspects of this research.
2 Her petition was lodged in a session of parliament that began in February in Drogheda and continued into the summer in Dublin: Richardson and Sayles, *The Irish Parliament in the Middle Ages* (Philadelphia, 1952), p. 357.
3 Richardson and Sayles, *Irish Parliament*, pp. 196–226; Steven Ellis, *Reform and Revival: English Government in Ireland, 1470–1534* (New York, 1986), pp. 143–164. For Ireland in a later period (but with useful comment on petitions in the later fourteenth century) see Coleman Dennehy, *The Irish Parliament, 1613–1689: The Evolution of a Colonial Institution* (Manchester, 2019), pp. 18–57. For England, see Gwilym Dodd, *Justice and Grace: Private Petitioning and the English Parliament in the Late Middle Ages* (Oxford, 2007); Mark Ormrod, *Women and Parliament in Later Medieval England* (Cham, Switzerland, 2020).
4 Joseph Biancalana, 'Widows at Common Law: The Development of Common Law Dower', *Irish Jurist*, 23:2 (1988), pp. 255–329; S.F.C. Milsom, *Historical Foundations of the Common Law* (London, 1981), pp. 167–168.
5 Widows merely had to prove that lands were held in jointure to ensure they were exempt from forfeiture for their husband's crimes: *CIRCLE (A Calendar of Irish Chancery Letters)*, 'Patent Rolls 13 Richard II, 40, 41', 'Close Rolls 48 Edward III, 87', 'Close Rolls 3 Richard II, 5, 6'; Paul Brand, '"Deserving' and 'Undeserving' Wives: Earning and Forfeiting Dower in Medieval England', *The Journal of Legal History*, 22:1 (2001), p. 15; Ormrod, *Women and Parliament*, p. 86; Mary O'Dowd, 'Women and the Law in Early Modern Ireland', in Christine Meek (ed.), *Women in Renaissance and Early Modern Europe* (Dublin, 2000), p. 102.
6 Ormrod, *Women and Parliament*, pp. 80–82, 85.
7 Michael Hicks, *Wars of the Roses* (Yale, 2010), pp. 78–80; Joel Rosenthal, 'Other Victims: Peeresses as War Widows, 1450–1500', *History*, 72:235 (1987), p. 221; Ormrod, *Women and Parliament*, pp. 79–85.
8 Ormrod, *Women and Parliament*, p. 77.
9 We do not have the original petitions, for example, which survive in significant numbers in England. See Philomena Connolly, *Medieval Record Sources* (Dublin, 2002), pp. 26–29. For the Irish records, see also Mary O'Dowd, below.
10 For the wars in Ireland see Steven Ellis, *Ireland in the Age of the Tudors, 1447–1603: English Expansion and the End of Gaelic Rule* (London, 1998), pp. 51–59 (and timeline pp. 1–4).
11 For the influence of the Wars of the Roses on these parliaments see Art Cosgrove, 'Parliament and the Anglo-Irish Community: The Declaration of 1460', in Art Cosgrove and J.I. McGuire (eds.), *Parliament and Community: Historical Studies XIV* (Belfast, 1983), pp. 25–41.
12 Peter Crooks, 'Factions, Feuds and Noble Power in the Lordship of Ireland, c.1356–1496', *Irish Historical Studies*, 35:140 (2007), pp. 425–454; Peter Crooks, 'The Ascent and Descent of Desmond under Lancaster and York', in Peter Crooks and Seán Duffy (eds.), *The Geraldines and Medieval Ireland: The Making of a Myth* (Dublin, 2016), p. 223.
13 The fourth earl of Ormond was a close associate of the Duke of York in his first stint in Ireland but professed his loyalty to Henry VI in 1451–1452; he died in 1452 before hostilities intensified. His son James the fifth earl adhered to Henry VI: Elizabeth Matthew, 'James Butler the 4th Earl of Ormond', *Oxford Dictionary of National Biography* (online); David Beresford, 'James Butler, 5th Earl of Ormond', *Dictionary of Irish*

Biography (online, accessed 4/11/2020); Vincent Gorman, 'Richard, Duke of York, and the Development of an Irish faction', *Proceedings of the Royal Irish Academy*, 85c (1985), pp. 169–171.
14 Crooks, 'Factionalism', p. 429.
15 See Crooks, 'Ascent and Descent of Desmond', pp. 223–228, 2547–2552; David Beresford, 'Thomas fitzMaurice FitzGerald', *DIB*; Mary Ann Lyons, 'The Kildare Ascendancy', in Patrick Cosgrove et al. (eds.), *Aspects of Irish Aristocratic Life: Essays on the Fitzgeralds and Carton House* (Dublin, 2014), pp. 47–59.
16 Gorman, 'Irish Faction', 169–179; John Watts, 'Richard of York, Third Duke of York', *ODNB* online (2011).
17 Hicks, *Wars of the Roses*, pp. 155–160.
18 Ellis, *Ireland in the Age of the Tudors*, pp. 70–97; Hicks, *Wars of the Roses*, pp. 243–248; F.X. Martin, 'The Crowning of a King at Dublin, 24 May 1487', *Hermathena*, 144 (1988), pp. 7–34.
19 See Richardson and Sayles, *Irish Parliament*, pp. 196–226, esp. 211–224.
20 For the most detailed overview of the court system see Geoffrey Hand, *English Law in Ireland, 1290–1324* (Cambridge, 1967). For the legal remit of the Irish chancery see: Ellis, *Reform and Revival*, pp. 143–164; *Statute Rolls of the Parliament of Ireland, Reign of King Henry VI*, ed. H. F. Berry (Dublin, 1910), pp. 169–170, 173–174; Steven Ellis, 'Parliament and Community in Yorkist and Tudor Ireland', in Art Cosgrove and J.I. McGuire (eds.), *Parliament and Community: Historical Studies XIV* (Belfast, 1983), pp. 45–51.
21 Robin Frame, '*Les Engleys nées en Irlande*': The English Political Identity in Medieval Ireland', *Transactions of the Royal Historical Society*, 6th series, 3 (1993), pp. 99–101; Sparky Booker, 'Moustaches, Mantles and Saffron Shirts: What Motivated Sumptuary Law in Medieval English Ireland?', *Speculum*, 96:3 (2021); Gwilym Dodd, 'Law, Legislation and Consent in the Plantagenet Empire: Wales and Ireland, 1272–1461', *Journal of British Studies* 56 (2017), pp. 237–246.
22 Paul Brand, 'Ralph de Hengham and the Irish Common Law', *Irish Jurist*, 19:1 (1984), p. 107; Paul Brand, 'The Birth of a Colonial Judiciary: The Judges of the Lordship of Ireland, 1210–1377', in W.N. Osborough (ed.), *Explorations in Law and History: Irish Legal History Society Discourses, 1988–1994* (Blackrock, Dublin, 1995), esp. pp. 46–48; Brand, 'Irish Law Students and Lawyers in Late Medieval England', *Irish Historical Studies*, 32:126 (2000), pp. 161–173.
23 See n. 21 above and Richardson and Sayles, *Irish Parliament*, pp. 174–175, 199.
24 Ellis, *Reform and Revival*, p. 146.
25 Richardson and Sayles, *Irish Parliament*, pp. 214–217. For women and the Irish court of chancery in a later period, see Mary O'Dowd, 'Women and the Irish Chancery Court in the late sixteenth and Early Seventeenth Centuries', *Irish Historical Studies*, 31:124 (1999), pp. 470–487.
26 For debates about access to women's voices through legal records and the 'storytelling' versus the 'translation' school of thought, see Joanne Bailey, 'Voices in Court: Lawyers or Litigants', *Historical Research*, 74:186 (2001), pp. 406–407; Richard Hillman and Pauline Ruberry-Blanc (eds.), *Female Transgression in Early Modern Britain: Literary and Historical Approaches* (Ashgate, Farnham, 2014), pp. 2–3. This author favours the combined approach suggested by Walker and Beattie: Garthine Walker, *Crime, Gender, and Social Order in Early Modern England* (Cambridge, 2003), pp. 5–6; Walker, 'Just Stories: Telling Tales of Infant Death in Early modern England', p. 112; Cordelia Beattie, 'I Your Oratrice: Women's Petitions to the Late Medieval Court of Chancery', in Bronagh Kane and Fiona Williamson (eds.), *Women, Agency and the Law, 1300–1700* (London, 2013), pp. 17–30.
27 Gwilym Dodd, Matthew Phillips and Helen Killick, 'Multiple-clause Petitions to the English Parliament in the Later Middle Ages: Instruments of Pragmatism or Persuasion?', *Journal of Medieval History*, 40:2 (2014), p. 187; Richardson and Sayles, *Irish Parliament*, pp. 91–92.

28 Richardson and Sayles, *Irish Parliament*, p. 88.
29 Ibid., pp. 88, 196–199. See James Graves (ed.), *Roll of the Proceedings of the King's Council in Ireland, 1392–3 Rerum Britannicarum Medii Aevi Scriptores*, 69 (London, 1877).
30 *Stat. Ire., Hen. VI*, pp. 277, 291, 521, 608–610, 626–629, 678–681, 689.
31 Ormrod, *Women and Parliament*, p. 99; Dodd, *Justice and Grace*, p. 214; Baker, J.H. Baker, *Introduction to English Legal History* (Oxford, 2007), p. 102.
32 Richardson and Sayles, *Irish Parliament*, pp. 216–219.
33 For Irish petitioners see Graves, 'Roll of King's Council', pp. 18–20, 50, 57–58, 111–112; Ormrod, *Women and Parliament*, p. 46; Sparky Booker, *Cultural Exchange and Identity in Late Medieval Ireland* (Cambridge, 2018), pp. 64–72.
34 Dodd, *Justice and Grace*, pp. 206–207.
35 Ormrod, *Women and Parliament*, pp. 10–11.
36 See n. 21 above for the evidence for a court of chancery in the fifteenth century. *Stat. Ire., Hen. VI*, passim, esp. pp. 286–291, 426–433, 631, 787.
37 Dodd has shown that in England MPs could 'forward private petitions into the upper house'; the procedure of the Irish parliament may have differed somewhat, but some backing from a temporal or spiritual lord or member of parliament seems to have been necessary or at least very common: Richardson and Sayles, *Irish Parliament*, pp. 91–92; Dodd, *Justice and Grace*, pp. 196, 206; Graves, 'Roll of King's Council', pp. 50, 150–154.
38 Gorman, 'Irish Faction', p. 175, 178; Malcolm Mercer, 'Select Document: Exchequer Malpractice in Late Medieval Ireland: A Petition from Christopher Fleming, Lord Slane, 1438', *Irish Historical Studies*, 36:143 (2009), pp. 407, 412.
39 *Stat. Ire., Hen. VI*, pp. 306–311. Jenet was probably the widow of the third lord of Killeen and her son would have been Christopher Plunkett the fourth lord.
40 *Stat. Ire., Hen. IV*, pp. 700–705.
41 For the legal activities of lower-status women, the surviving records of the ecclesiastical courts are the most informative. See John McCafferty (ed.), *The Act Book of the Diocese of Armagh, 1518–1522* (Dublin, 2020).
42 Dodd, *Grace and Justice*, pp. 211–214. Ormrod calculates that 11.7% of petitioners were women: *Women and Parliament*, p. 8.
43 The majority of the remaining petitions (70) came from laymen who most often petitioned alone but sometimes with co-petitioners. Eleven came from male leaders of monastic houses, 13 from clerics and 3 were lodged by city councils and officials. This count only includes petitions with named petitioners, not those that clearly favoured a given person or group of persons but were submitted under the name of the commons.
44 *Statute Ireland, Henry VI*, pp. 306–311, 337–339, 381–383, 404–407, 545–547, 586–589, 611–615, 699–701, 701–705, 715–719, 731–733, 773–779, 769, 787–789.
45 Dodd, *Grace and Justice*, p. 209; Ormond, *Women and Parliament*, pp. 44–45.
46 Mabina, wife of Gerald Tyrel, Matilda de Butler and Margaret de London were all permitted to answer singly in the Dublin bench when their husbands were unavailable or away on the king's business: *Calendar of Justiciary Rolls Ireland*, vol. 1, pp. 9, 211–214, 433–437; Cordelia Beattie and Matthew Frank Stevens (eds.), *Married Women and the Law in Premodern Western Europe* (Woodbridge, 2013), p. 9.
47 Ormrod, *Women and Parliament*, pp. 8, 11.
48 Margaret Griffith, 'The Talbot-Ormond Struggle for Control of the Anglo-Irish Government, 1414–1447', *Irish Historical Studies*, 2:8 (1941), pp. 376–397; David Beresford, 'Richard Nugent', *Dictionary of Irish Biography*.
49 David Beresford, 'Richard Nugent', *Dictionary of Irish Biography*; *Annals of Ulster, 1379–1588*, trans. B. Mac Carthy, celt.ucc.ie, 1458, 1460, 1475, 1478.
50 *Stat. Ire., Hen. VI*, p. 517.
51 James Lydon, *The Lordship of Ireland in the Middle Ages* (2nd edition, Dublin, 2003) pp. 208–211. William's brothers Edmund and Theobald rose for the Lancastrians but were pardoned: Butler, 'Barony of Dunboyne', pp. 109–113.

52 Thomas, earl of Kildare, oversaw this parliament as deputy lieutenant of the Duke of York: Vincent Gorman, 'Richard Duke of York, and the Development of an Irish Faction', *Proceedings of the Royal Irish Academy*, 85c (1985), 171; *Stat. Ire. Hen. IV*, pp. 336–339, 361–365.
53 'Nation' (*nacione* in the Hiberno-Middle English of this part of the letter) here describes the extended Butler family. See James Lydon, 'The Middle Nation', in James Lydon (ed.), *The English in Medieval Ireland* (Dublin, 1984), pp. 3–4.
54 C.J. Neville, 'The Law of Treason in the English Border Counties in the Middles Ages', *Law and History Review*, 9:1 (1991), p. 6; J.G. Bellamy, *The Law of Treason in England in the Later Middle Ages* (Cambridge, 2008), p. 62, 201.
55 *Stat. Ire., Hen. IV*, pp. 525–529.
56 *Stat. Ire., Hen. IV*, pp. 522–531.
57 Cormac Ó Cléirigh, 'The O'Connor Faly lordship of Offaly, 1395–1513', *Proceedings of the Royal Irish Academy*, 96c (1996), pp. 94–96; *Annals of Ulster*, 1459.
58 *Stat. Ire., Hen. VI*, pp. 715–719. See also Sue Sheridan Walker, 'Litigation as Personal Quest: Suing for Dower in the Royal Courts, circa 1271–1350', in Sheridan Walker (ed.), *Wife and Widow in Medieval England* (Ann Arbor, 1993).
59 Joseph Biancalana, 'Widows at Common Law: The Development of Common Law Dower', *Irish Jurist*, 23:2 (1988), p. 284.
60 These accusations of Lancastrians turning against the king made in a Yorkist controlled parliament while Henry VI remained on the throne seem richly ironic, but it is more accurate to see 'the king, his people and his laws' as metonymy for English order in Ireland rather than a specific reference to the individual monarch.
61 Dodd, *Justice and Grace*, p. 213; Hannah Worthen, 'Supplicants and Guardians: The Petitions of Royalist Widows during the Civil Wars and Interregnum, 1642–1660', *Women's History Review*, 26:4 (2017), pp. 531, 537.
62 Ormrod, *Women and Parliament*, p. 44.
63 *Calendar of the Justiciary Rolls of Ireland*, ed. James Mills (Dublin, 1905), pp. 34, 368; Gillian Kenny, *Anglo-Irish and Gaelic Women in Ireland, c.1170–1540* (Dublin, 2007), p. 45. For English parallels see Sara M. Butler, *Divorce in Medieval England: From One Person to Two Persons in Law* (Routledge, 2013).
64 Ormrod, *Women and Parliament*, pp. 80, 88 n. 26.
65 Widows petitioning the English parliament in this period (between 1440 anf 1480) used both formats: 'Cecily, late the wife of John Balle' or 'Joan, late the wife of Richard Stoneton' as well as 'Christine Brok, widow, sometime wife of John Brok' or 'Anne Stathom, late wife of Harry Stathom': TNA SC 8/31/1532; TNA SC 8/345/E1349; TNA SC 8/190/9489; TNA SC 8/334/E1302.
66 *Stat. Ire., Hen. VI*, pp. 306–310, 380–383, 453–457, 700–705. By 1393 in Ireland it appears that female petitioners were equally likely to describe themselves by their first and natal surname (#14, 126, 155, 179) as their first name only (#7, 20, 95, 136): Graves, 'Roll of King's Council'. English married women tended to describe themselves by their marital surname. The reason for this difference in naming practices for married women in Ireland (which mirrors Scottish and Welsh onomastic practice), has not yet been examined, but is under investigation by the author.
67 TNA SC 8/28/1383.
68 The records of the bishop of Meath's court do not survive.
69 The separation was not described as 'divorce (devorce in the French of the parliament rolls)', which is the usual term for annulments, but just in the form of the verb for separate, that is, William sued 'de estre departe del dit Maragrete': *Stat. Ire., Hen. VI*, pp. 776.
70 Charles Donohue, *Law, Marriage and Society in the Later Middle Ages: Arguments about Marriage in Five Courts* (Cambridge, 2007), pp. 33, 39, 522–536; Sara Butler, 'The Law as a Weapon in Marital Disputes: Evidence from the Late Medieval Court of Chancery, 1424–1529', *Journal of British Studies*, 43:3 (2004), p. 310.
71 *Stat. Ire, Henry IV*, P. 517.

72 Brand, 'Earning and Forfeiting Dower', pp. 8–9; Gwen Seabourne, 'Coke, the Statute, Wives and Lovers: Routes to a Harsher Interpretation of the Statute of Westminster II c.34 on Dower and Adultery', *Legal Studies*, 34:1 (2014), pp. 123–129.
73 Richardson and Sayles opined in relation to Margaret's successful dower claim that 'in the interests of justice, parliament set aside the judgement of an ecclesiastical court in a matrimonial case', but this was not necessary since a separation did not automatically negate a dower claim: Richardson and Sayles, *Irish Parliament*, pp. 218–219.
74 *Stat. Ire., Hen. VI*, p. 519.
75 Booker, *Cultural Exchange*, pp. 60–61; *Stat. Ire., Hen. VI*, pp. 314–317, 384–387, 408–413, 506–509, 530–534, 535–541, 556–571, 605, 787.
76 This freedom given by the crown to supposedly 'overmighty' magnates has been well rehearsed though Ellis has shown that such leeway was not a peculiarly Irish phenomenon: Maginn, 'English Marcher Lineages', pp. 128–129; Steven Ellis, 'Nationalist Historiography and the English and Gaelic Worlds', *Irish Historical Studies*, 25:97 (1986), p. 13. See also Steven Ellis, *Defending English Ground: War and Peace in Meath and Northumberland, 1460–1542* (Oxford, 2015).
77 *Stat. Ire., Hen. VI*, pp. 760–767; T. Blake Butler, 'The Barony of Dunboyne', *Irish Genealogist*, 2:4 (1946), pp. 111–112.
78 *Stat. Ire., Edw. IV*, i, pp. 24–27, 306–309, 543.
79 *Stat. Ire., Edw. IV*, i, pp. 689–691, 817.
80 Edmund Piersson was one of several names used by William Butler's brother: *Stat. Ire., Edw. IV*, i, pp. 306–307.
81 *Stat. Ire., Edw. IV*, i, pp. 687–689.
82 Baker, *Introduction English Legal History*, pp. 105–110; Richardson and Sayles, *Irish Parliament*, pp. 214–215.
83 *Stat. Ire., Edw. IV, 1–12*, p. 553.
84 There was a Dame Margaret Nugent who died in Dublin between mid-September and mid-October 1474. This Margaret was described as the widow of Thomas Newbury, ten times mayor of Dublin who was knighted in 1464 and died in 1469. A second marriage for our Margaret to Thomas Newbury after 1460 is possible. He was dead before her 1470 petition, so would not have to be named in it. The high status, title and name of Margaret the petitioner and Margaret the testator match but a Thomas Newbury and his wife Margaret (no surname given) were living in Dublin in 1436. This may have been a different Thomas Newbury, or he could have had two wives named Margaret, but the most likely explanation is that there were two different high-status women in the four shires region in this period named Margaret Nugent: H.F. Berry (ed.), *Register of Wills and Inventories of the Diocese of Dublin in the Time of Archbishops Tregury and Walton 1457–1483* (Dublin, 1896–1897), pp. 78–81; J.T. Gilbert (ed.), *Calendar of the Ancient Records of Dublin*, vol. 1 (Dublin, 1889), pp. 322, 327; William Arthur Shaw, *The Knights of England: A Complete Record from the Earliest Time*, vol. 1, (London, 1906), p. lx. Many thanks to Dr Brian Coleman for the 1436 reference: H.F. Berry, 'History of the Religious Gild of St Anne, in St Audeon's Church, Dublin, 1430–1740', *Proceedings of the Royal Irish Academy*, 25c (1904/5), p. 67.
85 Widowers only had this right to their wives' estates if there was a live child born from their marriage.
86 Gwen Seabourne, 'It is Necessary that the Issue Be Heard to Cry or Squall within the Four [Walls]': Qualifying for Tenancy by the Curtesy of England in the Reign of Edward I', *The Journal of Legal History*, 40:1 (2019), p. 47.

6
CHOOSING CHANCERY? WOMEN'S PETITIONS TO THE LATE MEDIEVAL COURT OF CHANCERY

Cordelia Beattie

> That it may please the same [the Chancellor] to grant a *corpus cum causa* to be directed to the mayor and sheriffs of the said city [London] commanding them by the same to bring the body of your said oratrice with the cause of her arrest before the king in his Chancery there to be ruled as right and conscience shall require.
> Chancery bill of Maria Moriana, c.1486–1493

> Grant your said beseecher a *procedendo* down to the sheriff of London to give judgment on the said condemnation.
> Chancery bill of Alice SeintJohn, 1433–1443 or 1462–1472[1]

In the above extracts from two Chancery petitions, we find one woman – Maria Moriana – requesting that her case be moved from a civic court to Chancery and another – Alice SeintJohn – requesting that her case be sent back to that same court for judgement. The difference between these two petitions, which is elided in scholarship that only distinguishes between women as petitioners and women as respondents, is crucial in thinking about how Chancery fitted into the overlapping legal jurisdictions that a female litigant might call on. While there is a long-running debate about whether Chancery as an equity court was 'better' for women than common law courts,[2] recent scholarship has paid more attention to the medieval female litigant in other jurisdictions such as church courts and customary courts (whether manor courts or civic courts of various levels).[3] This essay will briefly outline the debate about Chancery and make some remarks about how we might understand the 'agency' of a female litigant. It will then set out the nature of the surviving evidence – predominantly Chancery bills written from the perspective of the petitioner – and suggest that attention to the type of writ being sought (*corpus cum causa* and *procedendo* in the

DOI: 10.4324/9780429278037-7

examples above) is one way of distinguishing between female litigants to Chancery and revealing of why women approached this court and their interactions with the law more generally.

The debate

There is a historiographical debate about whether Chancery was a particularly attractive jurisdiction for women in premodern England as a result of restrictions that women faced under common law. The court emerged over the late fourteenth and fifteenth centuries as a place where plaintiffs could initiate procedure by complaint (the petition), rather than a writ as in a common law court, and that complaint could be made orally but increasingly it was made in written form, a bill.[4] It was presided over by the Chancellor and was always open (it could sit anywhere), whereas the central common law courts (King's Bench and Common Pleas) sat at Westminster in terms.[5] However, the key reason given for complaints to Chancery was not that it was easier but because justice could not be secured in the king's courts due to a lack of written evidence or the litigant was too poor or powerless.[6] The court of Chancery was an equitable jurisdiction, which means that cases were decided according to some notion of what was fair or just (informed by 'conscience'), as opposed to strict rules of evidence, which common law required.[7] It was also not bound by the common law doctrine of coverture, which held that husbands were the legal guardians of married women and their property.[8]

The debate about whether Chancery as an equity court was 'better' for women than common law courts, goes back to at least 1946. Mary Beard argued that the idea that married women had no legal personality was a distortion perpetrated by William Blackstone, whose *Commentaries on the Laws of England* (1765) were used to train lawyers in England and the United States. For Beard, if Blackstone had not been so hostile to equity courts (because they could be used to undermine or circumvent common law), he could have included a statement on how equity courts 'protected' married women's separate property rights.[9] This point was taken up in the 1980s by Maria Cioni who focussed on the English court of Chancery in the Tudor period. Cioni argued that women regularly sued in Chancery because it recognized their property rights when common law would not, for example, because they were married and under their husband's legal guardianship. Chancery influenced the development of particular equitable devices such as living trusts ('feoffments to use'), which might form part of a woman's family or marriage settlement.[10] In contrast, Eileen Spring, looking at the broader period 1300–1800, argued that Chancery could be used to defeat common law rules that were advantageous to potential heiresses in that strict settlements might enable daughters to be bypassed in favour of uncles or other collateral males.[11] The emphasis in this scholarship was largely on landed women, in part because in the late fifteenth century another equitable route emerged, now known as the Court of Requests, primarily to handle the cases of those who could not afford to get justice in the common law system and the number of such cases in Chancery declined as a result.[12]

For women and the medieval court of Chancery, a similar debate was initiated by Emma Hawkes. Hawkes argued that women were three times more likely to petition Chancery than to take a case to a central common law court, King's Bench or Common Pleas (15% as opposed to 5%). This finding was based on a very limited sample of cases from Yorkshire in the period 1461–1515, and the cases were largely about land.[13] However, it received some corroboration from Timothy Haskett's 'Early Court of Chancery in England Project (ECCE), 1417–1532', which sampled 6,850 cases of approximately 61,000 available in the National Archives document class C 1. His project found that 21% of petitioners to Chancery were female. It also found that only 7% of respondents were female, which suggests that when women appear in the court's records it is as instigators. The project demonstrated that land cases were the most numerous, followed by cases concerning money and trespass, but did not map these onto types of petitioner.[14]

The headline figures of 15% or 21%, which suggest late medieval women preferred Chancery over common law courts, can be challenged from a couple of directions. First, Haskett's project also found changes over the period, with a consistent decline in women's appearance as petitioners and a parallel increase in their appearance as respondents so that by 1515 the proportion of each was quite similar. He suggested that this might 'imply some diminished capacity to act at law' by the end of the period.[15] Second, Matthew Stevens has argued that such percentages hide the higher number of litigants who used courts like the Court of Common Pleas: 'the fifteenth-century Court of Common Pleas processed twenty to forty-five lawsuits for each one petition to Chancery'.[16] I would caution that there are problems with all such counting exercises, though. Stevens' proportions are based on Haskett's counting of bills but this approach likely undercounts how many cases Chancery actually heard. A study of extant Chancery writs suggests that the number of Chancery cases per year were much higher. As the opening examples indicate, writs were issued by Chancery during the course of a case. For 1441–1442, for example, there are an average of 136 bills but over 900 writs.[17] The number of extant writs, then, suggests that the vast majority of bills have not survived, although the survival rate of bills might have improved by the last quarter of the fifteenth century.[18] Further, attention to what writ was being requested – which indicates what petitioners wanted from Chancery – can challenge the binary of women as petitioner or respondent when thinking about women as legal agents. This essay will therefore take a more qualitative approach.

Agency and female litigants

Agency is a current buzzword in studies on women. For some it is synonymous with power. Mary Erler and Maryanne Kowaleski when revisiting the topic of women and power in 2003 argued that 'what we then [1988] called power ... is now often called agency'.[19] Similarly, RãGena DeAragon uses the formulation 'power and agency' throughout her 2019 essay on elite women in twelfth-century England.[20] But, as Martha Howell has recently pointed out, not all scholars use the term in the same way so it is important to define it clearly.[21] Anne Montenach and Deborah Simonton, for example, use the term 'agency' in the sense of 'capacity to act'.[22] But they are also careful to capture the nuance of recent debates. Rather than see humans as completely autonomous, they recognize that a person's capacity for action in the world is affected by internalised dispositions and structural constraints. For them agency 'is always embodied in power relations'.[23] Female agency, though, need not be about resisting male authority or patriarchy; there is a wider debate which argues that agency is not just about resisting the status quo.[24]

In a study of women as active litigants, the emphasis is on their 'capacity to act' within the constraints of that legal system and the patriarchal world in which they lived. These acts might take the form of subverting patriarchal structures but they might just as well be using the existing structures to their own advantage. Also, while bringing a case to court does show a 'capacity to act', we should note that many of these women would probably rather not have needed to take such legal action, for example, to recover lands promised to them. When Amy Erickson discussed the court for the early modern period she commented: 'While the number of women plaintiffs illustrates the extent of women's involvement with matters of property and business, the women themselves were not necessarily pleased to be exercising their right to appear before the court'.[25] Power is therefore not a term that readily springs to mind. Legal restrictions on women, and the fact that the legal system itself was entirely peopled by men, account for why collections such as this one focus on women. Yet women are not a homogeneous group with a shared way of dealing with the courts. In this essay I want to think about different kinds of female litigant, related to what they wanted from the court of Chancery.

The evidence

Our main source for how the late medieval court of Chancery operated is the petitioners' written bills. As the court did not make decisions based on legal precedents it did not have to store its records. While some of the bills have survived, it is rare that they are endorsed with process notes or stored with related records such as writs or depositions relating to the same case. Although this means we usually do not know how any individual case progressed, the evidence that we do have is written from the perspective of the litigant rather than the court, although the bills are clearly tailored towards it. The bills are very formulaic, both in terms of their structure and the language used. This means that the majority of petitioners probably used a professional scribe in order that the correct format and phrasing was used and the bill was not immediately dismissed. Dodd argues that these scribes might have been scriveners, notaries or lawyers.[26]

In terms of the format, petitions follow the same structure as medieval letters. They begin with a formal greeting to the addressee (*salutatio*) and then they introduce the petitioner (*exordium*). The most interesting section is perhaps the *narratio*, the narration of the circumstances leading to the bill, and it is this that social historians have often focussed on. Then there is the *petitio*, what the petitioner is requesting. The *conclusio* is the final part and most sign off by promising to pray for the Chancellor.[27] In the *petitio*, the usual request is for a writ. The key types are:

1 *sub pena* (attachias): to summon/secure an opponent
2 *corpus cum causa*: to officials/holders of courts asking them to produce the petitioner from prison
3 *certiorari*: to officials/holders of courts asking why the petitioner had been arrested
4 *procedendo*: to send the case back to a lower court.[28]

The rest of this essay will discuss requests for these types of writ, in turn, as the type of writ sought is a key indicator of what the women wanted from the court and is often reflective of their interactions with the law, prior to the bill's making. It is not possible to quantify here how common each type of request was. The National Archives catalogue does not consistently note this information, drawing as it does on the earlier *Lists and Indexes* series, and so it would be a major undertaking to determine this information from the thousands of bills that survive. Also, as discussed above, this would be to count what remains. In my own research, though, I have found that the most common requests for these writs were, in descending order: *certiorari*, *corpus cum causa*, *sub pena* and *procedendo*. A future project might look at the surviving writs to get a better sense of proportions.[29] The key element behind my fourfold division here is to reflect that the reasons women petitioned Chancery were complex and in part reflected their existing experience of the legal system, be it from a prison cell or a supportive lower court.

Sub pena writs

Petitioners that requested a *sub pena* writ were asking for a writ to compel the person of whom they complain to appear in Chancery. They were effectively asking for their case to be heard there so these are clear cases of women choosing Chancery. For example, the bill of Isabel, daughter of the late Thomas Cornseller, requested c.1432–1443 a writ of *sub pena* for Thomas Chosell and Hamund Cornseller.[30] In it Isabel stated that her father had made these two men executors of his testament and bequeathed her ten pounds to be paid at her marriage. Isabel feared that the men were wasting her father's goods so that there would not be ten pounds left at the point of her marriage. While an ecclesiastical court would normally deal with testamentary matters, in this case the condition stipulated in the will had not yet been met. Isabel clearly thought that she would have more chance of making the money secure by appealing to Chancery. In this case, singlewoman Isabel is a prime example of an active litigant in that she initiated this action rather than wait for the executors to waste her father's estate. In other Chancery cases, we see married couples pursuing executors for goods owed to the wives,[31] or husbands bringing such actions by themselves.[32]

A second example of a request for a *sub pena* writ is from a widow and it concerned her son. Around 1460–1465 Alice Wedon of Chalfont St Giles in Buckinghamshire asked Chancery to compel her son, Richard Wedon, to appear before the court.[33] According to the bill, Alice had made a testament, when very sick and close to death, bequeathing all her movable goods to her son and other persons. However, her son did not wait for her to die but took and carried away all her goods, including those she had intended to leave to others. Alice claimed that she was left with nothing, including food, drink and clothing, and was reliant on the charity of her neighbours. This is a case that could have been brought to a local court as her son had effectively stolen from her, but Alice does not discuss whether she pursued that option or, if she had not, why not. Instead, Alice's bill uses the line of extreme poverty to bring the case to Chancery instead. Again, we have a litigant choosing Chancery, this time over another jurisdiction. But, if we take Alice at her word, she was in quite a powerless position.

Corpus cum causa writs

The second type of writ requested was the *corpus cum causa* writ, literally 'body with cause'. The intent of such writs was to produce the petitioner from prison where they were being held. In these cases, as well as getting a case moved to Chancery, it was also a way of getting bail when one was unable to pay it or was being denied the opportunity to pay it. For example, a woman called Maria Moriana had been arrested and imprisoned in London on the grounds that she owed her master, a Venetian merchant, twenty pounds. Her bill (c.1486–1493) narrates how she had been in service with one Filippo Cini for more than twenty years.[34] She had not been paid any wages but had been provided with food, drink, clothing and presumably a place to sleep. However, Filippo fell into poverty and could no longer support himself, his wife and Maria and so he offered to sell Maria to a Genoese merchant for twenty pounds. Maria refused to agree to this sale. Filippo then told her that various people owed him money and he would sign those debts over to her as recompense for all her years of service. Maria accompanied him to the notary so he could put this agreement in writing. There he took advantage of her lack of English and Latin to have the notary draw up a document stating that she owed *him* twenty pounds, which – unaware of the document's contents – she agreed to seal. He then used this document to sue her in the sheriffs' court of London. Maria petitioned the Court of Chancery for help as her master had the sealed bond as evidence of the debt and so she was likely to be found guilty in the sheriffs' court. We can assume that Maria could not afford bail as she had not been earning wages for over twenty years. The bill is endorsed with a date, 29 May, at which her case was to be heard but we do not know what happened thereafter. We can still use the bill, though, to find out more about Maria Moriana and how she came to be a litigant in the court of Chancery.

Maria was probably a person of colour. While written sources at this date are not generally interested in marking out skin colour, Maria Moriana's name gives some us some clues. 'Morian' was a French borrowing for Moor with 'Moriana' as the feminine form. Europeans applied the term 'Moor' to Muslim Europeans, Arabs and North African Berbers and at least from the sixteenth century, if not earlier, 'moorish' was used to describe someone with darker skin.[35] Maria perhaps entered Filippo's household as a slave. The slave trade in Italy, although just one part of a broader trade in the Mediterranean with Catalan and Portuguese merchants dominant, was at its peak in the fifteenth century. Italian merchants, particularly from Venice and Genoa, supplied Muslim and Christian markets with slaves captured outside of the Latin West. While most slaves came from Eastern Europe and Central Asia, there were some black Africans.[36] Christians were not meant to take other Christians as slaves but they would often baptize their slaves and give them a Christian name: Maria is one such name.[37] Those who were bought within Italy tended to be young and female and used for domestic work. By the late fifteenth century in Italy it was becoming more common to pay for servants than to buy slaves, as the work that the two did was often comparable, and it is possible that Maria was a manumitted slave, hence her refusal to be sold.[38]

The bill also states, in Middle English, that Maria could not speak nor understand English. It is, indeed, possible that as the servant in an Italian-speaking household she had not learnt English, despite living in England for a long period of time. But this also raises questions about who then helped her with this bill. As discussed, the formulaic structure and language of such bills indicate the involvement of clerks or lawyers. We know that lawyers did tout their services at fairs and markets.[39] But did they also visit city prisons and offer their services? Were they fluent in Italian or did Maria have a contact outside of Filippo Cini's household? These are questions we cannot yet answer as most studies of legal records in late medieval England have focussed on the use of three languages: Latin, French, and English.[40]

That lawyers or clerks were involved in the drafting of Chancery bills for poor litigants held in prisons was not something confined to the capital.[41] To illustrate this, the next example hails from Coventry. The late fifteenth-century bill of Elizabeth Thornton alleges that one William Rowley had brought a false action of trespass against her husband, William Thornton, a labourer, in the court of the mayor and sheriffs of the city of Coventry[42]; trespass was a broad category that encompassed defamation, assault, and theft.[43] William Thornton was away working and could not respond. While Rowley had presumably brought this action in a personal capacity, he was one of the twenty-four men who made up the city's leet court, which by this date in Coventry had more of a role in making the law than policing it.[44] He then arrested Elizabeth Thornton, who had seemingly not been named in the original charge, and she had been held in prison for twelve weeks at the time the bill was drafted. The bill explains that, because of her 'great poverty' and Rowley's 'great might', she had no counsel and would be kept in prison forever without the Chancellor's intervention. There is a sense in this bill, as in others, that the claims are piled up to present the petitioner as completely powerless and so deserving of the Chancellor's attention. Rowley is presented as corrupt; one of the civic elite but motivated by 'malice and evil will'. Although this language is quite standard in Chancery bills, Meridee Bailey argues that the terminology of malice in particular was about pointing to the moral failings of an opponent, which the chancellor could take into account.[45] We are also presented with the paradox of a woman with no one to help her but able to submit a well-crafted Chancery bill.

Elizabeth Thornton's bill is particularly interesting in that one of her reasons for wanting the case moved to Chancery was that 'she cannot come answer without her husband' in Coventry's court.[46] Under the common law doctrine of coverture, a married woman could not bring or defend a lawsuit without her husband. Urban courts operated according to their own customs. They did not need to follow common law rules, but, influenced by the broader culture of the common law, they sometimes applied them.[47] For example, some borough customs specified that while a plea of trespass should be made against a husband and wife for an act of trespass committed by the married woman alone, the woman should be able to answer alone if her husband did not appear.[48] However, Teresa Phipps, in her study of the late medieval town court of Nottingham, found that married women were *more* likely to state that they could not answer without their husbands in trespass cases than in debt ones.[49] According to Elizabeth Thornton's bill she had not been originally sued and her husband was not able to appear with her even if they had been jointly charged. The bill does not use the language of coverture but that is what it alludes to here. Married women like Elizabeth Thornton could petition Chancery as individuals, although some still brought joint bills.[50] The request for the writ in this example, then, was in part because Elizabeth Thornton could not get bail but also so that the case could be moved to Chancery where she could answer alone. The bill is endorsed which indicates this initial request was successful.

A final example of a request for a *corpus cum causa* writ comes from a Cambridgeshire wife c.1462–1472. Her bill gives us an insight into what might happen *after* a successful petition to Chancery for such a writ. Eleanor, wife of Thomas Cotton, re-petitioned Chancery, even though her first bill had been successful.[51] The first bill is not extant but Eleanor's second bill relays the full story. It alleges that one Richard Lovell had taken a feigned action of trespass against her in London, leading to her arrest. She had then successfully gained a *corpus cum causa* writ from Chancery and been granted bail. However, the bill claims that Richard had Eleanor arrested for the same cause, while she was out on bail, leading to her being returned to prison in London. She again requested a *corpus cum causa* writ. One of her arguments was that the court in London was 'foreign' as she was from Cambridge and so unknown to the men who ran the court. Penny Tucker has argued that there were frequent requests for *corpus cum causa* writs because it would have been easier for strangers to get bail from Chancery than from London's city courts.[52] Eleanor seems to have been a frequent visitor to Chancery as there are surviving chancery writs relating to actions of debt and trespass taken against her.[53] When the Chancellor agreed to grant a writ, Eleanor undertook to appear when summoned (a recognizance). Patricia Barnes claimed that married women could take no part in their own recognizances because of coverture but Eleanor did.[54] Perhaps this is another way in which Chancery acted outside the scope of common law.

Certiorari writs

The third type of writ petitioners requested was that of *certiorari*, a writ directed to officials and holders of courts asking them why the petitioner had been arrested. By agreeing to such a writ, the Chancellor would be effectively moving the case up to Chancery, which is what the petitioners wanted. In these bills we see claims that the petitioner could not get justice in a lower court and we often get allegations of corruption, as we did in the Elizabeth Thornton bill, which gives some insight into how cases worked in lower courts which we do not get from the records of those courts themselves. We also see how litigants had to manoeuvre between different legal jurisdictions to manage their everyday lives and that women were well versed in these procedures. For comparison, I will give one example from the London area and one from another part of England.

The bill of Alice Parkyns sought to have a debt case, lodged with the manorial court of Southwark, moved to Chancery c.1475–1485.[55] Alice was being sued by one John Gould, brewer, for forty shillings, which she claimed was a false action 'to trouble and vex her', caused by his 'malice'.[56] In order to demonstrate the need to get the case heard in Chancery, the bill rehearses her dealings with an ecclesiastical jurisdiction and a civic court, before it turns to the case in the Bishop of Winchester's court in Southwark, which he ran as a manor. According to the bill, Alice's late husband, Roger Parkyns, had run up lots of debts including one for forty-seven shillings to John Gould but he had repaid that particular debt. In an effort to avoid other creditors, though, Roger took sanctuary at Westminster; a number of religious houses in late medieval England used their status as royally-chartered liberties to offer permanent sanctuary to debtors as well as accused criminals.[57] Roger was only there for three weeks before he died. As he died intestate, Alice paid for the cost of his burial, which suggests she had some money at her own disposal or was considered good for credit. Roger's goods, though, were sequestered by the Archdeacon of Westminster for the Abbot of Westminster, presumably so they could be used to pay back his creditors.[58] Alice's bill relates that she was not allowed 'to come within her doors ... under the seal of the archdeacon', as she was willing to show the Chancellor.[59] This suggests that a widow did not automatically get her share of her husband's property, including the marital home, in such bankruptcy cases.[60] The bill then turns to the actions of John Gould. According to the bill, he first took an action of debt against Alice in the City of London but did not see it through 'considering that he could have no remedy by the law'.[61] John then started an action of debt in the neighbouring area of Southwark, where he – unlike Alice – had important friends, and so was more likely to be successful there. This explains Alice's request for a writ of *certiorari* to get the case moved. The bill's endorsement reveals that the request was accepted.

For a non-London example of a request for a *certiorari* writ which also reveals the interpenetration of different legal jurisdictions, we can turn to the late fifteenth-century bill of widow Alice Smyth, alias Felton, from Much Wenlock in Shropshire.[62] This bill concerns a marital dispute that had been ruled on during the Bishop of Hereford's visitation to the diocese, which triggered an action before the bailiffs' court of Bridgnorth (probably a leet court), before it found its way to the court of Chancery. Alice's bill relates how her daughter, Margaret, had become pregnant within a year of marriage to one John Glover but had subsequently fallen out with her husband to the extent that she feared for her own life and that of her child. Margaret therefore fled to her father-in-law's home and he and some of her 'friends', which might include relatives, took up her cause before the Bishop of Hereford at the time of his visitation. The church had jurisdiction over matrimonial matters in this period and could authorize separations on the grounds of spousal abuse.[63] The bishop was clearly swayed by the arguments made as the woman and child were committed to Alice's custody. However, John – who was in service with one of the two bailiffs of Bridgnorth – began an action of detinue (the wrongful detention of goods or personal possessions) against Alice before the bailiffs of Bridgnorth for withholding his wife from him, to the damage of forty marks. The bringing of a detinue suit is unusual as it implies that the wife is the husband's property; in cases of runaway wives, husbands usually brought ravishment suits for the taking away of their wives and their goods.[64] Alice's bill explains that she would lose the case as she was 'a foreigner' and was facing 'the might of the said bailiffs'.[65] The bill follows the conventional line that Alice would not get a fair trial in Bridgnorth because she did not reside there (Much Wenlock is eight miles away) and because her opponent was well connected with those ruling on the case. Alice argues in her bill that this would be against 'right and conscience' as it would ignore the Bishop of Hereford's decision, thus directly appealing to Chancery's jurisdiction as a court of conscience but also playing to her audience. In 1475–1485 the Bishop of Lincoln was Chancellor.[66] Alice asked him for a writ of *certiorari* to be sent to the said bailiffs, so that the action could be decided in Chancery instead. The endorsement on the back of the bill reveals that this was successful in that her case was to be heard in Chancery.

Procedendo writs

The last type of writ is quite different; those who requested a *procedendo* writ wanted to get the case sent back down to a lower jurisdiction. In these cases, the litigants preferred their cases to be settled outside of Chancery, usually because the other court could require a financial settlement for the matter under dispute. These requests are less common in the surviving records and I have only found three examples of solo female litigants requesting one. The first is a widow from Norwich, Clemence Drewe, who sought a writ of *procedendo* because one Richard Elys of Great Yarmouth had three times sought a writ of *certiorari* against her.[67] Clemence Drewe's bill attests that Elys owed £47 for cloth and malt which he had bought from her late husband, Richard Drewe, and which she was now pursuing in the sheriffs' court in Norwich as the executrix of his will. However, the writs of *certiorari* obtained by Elys had led to delays of more than two years. Clemence Drewe's request for a *procedendo* writ was a response to Elys' third writ of *certiorari*. The bill notes that the debt was 'well known' locally and Elys had been outlawed in her shire (the standard response for a defendant failing to turn up to a court five times after being summoned).[68] The implication here is that Drewe would be likely to get satisfaction from a local court and so she saw no need for the case to be moved to Chancery.

The second example is the fifteenth-century bill of Alice, wife of John Seint-John, clerk, and is particularly interesting as her husband does not feature in any of her accounts of her legal actions but is only mentioned with reference to his 'great infirmity', presumably an explanation of why he was not involved.[69] The bill relates how Alice had long been seeking redress from one John Goldesburgh who had 'villainously' hit her on the leg, causing an injury which had prevented her from working for more than four years. They had tried extra judicial attempts to settle the matter through arbitration and 'lovedays' (days on which parties attempted to settle disputes amicably), before Alice had taken an action of trespass against John Goldesburgh in the sheriffs' court of London.[70] It was at this point that Goldesburgh tried to change the jurisdiction: first to the Mayor's court (it was sent back down to the sheriffs' court where a jury found against him); then *he* petitioned Chancery for a writ of *corpus cum causa*, which stopped the sheriffs' court enacting the jury verdict. Alice SeintJohn was therefore counter-petitioning Chancery to get a *procedendo* writ, which would send the case back down to the sheriffs' court so that she could recover her costs which included a 'foreign' physician who had healed her.

The third example is more complicated in that the female litigant requested both a writ of *procedendo* and a *certiorari* writ for different parts of her legal dispute. In the late fifteenth century, a widow in Bristol, Joan Martok, had successfully sued one Thomas Walssh in one of the city's courts and been awarded 51s. 8d.[71] However, Thomas delayed the execution of this decision by securing a writ of *certiorari* from Chancery. He then took an action of debt against Joan in Bristol for 43s., claiming that her late husband owed him this and that she was the administrator of his goods.[72] At this point Joan Martok petitioned Chancery, claiming she was 'of no power to hold plea' with him, asking for a *procedendo* writ so that the result of her initial case could be enacted and a *certiorari* writ so that Thomas's action of debt could be moved to Chancery. As with some of the other bills discussed, this is revealing of how a late medieval woman might have to negotiate a legal action and Chancery's role in this. In this case, it was not just a simple matter of suing a man in Bristol. Joan then had to deal with a counter suit of debt in one of Bristol's courts and had to use Chancery as a higher court, as had her opponent. Joan Martok was not the first one in this dispute to involve Chancery but her petition was a necessary next step in the dispute. Even then the bill shows awareness of which jurisdiction was better for which action in that it asked for one legal action to be sent back to the court in Bristol (so Joan could receive her 51s. 8d.) and the other to be decided in Chancery (so that Thomas's debt claim could be quashed).

Clemence Drewe, Alice SeintJohn and Joan Martok did petition Chancery, and would feature in Haskett's statistics as such, but we should note that they preferred their cases to be settled elsewhere, in lower, civic courts. While there do not seem to be many requests for such writs, by men as well as women, they offer another angle on the debate about whether Chancery was the most attractive venue for women.

Conclusion

While women faced some structural disadvantages in the late medieval legal system, in practice we find that different litigants experienced the courts in different ways. This essay has taken a qualitative approach to women's bills to the late medieval Chancery, focussing on what writs were requested, in order to think further about why women approached Chancery. It discusses Chancery as part of a broader legal system of which common law was but one important branch. In the consideration of *sub pena* writs we saw clear examples of women petitioning Chancery as their jurisdiction of choice, although in the case of Alice Wedon 'power' seems an unlikely synonym for agency. Some of the cases do point to limitations in common law practices, such as the reliance on written evidence when Maria Moriana was tricked into signing a bond, or Elizabeth Thornton who was unable to defend herself in a debt action because her husband was away labouring in the countryside. However, attention to the full range of cases in Chancery and what writ was being sought also reveals that women might petition because they could not afford bail, they did not know anyone in a city to stand as surety for them, or their opponents were well-connected and could ensure that they were refused bail. With the exception of Thornton's case which was affected by coverture, these are situations that male litigants could and did find themselves in. The bills do not just show poor, helpless petitioners, although that is a useful trope in a Chancery petition. Some of the bills reveal that the petition to Chancery might be relatively late in a legal dispute which had already played out in a number of jurisdictions (ecclesiastical, civic and manorial). When we think of the active litigant in late medieval England, we need to keep in mind that the instigator in one court might well be a respondent in another and that petitioning Chancery was not always an either/or option.

Notes

1 The National Archives, Kew (hereafter TNA), C 1/148/67; C 1/43/31. The bills are in Middle English but I have modernised the spelling in this essay for ease of reading. Bills are undated and so usually dated by the address to the Chancellor unless there is any additional information. Many of the Chancery bills have been photographed and can be accessed at the digital archive assembled by Robert C. Palmer, Elspeth K. Palmer, and Susanne Jenks, 'The Anglo-American Legal Tradition', <aalt.law.uh.edu/aalt.html>. I am grateful to the participants of the University of Michigan's Law and Society workshop and the James Lydon Research Seminar in Medieval History, Trinity College Dublin, where I tried out the ideas in this essay and to Teresa and Deborah for feedback on an earlier draft.
2 Judith Bennett has argued more generally that attempts to think about which groups of women were better off than others 'can provoke creative analyses among historians and energetic debates among students. But they can also lead to facile conclusions … that simplify quite complex differences': Judith M. Bennett, *Medieval Women in Modern Perspective* (Washington, 2000), p. 12.
3 See Jeremy Goldberg, *Communal Discord, Child Abduction and Rape in the Later Middle Ages* (New York, 2008); Bronach C. Kane, *Popular Memory and Gender in Medieval England: Men, Women and Testimony in the Church Courts, c.1200–1500* (Woodbridge, 2019); Miriam Müller, 'Peasant Women, Agency and Status in Mid-Thirteenth to Late Fourteenth-Century England: Some Reconsiderations', in Cordelia Beattie and Matthew Frank Stevens (eds.), *Married Women and the Law in Premodern Northwest Europe* (Woodbridge, 2013), pp. 91–113; Matthew Frank Stevens, 'London Women, the Courts and the "Golden Age": A Quantitative Analysis of Female Litigants in the Fourteenth and Fifteenth Centuries', *The London Journal*, 37:2 (2012), pp. 67–88; Teresa Phipps, *Medieval Women and Urban Justice: Commerce, Crime and Community in England, 1300–1500* (Manchester, 2020).
4 Strictly, the written document submitted to Chancery is a 'bill' but contemporaries also used the terms 'bill' and 'petition' interchangeably: Gwilym Dodd and Sophie Petit-Renaud, 'Grace and Favour: The Petition and Its Mechanisms', in Christopher Fletcher et al. (eds.), *Government and Political Life in England and France, c.1300-c.1500* (Cambridge, 2015), p. 241, n. 6.
5 W. Mark Ormrod, *Women and Parliament in Later Medieval England* (Cham, 2020), p. 10; John Baker, *An Introduction to English Legal History* (5th edn; Oxford, 2019), pp. 109–114. On oral petitions see P. Tucker, 'The Early History of the Court of Chancery: A Comparative Study', *English Historical Review*, 115 (2000), pp. 793–794.
6 For a useful summary of Chancery's remit but with examples from female religious houses see Elizabeth Makowski, '"*Deus est procurator fatuorum*": Cloistered Nuns and Equitable Decision-Making in the Court of Chancery', in Kenneth Pennington and Melodie Harris Eichbauer (eds.), *Law As Profession and Practice in Medieval Europe: Essays in Honor of James A. Brundage* (London, 2011), pp. 205–217.
7 For a discussion of conscience and the medieval court of Chancery, see Dennis R. Klinck, *Conscience, Equity and the Court of Chancery in Early Modern England* (Farnham, 2010), pp. 13–40.
8 On coverture see Tim Stretton and Krista J. Kesselring, 'Introduction: Coverture and Continuity', in Tim Stretton and Krista J. Kesselring (eds.), *Married Women and*

the Law: Coverture in England and the Common Law World (Montreal, 2013), pp. 3–19. On coverture in an equity court see Tim Stretton, *Women Waging Law in Elizabethan England* (Cambridge, 1998), pp. 129–154.
9 Mary R. Beard, *Woman as Force in History: A Study in Traditions and Realities* (New York, 1986; a reprint of the 1946 book), pp. 88–105. See also Tim Stretton, 'Coverture and Unity of Person in Blackstone's *Commentaries*', in Wilfrid Prest (ed.), *Blackstone and His Commentaries: Biography, Law, History* (Oxford, 2009), pp. 111–128.
10 Maria L. Cioni, 'The Elizabethan Court of Chancery and Women's Rights', in Delloyd J. Guth and John W. McKenna (eds.), *Tudor Rule and Revolution: Essays for G. R. Elton from His American friends* (Cambridge, 1982), pp. 159–182; Maria L. Cioni, *Women and Law in Elizabethan England with Particular Reference to the Court of Chancery* (New York, 1985). See also Amy Louise Erickson, 'Common Law versus Common Practice: The Use of Marriage Settlements in Early Modern England', *Economic History Review*, 43:1 (1990), pp. 21–39.
11 Eileen Spring, *Law, Land, & Family: Aristocratic Inheritance in England, 1300 to 1800* (Chapel Hill, 1993).
12 See Stretton, *Women Waging Law*, chs 4–8; Laura Flannigan, 'Litigants in the English Court of Poor Men's Causes, or Court of Requests, 1515–25', *Law and History Review*, 38:2 (2020), pp. 303–337. I focus on pre-1515 Chancery petitions and find requests from the poor.
13 Emma Hawkes, '"[S]he Will … Protect and Defend Her Rights Boldly by Law and Reason …": Women's Knowledge of Common Law and Equity Courts in Late-Medieval England', in Noël James Menuge (ed.), *Medieval Women and the Law* (Woodbridge, 2000), pp. 145–161.
14 Timothy S. Haskett, 'The Medieval English Court of Chancery', *Law and History Review*, 14:2 (1996), pp. 281–282, 286, 295–309.
15 Haskett, 'Medieval English Court of Chancery', p. 287 (52:48). However, Erickson's samples for 1558–1603 and 1613–1714 suggested that women made up 17% and 26% of plaintiffs respectively: Amy Louise Erickson, *Women and Property in Early Modern England* (London, 1993), p. 115.
16 Matthew Frank Stevens, 'London's Married Women, Debt Litigation and Coverture in the Court of Common Pleas', in Beattie and Stevens (eds.), *Married Women and the Law*, p. 124.
17 Tucker, 'Early History', pp. 798–799; Nicholas Pronay, 'The Chancellor, the Chancery, and the Council at the End of the Fifteenth Century', in H. Hearder and H. R. Loyn (eds.), *British Government and Administration: Studies Presented to S. B. Chrimes* (Cardiff, 1974), p. 89.
18 Tucker, 'Early History', p. 798.
19 Mary C. Erler and Maryanne Kowaleski, 'A New Economy of Power Relations: Female Agency in the Middle Ages', in Mary C. Erler and Maryanne Kowaleski (eds.), *Gendering the Master Narrative: Women and Power in the Middle Ages* (Ithaca, 2003), p. 1. The earlier volume was Mary C. Erler and Maryanne Kowaleski, *Women and Power in the Middle Ages* (Athens, 1988).
20 RāGena C. DeAragon, 'Power and Agency in Post-Conquest England: Elite Women and the Transformations of the Twelfth Century', in Heather J. Tanner (ed.), *Medieval Elite Women and the Exercise of Power, 1100–1400: Moving Beyond the Exceptionalist Debate* (Cham, 2019), pp. 19–43.
21 Martha Howell, 'The Problem of Women's Agency in Late Medieval and Early Modern Europe', in Sarah Joan Moran and Amanda Pipkin (eds.), *Women and Gender in the Early Modern Low Countries* (Leiden, 2019), pp. 21–31.
22 Anne Montenach and Deborah Simonton, 'Introduction: Gender, Agency and Economy: Shaping the Eighteenth-Century European Town', in Deborah Simonton and Anne Montenach (eds.), *Female Agency in the Urban Economy: Gender in European Towns, 1640–1830* (New York, 2013), p. 3.

23 Ibid., p. 4.
24 It is used in this more limited way in, e.g., Lindsay R. Moore, *Women before the Court: Law and Patriarchy in the Anglo-American World, 1600–1800* (Manchester, 2019), p. 10. But cf. Saba Mahmood, *Politics of Piety: The Islamic Revival and the Feminist Subject* (Princeton, rev. edn 2012), pp. 27–35.
25 Erickson, *Women and Property*, p. 116.
26 See Gwilym Dodd, 'The Rise of English, the Decline of French: Supplications to the English Crown, c. 1420–1450', *Speculum*, 86:1 (2011), p. 120. For a useful overview see Helen Killick, 'The Scribes of Petitions in Late Medieval England', in Helen Killick and Thomas W. Smith (eds.), *Petitions and Strategies of Persuasion in the Middle Ages: The English Crown and the Church, c.1200–c.1550* (Woodbridge, 2018), pp. 64–87.
27 See Gwilym Dodd, 'Writing Wrongs: The Drafting of Supplications to the Crown in Later Fourteenth-Century England', *Medium Ævum*, 80:2 (2011), pp. 223–227.
28 Tucker found requests for *attachias* writs (to secure an opponent's appearance in Chancery by arresting him/her or making that person find pledges to appear) were also common but noted that these were 'issued on behalf of chancery officials and their servants and .... rarely available to private litigants': Tucker, 'Early History', p. 799. There are occasional requests for different types of writ e.g. a writ for surety of the peace, to compel an opponent to keep the peace on pain of a fine (see TNA, C 1/15/189 [c.1443–1450], C 1/45/32 [1470]).
29 Pre 1428 writs are largely stored separately at TNA according to whether they were *corpus cum causa* (C 250), *sub pena* (C 253), *certiorari* (C 258) and *attachias 'non sunt inventi'* (person not found: C 251) and *'cepi corpus'* (person secured: C 252); writs after that date are often stored together in C 244, apart from writs of *sub pena* and *attachias 'non sunt inventi'* after 1447–1448: Tucker, 'Early History', p. 798, n. 1. See also Patricia M. Barnes, 'The Chancery corpus cum causa File, 10–11 Edward IV', in R. F. Hunnisett and J. B. Post (eds.), *Medieval Legal Records Edited in Memory of C. A. F. Meekings* (London, 1978), pp. 429–476.
30 TNA, C 1/11/68 (1432–1443).
31 E.g. see TNA, C 1/28/519 (1460–1465); C 1/151/116 (1486–1493 or 1504–1515); C 1/329/48 (1504–1515).
32 E.g. TNA, C 1/50/94 (1475–1480 or 1483–1485); C 1/61/269 (1480–1483); C 1/287/13 (1493–1500).
33 TNA, C 1/27/381 (1460–1465). For more testamentary cases in Chancery see Joseph Biancalana, 'Testamentary Cases in Fifteenth-Century Chancery', *Tijdschrift voor Rechtsgeschiedenis*, 76:3–4 (2008), pp. 283–306.
34 TNA, C 1/148/67. The master is named in the bill as Philip Syne but can be identified as the same man resident in Southampton between 1461 and 1469, paying taxes as an 'alien' (foreigner) 1463–1469, and involved in a number of other Chancery disputes so I have standardized his name: 'England's Immigrants 1330–1550', www.englandsimmigrants.com, entries for Philip Syny, Philip Syne, Filippo Tyny, Philip Deny; TNA, C 1/27/416 (1462–1463); C 1/29/150 (1462–1463); C 1/30/67 (1463–1467); C 1/32/52 (1466–1467 or 1483). See also Alwyn A. Ruddock, 'Alien Merchants in Southampton in the Later Middle Ages', *English Historical Review*, 61 (1946), pp. 14–15.
35 *Oxford English Dictionary*, online at https://www.oed.com, morian, n. and adj.; *Dictionary of the Older Scottish Tongue*, online at <https://dsl.ac.uk>, morien, a. and n. Maria is assumed to be black by Habib, Onyeka and Ormrod; Kaufmann is more circumspect: Imtiaz Habib, *Black Lives in the English Archives, 1500–1677: Imprints of the Invisible* (Farnham, 2008), p. 58, n.134; Onyeka, *Blackamoores: Africans in Tudor England, Their Presence, Status and Origins* (London, 2013), pp. 109–110; W. Mark Ormrod, Bart Lambert and Jonathan Mackman, *Immigrant England, 1300–1550* (Manchester, 2019), p. 190; Miranda Kaufmann, *Black Tudors: The Untold Story* (London, 2017), p. 316, n. 41. Habib argues that while identifications on the basis of nomenclature might lead to

uncertainty about 'the authenticity of their black content', they should be included 'to compensate for the over-conservative, mutually reinforcing, multilayered assumptions of traditional early modern history that have made black people in Tudor and Stuart England absent by default': Habib, *Black Lives*, p. 17.
36 Sally McKee, 'Domestic Slavery in Renaissance Italy', *Slavery & Abolition*, 29:3 (2008), pp. 305–326; Kate Lowe, 'Visible Lives: Black Gondoliers and Other Black Africans in Renaissance Venice', *Renaissance Quarterly*, 66:2 (2013), pp. 415–423.
37 See William D. Phillips Jr., *Slavery from Roman Times to the Early Transatlantic Trade* (Manchester, 1985), p.101.
38 McKee, 'Domestic Slavery', pp. 317–318; Lowe, 'Visible Lives', pp. 421–423.
39 E.g. see the 1455 complaint against this practice, quoted in Jonathan Rose, 'Medieval Attitudes toward the Legal Profession: The Past as Prologue', *Stetson Law Review*, 28:1 (1999), p. 360.
40 See Gwilym Dodd, 'Languages and Law in Late Medieval England: English, French and Latin', in Candace Barrington and Sebastian Sobecki (eds.), *The Cambridge Companion to Medieval English Law and Literature* (Cambridge, 2019), pp. 17–29.
41 See T. S. Haskett, 'Country Lawyers?: The Composers of English Chancery Bills', in Peter Birks (ed.), *The Life of the Law: Proceedings of the Tenth British Legal History Conference, Oxford, 1991* (London, 1993), pp. 9–23, although his definition of a 'country lawyer' includes non-Chancery legal professionals *in* London as well as those outside.
42 C 1/64/755 (1485). Rowley's wife was later tried for Lollardy: Shannon McSheffrey, *Gender and Heresy: Women and Men in Lollard Communities, 1420–1530* (Philadelphia, 1995), pp. 29–37, 123–124.
43 See Teresa Phipps, 'Misbehaving Women: Trespass and Honor in Late Medieval English Towns', *Historical Reflections/Réflexions Historiques* 43:1 (2017), pp. 62–76.
44 For the 24 see Charles Phythian-Adams, *Desolation of a City: Coventry and the Urban Crisis of the Late Middle Ages* (Cambridge, 1979), pp. 121–126. On the leet court see Levi Fox, 'Some New Evidence of Leet Activity in Coventry, 1540–41', *English Historical Review*, 61 (1946), pp. 235–243 and, more generally, Maryanne Kowaleski, 'Town Courts in Medieval England: An Introduction', in Richard Goddard and Teresa Phipps (eds.), *Town Courts and Urban Society in Late Medieval England, 1250–1500* (Woodbridge, 2019), pp. 29–32.
45 Merridee L. Bailey, '"Most Hevynesse and Sorowe": The Presence of Emotions in the Late Medieval and Early Modern Court of Chancery', *Law and History Review*, 37:1 (2019), pp. 13, 18–22.
46 C 1/64/755.
47 On borough courts see Kowaleski, 'Town Courts', pp. 17–42; Phipps, *Medieval Women and Urban Justice*, pp. 21–40. On the influence of common law see Sara M. Butler, *Divorce in Medieval England: From One to Two Persons in Law* (New York, 2013), p. 12; Phipps, *Medieval Women and Urban Justice*, pp. 11–12.
48 For London see Henry Thomas Riley (ed.), *Munimenta Gildhallae Londiniensis: Liber Albus, Liber Custumarum et Liber Horn*, 3 (London, 1862), p. 39; for York (c.1436) see Maud Sellers (ed.), *York Memorandum Book*, Surtees Society, 125 (Durham, 1915), p. 145; for Ipswich (1291), Lincoln (1481), Worcester (1467) see Mary Bateson (ed.), *Borough Customs*, Selden Society, 18 (London, 1904), pp. 223–224, 226–227. Phipps shows that this was enforced in the Ipswich courts 1290–1482: Teresa Phipps, 'Female Litigants and the Borough Court: Status and Strategy in the Case of Agnes Halum of Nottingham', in Goddard and Phipps (eds.), *Town Courts*, p. 89, n.63.
49 Phipps, 'Female Litigants', pp. 87–88.
50 E.g. see the bill of Humfrey Bawde and Johanne his wife (c.1480) which is discussed and transcribed in Cordelia Beattie, 'Your Oratrice: Women's Petitions to the Late Medieval Court of Chancery', in Bronach Kane and Fiona Williamson (eds.), *Women, Agency and the Law, 1300–1700* (London, 2013), pp. 23–29, 157.
51 TNA, C 1/46/424 (probably 1462–1472).
52 Tucker, 'Early History', p. 800.

53 TNA, C 244/112 no. 173–175 and no. 114 (all dated 1471–1472). See further Barnes, 'Chancery corpus cum causa File', pp. 454–455, 462–463.
54 Barnes, 'Chancery corpus cum causa File', p. 435 but see pp. 454, 463.
55 TNA, C 1/64/738 (1475–1485). On Southwark as an independent jurisdiction from London in this period see Martha Carlin, *Medieval Southwark* (London, 1996), pp. 108–114.
56 TNA, C 1/64/738. The bill refers to his 'verray malice' to emphasize the claim.
57 See Shannon McSheffrey, 'Sanctuary and the Legal Topography of Pre-Reformation London', *Law and History Review*, 27:3 (2009), pp. 483–513. For another Chancery bill about a husband going into sanctuary in Westminster, see TNA, C 1/78/1 (1485–1486).
58 See Richard H. Helmholz, 'Bankruptcy and Probate Jurisdiction before 1571', *Missouri Law Review*, 48:2 (1983), pp. 415–429.
59 For other bills which refer to the doors of the marital property being sealed see TNA, C 1/46/221 (1467–1472); C 1/48/60 (1473–1475).
60 Cf. Helmholz, 'Bankruptcy', pp. 424–425. A widow's dower might include a share of the tenement or she might get the property for life as 'freebench': see Mary Bateson (ed.), *Borough Customs*, Selden Society, 21 (London, 1906), pp. 120–128.
61 Falling 'non-sued' is a common strategy according to Chancery bills. E.g. see TNA, C 1/46/171 (1467–1472, possibly 1433–1443); C 1/48/43 (1473–1475); C 1/64/1130 (1475–1480 or 1483–1485); C 1/169/5 (1486–1493 or 1504–1515).
62 TNA: C 1/60/177 (c.1475–1485).
63 See Butler, *Divorce*, pp. 15–16, 32–34.
64 For a discussion of whether wives might have been viewed as property see Sara M. Butler, 'Discourse on the Nature of Coverture in the Later Medieval Courtroom', in Stretton and Kesselring (eds.), *Married Women and the Law*, pp. 33–35. On ravishment suits, see Sara Butler, 'Runaway Wives: Husband Desertion in Medieval England', *Journal of Social History*, 40:2 (2006), pp. 341–344.
65 For 'foreigner' as meaning an outsider to the locality see Ormrod, Lambert and Mackman, *Immigrant England*, p. 8.
66 Biancalana argued that petitioners sometimes expected the Chancellor (typically a bishop) to back up an ecclesiastical decision that was being challenged elsewhere: Biancalana, 'Testamentary Cases', p. 305.
67 TNA, C 1/71/14 (1386–1486).
68 On outlawry, especially in the late medieval period, see Anthony Musson, *Medieval Law in Context: The Growth of Legal Consciousness from Magna Carta to the Peasants' Revolt* (Manchester, 2001), pp. 171–172.
69 TNA, C 1/43/31 (1433–1443 or 1462–1472); unfortunately, the bill is damaged on the right-hand side and not all of it is legible.
70 On arbitration as a way of settling disputes, see Musson, *Medieval Law in Context*, pp. 16, 91–93.
71 TNA, C 1/64/1049 (1475–1480 or 1483–1485).
72 It was most likely the Mayor's Court, which could handle all civil pleas. On Bristol's courts see Peter Fleming, *Women in Late Medieval Bristol* (Bristol, 2001), pp. 1–2.

7
GENDERED ROLES AND FEMALE LITIGANTS IN NORTH-EASTERN ENGLAND, 1300–1530

Peter L. Larson

The law courts of medieval England were a man's world and for a long time scholars saw widows as the only women with any true scope for individual action.[1] The Common Law concept of coverture considered a wife to be 'covered' by her husband and unable to litigate except in very restricted situations. Nevertheless, more recent studies have shown that women overall were more active in medieval and early modern life and in the courts than the limited range of actions that Common Law theory would suggest, and historians continue to reveal how married women frequently appeared in court on their own.[2] The dissonance between prescriptions of women's roles and recorded activities is pronounced as historians have become aware of the difficulty of distinguishing between wives and singlewomen.[3] With Agnes Halum, Teresa Phipps recently demonstrates how a woman could appear in the records as a wife and apparently as single in fourteenth-century Nottingham. In her recent comparative study of borough courts, Phipps concluded, 'women's experiences of and engagement with the law were a product of local interpretations of legal practice'.[4] Thus, for women, the immediate matter and the locality influenced how they were recorded, whereas adult men were referenced consistently by a Christian name and a surname or occupation with no need to indicate marital status. As this chapter demonstrates, in some manorial and borough courts of north-eastern England most women who pursued claims did so on their own, even wives. Instances of coverture being invoked in these courts mostly were restricted to land, bearing out the arguments of the above scholars and others who have studied local courts. Many of the women who used the courts were tenants, yet not all their pleas involved their tenure and not all active female litigants were tenants. However, this chapter highlights the local and contingent nature of opportunities for women; Matthew Stevens, Chris Briggs and others have found elsewhere in England that improvements often were offset by new limitations. The experience of patriarchy varied from place to place,

DOI: 10.4324/9780429278037-8

and in north-eastern England women's opportunity to litigate and their success in doing so reflected their access to landholding, a predominantly male role.[5]

As this chapter will demonstrate, the variations in women's access to the courts derive less from changing contemporary views of women (generally and specifically about their legal status) or the 'tightening up of the patriarchal framework' than from the mediation of patriarchy by local customs and conditions. Sandy Bardsley has shown how little the number of women holding land changed despite the Black Death; Hare notes a small number of women holding land in Wiltshire, similar to Faith's findings in Berkshire, and the numbers tended to remain stable or decrease.[6] In the northeast, many manorial courts upheld the rights of a widow to her deceased husband's tenure, in many cases even if she remarried, and also the right of women to take up lands if they were the closest heir. Widows truly were relicts and some records even omitted the widow when the son took up his father's holding, even if she had held it for years.[7] After the Black Death until the late fifteenth century, when land was vacant, women as tenants were important for maintaining the stability of the manor. Whether tenants in widow-right or their own right, women were important as tenants; the role of landholder overrode their position as women in some respects. This would seem to conflict with theories about women and patriarchy in late medieval England, yet this strengthens those assertions. Barbara Hanawalt discussed a 'self-limiting patriarchy' that put the good of guild and community in London above that of individual family.[8] Similarly, courts in the northeast supported the rights of the family for the sake of the community; stability and prosperity were still the goal, protecting inheritances from other men in villages where families were resident for centuries until rising population and changing economy rendered such protections obsolete. Judith Bennett's concept of patriarchal equilibrium, in which social and cultural forces counteracted improvements in the condition of women, was also in play in the northeast; more women gained access to the standing of a tenant, but the overall position of women did not improve.[9] Women did not amass holdings and create larger farms as men did; a widow remained caretaker of holdings. The patriarchal equilibrium adjusted to the needs of the time, allowing more women into roles predominantly held by men and then pushed them out when the situation changed in the sixteenth century as yeomen increasingly dominated land and court. The shift of much business and litigation to the Quarter Sessions alongside lost records prevent a thorough evaluation of the effect on women and their litigation in the early modern northeast but there are suggestions that this was a general trend in the region. Landholding and litigation went hand in hand, largely an expression of local social and economic necessities.

The records

This chapter uses records from County Durham and all three ridings (divisions) of Yorkshire to explore these questions of women's litigation, its culture and its context in north-eastern England. As shown in Table 7.1, sufficient records from

TABLE 7.1 Manors and sources of north-eastern England examined

Manor	No. of villages or subdivisions	Estate	Historical County	Period covered	Years examined
Bishop Middleham	3	Durham Bishopric	Co. Durham	1349–1531	101
Billingham	1	Durham Priory	Co. Durham	1340–1501	91
Crossgate	1	Durham Priory	Co. Durham	1312–1531	13
Bolam	1	Earl of Suffolk	Co. Durham	1396–1434	17
St. Helens Auckland	1	Colville/Mauleverer	Co. Durham	1397–1401	4
Ingleby Arncliffe	1	Colville/Mauleverer	North Riding, Yorkshire	1368–1432	11
Daletown	1	Colville/Mauleverer	North Riding, Yorkshire	1376–1431	3
Wakefield	13	Earl of Surrey	West Riding, Yorkshire	1306–1331	19
Conisbrough	3	Crown	South Riding, Yorkshire	1324–1605	12

Source: Durham Bishopric Halmote Court Books; Durham Priory Halmote Court Rolls and Estreat Rolls; Mauleverer of Ingleby Arncliffe Records; Hospital of Jesus (Guisborough Grammar School) Records; *Court Rolls of the Manor of Wakefield*, vols. 2–5 (various eds.); *Records of the Borough of Crossgate, Durham, 1312–1531*.

several different courts survive to explore the interplay of gender, litigation, and society from the fourteenth to the early sixteenth century.

The manorial courts discussed offer a range of lived experiences, locations, and administrations. 'North-eastern England' includes here the counties of Durham and Yorkshire; aside from a few manors on the north side of the River Tyne belonging to Durham priory, there is little surviving material from Northumberland. The best record series comes from the Durham bishopric estate, with halmote court books surviving (with gaps) from 1349 to 1925: three villages have been examined for 1349–1360, 1388–1410, and 1439–1476, supplemented by sampling the years 1420–1424, 1488–1491, 1499–1501, 1509–1521, and 1529–1531.[10] The halmote court records for the Durham priory main estate are less plentiful but still provide a sample covering ninety-one years, focussing on the village of Billingham between 1364 and 1414.[11] The bishopric and priory halmote courts possessed both manorial and leet[12] jurisdiction, blending seigniorial oversight of lands and tenants (including interpersonal litigation) with the formerly royal franchise of peacekeeping and policing weights and measures; there is no evidence of a separate hundred court operating in Durham to carry out those public responsibilities. The bishop and priory had a court for tenants of free (as opposed to customary) land, but many free tenants conducted business at the more accessible halmotes. Limited manorial court records survive for two County Durham manors in lay hands: Bolam, held by the Earls of Suffolk, and St Helens Auckland, held by the Colville and then the Mauleverer family. Their free and customary tenants attended the same courts. Yorkshire is represented by manorial courts from each of its three Ridings (subdivisions). The Colville and

Mauleverer families held some manors in the North Riding as well; the Earls of Surrey held Wakefield manor, consisting of thirteen graveships (subdivisions of a large manor or parish) in the West Riding, and the fourteenth-century records have been supplemented with some later materials (1550–1552, 1583–1585, 1664–1665). A selection of ten manorial and leet court rolls between 1324 and 1605 for the royal manor of Conisbrough provides evidence for three graveships in the South Riding. Together, these provide evidence outside of Durham with the more traditional division of court baron (held to regulate the lord's tenants, such as the holding of land, payment of servile obligations, and what today would be considered 'civil' jurisdiction) and court leet/sheriff's tourn (a territorial jurisdiction over all persons, concerned with certain criminal matters and enforcing mercantile regulations such as the weight and quality of bread and ale).[13] Finally, the records of the Borough court of Crossgate, Durham from 1312 to 1531 represent an urban court with potentially different concerns than the rural manorial courts.[14] The preponderance of surviving material skews this essay toward Durham, but the more limited Yorkshire sources reveal similar patterns.

Women comprised a minority of litigants in these courts, as was the case across England, between 10% and 17% of all litigants depending on the years sampled.[15] Coverture, even when not part of the law (as these were not Common Law courts), nevertheless shaped women's access to courts and how their actions were recorded. In that sense, women were more active than the clerks suggested, as there are instances in the records used here where the wife was the one involved even though the husband was named. Thus, understanding how women accessed courts and how the clerks referred to them is necessary to understand the extent of women's litigation, and the appearance of women as litigants, particularly when they succeeded in their cases. Two patterns emerge from this sample. In courts where women rarely litigated, such as the Durham Priory halmote courts, the court records depicted women in a negative light, as scolds, fornicators, or in other disruptive roles; whereas in courts where women were more active as litigators, they were depicted similarly to male tenants. The opportunity for women to occupy male-gendered roles particularly as tenants explains these divergent patterns in north-eastern England. A person's role often mattered more than gender before the court: women were successful in court where local society allowed them to occupy roles such as tenant that normally were filled by men because it often was in the court's interest to support the broader group.[16] Women's access rested on social and economic need to fill such roles more than on positive views of women; as women lost the opportunity to occupy those roles as conditions changed in the early modern period, their activity and visibility in court decreased accordingly.

Women's litigation in the late medieval northeast: debt and trespass

Women appear in north-eastern court records in four main instances: 'breaking' the assize of ale; violation of local regulations; scolding and fighting; and interpersonal litigation for debt and detinue, broken contracts, and trespass. They do not appear in equal number, and local patterns can be discerned. For instance, in Wakefield, women appeared far more frequently than in the other courts in pleas of land and as buyers and sellers of land (see below). All these activities reveal the spectrum in which courts and society interpreted women's actions. The scope and truth of women's agency elude us; whether these women truly wished for, initiated, or voluntarily participated in this litigation is unknown. While the focus of this chapter is on litigation, the correlation with other aspects of women's lives in these localities reveals a flexible patriarchal culture when it came to the community's broader interest.

The most common type of interpersonal litigation for women in these courts was debt/detinue as both debtor and creditor, with trespass close behind, all revealing women's participation in agricultural and economic life. As commonly found with local courts, these patterns varied across England.[17] Women in the courts examined here were not involved in the largest debts (up to £11 13s. 9d. in Sedgefield, Durham in 1407) nor were they exclusively restricted to the smallest; most debts pursued by north-eastern men and women ranged between one and ten shillings.[18] The nature of those debts was the same for men and women: unpaid wages and unperformed work, items bought and sold or lost, and unpaid rents. For example, a certain Alice (last name illegible) in St Helens Auckland successfully pursued a debt for a quarter of oats, a quarter of barley, and 1s. in money versus a man in 1399.[19] Joan Mayland of Bolam sued the executors of John Pykard for 5s. for a quarter of malt that she sold him before his death.[20] Isabella Tidde of the Durham priory village of Billingham sued John Tidde for one mark.[21] And then there was Isabella Walsh of St Helen's Auckland. In 1398, the jury awarded her 9d. for the rent of lands let to William Symson and they also found William in mercy for breaking distraint of the oats seized from him at her behest to distrain him to answer. Later in 1399 John Symson recouped 4.5d. for wages Isabella owed him for ploughing a rod of her land, and then in 1400 she sued William Townend in a plea of debt and had him distrained to answer.[22] Likewise, Cecilia de Wakefield was an active tenant in the bishop's market village of Sedgefield circa 1400, suing and being sued for debts, breaking bylaws, and skipping court like many of her male counterparts.[23] Cecilia and Isabella were unusual; most women were involved in only one or two suits – but that was true for men too. The same was true in debt litigation over service, whether for work or provision of animals or goods, as in the case of Alice del Somerhouses of the village of Killerby who sued her village for failing to pay her for a horse taken for carriage duty in Scotland.[24] What we rarely know, however, is their marital status; even widows were not indicated consistently.

In the Crossgate borough court it is easier to identify married women as litigants, whether alone, with their husband, or through their husband (similar to coverture) thanks to the specificity of the clerks. Robert de Kirkham and Juliana his wife sued William Emery for 5s. in 1391 for hay William had purchased from Juliana three years before; William initially was going to wage his law, but then they compromised with him paying 2s. 6d. to Juliana. Other than Robert's mention in the record as appearing in court for the suit, he had no role; the transaction was between Juliana and William, and the record clearly has William paying Juliana with no mention of her husband.[25] That suit follows the practice of coverture, yet Juliana and not her husband was recognized as the creditor. Stevens suggested that debts such as this may have originated before marriage, but there is no evidence of Juliana's marital status (or to that of other women) when the debt was incurred.[26] When William de Bishopton sued Elena Ka because she had not returned wool that she had been given to card, this seems to be the opposite of Robert and Juliana de Kirkham, where in this case William's wife has little role in the underlying dispute.[27] Married women were also suing on their own in this period: in 1394, Alice wife of John de Bointon sued William Norris for a debt, and later through her attorney John Scharp they settled at 10s.[28] in 1529, however, Robert Smythirst sued Thomas and Elizabeth Robinson for a debt from when she was single (*dum ipsa sola fuit*).[29] This debt litigation demonstrates that north-eastern women, whether singlewomen, wives, or widows, were trading and litigating in the same ways that many men did, and that the courts were concerned with the role of the litigants and the transaction itself than the gender of the litigants.

The reason for many debts was not recorded. Of those that were, several involving women concerned the cloth trade, whether for wool as above, or for cloth in various stages – not unexpected given the suitability of the region for sheep. Others were for wages or small transactions of grain and flour. In the sixteenth century, debts appeared involving women as creditor and debtors over the payment for small quantities of prepared foodstuffs purchased from them – bread, mutton, ale – 6d. 11d., and the like.[30] Executrices were common in Durham, although the balance of executors and executrices needs further study. Pleas for debts owed to women in the sixteenth century frequently involved women functioning as executrices, such as the interestingly named Elizabeth Bruer Draver for her deceased husband Robert Draver, who sued John Gray for 3s. 3d. worth of items.[31] Even as women's litigation dwindled, executrices continued to be found suing for debt.

A woman's litigation usually involved her suing or being sued by a man, rather than another woman, particularly for debts. Women acting alone were far more likely to be the litigant than a husband and wife, or a woman with another relative. In Wakefield, 135 of 196 pleas litigated by women involved a woman on her own, with 54 of the rest a husband and wife.[32] Conisbrough had similar proportions although the sample size is much smaller. In a sample of three Durham bishopric villages from 1399 to 1407, fourteen of sixteen pleas involved single women, who won in eleven of the thirteen decisions.[33] The Durham priory village of Billingham had fifty suits involving women between 1364 and 1414 (the last suit involving a female litigant was recorded in 1413), with forty-eight involving a woman on her own as opposed to a husband and wife. Women identified by the clerks as wives usually appeared with their husbands; in Wakefield, only fourteen of the women who litigated debts and trespass on their own were identified as wives.[34] But it is very possible that many of the women litigating on their own were wives, and just not identified as such; this is clear in Durham, for example William and Marjory Tose of Sedgefield were both named individually in several suits in 1400, but their relationship was only indicated when she was fined for breaking the assize of ale.[35] The inconsistency in recording marital status further emphasizes how rarely it mattered in these courts, and that more attention should be paid to litigation where marital status is more consistently recorded.[36] There is too little detail and evidence to be certain, but in Durham courts, husbands and wives appeared jointly primarily in reference to land. In Wakefield, where women also litigated frequently on their own, a wife's marital status appeared to be critical only in relation to land: when Thomas Whatmod sued Emma del Storthes in 1315, she was acquitted and he amerced because he had failed to include her husband in the plea.[37] Here, coverture caused the suit to fail. Was this a regular application by the court or had Emma seized on the detail to derail the case, as Teresa Phipps observed in the Nottingham borough court?[38] Even the status of widows is not always clear or consistent in the records. Isabella de Carlton and Agnes Pollard sometimes were identified as widows, and Agnes Pollard was more often recorded in a way that suggested she was single and never-married, as when she answered for the profits of vacant tenures alongside seven men, rendering the second highest sum.[39] Most female litigants in the Crossgate borough court were not associated with a man; some were widows. Women identified as wives, either alone or with their husbands, appeared rarely yet may have been court. The lack of consistency is revealed by two examples from Billingham in the summer of 1381. Robert Faukes was named defendant and amerced because his wife had received a stolen sack, while John Miryman was amerced for a broken agreement over 10s. with the unnamed wife of William Stodow.[40] One unnamed wife's actions saw her husband named as defendant, while another unnamed wife litigated on her own, her husband invoked to identify her but not a litigant. Coverture was powerful but invoked specifically only when it was convenient for either side.

The plaintiff won more often if the case went to a decision (as opposed to default or non-prosecution), and this was true for women as well as men just as Briggs found in Oakington and Great Horwood. Unlike those manors, women in the northeast often settled suits through concord between the parties; 61 of 145 suits in Wakefield involving female litigants where the outcome is known were settled in such a way, compared to 27 by jury and 5 by waging one's law.[41] The waging of law, or using oath-helpers to swear to one's case, did not favour women on their own in Crossgate, where women on their own won only two of six cases that were settled in this way while wives with their husbands won both instances; in Wakefield, women won in cases of waging law half the time. In Billingham, of twenty-two cases with known outcomes involving an individual woman as litigant, she won fifteen. The different outcomes in Crossgate, Wakefield, and Billingham suggest the possibility of different local patterns in settling litigation that is worth examining, but if there was a general bias against women pleading in the manorial courts, either it was silent or it took place before the official plea.

Regulating women in court

Examining women as plaintiffs and defendants only tells part of the story of female participation and appearance in these courts. Women in the rural northeast comprised a regular but small proportion of tenants on the estates considered here, between 5% and 20% at any given time in the fourteenth and fifteenth centuries. Many were widows but the status is not always clear, and never-married and married women held lands in their own right. There were also regular numbers of female servants, both daughters of village families and immigrants from other counties and Scotland. In all the villages women formed a small proportion of those involved in court, however the balance of women as tenants, servants, and other inhabitants versus local politics and conditions shaped the roles of women in each estate's courts. Women appeared in court for more than debt and trespass: the assize of ale; as targets of social control; and for breaking manorial, village, and borough regulations. Nearly all persons targeted for scolding and leyrwite were women, as discussed below; the other two categories of appearance were more varied in gender balance, or at least recorded as thus.[42]

In most of the courts examined, women are recorded similarly to men when it came to violation of regulations, whether keeping their animals under control, their properties in repair, or other requirements. Men outnumbered women in these instances because most tenants were men; women were amerced relative to the number of male and female tenants, neither singled out nor ignored because of gender. Again, it was their role as tenant, not their gender, that determined their legal actions. Isabella Walsh of St Helens, discussed above, was also amerced for violating bylaws or failing to take part in communal works. Cecilia de Wakefield was one of several tenants in Cornforth, Bishop Middleham, and Sedgefield who refused to put their animals into the care of the common shepherd in the 1390s and 1400s; this was true even into the seventeenth century.[43] It may have happened, but there is no evidence of female tenants being treated differently than men, or participating less in agricultural affairs. The same was true in Yorkshire, where women were more involved in buying and selling land than in Durham. Durham priory was the exception here; male tenants dominated the presentments and orders but not to the extent that they outnumbered women as tenants. Unlike other villages examined here, in the priory villages the female tenants rarely appeared in the records outside of land transfers – or as fornicators and scolds, as discussed below. Women's absence from these might go unnoticed were it not for the contrast with other villages.

Women were treated differently when it came to social control. The Durham bishopric, priory, and Crossgate courts amerced men and women for hosting disruptive or misgoverned persons, usually women or Scots (usually *Scotos* with no name recorded) but sometimes men. All courts except Wakefield were concerned over quarrelling and disruptive speech, in line with the chronology established by McIntosh and Bardsley, but to varying extents. In post-plague north-eastern courts, clerks labelled women as *litigatrices* and *objurgatrices*, and both men and women as *garrulatores* and *garrulatrices*, arguing with their neighbours and stirring up trouble; likewise, this disruptive speech was gendered, as men predominated in confrontations with officers and jurors while rejecting authority.[44] Such activity was rare for women, whose disruptive behaviour took place outside of court against their neighbours in personal disputes. Men's disruptive speech tended to be recorded as action, as when John Sannifall of Billingham 'reviled the village pinder' (*maledixit ponderum villae*); women usually were recorded as disruptive beings, such as Alice Walker and five other Billingham women amerced for being 'common scolds' (*communes garrulatrices*).[45] The records from the borough court of Crossgate indicate greater concern than on the bishopric and lay manors of Durham regarding scolds and other disruptive women, although not as much concern as seen in the priory records. The Durham priory villages were very concerned over disorderly women, levying *leyrwite* into the late fifteenth century; from 1364 to 1414 in Billingham, where there were 48 suits involving individual women, 26 women were amerced for scolding and 127 paid leyrwite. Scolding appeared in bishopric court records less often, with an average of just over thirteen recorded fines per year *for the entire estate* in 1349–1360, with leyrwite all but disappearing by 1420.[46] In Billingham, the main cluster was 1376–1383, a time of considerable anxiety over violence and disorder in the village, in line with Bardsley's conclusions on increasing concern over 'sins of the tongue'. The Durham priory courts instructed men to keep their wives and servants in line, similar to late medieval London courts that looked to the household as the unit for social control: those who were (or should have been) responsible, and those who were not.[47] The Durham bishopric courts did not share these concerns, at least not in the surviving records.

The difference in social and moral regulation between Durham priory and bishopric appears linked with the presence and activity of female tenants, suggesting a correlation between litigation and tenancy. Between 1340 and 1396, the percentage of female priory tenants dropped from approximately 15% to less than 10%, similar to what Whittle found in Norfolk.[48] A similar comparison of the composition of the tenantry is not possible for the bishopric estate, but comparing the land markets in the two estates is revealing: women took land three to five times more often in the sampled bishopric villages than priory villages. In the priory village of Billingham, from 1388 to 1414, women took land six times, mostly in widow-right. In the nearby bishopric village of Sedgefield, with about 50% more tenants than Billingham, woman took land thirty-four times (nineteen times in widow-right); and in the bishopric villages of Bishop Middleham and Cornforth, together the same size as Billingham, women took land seventeen times (twelve times in widow-right).[49] A bishopric woman, even a wife, taking land in her own right was not unusual. While Durham women on both estates became tenants through inheritance or widow-right, more bishopric women fined in their own right: for example Margaret Othehough, wife of Patrick de Kreghton, took nineteen acres in the bishopric village of Benfeldside as a tenant in right, while Emma daughter of Walter Wyot in Heighington took a parcel on her own in 1358.[50] When in the fifteenth century it became increasingly common for groups of bishopric tenants to lease properties collectively, from the village brewhouse to the village itself, female tenants were found in the collective lease.[51] Instances of these were unusual but demonstrate that women were accepted as tenants, if grudgingly. This is reinforced by patterns in widow-right; 82% of widows of tenants taking holdings to hold in widow-right between 1349 and 1660, with the percentage rising to 89% from the mid-fifteenth century.[52] Some widows held lands for over twenty years; they did not forfeit the lands on remarriage nor could the new husband take the lands unless the original tenant had no heirs.[53] However, from the middle of the fifteenth century, bishopric women became less active in the land market so that most female tenants held in widow-right and landholding became more of a male preserve. This shift may have affected women's ability or opportunity to litigate. In the Yorkshire manors, women were more active in the early fourteenth-century land market than in Durham, both in taking land and in disputes over land, alone and with husbands; but the Wakefield land market also became almost exclusively male by the early modern period. Whether the different trajectories resulted from or generated a view of female tenants or for some other reason, tenure and law were connected.

Law and culture in the north-east

In many of the locations in north-eastern England examined here, female tenants were active in court much like their male counterparts; these north-eastern courts exhibited degrees of concern over women's behaviour alongside varying actions by and views of women. The exception was Durham priory, where female tenants were declining and women were more likely to appear as scolds or fornicators if they appeared in court at all. In the courts examined in this essay, women were more active in the lay-held manor of St Helens Auckland, and involved in more types of litigation, than any other estate. Unfortunately, there are so few records that there is no way to say if this is the random luck of surviving court rolls. The second distinction is that women on the bishopric estate and St Helen's Auckland usually were plaintiffs pursuing their own pleas, whereas on the Durham priory estate women were more likely to appear as defendants in pleas of trespass, or for disorder as perpetrators and victims. This pattern is rooted in or at least correlative with landholding, as discussed above. Along with this, the bishopric villages were more stable in terms of interpersonal relations than the priory villages, at least as reported to the court.

The ability of women to act in north-eastern courts seems to correlate with places with more female tenants. Where women were active and successful litigants, women also appear in other more visible activities such working the land, breaking bylaws, and marketing of agrarian produce – not selling food products such as bread and ale but the raw grains, or providing wool for processing. Most persons involved in these activities were men, and as such men dominated local society and the courts. But women had some access to these roles, could occupy them, and succeed in them (even if they could not rise as high as some men). When they encountered people not of this group, such as servants or the landless, their legal success is not surprising. Women who were not tenants, and especially female servants, appeared in court mainly for activities that were more domestic (such as brewing and selling ale out of the house) or for verbal and sexual misbehaviour; and they were more likely to fare poorly in court.

The connection between women as tenants and women as litigants indicates that the space for women to act as a litigant in the courts of north-eastern England depended on their access to roles predominantly occupied by men, which intersected with the intensity and focus of patriarchal culture in those localities. Women as tenants serve as the primary example of this argument. Where women formed a regular if small proportion of tenants and participated actively in the land market, namely in the Durham bishopric villages and Wakefield manor, men in authority focussed on tenant status rather than their gender. This correlated with a less negative view of women overall and a greater likelihood of women generally (and not just female tenants) litigating in court; tenancy and litigation by women who were not tenants were linked, and the nature of that link is a compelling question for further research. Where women tenants were fewer, such as in the Priory villages, women rarely initiated pleas and were more likely to be in court for disruptive behaviour such as fornication and scolding. Thus, rather than focus solely on gender, it is more accurate to think of a spectrum and assess the extent to which women were allowed to be tenants, and why. This access reflected the intersection of social, economic, and cultural factors and how these shaped the local expression of patriarchy. The greater presence of female tenants coincided with greater litigation by women. Whether one led to the other is unclear; did a less negative view of women encourage both tenancy and litigation, or did women's status as tenants lead to an improvement of how they were viewed?

The opportunity for a woman to sue, to be seen more neutrally or to face less discrimination in court, and to be identified by her own name depended on the balance between a patriarchal culture and economic pragmatism.[54] There was no single north-eastern patriarchal culture, let alone an English one, but a variety of expressions shaped by local contexts. On the bishopric estate, stability was prized but there was a serious shortage of tenants following the Black Death; even with female tenants, lands were vacant. Female tenants had access to court, and success, because they were tenants, while the control of the village elite played out in the rare presentation of women for scolding. But the preference for male tenants remained, and the practice of widow-right seems to support this: widows were tenants in right of their deceased husband, not on their own. As the population increased beginning late in the fifteenth century, widows retained their right but fewer women held lands in other ways. On the Durham Priory estate, however, conflicts often involved wives and daughters of leading tenants while vacant land was less of a concern; together with the instability of the villages this may have limited opportunities for a woman to hold land and increased the likelihood of women appearing in a more negative light as scolds and fornicators.

The roots of that difference need to be studied. The size of a holding was not a factor. While tenures remained intact in Bolam, St Helens Auckland, and in the Durham bishopric into the fifteenth century and beyond, in Yorkshire there was a market in parcels of many sizes throughout the period; the Durham priory villages fell in the middle. The style of lordship could have been a factor. The Durham priory administrators were active in the affairs of the village, but those of the Durham bishopric were not, leaving much of the governance of the villages to the tenants, resulting in the appearance of stability while priory communities were riven by faction.[55] Later, syndicates of tenants took over the management of priory villages in the fifteenth century and less strife was recorded, but whether litigation disappeared because of that stability or from settlement outside of court needs to be established more firmly.

The link between landholding by women and litigation likely persisted into the late fifteenth and sixteenth centuries, although this requires analysis on its own; the bishopric and priory villages examined here suggest a decline in women's litigation in the fifteenth century, which would be in line with other recent studies on women's litigation. Interpersonal litigation in general disappeared from many manorial courts in these centuries, leaving them primarily vehicles for recording land transfers and enforcing village bylaws. In Wakefield, this occurred in the sixteenth century.[56] In Durham, debt and trespass pleas disappeared in the mid-fifteenth century to reappear in the middle of the sixteenth century with women involved in similar proportion as the fourteenth and fifteenth centuries. The ways in which women were referred to in the courts changed underwent a significant transformation, however. In the thirteenth and fourteenth centuries, most women in the bishopric courts were identified by a first and last name, or by their first name and a connection to an adult male (as was also done with servants and even many sons), while widows were linked to their deceased husband, for example, Annabilla widow of Thomas Headlam. Wives and widows could be recorded by first and last names, like never-married women. Often it was situational; when John Smith convinced Joan Proudlok to work for him and not her father in 1411, she was 'Joan daughter and servant of John Proudlok', but when she was amerced for leyrwite she was simply 'Joan Proudlok'.[57] When the widows Isabella Hanslap and Agnes del Gate failed to maintain their buildings, or when the pinder failed to distrain Agnes Pillok, their deceased husbands were not named, suggesting that marital status was not relevant and/or that their names alone sufficed to identify them as with men.[58] In the middle of the fifteenth century, however, the first names of wives and widows began to disappear. The identification of widows was truncated further, omitting the first name, such as widow Gibson or widow Coky.[59] Unfortunately, the loss of records and the overall decline of litigation precludes analysis of this change for comparison with other studies showing a decline or in women's litigation in the fifteenth century.[60] The change in naming conventions in the later fifteenth century and the likely decline in numbers of female tenants as population increased suggests that the link between female landholding and litigation argued for in this chapter continued – negatively – into the early modern period.

The appearance and activity of women in north-eastern courts, whether single, married, or widowed, depended on how law and legal culture intersected with the options afforded to women. That local conditions had a profound effect on the lives of pre-modern women is far from new. The strikingly different experiences in the two major Durham estates reflected differences in seignorial attitudes, but it may well have run deeper; the persistence of widow-right on the bishopric estate despite centuries of change indicates that women's roles were deeply rooted in local economic and demographic systems as much as culture.[61] What these north-eastern courts demonstrate is that the general late medieval English perceptions of gender did not change but could be overridden by local concerns – whether economic, demographic, or seignorial – temporarily allowing women more autonomy and choice. If there was any improvement for women following the Black Death, then it was local, situational, and temporary.

Notes

1 For example, see Doris Stenton, *The English Woman in History* (London, 1957), p. 97. The 'liberation' of widowhood is a frequent trope, for example, Sue Sheridan Walker, 'Introduction', *idem* (ed.), *Wife and Widow in Medieval England* (Ann Arbor, 1993), pp. 11–12, and Peter Franklin, 'Peasant Widows' "Liberation" and Remarriage Before the Black Death', *Economic History Review* n.s., 39:2 (1986), pp. 186–204. The focus on the *fem(m)e sole*, the married woman with the right to trade on her own in cities, is another variant on this assumption; for an overview of the concept and historiography, see Sara Butler, 'Femme Sole Status: A Failed Feminist Dream?, *Legal History Miscellany*, February 8, 2019 https://legalhistorymiscellany.com/2019/02/08/femme-sole-status-a-failed-feminist-dream/ (accessed August 1, 2020). These views on the limitations of married women at law date back to William Blackstone's *Commentaries on the Laws of England* (Oxford, 1765), Book 1, p. 430, and the spread of that doctrine is analysed by Tim Stretton in 'Coverture and Unity of Persons in Blackstone's Commentaries', in Wilfrid Prest (ed.), *Blackstone and His Commentaries: Biography, Law, History* (Oxford, 2009), pp. 111–127.

2 Matthew Stevens concluded that 'there is in truth little evidence to sustain this argument' that 'women were mostly named in common law actions where a husband claimed lands in right of his wife': Matthew Frank Stevens, 'London's Married Women, Debt Litigation and Coverture in the Court of Common Pleas', in Cordelia Beattie and Matthew Frank Stevens (eds.), *Married Women and the Law in Premodern Northwest Europe* (Woodbridge, 2013), pp. 120–131 (quotation on p. 131). On the Common Law of coverture, see J. H. Baker, *An Introduction to English Legal History*, 3rd edition (London, 1990), and William C. Sprague, *Blackstone's Commentaries, Abridged*, 9th ed. (Chicago, 1915), vol. 1, p. 82. In addition to the volume edited by Beattie and Stevens, there is another recent collection on wives and the law: Tim Stretton and Krista J. Kesselring (eds.), *Married Women and the Law: Coverture in England and the Common Law World* (Montreal, 2013).

3 Miriam Müller, 'Peasant Women, Agency and Status in Mid-Thirteenth to Late Fourteenth-Century England: Some Reconsiderations', in Beattie and Stevens (eds.), *Married Women and the Law*, pp. 91–113; Judith Bennett, *Women in the Medieval English Countryside: Gender & Household in Brigstock before the Plague* (Oxford, 1989), pp. 144–145.
4 Teresa Phipps, 'Female Litigants and the Borough Court: Status and Strategy in the Case of Agnes Halum of Nottingham', in Richard Goddard and Teresa Phipps (eds.), *Town Courts and Urban Society in Late Medieval England, 1250–1500* (Woodbridge, 2019), p. 87.
5 Matthew Frank Stevens, 'London Women, the Courts and the "Golden Age": A Quantitative Analysis of Female Litigants in the Fourteenth and Fifteenth Centuries', *The London Journal*, 37 (2012), p. 83. Briggs concluded that 'a relatively high proportion of not-married female landholders in the local population …at least partly explains the unusually pronounced degree of female participation': 'Empowered or marginalized? Rural women and credit in later thirteenth- and fourteenth-century England', *Continuity and Change* 19 (2004), p. 34. This supports the current state of the 'golden age for women' debate, focussing on the subtle changes and regional variations. Stevens provides an overview of the Golden Age debate as regards London, pp. 67–71. See also Judith Bennett, *History Matters: Patriarchy and the Challenge of Feminism* (Philadelphia, 2006); Barbara Hanawalt, *The Wealth of Wives: Women, Law, and Economy in Late Medieval London* (Oxford, 2007).
6 Stevens, 'London Women', p. 83; see also pp. 69–70; Sandy Bardsley, 'Peasant Women and Inheritance of Land in Fourteenth-Century England', *Continuity and Change*, 29 (2014), p. 297; R. M. Smith, 'Women's Property Rights under Customary Law: Some Developments in the Thirteenth and Fourteenth Centuries', *Transactions of the Royal Historical Society* 36 (1986), pp. 181–186, and Smith, 'Coping with Uncertainty: Women's Tenure of Customary Land in England c. 1370–1430', in Jennifer Kermode (ed.), *Enterprise and Individuals in Fifteenth-Century England* (Stroud, 1991), pp. 43–67, Rosamund Faith, 'Berkshire: Fourteenth and Fifteenth Centuries', in P.D.A. Harvey (ed.), *The Peasant Land Market in Medieval England* (Oxford, 1984), pp. 114, 161, and John Hare, *A Prospering Society: Wiltshire in the Later Middle Ages* (Hatfield, 2011), pp. 134–136. See also Jane Whittle, 'Inheritance, Marriage, Widowhood and Remarriage: A Comparative Perspective on Women and Landholding in North-East Norfolk, 1440–1580', *Continuity and Change* 13 (1998), pp. 35–36. The decline in women's customary holdings is mirrored by declining rights in Common Law: Michael Phifer, 'Property, Power, and Patriarchy: The Decline of Women's Property Right in England after the Black Death', Unpublished Ph.D. dissertation, University of Houston, 2014.
7 Peter L. Larson, 'Widow-Right in Durham, England (1349–1660)', *Continuity and Change*, 33 (2017), pp. 178–179.
8 Judith Bennet, *Ale, Beer, and Brewsters in England: Women's Work in a Changing World, 1300–1600* (Oxford, 1996), and *History Matters*, esp. pp. 54–81; Hanawalt, *The Wealth of Wives*, p. 12. Amy Louise Erickson identified a similar contrast between ideology and practices in early modern England, writing that 'limiting a wife's bequest to her widowhood was considered the natural result of a man's desire to protect his own and his children's property from the grasp of any future husband of his widow's, or of her children by another man' but then notes that 'more than half of all men – and in some places up to three quarters of all men – imposed no limitation on their wives' bequests': *Women and Property in Early Modern England* (New York, 1995), pp. 166, 162–169.
9 Bennett, *History Matters*, pp. 54–81.
10 The National Archive: Public Record Office, DURH 3/12–28 Palatinate of Durham: Chancery Court: Cursitor's Records: Halmote Court Books; Durham University Library Special Collections, Durham Bishopric Halmote Court Records, Durham Halmote Court Books, DHC1/I/1–91 (hereafter DHC).
11 Durham University Library Special Collections, Durham Cathedral Archive: Court Records, Halmote Court Rolls (hereafter Durham Priory Halmote Court Rolls) c.

1295 to Autumn 1507, and Loc.IV, Prior's and Other Courts, Halmote Court Estreat Rolls, Loc.IV.149, 158, 162, 163, 165, 166, 167, 168, 174, 178, 180, 182, 184, 185, 187, 211, 213–215, 217, 220, 221, 223, 224, 227, and 240.

12 The court leet, or sheriff's tourn, had jurisdiction over some criminal matters and the enforcement of weights and measures used for bread and ale; some had the right over some capital offenses.

13 William Baildon (ed.), *Court Rolls of the Manor of Wakefield*, vol. 2: *1297 to 1309* (Leeds, 1906; reprinted Cambridge, 2013); John Lister (ed.), *vol. 3: 1313 to 1316, and 1286* (Leeds, 1917; reprinted Cambridge, 2013) and *vol. 4: 1315 to 1317* (Wakefield, 1930; reprinted Cambridge, 2013); and John William Walker (ed.), *vol. 5: 1322 to 1331* (Wakefield, 1945; reprinted Cambridge 2013); C.M. Fraser and Kenneth Emsley (eds.), *The Court Rolls of the Manor of Wakefield from October 1639 to September 1640* (Norwich, 1977); Ann Weikel (ed.), *The Court Rolls of the Manor of Wakefield from October 1583 to September 1585* (Leeds, 1984); 'Conisbrough Court Rolls', https://www.dhi.ac.uk/conisbrough/index.html (accessed 29 September 2019); court rolls for 1324–1325, 1349–1350, 1380–1381, 1480–1486, 1536, and 1605; NYCRO Maulverer of Ingleby Arncliffe Records, ZFL 107, 109, 123 (MIC 1290–1291) for the manors of Dale and Ingleby Arncliffe.

14 Richard H. Britnell (ed.), *Records of the Borough of Crossgate, Durham, 1312–1531*, Surtees Society vol. 212 (Woodbridge, 2008).

15 Ten percent of litigants in Wakefield in 1315 and Bishop Middleham from 1399 to 1403 were women, while at the height of litigation by women in Billingham, they comprised 17% of litigants; the remaining courts have too few records for precise analysis. Women comprised only about 8% of litigants in pre-plague Brigstock, while participation was twice as high in Oakington (Cambs.) and Great Horwood: Bennett, *Women in the Medieval English Countryside*, pp. 194–195; Chris Briggs, 'Empowered or Marginalized', p. 19. Woman's participation in borough courts varied; see Phipps, *Medieval Women and Urban Justice*, Kindle version, Chapter 2, 'The nature of women's litigation'.

16 S.H. Rigby, *English Society in the Later Middle Ages* (Basingstoke, 1995).

17 Many courts used debt and detinue interchangeably. Women's litigation varied greatly from place to place, often with significant changes over time; for examples see Bennett, *Women in the Medieval English Countryside*, pp. 194–195; Briggs, 'Empowered or Marginalized', pp. 17–18; Phipps, 'Female Litigants', pp. 82–83, and *Medieval Women and Urban Justice*, Kindle edition, Chapter 2; Erin McGibbon Smith, 'The Participation of Women in the Fourteenth-Century Manor Court of Sutton-in-the-Isle', *Marginalia* 1 (2005), II, http://merg.soc.srcf.net/journal/05margins/smith.php (accessed 11 June 2020); and Stevens, 'London Women', pp. 77–83, and 'London's Married Women', p. 117.

18 DURH 3/14 f. 65v. This was one of many debts pursued by the executors of Bishop Walter Skirlaw.

19 ZFL 192 fol. 4r.

20 ZJB 2/1.

21 Durham Priory Halmote Court Rolls, Summer 1380. As late as 1587, widow Agnes Hutcheson pursued debts of 25s. and 35s. in the Durham bishopric village of Bishop Middleham: DHC1/I/39 fol. 234v.

22 ZFL 192 fol. 1v ff.

23 DURH 3/13 fol. 309r -348v *passim*.

24 DURH 3/12 fol. 138r.

25 *Records of the Borough of Crossgate*, pp. 13–14.

26 Stevens, 'London's married women', pp. 118–119. Phipps found that such debts were incurred post-marriage: *Medieval Women and Urban Justice*, Kindle edition, Chapter 2.

27 *Records of the Borough of Crossgate*, p. 52.

28 *Records of the Borough of Crossgate*, p. 42.

29 *Records of the Borough of Crossgate*, p. 326

30 *Records of the Borough of Crossgate*, pp. 148, 152, 160.
31 *Records of the Borough of Crossgate*, p. 170.
32 'Conisbrough Court Records.'
33 DURH 3/13 fol. 266v - 468r, to 3/14 fol. 1r-75v *passim*.
34 *Court Rolls of the Manor of Wakefield*, *passim*.
35 DURH 3/13 fol. 309r.
36 Phipps, *Medieval Women and Urban Justice*, Kindle edition, Chapter 2.
37 *Court Rolls of the Manor of Wakefield, vol. 3: 1313 to 1316*, p. 96.
38 Phipps, 'Female Litigants', pp. 87–91.
39 DURH 3/13 fol. 288v-289r, 309v, 313r, 342v, 348v.
40 Durham Priory Halmote Court Rolls, Summer 1381.
41 Briggs, 'Empowered or Marginalized', pp. 26–27.
42 A very small number of Durham men were fined for leyrwite, such as William Davison 'for leyrwite committed with Isabella the tenant of William White': Durham Priory Halmote Court Rolls, Summer 1478.
43 ZFL 192 fol. 1v ff.; DURH 3/13 fol., 309r-v, 3/14 fol. 66r, 156r. Even in the seventeenth century, female bishopric tenants were treated similarly to male tenants as in 1642 when three women and five men were cited for failing to keep their fences in repair: DHC1/I/79 fol. 436r.
44 Sandy Bardsley, *Venomous Tongues: Speech and Gender in Late Medieval England* (Philadelphia, 2006), esp. pp. 36–38, 82–89, and 99–105; Marjorie McIntosh, *Controlling Misbehavior in England, 1370–1600* (Cambridge, 1998), pp. 31–32, 57–62; Phipps, *Medieval Women and Urban Justice*, Kindle version, Chapter 5.
45 Durham Priory Halmote Court Rolls, Summer 1390, Autumn 1391.
46 P. L. Larson, *Conflict & Compromise in the Late Medieval Countryside: Lords and Peasants in Durham, 1349–1400* (New York, 2006), pp. 105–106; on the emergence of scolding 'as a legal category' see Bardsley, *Venomous Tongues*, pp. 82–89 and 99–105. McIntosh found increasing concern over sexual misbehavior starting only in 1460: *Controlling Misbehavior*, pp. 68–74 (quotation on p. 70).
47 Larson, *Conflict & Compromise*, pp. 186–189; Bardsley, *Venomous Tongues*, esp. pp. 34–44; Cordelia Beattie, 'Governing Bodies: Law Courts, Male Householders, and Single Women in Late Medieval England', in *idem*, Anna Maslakovic, and Sarah Rees Jones (eds.), *The Medieval Household in Christian Europe, C. 850-C. 1550: Managing Power, Wealth, and Body* (Turnhout, 2003), pp. 199–220; on the interconnection of assault with interfamilial disputes see Phipps, *Medieval Women and Urban Justice*, Kindle version, Chapter 4.
48 R.A. Lomas and A.J. Piper (eds.), *Durham Cathedral Priory Rentals, volume I: Bursars Rentals*, Surtees Society vol. 198 (Newcastle, 1989), pp. 32–65, 71–128; Whittle, 'Inheritance, marriage, widowhood, and remarriage', pp. 35–36.
49 Durham Priory Halmote Court Rolls, 1388–1414 *passim*; DURH 3/13 ff. 4r-494r *passim*, 3/14 ff. 21v-334r *passim*.
50 DURH 3/12 ff. 61r, 185r.
51 DURH 3/17 fol. 47v, 48v: one woman and five men leased the village of Burdon.
52 Larson, 'Widow-right', p. 184.
53 Larson, 'Widow-right', pp. 185–188.
54 That tension was part of the original 'golden age for women' debate and now features in analysis of the European Marriage Pattern in the Little Divergence; see Tine De Moor and Jan Luiten Van Zanden, 'Girl Power: The European Marriage Pattern and Labour Markets in the North Sea Region in the Late Medieval and Early Modern Period', *EcHR*, 63:1 (2010), pp. 1–33; Jane Humphries and Jacob Weisdorf, 'The Wages of Women in England, 1260–1850', *Journal of Economic History*, 75:2 (2015), pp. 405–477, and Judith M. Bennett, 'Wretched Girls, Wretched Boys and the European Marriage Pattern in England (c. 1250–1350)', *Continuity and Change*, 34 (2019), pp. 315–347.
55 Larson, *Conflict and Compromise*, pp. 171–223.

56 *Court Rolls of the Manor of Wakefield from October 1639 to September 1640*, p. x.
57 DURH 3/14 fol. 211r, 229r.
58 DURH 3/14 fol. 175r, 186r, 204v, 315v.
59 DHC 1/I/1 fol. 5v, 16v. See Barbara Todd, 'The Remarrying Widow: A Stereotype Reconsidered', in Mary Prior (ed.), *Women in English Society 1500–1800* (Methuen, 1985), p. 58.
60 Stevens compares several studies of women's participation in litigation: 'London Women', p. 84; Phipps, *Medieval Women and Urban Justice*, Kindle Version, Chapter 2, and Conclusion.
61 Larson, 'Widow-right'.

8
PROPERTY OVER PATRIARCHY? REMARRIED WIDOWS AS LITIGANTS IN THE RECORDS OF GLASGOW'S COMMISSARY COURT, 1615–1694

Rebecca Mason[1]

In the spring of 1670, Jonet Love, the twenty-year-old daughter and heiress of her late father William Love, a maltman in Paisley, embarked on a bitter legal battle before Glasgow's commissary court. Jonet was litigating against her father's widow, Agnes Montgomerie.[2] (It is unclear if Agnes was Jonet's mother or stepmother, as Agnes was referred to as William's 'relict' [widow] throughout the case.) Agnes had remarried since William's death, with the clerk noting that her new husband John Fork, a lawyer's clerk in Paisley, appeared 'for his interest'. Jonet – with the support of her uncles in their capacity as legal guardians – accused Agnes of refusing to deliver her inheritance, consisting of various household items, books, weaponry, riding gear, and pieces of gold and silver jewellery. John – a man seemingly well-versed in the intricacies of the law, presumably due to his occupation – is noted to have replied on behalf of his wife Agnes, alleging before the commissar judge that the goods had passed to Agnes as her widow's share of goods, and that she was not expected to answer as a response would 'prejudg [prejudice] him' as her husband. John also argued that his wife Agnes had transferred ownership of the goods in question to him at 'the tyme of her mariage'. According to marital property law, the goods now rightfully belonged to him. Despite this, and after much deliberation, the commissar judge ordered Agnes and her husband John to return the property to Jonet as the rightful heir of the estate.[3]

Property quarrels between Jonet, Agnes and John were to last many years. In the summer of 1673, three years after the initial litigation, Jonet appealed to the commissar judge yet again; however, on this occasion she appeared as a married woman, with her husband William Fyff named 'for his interest'. In the records, Jonet further escalated her grievances, accusing Agnes of 'maliciouslie' hiding and embezzling her late father's deeds. She also accused John of borrowing a large sum of money from her late father shortly before his death, and asserted that

DOI: 10.4324/9780429278037-9

Agnes and John had contracted a marriage 'within ane verie short space eftir the defuncts [William's] deceas', insinuating, perhaps, that their hasty marriage was forged in an attempt to divert property away from her as the rightful heir of the estate. She further accused Agnes and John of misappropriating goods beyond the specific allegations she had made in 1670, and asserted that Agnes and John had repeatedly refused to appear before the commissary court when summoned, on numerous occasions, to answer to these allegations.[4]

This ongoing disagreement between a married daughter and a remarried widow exemplifies the ambiguities within the operation of marital property law and married women's legal status that have been highlighted by recent research into the realities of women's access to justice in Scotland and Europe.[5] Even though women's legal status and property rights were significantly regulated in Scottish legal handbooks on marriage, women regularly appeared as pursuers and defenders in a range of disputes related to their rights to property, although to varying degrees.[6] Married daughters (like Jonet) demanded their share of inheritance and remarried widows (like Agnes) claimed a customary share of their late husbands' property. Husbands (like William) supported their wives' litigation as they held a vested interest in their wives' inherited goods, while other husbands (like John) attempted to exploit the strictures of marital property law by emphasising their patriarchal control over their wives' property and person. In early modern Scotland, a husband was considered the legal, economic, political and moral head of his household; dependents – notably his wife, children and other subordinates (male and female) – were deemed to have inferior, restricted legal rights while living under his authority.[7] Yet, as the above dispute demonstrates, married women were intrinsically involved in their property dealings, and could be named as pursuers or defenders in disputes surrounding their inheritance, marriage and widowhood rights. Moreover, litigation concerning a remarried widow and her property not only threatened to disrupt relationships within and between families but also overtly challenged her new husband's patriarchal authority as superior manager of their marital property.

In broader contexts, however, the legal battle between Jonet and Agnes touches on some of the complex legal circumstances experienced by remarried widows as litigants in early modern Scotland. The distribution of a household's patrimony on the death of a husband, as well as the organisation of a new household following a widow's remarriage, involved complex negotiations between unequal actors with multiple and often competing interests. Widows were required to transfer or secure inheritance portions to their children (or to their children's legal guardians if they were minor) on remarriage, primarily to prevent the stepfather from seizing control of assets.[8] Yet, as can be seen from the opening dispute between Jonet and Agnes, remarriage sometimes brought into conflict opposing claims to the same property, with disputes often lasting many years. Heirs (either children or kin relations) brought remarried widows (who were often their mothers or stepmothers) to court to assert their claim to property that they considered had been misappropriated. The husbands of remarried widows, with their own interests in the property that marriage provided, asserted ownership of their wives' customary share of the marital estate, citing – and thereby attempting to reinforce – their patriarchal control over their wives and their households.[9]

This chapter will demonstrate, quantitatively and qualitatively, that remarried widows were visible litigants in a wide range of issues concerning their blended marital status and diverse property rights, and that court clerks carefully mapped their varied identities within the records of Glasgow's commissary court. Remarried widows are often reclassified as married women within historiography on women's access to law, mainly due to their married status.[10] Yet, as this chapter will show, concealing remarried widows within the broad category of 'married women' is a methodological oversight that overlooks their complex marital identities, as well as their legal obligations to children and kin relatives from previous marriages. Moreover, looking closely at remarried widows' litigation in court records sheds further light on the roles and interests of their new husbands, including the specific challenges they faced when entangled in litigation concerning their wives' blended marital status. In doing so, this chapter argues that remarried widows should be considered as a distinctive category of married female litigant in order to explore the diversity of married women's backgrounds and life-choices that influenced their access to justice in early modern Scotland. Female litigants are here defined as women who pursued actions (pursuers) or defended actions (defenders). Detailed analysis of nearly two-thousand lawsuits recorded in Glasgow's commissary court between 1615 and 1694 reveals the myriad ways in which remarried widows and their new husbands contested and negotiated their varied rights to property in daily life. By locating and categorising remarried widows as a distinctive group of married female litigant, this chapter provides a more nuanced picture of the operation of marital property law and negotiation of patriarchy in relation to women's rights on remarriage in early modern Scotland.

Property and status

The Scottish context provides a particularly compelling case study to explore remarried widows as litigants because Scottish women retained their family surname on marriage.[11] In fact, throughout the early modern period, England was the only country in Europe in which married women routinely took their husbands' surname.[12] Unlike their counterparts in England, whose status, wealth and property became subsumed by their husbands on marriage under coverture, Scottish women retained greater control over their property, thus assisting them in remaining economically and legally active. John Finlay and Elizabeth Ewan uncovered married women acting as procurators (lawyers) in Scottish courts for their husbands and children during the late medieval period.[13] Cathryn Spence found that married women formed the largest proportion of female litigants in the debt records of the burgh (town) courts of Edinburgh, Haddington and

Linlithgow between 1560 and 1640, locating wives – including remarried widows – as producers and consumers of a wide range of goods and foodstuffs.[14] Yet, while it is now accepted that married women were considerably active in legal actions and property networks in early modern Scottish towns, less attention has been paid to the ways in which Scottish women came into contact with property through inheritance, marriage and widowhood, or how remarriage affected women's property rights and legal status as litigants in the courts.[15]

Much of what we know about widows and remarriage during the early modern period relies on scholarship that is focussed on England. Historians of early modern England have primarily investigated the range of choices available to those women who sought another partner, crediting their socioeconomic status, their stage of lifecycle, the presence (or absence) of children and their place of residence in dictating their marriage choices.[16] To date, only a handful of studies have considered the unique status and experiences of remarried widows in early modern Scotland. Winifred Coutts' study of the considerable use of litigation made by elite remarried widows in the Court of Session – Scotland's central civil court – in Edinburgh has brought to light the extent and nature of their litigating activities. Coutts estimated that around 17% of female litigants who appeared before the court in 1600 were remarried widows, with many embroiled in property disputes connected to their previous marital estates.[17] Unfortunately it is quite difficult to ascertain the rate of remarriage among the lower orders in Scotland as civil registration was not mandatory until the nineteenth century.[18] It has been estimated, however, that in early modern England, at least a quarter of all marriages involved at least one party remarrying.[19]

Much work has been done in recent years to dispel the persistent narrative that women were legally and economically incapacitated within marriage, particularly for the English context.[20] Yet, despite significant developments in understanding the reasons as to why a widow would (or could) remarry, more research is clearly needed to fully understand the impact of remarriage on women's legal status and property rights during the early modern period. Further, much less is known about remarriage in the context of early modern Scotland, especially for the middling to lower orders. In addition to further strengthening existing conclusions regarding women's access to justice during the early modern period, this chapter investigates the status of women in relation to their diverse family relationships, socio-economic status and blended marital careers, further highlighting that women – especially married women – were not a homogenous group with a shared way of dealing with the court. This chapter therefore contributes to a burgeoning literature that investigates the reintegration of the role of women into legal histories.

As previously mentioned, Scottish women retained their family surname on marriage. As such, Scottish women are easily traceable in court records, documented by clerks in relation to their marital status and their kin networks. Scribal conventions in Scottish court records assist in determining the cause and nature of women's legal actions. Rather than simply recording women in relation to their marital status – as single, married or widowed – clerks and notaries recorded women in relation to a wide range of descriptors, including details surrounding their blended marital careers and diverse family relationships.[21] The reality of married women's access to courts in early modern Scotland was much more complex than previously imagined, depending on whether she was an unmarried heiress seeking restitution of her inheritance, a wife participating in credit arrangements on behalf of her absent husband, or a remarried widow safeguarding her widow's estate within a subsequent marriage. When claims to property were tenuous or left unrecorded outside the realms of the law, remarriage introduced significant financial complications that could be escalated before the courts.

The reasons why it is important to disentangle remarried widows' litigation from the legal actions of married women are twofold. First, married women theoretically required their husband's consent before engaging in legal action, while widows were considered as independent legal persons.[22] Second, alongside the loss of their independent legal status, married women surrendered much of their property (including the rents of their inherited and liferent land) to their husbands under the doctrine of *jus mariti*, while widows assumed full ownership of one-third of their husbands' goods (which increased to one-half if no children were born of the marriage).[23] Widows were also entitled to claim the custom of terce (lifelong rights to one-third of the husband's landed estate) or the lifelong use of their jointly-owned land (known as land held in 'conjunct fee').[24] The Scottish legal writer Sir James Balfour in his 1579 legal treatise *Practicks* even asserted that a widow's entitlement to a share of her husband's property – in this context, terce land – was so she 'may the mair easilie be maryit with ane uther man.'[25] Yet a woman's transition from widowhood back to wifehood, and her resubjugation within the marital household, clearly raises pertinent issues surrounding her property and status. How did remarried widows and their new husbands navigate the prevailing rights of the late husbands' children and/or heirs, who maintained a vested interest in property? How did the theoretical requirement for consent function in practice when remarried widows were called to court as defenders? And how did the husbands of remarried widows assert their patriarchal authority when faced with overlapping claims to their wives' – and, by extension, their own – property? While this chapter does not claim to provide all the answers to these complex questions, it does attempt to address many of these pertinent issues in the context of remarried widows' litigation in Glasgow's commissary court.

Women and litigation in Glasgow's commissary court

The legal business of Scotland's commissary courts has received scant attention in historical scholarship, especially in relation to women's litigation.[26] After the Scottish Reformation of 1559–1560 – when the country transformed from a Catholic nation to a Protestant state – the commissary courts were in disarray, and attempts to restructure them in the years that followed led to episodes of jurisdictional chaos and confusion.[27] By the start of the seventeenth century, the principal commissary court in Edinburgh exercised exclusive jurisdiction over matrimonial law; only the four commissar judges in Edinburgh could theoretically decide if a marriage could be dissolved on the grounds of adultery and desertion. The inferior commissary courts – twenty-three of which were scattered across the country – inherited much of the jurisdiction of the courts of the bishops' officials, and their main business remained the confirmation of testaments.[28] They also dealt with other executry and civil matters relating to property, such as the confirmation of tutorial and curatorial inventories (given up by the legal guardian of a fatherless child), actions for aliment (maintenance of an abandoned wife, fatherless child or close relative) and suits for debt up to a limit of £40 Scots. Disputes raised in the inferior commissary courts involving women included the administration of testaments, claims for the mishandling of heirship goods, the recovery of debts, claims for care provision (of both legitimate and illegitimate children), and the implementation of the provisions of marriage contracts, to list a few. As the inferior commissary courts were mainly concerned with determining the legal responsibility of individuals for debts and the rightful transmission of property following a person's death, they heard a wide range of disputes involving women and their property.

In Glasgow, the commissary court was situated in the south-west tower of Glasgow's Cathedral, and was headed by a commissar judge and his deputy.[29] The commissary court was one of many courts in Glasgow, and administered civil law alongside the regality, sheriff and burgh (town) courts. While the records of Glasgow's commissary court are fairly formulaic, they are also rich in detail. The Register of Decreets and Decrees Dative mainly recorded cases that reached the final stages of litigation; cases that were settled outside of court are therefore largely missing from the register. The majority of recorded cases in the register were successful actions (where the commissar judge pronounced his 'decreet' in favour of the pursuer); however, on a number of occasions the defender was absolved. Unfortunately, depositions (witness statements from litigants and witnesses) in support of these suits have not survived. Clerks did include, however, the pleas and responses of pursuers, defenders and their legal counsel, making it possible to ascertain the context and nature of a dispute.

The challenges of using early modern court records are well-known.[30] Specific details within the records, such as particular behaviours and motives, cannot be taken as accurate accounts of events. Rather than attempting to locate true statements from narratives created and mediated through judicial processes, Cordelia Beattie has suggested that historians who rely on legal records should 'move beyond the alleged truths of the dispute itself on to broader cultural attitudes', such as the depiction and interpretation of attitudes to gender.[31] Tim Stretton has urged similar caution, advising historians to 'pay closer attention to language – our own as well as that of our subjects' to allow for alternative readings and possibilities.[32] Stretton has also suggested that using measured phrases, such as 'according to the plaintiff's bill', or 'the alleged assault', avoids making bold statements about what happened or who was at fault.[33] Rather than fixating on the authenticity of constructed narratives in the commissary court records, this chapter acknowledges the influence of legal counsel and officials in constructing and dictating women's legal claims to property. While remaining mindful of the limitations of records that were filtered through the male-dominated legal profession, attention is instead focussed on legal 'facts', such as the percentage of remarried widows as litigants, and the subjects and outcomes of their disputes and trials.

Remarried widows appeared personally, with (or through) their husbands or by way of an appointed procurator (lawyer) in the commissary court, not only to pursue or defend actions but to register deeds or take part publicly in legal actions as interested parties.[34] As a pursuer, a remarried widow could begin judicial proceedings by obtaining a formal written order from the court, such as a 'libel precept'. A libel precept was a formal statement of the grounds on which a civil prosecution was made, and it contained the name of the judge, the name of the pursuer(s) and defender(s), and specific details surrounding the case. The libel precept would then be delivered to the defender's dwelling place in the presence of 'diverse witnesses', summoning him or her to 'compeir [appear] in judgment' and answer at the instance of the other party.[35] If the defender failed to appear before the court on a specified day, further details of the summons were then read out at the Market Cross on a market day or at the kirk on the Sabbath as a form of public proclamation.

Due to Glasgow's distinctively mercantile and urban culture, many Glaswegian widows conducted subsequent marriages with men. Prospect of social advancement and economic improvement in Glasgow attracted opportunist men from all corners of Scotland, with the city's population more than doubling from 6,000 inhabitants in 1600 to 15,000 in 1700.[36] A widow's remarriage, in particular, supported the city's economy by encouraging the flow of goods within and between marriages and families. As a consequence of war, famine, plague, and merchant seafaring, Scottish women were frequently widowed, with many choosing to conduct a subsequent marriage when possible. Margaret Sanderson, in her study of individuals, families and communities in sixteenth-century Scotland, found that widows who lived in lively, populated Scottish towns – like Glasgow – tended to conduct subsequent marriages with men from the same mercantile or craft background as their former partners.[37] Despite a lack of information on the rate of remarriage in Scotland, it is possible to piece together details captured in commissary court records with information recorded in local parish registers to trace the marital careers of individual Glaswegian widows who remarried. Lilias Young, aged around twenty, wed John Wallace, a maltman of Glasgow, in February 1653, was widowed in 1656, then married the merchant Alexander Watson less than a year later.[38] Dorothy Dunlop wed the merchant James Stewart in 1614, was widowed after thirty years of marriage in 1644, then married the merchant Cuthbert Campbell three years later in 1647.[39] Margaret Hamilton married Patrick Bell, son of the provost of Glasgow, in 1634, was widowed twenty-two years later in 1656, then married Robert Hamilton less than a year later.[40] While these three women had varying experiences of widowhood and remarriage— Lilias was widowed for a short period of time in her early twenties, while Dorothy and Margaret were married to their first husbands for decades before returning to married life once again as older widows – each sought another husband for reasons that remain elusive in the records.

Table 8.1 details the range of cases heard before Glasgow's commissary court throughout the seventeenth century. As expected, most of the business of the court related to testamentary and other civil disputes. Nearly one-third of all lawsuits were testamentary disputes, mainly relating to an outstanding debt when a person had died. A dispute was identified as testamentary when the pursuer or defender produced a testament-dative (intestate) or testament-testamentar (will and legacy) as part of their evidence. The court also dealt with a wide range of credit and debt-related disputes that involved both living and deceased persons. Aside from hearing testamentary and debt-related disputes, which routinely pulled in women from all social backgrounds, the commissary court also heard cases directly relating to women and the transmission of property through inheritance, marriage and widowhood. Matters raised in Glasgow's commissary court involving remarried widows included claims for inheritance, provisions

TABLE 8.1 Types of court cases dealt with by Glasgow's commissary court, 1615–1645 and 1658–1694

Type of court case	Number of cases
Testamentary	552 (29%)
Credit and debt	451 (23.7%)
Food and drink	253 (13.3%)
Merchandise	201 (10.6%)
Landlord-tenant relations, including removal of tenants	97 (5.1%)
Family/inheritance business	81 (4.3%)
Widows' interests of terce/conjunct-fee land and *jus relictae*	63 (3.3%)
Service and apprenticeship, including breach of contract	59 (3.1%)
Land-related issues, including boundary disputes and damage to crops	35 (1.8%)
Handling of goods, including recovery of heirship goods and goods pledged for credit	31 (1.6%)
Exhibition of legal documentation	24 (1.3%)
Actions for aliment	24 (1.3%)
Unpaid marriage portions	19 (1.0%)
Defamation	7 (0.4%)
Miscellaneous legal matters	4 (0.2%)
Matrimonial business, including action of adherence	1 (0.1%)
Total number of cases	**1902 (100%)**

Source: National Records of Scotland, Glasgow Commissary Court, Register of Decreets and Decrees Dative, CC9/3/vols. 7, 17, 23, 33.

for widows' estates, actions for aliment, the recovery of heirship goods and the exhibition of legal documentation, which formed roughly 13% of the business of the court.

When considered as a whole, women maintained a strong presence as both pursuers and defenders in Glasgow's commissary court. Tables 8.2 and 8.3 show a detailed breakdown of the sex of pursuers and defenders in the court. Across the period, women appeared as pursuers in approximately 20% of property disputes between 1615 and 1694. During the first half of the seventeenth century, female pursuers appeared in as many as one-quarter of all cases heard before the court. What the data reveals, however, is that women were more likely to be called to defend actions as defenders than pursue cases as pursuers. Women were recorded as defenders in nearly 30% of disputes across the period, increasing from 25% during the first half of the seventeenth century to as many as one-third of defenders in the latter half of the seventeenth century. This high-level of female litigation is rather surprising, mainly because the commissary court overwhelmingly dealt with issues relating to property. The regulation and discipline of women's bodies, actions and speech was instead left to lower-level secular and church courts (such as the burgh court, the kirk sessions and the presbyteries).[41] As a result, women's participation as litigants in the commissary court largely mirrored the activities, pursuits and concerns of men, though to a lesser extent.

Table 8.4 details the marital status of female litigants in the court records. Married women formed the majority of women pursuing cases across the period, accounting for nearly 43% of female pursuers. Wives were also highly visible as defenders, accounting for over 37% of female defenders. The legal actions of wives can be further divided into three categories: wives as sole litigants; wives

TABLE 8.2 Sex of pursuers in litigation in Glasgow's commissary court, 1615–1645 and 1658–1694

Pursuers	Male	Female	Total cases examined
1615–1645	635 (75.5%)	206 (24.5%)	841
1658–1694	893 (84.2%)	168 (15.8%)	1061
Total	**1528 (80.3%)**	**374 (19.7%)**	**1902**

TABLE 8.3 Sex of defenders in litigation in Glasgow's commissary court, 1615–1645 and 1658–1694

Defenders	Male	Female	Total cases examined
1615–1645	624 (74.2%)	217 (25.8%)	841
1658–1694	715 (67.4%)	346 (32.6%)	1061
Total	**1339 (70.4%)**	**563 (29.6%)**	**1902**

Source: National Records of Scotland, Glasgow commissary court, Register of Decreets and Decrees Dative, 1615–1694, CC9/3/vols. 7, 17, 23, 33.

TABLE 8.4 Marital and relational status of female litigants in Glasgow's commissary court, 1615–1645 and 1658–1694

Marital status	Pursuers	Defenders
Widowed	122 (32.6%)	239 (42.5%)
Married	159 (42.5%)	209 (37.1%)
named as primary litigant (husband 'for his interest')	62 (16.6%)	83 (14.7%)
named as co-party with husband	64 (17.1%)	85 (15.1%)
named as remarried widow (husband 'for his interest)	33 (8.8%)	41 (7.3%)
Daughter	52 (13.9%)	44 (7.8%)
Female kin (mother, aunt, sister)	10 (2.7%)	8 (1.4%)
No marital or relational classification	31 (8.3%)	63 (11.2%)
Total	**374**	**563**

Source: National Records of Scotland, Glasgow commissary court, Register of Decreets and Decrees Dative, 1615–1694, CC9/3/ vols. 7, 17, 23, 33.

as co-parties with their husbands; and remarried widows. Sheenan Hutton, in her study of women's economic activities in fourteenth-century Ghent, similarly classified women as 'active women, passive women, and consenting wives' in court records, differentiating between wives who were named after their husbands from those who appeared as principal litigants in disputes.[42]

Aside from married women, widows were highly visible as female litigants, accounting for nearly one-third of pursuers and over 43% of female defenders across the period. When recorded in litigation, widows primarily appeared as executrices to their former husbands' estates, which entitled them to sue debtors and uplift rents owed to their former husbands, and made them liable for settling outstanding credit arrangements.[43] Table 8.4 also reveals the extent to which court clerks recorded relational descriptors when women appeared as litigants. Aside from marital status, nearly 17% of pursuers and over 9% of defenders were identified as daughters, mothers, aunts, sisters and nieces in the court records. A significant number of women were not assigned a marital or relational descriptor, accounting for over 8% of pursuers and 11% of defenders. It is possible that women without a marital or relational descriptor were single women, wives, widows or remarried widows, but this cannot be ascertained.

When a wife appeared as a primary pursuer or defender in the commissary court, her husband was always named 'for his interest'. For instance, when Jonet Wood, the wife of Alexander Mayne, appeared as a pursuer in 1625 concerning unpaid rent on a brewhouse she had inherited and subsequently leased, her husband was named 'for his interest'.[44] A wife was categorised as a co-party in a suit when her name was included after her husband's name in the record. Catherine Cauldwell, for instance, was named after her husband Patrick Wilson in a suit initiated by Patrick before the commissary court in 1625.[45] Patrick, as the primary pursuer, alleged that he had purchased a horse from John Cauldwell and his wife (who remained nameless) at the Glasgow Fair and that he was still waiting for the animal to be delivered to his dwelling place. If Patrick died before receiving the horse, his wife Catherine would have been entitled to pursue John through the courts as a co-party to the transaction. When a remarried widow was identified in the court record, her blended marital status was recorded, with her current husband named 'for his interest'. When Merry King, the widow of Patrick Aikenhead, a bookbinder in Newcastle and resident of Glasgow, appointed her father Nicolas King as her son's legal guardian in 1694, her new husband David Longdale was named 'for his interest'.[46] Remarried widows were recorded as nearly 9% of female pursuers and over 7% of female defenders across the period. When focussing solely on those female litigants who were married, remarried widows formed 21% of married female pursuers and 20% of married female defenders. While these figures are not drastically high, they warrant specific attention as remarried widows' litigation primarily concerned the negotiation of relationships within blended families and the transmission of property within and between marriages.

Inclusion of the stock phrase 'for his interest' in Scottish court records has garnered specific attention among historians in recent years. Gordon DesBrisay and Karen Sander Thomson, in their study of married women and debt litigation in seventeenth-century Aberdeen, argue that the phrase 'for his interest' signalled 'both the nominality of the husband's role in the transaction and his legal responsibility for it.'[47] Cathryn Spence, in her study of women's credit networks in early modern Edinburgh, similarly argues that while the phrase 'for his interest' rarely appeared in debt records in Edinburgh, clerks often named a woman 'for her interest', with the phrase denoting legal responsibility for a debt, but not solely between husbands and wives.[48] In the cases analysed for this chapter, however, clerks frequently employed the phrase 'for his interest' when signalling married women's obligations to pursue or answer for property received, due or taken through inheritance, marriage or widowhood. The circulation of property within and between marriages and families somewhat alleviated the general legal principle that married women were subjugated to their husbands, especially when their legal actions concerned inheritance from kin, care provision for children from previous marriages, or marital property tied to previous marital estates. In Glasgow's commissary court, the phrase 'for his interest' therefore alludes to married women's *de facto* legal capability and responsibility to pursue actions or defend cases relating to property, as we will see further below in the context of remarried widows' litigation. Remarriage, in particular, sparked a series of negotiations that, if left unchecked, could result in significant levels of interfamilial discord before the courts. Key issues – such as transferring or securing children's inheritance portions in deeds, safeguarding care provision for infants from kin relatives, and protecting the widow's estate and other forms of marital property – frequently drew in remarried widows and their new husbands as litigants. When disputes were escalated before the courts, the husbands of remarried widows, in particular, could potentially gain or lose out on a significant proportion of the property their wives had accumulated from previous marriages.

Access to resources

When appearing as pursuers in the records, remarried widows frequently accused their late husbands' heirs of refusing to honour the property arrangements agreed in their marriage contracts. In a case heard before Glasgow's commissary court between December 1693 and February 1694, Anna How, the widow of John How, alongside her new husband William Miller, pursued her late husband's nieces and heirs, Anna and Mary Marshall, for her liferent payments.[49] Anna had wed John in 1682, was widowed in 1688, then remarried in 1690.[50] As John's nieces were jointly served as heirs to his estate, it appears that John did not have any living children at the time of his death. Anna alleged that her first husband John had placed her in 'conjunct fee' (joint ownership) of lands in Renfrewshire worth £100 Scots in liferent per year in their marriage contract, and that she had attempted to retrieve payment from her late husband's nieces ever since his death in 1688. William, appearing 'in name and behalf of' his wife Anna, also informed the commissar judge that he had (allegedly) visited Anna and Mary Marshall at their dwelling place on numerous occasions and implored them to deliver the yearly liferent payments, to no avail. As well as the outstanding sum of £700 Scots in liferent, the clerk also noted that Anna 'and her said husband for his entres' had requested further payment of 500 merks as a late penalty fee.

In response, the defenders Anna and Mary Marshall, through their legal counsel, alleged that Anna's liferent was only worth £60 Scots per year. They also accused Anna's new husband William of uplifting rents from the land totalling £54 Scots per year since their marriage in 1690, a claim which he denied under oath. Anna also denied any knowledge of her late husband's credit arrangements, and insisted that her former husband John did not provide her with bonds or deeds worth her liferent payments before his death. The commissar judge, on this occasion, ruled in favour of Anna and her husband, ordering the defenders to deliver the outstanding liferent amount, and to continue to pay £100 Scots yearly to Anna during her lifetime. Favourable legal decisions did not mean that pursuers were guaranteed immediate payment, however. Four months later, William reappeared on Anna's behalf before the commissary court, alleging that his wife's nieces were still refusing to honour the property arrangements detailed in his wife's first marriage contract.[51] This time, however, William asked the court to send town officers to their dwelling place in order to seize assets worth the outstanding sum. The transmission of women's property between marriages was clearly not always smooth.

Remarried widows were expected to relinquish control of their children's inheritance to appointed legal guardians on their remarriage.[52] Sir John Erskine, in his 1773 *Institutes of the Law of Scotland*, cited 'both the impropriety of a woman's having one under her power who is herself subjected to the power of another' and 'from the bad consequences that might be dreaded from leaving a [child's] estate to the management of one under the influence of his stepfather.'[53] Second marriages were financially complicated, and heirs frequently accused remarried widows of carrying away goods or concealing legal documents that they considered to rightfully belong to them before the commissary court.[54] In 1620, Andro and Christian Anderson, children and heirs of the late John Anderson, accused their father's widow Margaret Anderson and her new husband Matthew Wood 'for his interest' of refusing to deliver household goods left to them in their father's testament. Margaret and her new husband Matthew, through their legal counsel, replied that the property had passed to Margaret as her widow's share of goods, and that ownership of the property was automatically transferred to Matthew on their marriage. After considering the various arguments offered by legal counsel, the commissar judge ordered Margaret and her new husband to return the requested goods to her late husband's children.[55] Later that very same month, the five children and heirs of the deceased George Leggat accused their father's widow, Isobel Thompson, and her new husband, James Hamilton, 'for his interest' of withholding their inheritance portions and misappropriating goods that they considered belonged to them as heirs of their father's estate. With the assistance of their legal guardians and counsel, the children alleged that Isobel had failed to adequately divide George's moveable estate before her remarriage, and that she had taken more than she was due as her widow's share. Ruling in favour of the pursuers, the commissar judge ordered Isobel and her new husband James to return the property or else to pay the requested amount, totalling a hefty 1,280 merks.[56]

The husbands of remarried widows clearly supported their wives' litigation when claims to property due to them as widows were contested; however, they were also drawn into disputes that threatened their control of their wives' goods. Moreover, these cases represent a significant difference in the conceptualisation of married women's status in theory and practice, where a remarried widow's responsibility to negotiate the interests of her late husband's children and heirs threatened to undermine her newly formed household economy, as well as her new husband's patriarchal authority.

Many remarried widows brought young children from their previous marriages into subsequent marriages. Children under the age of seven typically resided with their mother after their father's death, while older children came under the care of members of their father's kingroup before entering apprenticeships and service in their early teens.[57] A mother's financial obligation towards her children after the death of a father was subject to much deliberation in legal handbooks. The legal writer Erskine noted that mothers should only be liable to provide care provision for the children after paternal ascendants had been obliged to contribute (grandfathers, uncles and so on).[58] Blended families clearly had the best chance of living in harmony when contracts secured the inheritance and provisions of all children. In 1664, John Connell drew up a contract concerning his forthcoming marriage to Jean Dunlop, a widow. Her three children – James,

Jean and Barbara Dunlop – born from her previous marriage to John Dunlop, a landowner from Ayrshire, were all named in the contract.[59] John swore to receive Jean and her children 'all in familie with me', promising that he would provide food and shelter for his new wife and stepchildren, and that each of the children were to be 'put to the scholles for learning', according to their rank and degree. In return, however, John noted that the children's 'friends' (i.e. former husband's kin relatives) were required to pay him twenty merks yearly per child until each child had reached the age of fourteen.

The reliance on their former husband's kin relatives meant that many remarried widows and their new husbands frequently appeared as pursuers when embroiled in litigation surrounding actions for unpaid care provision. In 1620, Agnes Halden, the widow of Gabriel Maxwell, and new wife of James Mowet 'for his interest', pursued William Maxwell – her daughter's legal guardian – for unpaid child maintenance. James, appearing on behalf of his wife Agnes, alleged that his stepdaughter Grissell was in 'his custodie and keiping', and that ever since his marriage to Agnes in October 1617, he had kept her in 'meit, drink, cleithing and bedding' relative to her estate. William, as Grissell's uncle and legal guardian, had control of her inheritance while she was a minor, and was liable to pay for her sustenance. James requested, and was granted, a yearly payment of £100 Scots per year, with expenses to continue for a further one year and ten months, when Grissell turned fourteen.[60]

Disputes surrounding the care of older children also sparked heated arguments between remarried widows and their late husbands' kin relatives. In the spring of 1670, Margaret Mathie, the widow of James Brock, now married to John Crun, alleged before the court that since her former husband's death in 1666, she and her new husband had maintained her former husband's three children 'in household and Familie', providing them with 'meit, drink, bedding and abulziementis [clothing]'. She alleged that her children's uncle legal guardian – John Brock – had promised on multiple occasions to pay her eighty merks per child as compensation for childcare; a claim which he denied. In fact, John Brock, appearing on behalf of two of Margaret's children, disputed Margaret's claims, insisting that the children's 'labour and work' was, in fact, 'worth the[i]r intertainement'. John also informed the commissar judge that Margaret's eldest daughter had left the household shortly after her father's death, and that she was now 'hyred as ane ordinarie servant' in another household where she also 'works for hir meit'. The commissar acquitted Margaret Brock from paying for her care, but ordered John to deliver eighty merks to Margaret and her new husband in satisfaction of the care they had provided to her two remaining children.[61] Three months later, however, Margaret's new husband John Crun reappeared before the commissary court, alleging that he was still awaiting the payment.[62]

The provisioning of children was also mentioned in broader disputes that drew in remarried widows as litigants. In 1694, Jean Findlay, the widow of John Ritchie, now the new wife of James Reid, appeared as a pursuer before the commissary court, with her five children and their appointed legal guardians named as defenders in the lawsuit.[63] Jean, appearing before the commissar judge by herself, alleged that she was owed various sums of money, including £400 Scots for her husband's funeral expenses and care during his protracted illness, £50 Scots for 'alimenting and intertaining' four of their children with a nurse and servant, and various other expenses for 'maintenance of the defuncts familie fra the tyme of his deceis'. Jean also alleged that she was owed 300 merks for baptising and burying a child born shortly after her husband's death. Finally, Jean alleged that her late husband's kingroup had sold much of her husband's property, and that she was owed £30 Scots for the sale of goods due to her as part of her widow's share. In response, her children's legal guardians – members of her late husband's kingroup – alleged that Jean's husband had gifted her with a gold purse with £30 Sterling in cash shortly before his death, and that she was not due any further payment from his moveable estate. Appearing under oath, Jean conceded that while her husband had gifted her the purse, she had used the money for 'what was needful during her said husbands seikness', purchasing brandy, wine, medicines and other 'necessaries'. The commissar judge accepted Jean's plea, but modified and reduced her claim after learning she had received cash shortly before her first husband's death. Moreover, Jean's new husband James is only briefly mentioned 'for his interest' at the start of the dispute, suggesting that he was either absent from Glasgow or that Jean – due to her blended marital status and pressing need for payment – was entitled to pursue her own actions without her husband's direct assistance.

Conclusion

This chapter has sought to argue for locating and categorising remarried widows as a distinctive group of married female litigant in early modern Scotland. While commissary court records cannot fully reveal the intricacies of remarried widows' diverse interactions with the law, these legal documents do provide a valuable insight into the varying types and nature of litigation that remarried widows were embroiled in. Unlike with women married for the first time, remarried widows' experience of litigation – both as pursuers and defenders – was, in many cases, dictated by their particular marital status. Remarried widows pursued their late husbands' kin for care provision for children, fought with children or step-children of the previous marriage over heritable property rights, and sought to protect what they deemed as their widow's share of goods within subsequent marriages. Rather than simply grouping married women and remarried widows together in relation to their legal status as 'wives', this chapter has highlighted the importance of eschewing the homogeneity of collective 'women's experiences' at law during the early modern period, especially in relation to married women.[64] Furthermore, this chapter has also shone a light, albeit briefly, on the experiences of the husbands of remarried widows, a group previously overlooked or homogenised with married men more widely. When considering how property and patriarchy overlapped and interrelated, there needs to be a consideration of how marriage and remarriage affected men's access to property and how their patriarchal authority over their households was perhaps challenged, threatened or even undermined by the complex marital status of their wives.

Notes

1 This research was kindly funded by the Arts and Humanities Research Council [Ref: AH/L013568/1] and the Economic and Social Research Council [Ref: ES/V011847/1]. I am also grateful to the Economic History Society and the Institute for Historical Research for a postdoctoral research fellowship during which this chapter was completed. Special thanks are due to Karin Bowie, Hannah Telling, and the editors of this volume for their comments on earlier drafts of this chapter.
2 Only William is named as Jonet's parent in the birth register. See National Records of Scotland (hereafter NRS), Old Parish Register of Births, Hamilton, 647/10/21.
3 By 1600, £12 Scots was worth £1 sterling; £1 Scots was worth 1s 6d sterling; 1 Scottish merk was worth 1s 1d sterling. English monetary values have been included in parentheses throughout for ease of reference. See A. J. S. Gibson and T. C. Smout, *Prices, Food, and Wages in Scotland, 1550–1780* (Cambridge, 1995). NRS: CC9/3/23/fols. 467–469.
4 NRS: CC9/7/39/fols. 673–678.
5 For married women's legal status in Scotland see Gordon DesBrisay and Karen Sander Thomson, 'Crediting Wives: Married Women and Debt Litigation in the Seventeenth Century', in Elizabeth Ewan and Janay Nugent (eds.), *Finding the Family in Medieval and Early Modern Scotland* (Aldershot, 2008), pp. 85–98; Cathryn Spence, '"For His Interest?" Women, Debt and Coverture in Early Modern Scotland', in Cordelia Beattie and Matthew Frank Stevens (eds.), *Married Women and the Law in Premodern Northwest Europe* (Woodbridge, 2013), pp. 173–190; Cathryn Spence, *Women, Credit and Debt in Early Modern Scotland* (Manchester, 2016); For married women's legal status under coverture in England see Tim Stretton, 'The Legal Identity of Married Women in England and Europe 1500–1700', in Andreas Bauer and Karl H. L. Welker (eds.), *Europa Und Seine Regionen: 2000 Jahre Rechtsgeschichte* (Cologne, 2007), pp. 309–322; Cordelia Beattie and Matthew Frank Stevens (eds.), *Married Women and the Law in Premodern Northwest Europe* (Woodbridge, 2013); Tim Stretton and Krista J. Kesselring (eds.), *Married Women and the Law: Coverture in England and the Common Law World* (Montreal, 2013); Bronach Kane and Fiona Williamson (eds.), *Women, Agency and the Law, 1300–1700* (London, 2013), see Introduction; Alexandra Shepard and Tim Stretton, 'Women Negotiating the Boundaries of Justice, 1300–1700: An Introduction', *Journal of British Studies*, 58:4 (2019), pp. 677–683.
6 *The Practicks of Sir James Balfour of Pittendriech*, 2 vols., ed. P.G. B. McNeill (Edinburgh, 1962–1963), 93, 163; Sir Thomas Hope of Craighall, *Major Practicks*, ed. James Avon Clyde, 2 vols (Edinburgh, 1937–1938), II, 17, 1; Sir James Dalrymple, *Institutions of the Law of Scotland, Deduced from Its Originals, and Collated with the Civil, Canon, and Feudal Laws, and with the Customs of Neighbouring Nations, in Four Books* (Edinburgh, 1693), I, IV, IX, pp. 27–28.
7 Alexandra Shepard, 'From Anxious Patriarchs to Refined Gentlemen? Manhood in Britain, circa 1500–1700', *Journal of British Studies*, 44:2 (2005), pp. 281–295, at p. 283; Janay Nugent, 'Reformed Masculinity: Ministers, Fathers and Male Heads of Households, 1560–1660', in Lynn Abrams and Elizabeth Ewan (eds.), *Nine Centuries of Man: Manhood and Masculinities in Scottish History* (Edinburgh), pp. 39–57.
8 Balfour in his 1579 *Practicks* stated that a widow was expected to 'offer all hir gudis and geir, moveabill and unmoveabill, to renounce and discharge the office of tutorie, gif scho thairefter maryis ane husband.' He also noted that 'the woman may be tutrix testamentar [legal guardian] to hir bairns [children], sa lang as scho remains wedow.'

See Balfour's *Practicks*, p. 116; Sir John Erskine, *Institute of the Law of Scotland in Four Books: In the Order of Sir George Mackenzie Institutions of that Law* (Edinburgh, 1773), I, VII, XXIX, p. 129.

9 Alexandra Shepard has also cited instances of married women who declared themselves worth little or nothing before English courts in a bid to reinforce the strictures of marital property law. Shepard has suggested that 'a woman's marital status may have aided evasion strategies by which witnesses avoided providing an estimate of their means.' See Alexandra Shepard, *Accounting for Oneself: Worth, Status and the Social Order in Early Modern England* (Oxford, 2015), pp. 58–59.

10 These identifications reflected the effects of marriage on women's legal and social status. See Spence, *Women, Credit and Debt*, pp. 12–15; Amy M. Froide, *Never Married: Singlewomen in Early Modern England* (Oxford, 2005), pp. 17–24; Cissie Fairchilds, *Women in Early Modern Europe, 1500–1700* (Harlow, 2007), pp. 35–122; Merry E. Wiesner-Hanks, *Women and Gender in Early Modern Europe*, 3rd ed. (Cambridge, 2008), pp. 55–110; Lyndan Warner, 'Before the Law', in Jane Couchman, Allyson M. Poska, and Katherine A. McIver (eds.), *The Ashgate Research Companion to Women and Gender in Early Modern Europe* (Farnham, 2013), pp. 234–254, at pp. 237–238.

11 For a discussion of this practice, see Jenny Wormald, 'Bloodfeud, Kindred and Government in Early Modern Scotland', *Past & Present*, 87:1 (May 1980), pp. 54–97, at p. 67; Katie Barclay, *Love, Intimacy and Power*, p. 72.

12 Amy L. Erickson, 'Mistresses and Marriage: or, a Short History of the Mrs', *History Workshop Journal*, 78 (Autumn 2014), pp. 39–57, at p. 48.

13 Elizabeth Ewan, 'Scottish Portias: Women in the Courts in Mediaeval Scottish Towns', *Journal of the Canadian Historical Association* 3:1 (1992), pp. 27–43, at pp. 35–36; John Finlay, 'Women and Legal Representation in Early Sixteenth-Century Scotland', in Elizabeth Ewan and Maureen M. Meikle (eds.), *Women in Scotland: 1100–1750* (East Linton, 1999), pp. 165–175, at p. 172.

14 Spence, *Women, Credit and Debt*, p. 47.

15 Tim Stretton has argued that much of the litigation involving stepmothers (who were sometimes remarried widows) centred on the death of a husband and the destination of his property. See Stretton, 'Stepmothers at Law in Early Modern England', pp. 91–107.

16 For scholarship on remarried widows in England, see Barbara J. Todd, 'The Remarrying Widow: A Stereotype Reconsidered', in Mary Prior (ed.), *Women in English Society 1500–1800* (London, New York, 1985), pp. 54–92; Barbara J. Todd, 'Demographic Determinism and Female Agency: The Remarrying Widow Reconsidered… Again', *Continuity and Change*, 9:3 (1994), pp. 421–450; Barbara Hanawalt, 'Remarriage as an Option for Urban and Rural Widows in Late Medieval England', in Susan Sheridan Walker (ed.), *Wife and Widow in Medieval England* (Michigan, 1993), pp. 141–164; Sandra Cavallo and Lyndan Warner (eds.), *Widowhood in Medieval and Early Modern Europe*, 2nd ed. (Abington, 1999), especially chapters 6, 7 and 12; Jane Whittle, 'Inheritance, Marriage, Widowhood and Remarriage: A Comparative Perspective on Women and Landholding in North-East Norfolk, 1440–1580', *Continuity and Change* 13:1 (1998), pp. 33–72; Shannon McSheffrey, 'A Remarrying Widow: Law and Legal Records in Late Medieval London', in Kim Kippen and Lori Woods (eds.), *Worth and Repute: Valuing Gender in Late Medieval and Early Modern Europe: Essays in Honour of Barbara Todd* (Toronto, 2011), pp. 231–252.

17 Winifred Coutts, 'Women and the Law', in *The Business of the College of Justice in 1600: How It Reflects the Economic and Social Life of Scots Men and Women* (Edinburgh, 2003), pp. 135–205.

18 For a discussion of remarriage among the Scottish elites, see Katie Barclay, *Love, Intimacy and Power: Marriage and Patriarchy in Scotland, 1650–1850* (Manchester, 2011), pp. 20–21.

19 Amy Erickson, *Women and Property in Early Modern England* (London, 1993), p. 72.

20 Erickson, *Women and Property*; Tim Stretton, *Women Waging Law in Elizabethan England* (Cambridge, 1998); Beattie and Stevens, *Married Women and the Law in Premodern*

Northwest Europe; Stretton and Kesselring, *Married Women and the Law: Coverture in England and the Common Law World*.
21 Rebecca Mason, 'Women, Marital Status and Law: The Marital Spectrum in Seventeenth-Century Glasgow', *Journal of British Studies*, 58:4 (2019), pp. 787–804, at p. 791.
22 Balfour, *Practicks*, p. 93.
23 Balfour, *Practicks*, pp. 93, 217–218, 294.
24 Dalrymple, *The Institutions of the Law of Scotland*, 2: ii, vi, x, pp. 275–277.
25 Balfour, *Practicks*, pp. 93, 105.
26 Leah Leneman and Thomas Green have both produced detailed studies on the business of Edinburgh's commissary court in relation to matrimonial law. See Leah Leneman, *Alienated Affections: The Scottish Experience of Divorce and Separation 1684–1830* (Edinburgh, 1998); Leah Leneman, *Promises, Promises: Marriage Litigation in Scotland 1698–1830* (Edinburgh, 2003); Thomas Green, *Consistorial Decisions of the Commissaries of Edinburgh 1564 to 1576/7* (Edinburgh, 2014).
27 Green, *Consistorial Decisions*.
28 Gordon Donaldson, 'The Church Courts', in *An Introduction to Scottish Legal History* (Edinburgh, 1958), pp. 363–373, at p. 369.
29 Thomas Green, 'Romano-Canonical Procedure in Reformation Scotland: The Example of the Court of the Commissaries of Edinburgh', *The Journal of Legal History*, 36:3 (2015), pp. 217–235.
30 Natalie Zemon Davis, *Fiction in the Archives: Pardon Tales and Their Tellers in Sixteenth-Century France* (Stanford, 1987), pp. 1–6; Joanne Bailey, 'Voices in Court: Lawyers' or Litigants'?', *Historical Research* 74:186 (November 2001): 392–408; Bronach Kane and Fiona Williamson (eds.), *Women, Agency and the Law, 1300–1700*, pp. 7–8; Tim Stretton, 'Women, Legal Records, and the Problem of the Lawyer's Hand', *Journal of British Studies* 58:4 (October 2019), pp. 684–700.
31 Cordelia Beattie, 'Single Women, Work, and Family: The Chancery Dispute of Jane Wynde and Margaret Clerk', in Michael Goodich (ed.), *Voices from the Bench: The Narratives of Lesser Folk in Medieval Trials* (New York, 2006), pp. 177–202.
32 Stretton, 'Women, Legal Records, and the Problem of the Lawyer's Hand', p. 695.
33 Stretton, 'Women, Legal Records, and the Problem of the Lawyer's Hand', pp. 695–696.
34 Sanderson, *A Kindly Place?*, pp. 102–103.
35 Balfour, *Practicks*, 303.
36 George Smith Pryde, 'The City and Burgh of Glasgow: 1100–1750', in Robert Miller and Joy Tivy (eds.), *The Glasgow Region: A General Survey* (Glasgow, 1958), p. 144.
37 Margaret Sanderson, *A Kindly Place? Living in Sixteenth-Century Scotland* (East Linton, 2002), p. 122.
38 Lilias's first marriage was registered in Glasgow in 1653 (NRS, Register of Banns and marriages, Glasgow, 644/1/230/216). Her first husband died in May 1656 (NRS: CC9/7/32/fols. 101–102. She appeared as a remarried widow before the commissary court in January 1658 (NRS: CC9/3/17/fols. 84–86).
39 Dorothy's first marriage was registered in Glasgow in 1614 (NRS, Register of Banns and marriages, Glasgow, 644/1/230/12). Her second marriage was registered in 1644 (NRS, Register of Banns and marriages, Glasgow, 644/1/230/185).
40 Margaret's multiple marriages were noted in a dispute concerning her widow's estate in 1658. See NRS: CC9/3/17/fols. 173–174.
41 Leah Leneman and Rosalind Mitchison, *Girls in Trouble: Sexuality and Social Control in Rural Scotland, 1660–1780* (Edinburgh, 1998); Leah Leneman and Rosalind Mitchison, *Sin in the City: Sexuality and Social Control in Urban Scotland 1660–1780* (Edinburgh, 1998); Elizabeth Ewan, 'Impatient Griseldas: Women and the Perpetration of Violence in Sixteenth-Century Glasgow', *Florilegium* 28 (2011), pp. 149–168; Alice Glaze, 'Women and Kirk Discipline: Prosecution, Negotiation, and the Limits of Control', *Journal of Scottish Historical Studies*, 36:2 (2016), pp. 125–142.

42 Shennan Hutton, '"On Herself and All Her Property": Women's Economic Activities in Late Medieval Ghent', *Continuity and Change*, 20:3 (December 2005), pp. 325–349.
43 Balfour, *Practicks*, pp. 219–221.
44 NRS: CC9/3/7/ fol. 342.
45 NRS: CC9/3/7/fol. 328.
46 NRS: CC9/3/33/fols. 523–524.
47 DesBrisay and Sander Thomson, 'Crediting Wives', p. 89.
48 Cathryn Spence, '"For His Interest?" Women, Debt and Coverture in Early Modern Scotland', p. 180.
49 NRS: CC9/3/33/fols. 419–421.
50 NRS, Register of banns and marriages, 568/20/fols. 30, 35.
51 NRS : CC9/3/33/fols. 525–527.
52 Balfour, *Practicks*, p. 227.
53 Erskine, *Institute* I, VII, XXIX, p. 129.
54 For scholarship exploring property disputes between remarried mothers and children, see Stretton, 'Stepmothers at Law in Early Modern England', pp. 91–107; Katie Barclay, 'Natural Affection, Children, and Family Inheritance Practices in the Long Eighteenth Century', in Janay Nugent and Elizabeth Ewan (eds.), *Children and Youth in Premodern Scotland* (Woodbridge, 2015), pp. 136–151.
55 NRS: CC9/3/4/fol. 234.
56 NRS: CC9/3/4/fol. 263–264.
57 Balfour, *Practicks*, pp. 336–337.
58 Erskine, *Institute*, I, VII, LVI, p. 112.
59 NRS: CC9/14/20/208.
60 NRS: CC9/3/4/fols. 212–213.
61 NRS: CC9/3/23/fols. 489–490. See also Mason, 'The Marital Spectrum', p. 800.
62 NRS: CC9/3/23/fols. 555–556.
63 NRS: CC9/3/33/fols. 503–506.
64 Kane and Williamson, *Women, Agency and the Law, 1300–1700*, p. 15.

9

WOMEN NEGOTIATING WEALTH

Gender, law and arbitration in early modern southern Tyrol

Margareth Lanzinger and Janine Maegraith

Conflicts between family members, spouses, or neighbours were ubiquitous and can be regarded as an integral element of social relationships in previous centuries as well as today. However, the reasons for disputes and the specific configurations of the disputants could be very different. A distinctive arena of conflict in marital, familial, and kinship contexts related to wealth.[1] The potential points of conflict were manifold: they could be about property rights and rights of use, about the clarification of claims, about the appropriate distribution of assets, especially of inheritances, or about the type and amount of compensation, about problems of payment of adjudicated funds, about debts, and more. Conflicts took place in domestic contexts but could also extend into the neighbourhood, into further kinship, into the village, into the town district, or into other localities. When it came to wealth, the dispute configuration was often inter-gender and involved inter- and intragenerational relations. Such 'civil law' cases show a multitude of possible conflicts between different family members and consistently point to the aspects of women's wealth that were either not documented or evidenced, to usage rights of property brought into the marriage by the spouse, to inheritance disagreements, or to widows' entitlements. The causes, logics, and patterns of such conflicts are directly connected with the prevailing marital property regime and inheritance practice.

The aim of this chapter is to reconstruct conflict contexts of this kind and to relate them to modes of conflict resolution. The main question hereby is how women have acted in these settings. Our contribution consists of two parts: first, we look at the German speaking areas in general to provide insight into current research on women's involvement in conflict situations to provide a comparative perspective focussing on arbitration procedures and family conflicts. This shines light on the link between marital property regimes, inheritance practices, and

DOI: 10.4324/9780429278037-10

litigation – a triangle that is central to understanding marital, familial, and kinship conflicts over wealth. Second, we present and interpret a set of cases from southern Tyrol from the sixteenth century to the 1780s. In the County of Tyrol, a *Landesordnung* or territorial law code was introduced in the sixteenth century and remained in force until 1787. It also regulated 'civil law' matters including inheritance and marital property. The *Verfachbücher* or court records, extant from the early sixteenth century onwards, contain arrangements, contracts, and court proceedings pertaining to property related matters such as inheritance, marriage, and widowhood contracts, probate proceedings and inventories, purchase deeds and other property transfers, and litigation documents. These documents refer to non-adversarial proceedings. The case studies in the second section as well as references throughout the discussion are based on the analysis of documents for the court districts of the town Brixen, the village and court district of Kastelruth, and the rural territory of the abbey of Sonnenburg in the Puster valley from the sixteenth to the eighteenth century.

The early modern period is considered to be a time in which courts were characterised by the fact that they were a self-evident part of social life, that is, that they were present and accessible in everyday life across the various social milieus.[2] In our study area in southern Tyrol, this was ensured, for example, by the court sitting on market days for those who lived outside court locations, or by appointing local men as court representatives. These then acted as intermediaries between the residents and the relevant court by forwarding information and documents, such as contracts. In this way, long or difficult routes could be overcome. And the courts were accessible to men *and* women. In the process, courts not only functioned as 'punitive instances' but were also 'used to enforce one's own interests'.[3] Research has shown how early modern women used the courts to challenge legal restraints to defend their property, living conditions, families, and children.[4] Women sometimes exploited restrictions to avoid tax or debt payment or to enforce securities. With this, authorities could face the choice between unwanted economic consequences to defend patriarchal structures or opting for economic sense but risking a disruption of the gender balance. Interpretations, however, could vary. One example is the *Senatus Consultum Velleianum*, which, although much debated academically, was found by Hendrikje Carius to have had little influence in legal practice at Saxon courts.[5] Siglinde Clementi showed in her study of Maria Anna Trapp, née Thun, how an appeal and reference to female weakness and the 'poor widow' could be a legal strategy: 'Maria Anna described herself as a poor, undefended (*indefesa*) widow who deserved, and was in need of, special protection from the *Landesfürstin*'.[6] Thus, women appear frequently as litigants in the court records defending or claiming their entitlements. In our context of separation of marital property, women defended their wealth in almost equal numbers as men.

Within legal spaces, in the Middle Ages and in early modern times, different laws could coexist – customary law, canon law, Roman law, royal and town statutes, and so on[7] – which men and women also used instrumentally. There was a change at the transition from the fifteenth to the sixteenth century, as Regina Schäfer shows. In fifteenth-century Ingelheim, legal plurality and the coexistence of legal systems and statutes left a larger scope for the courts to use adjournment, postponement, and delegation, or enabling extrajudicial settlements.[8] The Ingelheim court records reveal many intra-family conflicts that frequently related to inheritance and marital wealth disputes. Thus, women of all ages and marital status were present in these records. Women could even represent their husbands at court. But Schäfer emphasises that women's legal status experienced a decline from the sixteenth century onwards with increasing codifications of laws and thus fewer opportunities for negotiation.[9] But in some areas even codified law codes could leave scope for legal plurality in early modern times, visible in the significance of customary rights and differing legal practices. Written law such as the Tyrol Law Code of 1532, extended in 1573, for example, did not stipulate the type of succession to property and thus allowed for undivided transmission as well as partible inheritance or undivided fraternal inheritance.[10] The complexity of different forms of ownership and nuances in the entitlements linked to ownership variants and the resulting competing property rights is illustrated by Hendrikje Carius for the early modern court in Jena in Saxe-Weimar-Eisenach.[11] In early modern continental Europe, law codes and legal procedures were increasingly codified and aligned with Roman law and in many regions, including in German speaking territories, women were required to be represented or accompanied by a gender guardian at court.[12] As research findings show, the more open negotiation mode in court changed again in many places at the transition from the eighteenth to the nineteenth century or in the course of the nineteenth century. Various changes in the law, such as the increasing centralisation of the law, and in the organisation of courts towards a greater formalisation of procedures, led to courts becoming less and less a place of negotiation but a place of adversarial proceedings – be it in relation to marital conflicts, or in the context of property disputes.[13]

The way conflicts were resolved also varied.[14] Beyond personal attitudes, the way conflicts were settled is likely to be related to different dispute cultures and to different legal cultures, and above all to how courts functioned. In our research context of southern Tyrolean wealth litigations, however, these disputes did not lead to an indictment and were not concluded by a sentence but by arbitration or court settlement and therefore resemble non-adversarial proceedings. It was in the interest of the local courts in early modern Tyrol to settle disputes and to avoid indictments. This was primarily aimed at avoiding costs that a court case would have entailed.[15] As a result, this may have had a lasting impact on the legal culture – in contrast to very disputatious societies or communities. This arbitration procedure included a multitude of participants. Consequently, every female litigant's experience varied due to the differing family settings, property situation and social standing, the use of attorneys or gender guardians, and the objective of the judge and his assessors.[16]

The requirement for a *Geschlechtsvormund* or *Anweiser* (gender guardian) raises the question of legal inequality in relation to women's position in court and in the context of legal transactions.[17] Whether women could appear in court and conclude transactions in their personal capacity or whether they needed a representative or gender guardian and what this meant, are important questions, especially from the perspective of gender history. Our working hypothesis is that while the gender guardian function reflects women's limited legal subjectivity, it has not necessarily limited women's legal involvement in terms of asserting their claims and concerns. The presence of a gender guardian in Tyrol ensured the validity of legal transactions concluded with women – such as purchases or sales – and could strengthen the position of women in cases of dispute. Often the gender guardian was a man from the community with court experience and considerable standing, and in some cases, the husband, brother, or father assumed that role. In numerous of our analysed cases, it is explicitly noted that the gender guardian was chosen by the woman and then confirmed by the court. And in the case of conflicts over property, it can be assumed that women chose a gender guardian to represent their interests and for this, women probably chose men with experience and good track records. It is therefore important to know who was in competition with whom and who formed alliances. In our project, we assume that the axes of competition were, on the one hand, structurally laid out and particularly shaped by the wealth competition between marriage, family, and kinship, and, on the other hand, that they were closely related to the respective configuration of the persons involved: existence and age of children or childlessness, marital status, age, financial position, and so on. With Ute Gerhard's edited volume on women in the history of law, an important step was made towards establishing women's presence in the world of law in a broad approach that also embraces areas of civil law.[18] There still needs to be more research done to understand the impact of the different legal contexts of women litigants – legal framework, marital property regimes, inheritance laws and practice, gender guardian regulation – and how they can be compared.

Women as litigants in property and household matters: research perspectives

Arbitration procedures can be described with reference to Franziska Loetz as an 'alternative' to court proceedings and as a 'social practice of conflict regulation'.[19] The conflicts over property that we see in the sources were settled in the interplay between courts and extrajudicial arbitration bodies. The 'neighbourhood' could function as such in the sense of a legal organisational unit and seek to settle a dispute on behalf of the court, as well as relatives or local representatives of the court.[20] Courts functioned not only as a 'frame of reference' but also as a place for various stages of arbitration.[21] The court offered regular court days for people to come forward with their cases, it commissioned arbitrations, had them reported, heard witnesses, and wrote up settlements. The Saxon Code of

Procedure of 1622, for example, provided that differences between close relatives were to be settled 'on equitable terms, in amicability, or, if such did not take place, at least the trial with their mutual consent per *modum compromissi*'.[22]

The logic of this interplay is shown by Inken Schmidt-Voges's research on conflict regulation at the household level by providing insights into its pattern of general procedures, aims, solutions, and norms. She stresses the importance of witness statements to establish the prehistory of conflicts and infrajudicial attempts to regulate conflicts.[23] Many women were called on as witnesses. The aim was to document the conflict biography and to reach a settlement of the conflicting interests. Schmidt-Voges identifies several aspects for further research, among them the analysis of the knowledge of the actors, their language, how the judiciary was used, infrajudicial aspects of conflict regulation, symbolic communication, the significance of violence in communication, and, last but not least, a stronger emphasis on gender specific aspects.[24] Katharina Simon-Muscheid with her analysis of Upper Rhenish theft cases carefully looks at the language used at court and any underlying stereotypes. In cases where a maid servant was accused of theft, an unequal power relation was prevalent between the employer and the employee, but also an underlying gender asymmetry as to how women were expected to comply with the 'catalogue of virtues'. However, this – and especially female weakness – could be instrumentalised by the accused or accusing women as well. Simon-Muscheid stresses that going to court was often a last solution which people sought to avoid because it meant that the dispute would become public and with it the contextual (personal) information about the household in question.[25]

Past and current research on women and gender at late medieval and early modern courts of law in the German speaking areas uncovers various conflict situations negotiated at different courts, from the lower to the Imperial courts. This body of research has made women visible not only as defendants and witnesses but also as independent litigants. In her research on the courts of the Holy Roman Empire, Siegrid Westphal revises the older historiography's impression that suggests a general subordination of women in early modern times, and that argues that women needed a gender guardian and were without legal capacity. The quantitative analysis of cases brought before the Imperial Chamber Court, for example, evidences women's considerable legal participation at the courts. Irene Jung analysed cases from 1690 to 1806 of the Prussian district of Wetzlar and found that women were litigants in 17% of cases.[26] This ratio rises when looking at the town of Wetzlar where she identified c. 31% female litigants. Sixty per cent of the litigating women were widows, 25% were married, and 15% unmarried. The themes negotiated at court remained consistent with money and loans, and marital, family, and inheritance law. This research shows that a significant number of women addressed the highest courts coming from all social groups in spite of their constrained legal status. Women possessed court capacity as victim as well as delinquent and they also made use of the courts to address their unequal treatment.[27]

Women, whether in the context of marital disputes and separation, inheritance shares, or restitution of their wealth as widows, often turned to the courts to defend their wealth and secure their entitlements. Nicole Grochowina presents a broad spectrum of property disputes that were fought before the Jena *Schöppenstuhl* at the end of the eighteenth century: women went to court here to secure access to property and its protection or to fight against the loss of property.[28] Wealth in the context of marriage was particularly important and at the same time highly conflictual. The husband's authority to administer marital wealth including his wife's marriage portion was a centre of conflict. Here, positions and gender relations could change, all the more if the wife's portion exceeded the husband's property in value, 'inverting' the marital constellation.[29] Many lawsuits of various women concerning marital disputes are extant where women tried to sue for restitution of their wealth or parts of their wealth or at least for alimony – especially in the aftermath of divorce.[30]

Property and usage rights and maintenance claims were also highly conflictual in early modern times, not least because these rights were rooted in the prevalent marital property and inheritance regimes whereby their legal codification and legal practice created differing entitlements and ideas of entitlements that were not necessarily shared by all. This led to competing interests between all persons concerned, such as siblings, in-laws, children, parents, step-parents, widowed spouses, further relations, or guardians.[31] These constellations could vary by locality and region with many different property regimes in place in the German-speaking areas.[32] Marital property regimes, for example, differed widely from communion to separation of property with significant implications for wives and widows, as community of property favoured the married couple in terms of property claims, while separation of marital property gave children and relatives a privileged position. Grethe Jacobsen stresses that changes within marital property would necessarily lead to re-negotiations or shifts and the resulting conflicts would then be negotiated at the lower courts or by notaries.[33] And Gesa Ingendahl shows how marriage contracts in an urban context were used by couples to validate negotiated marital property agreements often divergent from the legal marital property regime.[34]

Inheritance laws and practices, and especially discrepancies between them, created another area of conflict. The whole range between partible and impartible inheritance contained the problem of gender allocation and disbursement of inheritance shares, whether the shares could be paid out or whether they had to stay invested on the estate, and how the shares were distributed between sisters and brothers. This all mattered as inheritance was linked with wealth and access to landed property which, in turn, meant access to power. This gives transfer of property and its control even more significance. Given the existence of different inheritance laws and practices and also marital property regimes, remarriages and children of different marriages produced different claims and with them conflict potential.[35] Sisters and daughters could and did revert to the courts to enforce their inheritance share and entitlement. Thus, women in rural areas in the district of Goslar, for example, sued their brother who inherited the farm.[36] Hendrikje Carius examined in her study, among other things, fifty-two cases of inheritance disputes involving women before the Jena court. In 18.9% of the cases, the conflicts revolved around debts and protection of property. The appearance at the Jena *Hofgericht* (Court of Justice) had already been preceded by several stages in lower courts, including elaborate evidentiary proceedings and the use of various legal remedies.[37] 'Claims to inheritance shares from testamentary dispositions and inheritance settlements' accounted for a total of more than 70% of the cases.[38]

Steven Ozment's reconstruction of Anna Büschler's lifelong struggle to regain her full inheritance share in sixteenth-century Hall illustrates three important aspects relevant to the study of litigating women: first, although women had fewer economic opportunities and could not directly participate politically (with few exceptions), they had 'inalienable rights and significant access to the courts'. Anna Büschler brought her case against her father (and later against her siblings) to three different courts including an Imperial court and was heard at all of them, even if only partially successful from her perspective.[39] Second, in addition to gender, social standing and wealth of a person determined their entitlements and access to public office or citizenship, for example.[40] And third, access to personal resources or supporters and legal counsellors could be crucial to assert oneself during the proceedings, especially in cases like hers where strong kinship entitlements were involved.[41] Ozment's interpretation might be too positive when he stresses that gender alone did not determine access to and the outcome of legal proceedings. But all three aspects certainly play into each other and have to be considered when researching women who negotiated wealth at the courts.

Women negotiating wealth: case studies from southern Tyrol

The axes and logics of the conflicts we analyse in the following cases are closely related to the specific legal situation. Their implications for wives, unmarried women, and widows are always inextricably linked to the interplay of inheritance practices and marital property regimes. The legal basis is the above-mentioned Tyrolean law code of 1526, significantly amended in 1532 and in 1573. The provisions on inheritance were relatively open and did not provide for a specific model of inheritance – whether undivided or divided – but there existed a preference for sons. Therefore, daughters were at a disadvantage compared to sons regarding succession, creating the potential for conflict between brothers and sisters. The separation of marital property, on the other hand, was clearly stipulated. The assets that women brought into the marriage remained their property but were managed by the husband. On the death of the husband, his own property fell to the children or to his relatives, while the widow was entitled to restitution of what she had brought into the marriage, but only time-limited provision rights in the deceased husband's house until restitution was made. If the children were minors, widows could manage their late husband's wealth on the basis of a usufruct contract, usually until the children reached the age of majority.[42] By the eighteenth century at the latest, the practice of life estate (*Ausgedinge*) replaced restitution of the marriage portion and other assets of the widow: the money remained on the house and the widow received a right of residence and maintenance in return, often with an interest payment on her invested assets.

Separation of marital property means that the central axis of conflict ran between the widow and the children with their guardians or – in the case of childlessness – between the widow and the relatives of the deceased husband.[43] In contrast to community of property, the origin of the property – whether inherited or acquired, and by whom – and its legal quality – whether defined as marriage property, trousseau, or just generally as wealth – remained much more important during and at the end of a marriage, but also for the unmarried. The starting point of the case analyses is that separation of marital property not only largely structured the configuration of the persons in dispute but also the potential for conflict and the objects of conflict. On the one hand, the question focusses on which concrete conflict settings can be identified, and on the other hand, which spaces for action and empowerment women were able to use in the process. The reconstructed cases originate from court books (*Verfachbücher*) of various courts in present-day South Tyrol, which contain all relevant civil law agendas – contracts of all kinds, probate proceedings, inventories, guardianship accounts, obligations (*Schuldscheine*), receipts, and so on – in the form of minutes and copies.[44] In addition, numerous disputes are recorded in the court books of the sixteenth and seventeenth centuries. The court books of the eighteenth century, on the other hand, are visibly larger or have been divided into several volumes per year, but the proceedings of conflicts have been incorporated far less overall, tending only towards settlements or contracts documenting the outcome of a dispute. The court books are fairly representative for the contemporary population in these areas, where values between zero and 10,000 gulden, and in the eighteenth century up to 20,000 gulden were dealt with. In most extracted cases, around 60% in Brixen and Sonnenburg, people negotiated values of below 300 gulden and thus represented the lower and middle strata of society. People of different social backgrounds addressed the court, from day labourers, peasants, artisans, to merchants. Only the unpropertied are underrepresented, as they had too few assets to negotiate.[45] For this contribution we have selected cases representing key constellations which could lead to women litigating for their entitlements: inheritance and provision contracts, securing marital wealth and provisions for children, reconstitution of wealth and widow's rights, and the competition between children's guardians and widows. On the basis of the wording copied into the court books, we reconstructed the parties' approaches. While it is clear that this cannot reflect the exact wordings or intentions of the women at court, especially since they had to be represented by a gender guardian and all statements were 'filtered' and adjusted by the court clerk according to his reasoning, it nevertheless reveals the social logics and instruments agreed on by the women litigants and their representatives.

Sister versus brother: securing inheritance shares – 1565–1581

Family money, whether from inheritance shares or marriage portions, was secured on landed property as hypothecary loan or mortgage. Thus, a demand for reimbursement of wealth created the problem of liquidating money, and inheritance proceedings as well as widows' endowment contracts contain payment agreements that address the scarcity of cash with deferred payments and long-term instalments to avoid having to sell land. This was a common problem in inheritance cases where succession entailed the payout of the siblings' inheritance shares and the demand for payment by siblings could lead to contention. But securing entitlement to or payout of the shares could be vital for the siblings' future, for example as marriage portions for sisters. Margaretha Hofer, sister of Urban Hofer in Weitenthal, court district of Sonnenburg,[46] appeared at the court together with her gender guardian in December 1565 to claim her outstanding parental inheritance share from her brother.[47] Her brother Urban was the successor to the parental estate and owed her fifty gulden according to a contract from November 1565. An interim settlement was achieved whereby Margaretha's fifty gulden should remain invested and secured in her brother's farmstead against an interest payment of two gulden thirty kreuzer, free lodging and firewood, and care in case of illness. For her work on the farmstead, she would receive food and drink, but for this she should behave as befits a sister, 'friendly and without complaint'.

Margaretha must have been content with this solution and decided not to marry, because in January 1570, she augmented the existing settlement with a new one in presence of her gender guardian.[48] According to an inheritance contract from 1558, Margaretha was also entitled to a maternal inheritance share of 170 gulden. She now abstained from her claim on her mother's inheritance because of her physical and mental 'deficiency' (*mangelhafft*) which left her inept to provide for herself. She transferred 120 gulden to her brother for his use during his lifetime. She retained fifty gulden for her own use. In exchange, Margaretha received a provision contract for life which entitled her to free lodging, food and drink, an annual allowance on her brother's farmstead, and after her death a Christian burial. But she should not be urged to do work beyond her capability. In case of dispute, four arbiters would be called to renegotiate her provision and thus an infrajudicial solution. With this, her wealth was again secured on her brother's property and a transfer contract was drawn up.

But five years later, April 22, 1575, Margaretha went to court to litigate against her brother Urban. She had the support of her new gender guardian, Christan Kopfguter now Pitschelin in Pflaurenz, who acted as legal advocate in many cases, and her brother-in-law Sigmund Frennes in Enneberg.[49] She complained that Urban had hit her and that he did not adhere to the contractual conditions.

Therefore, she was not willing to continue to live on his property and demanded to be paid out with her money to which she was contractually entitled. Urban, however, replied that he did provision her according to contract but accused her of begging for alms from strangers. This was followed by an even worse act of defamation on the same day: Urban Hofer registered at court that Margaretha had called his wife a 'whore'. But the judge ordered Urban to prove this accusation within four weeks or face appropriate punishment for defamation. Both accusations made it more important for Margaretha to revert to the court again just a few days later on April 27. She filed the same claim against her brother and this time the case was heard, and the dangerous behaviour of her brother acknowledged. Her brother protested and defended himself, but he did not repeat any of the earlier accusations against his sister. He probably could not prove them and Margaretha was able to clear her name.[50] After another hearing, the judge Augustin Neuner and his four assessors settled the case: Margaretha was to be paid out her provision for one year in money, and then, based on their agreement, fourteen gulden annually. With this settlement, sister and brother were to be reconciled and should not come forward with a complaint in this matter again. Here, the court probably referred to the clause in the first contract, whereupon arbiters should be consulted in case of dispute — and not the court.

The co-residence of sister and brother must have been highly contentious for Margaretha to resort to the court twice and to bring their dispute out into the public — instead of choosing an infrajudicial solution. A lot was at stake: she had claimed to be inept to provide for herself and was dependent on the provision provided by her brother who, in turn, enjoyed usufruct of her wealth. But in the context of their dispute, she remained in the weaker position as she lived on his property and this was probably the reason why her first provision contract provided for arbiters to be called on in case of arising disputes. She chose to go to court directly, and with the accusation of her brother's physical violence against her, illustrated this unequal power relationship. By exposing their difficult situation to the public and with the help of her experienced gender guardian and her brother-in-law achieved acknowledgment of her rights rooted not only in her provision contract but also in the Tyrolean law code and customs of the court district.[51] She could also clear her name against her brother's defamations.

The order to pay out the annual provision in money probably worked as a threat to her brother and led to an arrangement whereby she could stay on his property. Urban Hofer's transfer and retirement contract from 1581 attests that Margaretha still enjoyed lifelong provision which was underwritten with 170 gulden on this property.[52] Obviously, the earlier settlement of 1575 made a renewed co-habitation possible. By repeatedly reverting to the court and claiming her rights, Margaretha had ensured her entitlement to lifelong provision, forced her brother to adhere to its conditions, and resolved the disputes that arose between her and her brother successfully. As a sister, it paid off not to be too 'friendly and without complaint'.

Securing marital wealth and children's maintenance – 1600

Young families often found themselves under economic pressures while the children were still small, and the household had to rely on a reduced income due to the need of childcare.[53] In such cases, income from interest stemming from wealth such as marriage portions could be a welcome relief. In 1600, Anna Maria Säbin took matters into her own hands to secure income from her marriage portion that was administered by her father-in-law.[54] Anna Maria Säbin was married to Caspar Vilscheider who became citizen of Brixen in 1592.[55] They had several children but their number and age is not specified. Caspar's father, Hans Vilscheider, was a tinsmith in Brixen and his mother Ursula was deceased.[56]

After much disagreement with her father-in-law, Anna Maria went to the town court in Brixen in November 1600, assisted by her gender guardian, to assert that she had brought in a marriage portion of 100 gulden. Her father-in-law Hans had received the money at her wedding, acknowledged receipt and promised the allowance or payment – in this case probably to his son as Anna Maria's husband. In a contract concluded in 1598, he had also promised to pay out his son's maternal inheritance share of seventy-five gulden and to pay back seven gulden he borrowed from Anna Maria. Anna Maria now demanded the payout of her money because none of this had happened with her prior knowledge nor with her approval. Because of her husband's 'negligence' and for want of her and her children's maintenance, she demanded from her father-in-law not only the payout of her 107 gulden but also that he should take the children into his maintenance so that she could apply for employment in service – a demand in line with the logic of separation of marital property where the maintenance of children lay with the paternal side. From her demands we can deduce that her husband was not able to support his family,[57] but we do not learn why. It could be that he was either injured or the couple lived in Hans Vilscheider's house and thus under his authority. If the father had not consigned the domestic economic management to his son, then the father retained the financial management of his daughter-in-law's marriage portion as well. In this case, he should have been liable for the upkeep of the children.[58] It is likely that the father retained full authority, because he claimed administration rights over the couple's finances, though he held back money for the upkeep of the children which is why Anna Maria saw the need to earn additional income. In response, Hans claimed not to remember promising payment of her marriage portion to his son. What he had received of his late wife's estate in his son's place, he had handed on to his son as his maternal inheritance according to contract. He also excused himself from taking his grandchildren into his maintenance.

Both parties agreed that the town judge and his assessors should settle this case to save costs and preserve good friendship. The settlement confirmed Anna Maria's view of her husband's 'negligence': Caspar Vilscheider admitted that his inheritance share of seventy-five gulden was not fully paid and that he had used previous partial payments from his father for the repair of the roof – undertaken by his father. Father and son would have to account for the paid money first and had obviously no documentation for this – probably because it was invested into the repair of the father's house which, in turn, would have been the son's future inheritance. But the court assumed that the money was fully reimbursed and thus settled the matter. Concerning Anna Maria's marriage portion and loan, the court found that her father-in-law, indeed, owed her eighty gulden (seventy-five gulden marriage portion and five gulden loan), but that those should remain mortgaged on his house. To secure the maintenance of his grandchildren, he was obliged to pay annual interest on this money of four gulden or 5%. Should he sell his house, he had to reinvest her money so that its interest could pay for his grandchildren's upkeep. The court also found that although the contract recorded that all 100 gulden of Anna Maria's marriage portion were received by her father-in-law, in fact, only 75 gulden had been paid. She authorised him to call the remaining 25 gulden from her family. And finally, it was settled that father and mother were 'naturally' obliged to provide for their children and not their grandfather, except for what he was willing to give, freeing Hans Vilscheider from any obligations towards his son's children.

This case shows the economic importance of marital property especially in times of need. But the administration of this money was not in the hands of the wife but of her husband. In this case, however, her father-in-law retained household authority. This opened up another axis of competition with high conflict potential especially since proper documentation was missing and hence the financial matters were not transparent.[59] Reverting to the court provided the opportunity to document the current financial status as the father-in-law had to declare his dealings. This, in turn, facilitated a settlement between the two parties, securing at least regular interest payments for the maintenance of the children. Anna Maria was forced to make this step also because her husband could not assert himself against his father. The recorded wording suggests that she emphasised the weakness of her husband and her own strength, not only demanding her own share but also standing in for his – almost a reversal of expected gender roles. But because the legal provision of separation of marital property in Tyrol ensured Anna Maria's rights over her marital property, the court responded to her complaint in favour – with the reservation of the administration rights which were not legally in her hands. The presence of small children probably also helped her case.

Reconstitution of wealth and widow's rights – 1669/1670

Anna Maria Säbin's case shows that a wife's marriage portion came into the administration of her husband (or her father-in-law) who was obliged to secure her money on his landed property.[60] In the case of widowhood, she could claim her marriage portion back and she had priority before all other creditors to ensure that she received her full share. Anna Maria Säbin's case illustrates the consequences when no documentation or guarantee were drawn up or the property changed ownership. The next case shows that the payout of the widow's marriage portion invested in her late husband's estate was not always administered.[61]

Christina Gebhartin, widow of Franz Huber, remarried Ulrich Tschaueller, physician in Brixen. But by the time of their marriage (probably in 1669), she had not been fully reimbursed with her marriage portion of her first marriage. In 1669, she went to the town court in Brixen to claim back part of her marriage portion that was still invested in her late husband's mill that Hans Adam Purwalder, citizen and merchant in Brixen, had purchased. But she was turned down. In January 1670, she went to the princely chamber in Brixen against Purwalder, *in causa et actione Hypothecaria*. The chamber decided partly in her and partly in Purwalder's favour. He protested, but after his purchase of the mill, Purwalder would have had to settle with Huber's widow Christina whose property was secured on it; her entitlement had precedence before the creditors' demands if she could produce evidence.[62] After ongoing dispute and Christina's insistence, a settlement was reached at the town court in July 1670.[63] It found that part of Christina's marriage portion was, indeed, mortgaged on the mill and to avoid additional costs and to bring the case to a close the parties came to an agreement. The couple's advocate and Christina's gender guardian, Melchior Puger, innkeeper in Brixen, was present and the couple also gained the assistance of Johann Michael Bachmiller, princely court judge in Brixen.

The court settled that her claim should be extracted from the value of the mill: of the 2,000 gulden purchase price, Purwalder had paid 1,735 gulden 11 kreuzer. Christina was to receive back the remaining difference of 264 gulden 49 kreuzer and the full documentation of the transactions. In addition, Christina and her husband won their claim to get the interest payment for the period since the chamber's decision in January amounting to six gulden two kreuzer (c. 4.5% per annum). They also claimed their expenses of four gulden twenty kreuzer. In total, Purwalder was to pay 275 gulden 45 kreuzer. This case highlights the importance of legal and financial knowledge: people were well aware of their entitlements and knew how much they were due.

Christina Gebhartin and her husband gained not only payment of her share from Purwalder but also transparency with documentation of all payments made concerning the mill. She argued on the grounds of her legal entitlement to get back her marriage portion that was mortgaged on the mill previously in her late husband's possession. She did so with the help of her husband, her gender guardian and legal aid, and the assistance of the princely court judge in Brixen. She needed this help to settle with Purwalder, who as citizen and merchant in Brixen had a strong social position. But she also showed persistence, went to two different courts, and contested previous decisions. Christina always appeared in company of her husband and they put in her claims as a couple. She probably brought the marriage portion from her last marriage into her second marriage and hence her new husband had an interest in its restitution. Why she was not compensated with her wealth after Huber's death is not documented and the share on Purwalder's mill was not the only one. Franz Huber, Christina's late husband, had pledged his whole property on her marriage portion as was custom and law in early modern Tyrol. Since he had possessed several pieces of land, her wealth was mortgaged not only on the mill and so she took on another court case.

Parallel to her case against Purwalder, in March 1670, Christina and her husband went to the town court to demand back an arable field now in possession of Martin Pichler, *Haußvater* or director of the hospital in Brixen.[64] Christina claimed that she still had a pledge on this field deriving from her late husband Franz Huber. Pichler, on the other hand, claimed that he had bought the field from Anna Huberin. Therefore, Christina should not demand her share from him but from Anna Huberin. The case was deferred until May 1670 and its history reconstructed.[65] Christina could prove with her marriage contract with Franz Huber that the wedding took place before the field was sold and that it was therefore part of her pledge. Huber had mortgaged her wealth on all his wealth including the field and she had not been reimbursed yet. Interestingly, she referred to her ongoing case against Purwalder and the decisions to date to substantiate her case. Anna Huberin, possibly a relative of the deceased Franz Huber, had acquired the field by claiming her pre-emption right from the buyer Caspar Häusler (ca. 1660), and Pichler then bought the same field from Anna Huberin. The court recognised on these grounds that Christina's 'hypothecary case' (*Hipothecierte Clag*) was legal. The defendant Pichler was granted adjournment.

In June 1670, the court reconvened and concluded that Pichler had to assign his field to Christina referring also to the case against Purwalder. Pichler protested arguing that he bought the field from Anna Huberin in 1663 – nine years after Christina's wedding – and not from Franz Huber and he therefore should not be prosecuted. For the couple's claim against Pichler to be valid, they were required to prove how much of the money was still pledged on the field and whether the outstanding sum of her wealth was the same or more than the purchase price of the field. Until they produced the documentation for this, Martin Pichler was not obliged to assign his field to Christina. In August, the couple produced enough written evidence that the case was settled in their favour.[66]

Christina's strategy – supported by her husband and gender guardian – to appeal to two different courts and to follow two cases in parallel strengthened her argument: in the case against Martin Pichler, the town court judge repeatedly referred to the findings concerning Purwalder's case at the chamber and town court. But Pichler protested and referred to his property rights as an approved buyer of the field. This illustrates that although the Tyrolean territorial law prescribed that a woman's marriage portion should be mortgaged on her husband's property and that her entitlement to a payout as a creditor after his death was protected, uncertainties could remain especially if such properties were sold during the marriage (Pichler) or the widow's claim on the pledge was not regarded (Purwalder). Here, the entitlement to wealth secured on land collided with property rights on land. Christina was able to assert her claims with perseverance, legal support, appealing to two courts, and producing written documentation. She also appeared with her husband and as a couple, they did not appeal to her female weakness but insisted on her rights established in the Tyrolean law code.

Guardian versus widow – 1781

Litigation is comparatively rare in the court books of the eighteenth century, as already mentioned – so too around the 1780s. The subject of conflicts related mainly to disputes between the guardian (*Gerhab*) of children and widows. One such case is that following the death of Martin Schenk, innkeeper of the inn 'Zum Lamm' in Kastelruth. He was torn from life in mid-February 1781 at the age of forty-two due to illness, leaving behind his widow Ursula Schenkin and three children, two sons and a daughter, aged between six and fourteen years. The minutes of the judicial proceedings that followed cover 278 pages.[67] The extensive nature of the probate proceeding was undoubtedly due to the fact that this was a very wealthy family of innkeepers, members of the local elite, so that there was a lot to inventory and settle, not least as a result of the guardian's challenge to the will. At the same time, this elaborateness can also be interpreted as an act of performing social status. In this case, the specific procedures in court and in the inn as well as the actions of the various parties involved are explicitly recorded.

Despite the extremely extensive material, one document that is central to the conflict is missing, namely the will of the deceased Martin Schenk. The documents with the guardian's counter-position and with the arguments of the widow in favour of the fulfilment of the will were unfortunately not included in these court records either.[68] But the existing records allow the following conclusions: the guardian was of the opinion that from the will 'a character that does not exist in law emerges', calling it a *unstandhaftes Werk* – a work that could not stand – and which he had to contest. His objection was aimed at the fact, as he later elucidated, that the provisions in the will favoured the widow too much. From his position as guardian, this would imply that the paternal will was to the detriment of the children. The widow, in contrast, stood up for the fulfilment of the provisions and reserved 'all legal remedies for the manutention of the husband's will'. The guardian, on the other hand, demanded certain restrictions on the widow's entitlements. The point of contention was that Ursula Schenkin should be able to manage the real estate, including the inn, on the basis of a usufructuary contract. How exactly this was formulated in the will must remain open, because changes had been made in the design of the usufructuary rights. However, the usufruct contract itself came about after the guardian had agreed in principle to the administration of the property by the widow, despite his 'apprehensions' (*bedenklichkeiten*). The administration by the widow was arranged for eleven years and thus until the eldest child would have reached majority at the age of twenty-five.[69] The widow had undoubtedly achieved success with this. For the time being, one can only speculate about the extent of the restrictions on the rights granted to her in the will. It is conceivable that the deceased husband granted her discretionary power over the duration of her administration. In this period, such an option, which tends towards reciprocity between the sexes, is found in marriage contracts in some places, especially among craftsmen and tradesmen.[70]

Three aspects are of particular interest here. First, the procedure for dispute resolution: called to court on 31 March 1781 were, on the one hand, the guardian and curator of the children Anton Gasser as well as Johann Schenk, a paternal uncle and thus the closest male relative of the children, and on the other hand, the widow with the obligatory gender guardian and her father Kristian, also Schenk, an innkeeper from a neighbouring court district. This illustrates that in property separation regimes, the family of origin continued to play an important role for married and widowed women when it came to property issues. The court instructed both parties to 'draw up their pleadings against each other' so that the matter could be 'mediated in good faith'. These should be sent to the court within eight days so that the court could communicate them to the other side. At the court hearing on 6 April 1781, the factual situation and the parties' disputes in the meantime were presented once again. Thereupon, 'interested parties had been talking for a longer time' and the dispute could be settled by finding a compromise in the form of certain restrictions on the widow's rights. The guardian was ready to make concessions, as he 'disliked' the idea of 'getting into a quarrel with the children's mother Ursula Schenkin'. The arguments here were not the interests of the lineage, but rather the widow's position as a mother and family peace. The endeavour to find a peaceful solution was also emphasised yet again before the usufruct contract was drawn up: it had been 'agreed to bring the matter to a peaceful end in a desired manner, and to maintain good harmony'.

Second, it is striking that the children's uncle, the braid maker Johann Schenk, a brother of their father, who was present at all important court hearings, largely kept out of this dispute. In the property separation logic, he represented the paternal line, so he would be expected to act and advocate for the protection of the children's interests against the widow. Instead, at the first court hearing in this matter on 23 February 1781, he merely declared that he was 'not opposed' to the guardian's response and 'reserves the right to be able to present several things afterwards'.[71] However, no further statement on his part is on record.

Third, it should be noted that at no point in the detailed negotiations is it mentioned that the contentious guardian Anton Gasser was the brother-in-law of the deceased Martin Schenk. He had married Martin's sister Maria in 1770 and, thanks to the considerable wealth she brought into the marriage, had risen from being a farmer to becoming an innkeeper and merchant as a result of the purchase of the Inn 'Zum Kreuz' in 1773. Thus, in conclusion, it remains to be asked whether he only represented the interests of the children or whether he did not also pursue his own agenda and, together with his wife, perhaps had aspirations for the Inn 'Zum Lamm' or other properties. Similar such occupational interests and competition between a widowed spouse and the kin of the deceased can be seen in a sixteenth-century case in Brixen, for example, where the husband of an apothecary's daughter – himself an apothecary – sued her widowed step-father in order to gain control and management of the apothecary shop.[72]

Conclusion

Past and ongoing research concerning women negotiating wealth in early modern German-speaking territories reinforces the view that women did not shy away from litigating even against their neighbours, brothers, or in-laws. This frequent recourse to the courts often had a positive outcome for women. But to understand the aims and options litigating women in wealth-related cases had, the prevailing property laws have to be considered. They could determine whether women took up the opportunity to appeal to a court in the first place, which wording they chose and how they argued, who advised and represented them, which axes of competition existed, and what the objectives of the courts were. The wealth-related legal framework was crucial as it had direct implications on inheritance and succession practices and marital property systems and thus on a substantial part of pre-modern wealth transfer.

In the County of Tyrol, property rights were legally secured especially with the introduction of the Tyrolean law code in the sixteenth century, but various forms of property and usage rights led to competition and conflict. Relatively open inheritance laws and strict separation of marital property – and thus a prevalence of lineage property – combined with hereditary land tenure facilitating rights of disposal of one's property, for example, created complex layers of ownership. Separation of marital property had consequences and reinforced unequal and gendered property distribution. But to some extent this could also protect women's property from their (late) husband's kin and creditors. With such protection of their lineage as well as acquired property, women did not need to employ gendered language but insisted on their inherent rights. Owing to the property's origin, kin members were present in most of the cases, either in support of women (as their father or brother, for example) or in competition to them (as kin of the late husband or the children's guardians on behalf of him). Wills were decisive in transferring usage rights to a spouse thus counteracting consequences of separate property and showing reciprocity, but since such arrangements delayed the property to revert to the deceased kin, they were often contested by them. However, the court aimed for a compromise often securing a preferable outcome for women whether or not a husband's will existed.

In our research area, the relatively open negotiation mode in court during the sixteenth and seventeenth centuries changed at the transition from the eighteenth to the nineteenth century with increasing centralisation of the law and formalisation of procedures. This led to more adversarial proceedings. How far the use of infrajudicial solutions mitigated this process needs to be investigated. They are referred to in the records, for example with the designated role of neighbours as arbiters to prevent cases returning to the court, but actual infrajudicial proceedings were not necessarily written down, thus calling for more research.

Throughout the period, the mandatory gender guardian, however, did not necessarily weaken women's positions but could strengthen their presence at court. A woman could choose her own gender guardian and in addition he would not be fixed for future negotiations because she could choose a new one every time. Although the fact that women could not represent themselves independently reflects unequal gender rights, analysis of the practice and use of this institution is important. The same is true of the objectives of the courts. Earlier research into marital disputes and domestic violence established the thesis that courts tended to side with the women.[73] We found in our study that keeping the peace with amicable settlements and compromises was the main aim of the courts. Since the composition of the litigating parties, the subject matter and context of the dispute always changed, it is necessary to ask about the rationale of the courts, because it could always be different.

Notes

1 This article builds on research and source material from the research project 'The Role of Wealth in Defining and Constituting Kinship Spaces from the 16th to the 18th Century', funded by the Austrian Science Fund FWF (P 29394 and P 33348-G28, 2016–2020 and 2020–2023), see http://kinshipspaces.univie.ac.at/en/.
2 See for example Craig Muldrew, *The Economy of Obligation. The Culture of Credit and Social Relations in Early Modern England* (Basingstoke, 1998), esp. Map 1, The Catchment Areas of Chartered Boroughs with Active Courts of Records, p. 212.
3 Ulrike Gleixner, 'Frauen, Justiznutzung und dörfliche Rechtskultur – Veränderungen nach dem Dreißigjährigen Krieg', in Klaus Garber and Jutta Held (eds.), *Der Frieden. Rekonstruktion einer europäischen Vision, vol. 1: Erfahrung und Deutung von Krieg und Frieden. Religion – Geschlechter – Natur und Kultur* (Munich, 2001), pp. 453–461, p. 454.
4 Grethe Jacobsen, 'Women and Men in Legal Proceedings: A European Historical Perspectives', *NAVEIÑ REET: Nordic Journal of Law and Social Research* 3 (2012) (published 2015), pp. 97–111, p. 103.
5 Hendrikje Carius, 'Strategien vor Gericht? Die "velleianischen Freyheiten" im sächsischen Recht (1648–1806)', in Grethe Jacobsen, Helle Vogt, Inger Dübeck, and Heide Wunder (eds.), *Less Favored – More Favored: Proceedings from a Conference on Gender in European Legal History, 12th–19th Centuries, September2004*: http://www5.kb.dk/export/sites/kb_dk/da/nb/publikationer/fundogforskning-online/pdf/A07_Carius.pdf.
6 Siglinde Clementi, 'A Dispute over Guardianship. The Trentino-Tyrolean Noble Trapp Family between 1641 and 1656', in Margareth Lanzinger, Janine Maegraith, Siglinde Clementi, Ellinor Forster, and Christian Hagen (eds.), *Negotiations of Gender and Property through Legal Regimes (14th–19th century). Stipulating, Litigating, Mediating* (Leiden, 2021), pp. 282–308.
7 Jacobsen, 'Women and Men in Legal Proceedings', p. 101.
8 Regina Schäfer, 'Inheritance Disputes from Ingelheim Court Records on the Threshold of the Early Modern Period (Fourteenth to Fifteenth Centuries)', in Lanzinger, Maegraith, Clementi, Forster, and Hagen, *Negotiations of Gender and Property*, pp. 52–83.
9 Schäfer, 'Inheritance Disputes from Ingelheim Court Records'.
10 Margareth Lanzinger and Janine Maegraith, 'Houses and the Range of Wealth in Early Modern Gender- and Intergenerational Relationships', *Jahrbuch für Europäische Geschichte / European History Yearbook*, 18 (2017), pp. 14–34, pp. 17–18 (open access https://doi.org/10.1515/9783110532241-002).
11 Hendrikje Carius, *Recht durch Eigentum. Frauen vor dem Jenaer Hofgericht 1648–1806* (Munich, 2012), pp. 149–192, p. 50 and ch. 3.2.3.
12 Jacobsen, 'Women and Men in Legal Proceedings', p. 102; Ernst Holthöfer, 'Die Geschlechtsvormundschaft. Ein Überblick von der Antike bis ins 19. Jahrhundert', in Ute Gerhard (ed.), *Frauen in der Geschichte des Rechts. Von der Frühen Neuzeit bis zur Gegenwart* (Munich, 1997), pp. 390–451.

13 Jacobsen, 'Women and Men in Legal Proceedings', pp. 102–103; on marriage in Switzerland, Arno Haldemann, 'Prekäre Eheschliessungen: Eigensinnige Heiratsbegehren und Bevölkerungspolitik in Bern, 1742–1848' (PhD diss., University of Bern, 2019); on wealth in Greece, Evdoxios Doxiadis, *The Shackles of Modernity. Women, Property, and the Transition from the Ottoman Empire to the Greek State* (Cambridge, MA/London, 2011).

14 See Inken Schmidt-Voges and Katharina Simon, 'Managing Conflict and Making Peace', in Joachim Eibach und Margareth Lanzinger (eds.), *The Routledge History of the Domestic Sphere in Europe, 16th to 19th Century* (London, 2020), pp. 254–268, p. 256.

15 This is set out in many court records in sixteenth and seventeenth century Tyrol as a reason to conclude the proceedings with a settlement. See also Tiroler Landesordnung (TLO) 1573, 2.20 which urged the judges of the district courts not to unnecessarily lengthen procedures to protect the parties from rising costs.

16 See for different legal spaces, Lanzinger, Maegraith, Clementi, Forster, and Hagen, *Negotiations of Gender and Property*, especially the chapter by Isabelle Chabot, 'Family Justice and Public Justice in Dowry and Inheritance Conflicts between Florentine Families (Fourteenth to Fifteenth Centuries)', pp. 225–253.

17 Holthöfer, 'Die Geschlechtsvormundschaft'. In Tyrol, women, especially unmarried or widowed women, were legally obliged to have a gender guardian, TLO 1532, 1573, 3.53.

18 Gerhard, Ute (ed.), *Frauen in der Geschichte des Rechts: Von der Frühen Neuzeit bis zur Gegenwart* (Munich, 1997).

19 Franziska Loetz, 'L'infrajudiciaire. Facetten und Bedeutung eines Konzepts', in Andreas Blauert and Gerd Schwerhoff (eds.), *Kriminalitätsgeschichte. Beiträge zur Sozial- und Kulturgeschichte der Vormoderne* (Konstanz, 2000), pp. 545–562, 553, 555. First impulses came from Benoît Garnot, 'Justice, infrajustice, parajustice et extrajustice dans la France d'Ancien Régime', *Crime, Histoire & Sociétés/Crime, History & Societies* 4 (2000), pp. 103–120.

20 Benoît Garnot names the *apaiseurs* as institutionalised *médiateus-arbitres*, which existed in all districts of northern French cities. Garnot, 'Justice, infrajustice', p. 111; see also Benoît Garnot (ed.), *L'infrajudiciaire du Moyen Age à l'époque contemporaine* (Dijon, 1996).

21 That the 'two spheres […] can hardly be sharply separated' is pointed out by Karl Härter, here with a focus on criminal justice: Karl Härter, 'Konfliktregulierung im Umfeld frühneuzeitlicher Strafgerichte: Das Konzept der Infrajustiz in der historischen Kriminalitätsforschung', *Kritische Vierteljahresschrift für Gesetzgebung und Rechtswissenschaft* 95:2 (2012), pp. 130–144, p. 132.

22 Carius, *Recht durch Eigentum*, p. 153.

23 Inken Schmidt-Voges, 'Familie' in Wim Decock (ed.), *Konfliktlösung in der Frühen Neuzeit* (Berlin, 2021), pp. 333-341; Inken Schmidt-Voges, *Mikropolitiken des Friedens. Semantiken und Praktiken des Hausfriedens im 18. Jahrhundert* (Berlin, 2015).

24 Schmidt-Voges, 'Instrumente und Strategien', p. 339.

25 Katharina Simon-Muscheid, 'Frauen vor Gericht. Erfahrungen, Strategien und Wissen', *Historische Zeitschrift*, Beihefte 31 (2001), pp. 389–399, pp. 394–396.

26 Siegrid Westphal, 'Frauen in den höchsten Gerichten des Alten Reiches: Eine Einführung', in Siegrid Westphal (ed.), *In Eigener Sache: Frauen vor den Höchsten Gerichten des Alten Reiches* (Cologne/Weimar/Vienna, 2005), pp. 1–17, p. 12; Irene Jung, '*Ihrem Herzen Und Charakter Ehre Machen': Frauen wenden sich an das Reichskammergericht* (Wetzlar, 1998); for comparable results see Anette Baumann, *Die Gesellschaft der Frühen Neuzeit im Spiegel der Reichskammergerichtsprozesse: Eine sozialgeschichtliche Untersuchung zum 17. und 18. Jahrhundert* (Cologne/Weimar/Vienna, 2001).

27 Westphal, 'Frauen in den höchsten Gerichten', pp. 1–3. This can be verified in other European legal areas as well.

28 Nicole Grochowina, *Das Eigentum der Frauen. Konflikte vor dem Jenaer Schöppenstuhl im ausgehenden 18. Jahrhundert* (Cologne/Weimar/Vienna, 2009), pp. 181–346.

29 Margareth Lanzinger, Ellinor Forster, Janine Maegraith, Siglinde Clementi, and Christian Hagen, 'Konfliktpotenzial und Streitgegenstände im Kontext ehelicher Vermögensregime', *Frühneuzeit-Info* 26 (2015), pp. 104–115, p. 112.
30 Sylvia Möhle, *Ehekonflikte und sozialer Wandel. Göttingen 1740–1840* (Frankfurt a. M./ New York, 1997), p. 189–191.
31 Lanzinger, Maegraith, Clementi, Forster, Hagen, *Negotiations of Gender and Property*.
32 Gabriela Signori, *Von der Paradiesehe zur Gütergemeinschaft. Ehe in der mittelalterlichen Lebens- und Vorstellungswelt* (Frankfurt a. M./New York, 2011); Margareth Lanzinger, Gunda Barth-Scalmani, Ellinor Forster, and Gertrude Langer-Ostrawsky, *Aushandeln von Ehe: Heiratsverträge der Neuzeit im europäischen Vergleich* (Cologne/Weimar/ Vienna, 2015, 2nd edition).
33 Jacobsen, 'Women and Men in Legal Proceedings', p. 105.
34 Gesa Ingendahl, 'Verträgliche Allianzen. Verwandtschaftsbeziehungen in Heiratsverträgen der Freien Reichsstadt Ravensburg', in *Geschichte und Region / Storia e regione* 27:2 (2018), pp. 102–122, special issue on *Vermögen und Verwandtschaft / Parentela e patrimonio*.
35 Jacobsen, 'Women and Men in Legal Proceedings', p. 105; Margareth Lanzinger, 'Emotional Bonds and the Everyday Logic of Living Arrangements: Stepfamilies in Dispensation Records of Late Eighteenth-Century Austria', in Lyndan Warner (ed.), *Stepfamilies in Europe, 1400–1800* (Abingdon/New York, 2018), pp. 168–186, here pp. 179–182.
36 Ulrike Gleixner, 'Das Gesamtgericht der Herrschaft Schulenberg im 18. Jahrhundert. Funktionsweise und Zugang von Frauen und Männern', in Jan Peters (ed.), *Gutsherrschaft als soziales Modell. Vergleichende Betrachtungen zur Funktionsweise frühneuzeitlicher Agrargesellschaften* (Munich, 1995), pp. 301–326, p. 316.
37 Carius, *Recht durch Eigentum*, p. 152.
38 Carius, *Recht durch Eigentum*, p. 154.
39 Steven Ozment, *The Bürgermeister's Daughter. Scandal in a Sixteenth-Century German Town* (New York, 1998), pp. 188, 193.
40 For similar findings, see Carius, *Recht Durch Eigentum*; Westphal, 'Frauen in den höchsten Gerichten'.
41 Ozment, *The Bürgermeister's Daughter*, p. 193; see also Gesa Ingendahl, *Witwen in der frühen Neuzeit: Eine kulturhistorische Studie* (Frankfurt a. M., 2006).
42 Lanzinger and Maegraith, 'Houses and the Range of Wealth'; Margareth Lanzinger and Janine Maegraith, 'Konkurrenz um Vermögen im südlichen Tirol des 16. Jahrhunderts', *L'Homme. Z.F.G.*, 27:1 (2016), pp. 15–31.
43 Christian Hagen, Margareth Lanzinger and Janine Maegraith, 'Competing Interests in Death-related Stipulations in South Tirol ca. 1350–1600', in Mia Korpiola and Anu Lahtinen (eds.), *Planning for Death: Wills, Inheritance and Property Strategies in Medieval and Reformation Europe* (Leiden, 2018), pp. 88–118; Clementi, 'A Dispute over Guardianship'.
44 Wilfried Beimrohr, *Mit Brief und Siegel: die Gerichte Tirols und ihr älteres Schriftgut im Tiroler Landesarchiv* (Innsbruck, 1994), pp. 97–101.
45 These results are based on the database for Sonnenburg and Brixen, compiled by Janine Maegraith. For a more detailed discussion of the sample's representativeness, Janine Maegraith, 'Selling, Buying and Exchanging Peasant Land in Early Modern Southern Tyrol', in Thomas Ertl, Thomas Frank, and Samuel Nussbaum (eds.), *Busy Tenants. Peasant Land Markets in Central Europe (15th to 16th centuries)* (Stuttgart, 2021), pp. 193–229, p. 197.
46 The court district of Sonnenburg, Benedictine convent, was situated in the Puster valley/Val Pusteria.
47 Südtiroler Landesarchiv (SLA), A 742, Verfachbuch (VfB) Sonnenburg, 1564–1567, no fol., 17.12.1565, no title.
48 SLA, A 742, VfB Sonnenburg, 1568–1573, 28.1.1570, no fol. no title.

49 SLA, VfB Sonnenburg, 1573–1575, no fol., 22.-27.4.1575, no title.
50 See on restitution of female honour Simon-Muscheid, 'Frauen vor Gericht', pp. 398–399.
51 TLO 1532, 1573, 3.2.
52 SLA, VfB Sonnenburg, 1580–1581, no fol., 8.4.1581, no title.
53 See, for example, Sheilagh Ogilvie, *A Bitter Living: Women, Markets, and Social Capital in Early Modern Germany* (Oxford, 2003), esp. pp. 194–200.
54 SLA, VfB Brixen Stadtgericht, 1599–1601, fol. 201v-204r, 29.11.1600, 'Güettige Vergleichung Zwischen Anna Maria Säbin und Hannsen Vilscheider'.
55 Philipp Tolloi, 'Das Bürger- und Inwohnerbuch der Stadt Brixen von 1500–1593. Edition und Kommentar' (Magisterarbeit, Wien, 2012), p. 207, no. 1311.
56 Tolloi, 'Das Bürger- und Inwohnerbuch', p. 150, no. 857.
57 On this discussion see, for example, Angiolina Arru, 'Die nicht bezahlte Mitgift. Ambivalenzen und Vorteile des Dotalsystems im ausgehenden 19. und beginnenden 20. Jahrhundert', *L'Homme Z.F.G.*, 22:1 (2011), pp. 55–69, pp. 57–58.
58 Unfortunately, no further evidence could be found in the court books. For a similar case see Margareth Lanzinger, *Das gesicherte Erbe. Heirat in lokalen und familialen Kontexten, Innichen 1700–1900* (Vienna/Cologne/Weimar, 2003), pp. 261–263.
59 On consequences of missing documentation see also Janine Maegraith, 'Gender Imbalance in the Use, Ownership, and Transmission of Property in Early Modern Southern Tyrolean Urban and Rural Contexts', in Lanzinger, Maegraith, Clementi, Forster, and Hagen, *Negotiations of Gender and Property*, pp. 193–222.
60 TLO 1573, 3.1; Christian Hagen, Margareth Lanzinger, and Janine Maegraith, 'Verträge als Instrumente der Vermögensabsicherung im südlichen Tirol vom 14. bis zum 18. Jahrhundert', *Historische Anthropologie*, 25:2 (2017), pp. 188–212, here pp. 198–199.
61 On this see also Anna Bellavitis, *Famille, genre, transmission à Venise au XVIe siècle* (Rome, 2008); Chabot, 'Justice', pp. 225–253.
62 SLA, VfB Brixen Stadtgericht, 1670, fol. 32v–34v, 30.1.1670, 'Herrn Hans Adamen Purwalder, contra Christina Gebhartin und Ires Ehemans Ulrich Tschauellers'. This case refers to the town court case in 1669; TLO 1573, 3.38.
63 SLA, VfB Brixen Stadtgericht, 1670, fol. 179r–188v, 27.7.1670, 'Vergleichung Ulrich Tschaueller und sein Ehewirthin Christina Gebhartin, Hanns Adam Purwalder'.
64 SLA, VfB Brixen Stadtgericht, 1670, fol. 70v–72r, March 1670, 'Christina Gebhartin, Martin Puhler Firkhomen'.
65 SLA, VfB Brixen Stadtgericht, 1670, fol. 205r–211v, 17.5.–7.6.1670, 'Christina Gebhartin und Ir Ehemann Ulrich Tschaueller Contra Martin Pichler'.
66 SLA, VfB Brixen Stadtgericht, 1670, fol. 212r–212v, 23.8.1670, no title.
67 SLA, VfB Kastelruth 1781, fol. 404r–544v. The following references to this source can be found on fol. 517v–520v.
68 This is a work in progress. The hope is that these documents will turn up in the court records in later years or that they will be found in the Kastelruth municipal archives.
69 SLA, VfB Kastelruth 1781, fol. 521r–530v, 521v. The usufruct contract comprises a total of 18 points and is thus comparatively detailed.
70 Margareth Lanzinger, 'Von der Macht der Linie zur Gegenseitigkeit. Heiratskontrakte in den Südtiroler Gerichten Welsberg und Innichen 1750–1850', in Lanzinger, Barth-Scalmani, Forster, and Langer-Ostrawsky: *Aushandeln von Ehe*, pp. 205–367, pp. 290–293.
71 SLA, VfB Kastelruth 1781, fol. 409r.
72 Lanzinger and Maegraith, 'Houses and the Range of Wealth', pp. 28–32.
73 Heinrich Richard Schmidt, 'Hausväter vor Gericht. Der Patriarchalismus als zweischneidiges Schwert', in Martin Dinges (ed.), *Hausväter, Priester, Kastraten. Zur Konstruktion von Männlichkeit im Spätmittelalter und Früher Neuzeit* (Göttingen, 1998), pp. 214–236, pp. 224, 226, 239.

10

A LITIGATING WIDOW AND WIFE IN EARLY MODERN SWEDEN

Lady Elin Johansdotter [Månesköld] and her family circle[1]

Mia Korpiola

In medieval and early modern Sweden, unmarried maidens and wedded wives were represented in court by law by their legal guardians (Sw. *målsman*, literally 'spokesman'), who were to speak and answer for them in court. Minors could also have guardians (Sw. *förmyndare*) appointed for them. At marriage, husbands became their wives' legal guardians until widowhood, resembling to some extent the English common law institution of coverture. Only widows were empowered to litigate themselves, having been freed of legal guardianship through their guardian's death. But did this legal framework actually correspond with real life and legal practice? Current research suggests that the practice was rather fluid and pragmatic, and there were regional patterns and changes in time. To investigate this question further, and the extent of women's legal agency[2] or capacity to act in early modern Sweden, this chapter will focus on a particular noblewoman, Elin Johansdotter [Månesköld] (d. 1640).[3] She was involved in several lawsuits in the most important court in Sweden in the first decades of the seventeenth century. The Svea Court of Appeal, the country's first royal appellate court, was established in 1614 and remained without sister courts until 1623 when the next new appellate court was established.[4]

Maria Sjöberg has characterised Swedish sixteenth- and seventeenth-century history largely as a fight for land, the main resource of power, between crown, the nobility, and the peasantry.[5] The proportion of land in possession of the Swedish nobility increased during the seventeenth century so that in its heyday on the advent of the Great Repossession of 1680,[6] about two-thirds of all land was in noble hands. Thus, it is only natural that more than half of all Svea Court of Appeal disputes involving nobles were land- or family-related with roughly equal proportions.[7] Thus, Elin Johansdotter's suits involving landed property more generally were relatively typical noble causes in the court.

This chapter will first scrutinise what we know about Lady Elin's life and the court cases she was involved in. The piecing together of this family history

DOI: 10.4324/9780429278037-11

is essential to our understanding of the legal struggles that arose after multiple marriages, the blending of families involving many children and stepchildren, and the effects of partible inheritance. It will then analyse how Elin conducted her litigation during a period where her civil status changed from widow to wife, then to widow, and again to wife. Did this have an effect on her capacity to act? How did Swedish law regulate female agency in legal matters and how did this work in practice? Did Lady Elin use legal representatives or attorneys? Her agency will also be contextualised with examples of other women in her own family circle and with evidence from other Swedish courts and social classes.

Lady Elin Johansdotter [Månesköld] and her family

Elin Johansdotter was born by 1580, and probably earlier – perhaps already in the latter half of the 1570s – as she was married to her first husband, Tönne Eriksson [Tott] (1553–1608), on 9 October 1592.[8] This would have made her husband over twenty years her senior and belonging to the generation of her father Johan Carlsson [Månesköld, d. 1613]. There has been some confusion about the origins of the Månesköld [af Seglinge] family, but it now seems certain that the family's fifteenth-century noble progenitor was Jöns Pedersson of Seglinge (active 1425–1472) from the province of Uppland. His descendants married into local minor nobility.[9] Elin's father Johan Carlsson and his brothers Arent and Christer were all listed as members of the Uppland nobility in November 1582.[10] Since the mid-sixteenth century, the family's coat of arms – also used by Elin – had a star and a crescent moon which gave the family its surname.[11] Johan Carlsson had been married twice, and all his seven surviving children – of whom Elin seems to have been the eldest – were from his first union to Anna Isaksdotter, daughter of Isak Nilsson [Banér] (b. bef. 1521–1589) and Brita Lagesdotter.[12]

One of the lawsuits we will be investigating in detail was between Elin and her stepchildren from her husband Tönne Eriksson's [Tott] first marriage, for the property she was entitled in widowhood. Originally a Danish aristocratic family, the Totts had become very influential through important marital alliances and extensive kinship networks during the so-called Kalmar Union in late medieval Sweden. They had also received important enfeoffments and administrative positions before the 1520s. Tönne Eriksson [Tott the Elder], 'our' Tönne's grandfather and namesake, was a member of the Council of the Realm indicating he belonged to the politically influential ruling aristocracy. His son Erik (d. 1570) also married well as his wife Ermegård Larsdotter [Sparre af Rossvik], who died after a short marriage having given birth to Tönne and another son, was also daughter of a Councillor.[13] Tönne Eriksson [Tott the Younger] contracted a prestigious first marriage with Brita Henriksdotter [Horn], daughter of knight and provincial judge (*lagman*) Henrik Klasson Horn (1512/1513–1595) and Elin Arvidsdotter [Stålarm], in 1578. However, apparently after less than a decade together, Brita died (1587 at the latest) after giving birth to at least five surviving children: Erik (d. 1629), Karin (d. 1631), Elin (d. in or after 1638), Gunilla (lived in 1645, possibly even 1656) and Ermegård (lived in 1645).[14] These became Elin's stepchildren.

In addition, Tönne Eriksson and Elin Johansdotter together had three daughters, Brita (1600–1660), Ingeborg and Kerstin (d. 1643), and a son called Lars, who having outlived his father was dead by 1616.[15] All in all, when he died in 1608 after a sixteen-year marriage, Tönne had an unusually large number of direct heirs: seven living daughters and two sons. Sweden practiced partible inheritance and while sons inherited double the amount of daughters in the countryside, this could lead to the division of noble estates, and trigger litigation.[16] As the Totts were not among the aristocratic families that reaped the fruits of royal favour through enfeoffments, land grants, and offices, this made their claims to the existing family estates all the more important. In addition, the Måneskölds had backed the wrong side in the power struggle between King Sigismund Vasa (r. 1592–1599) and his uncle, Duke Karl of Södermanland, later King Charles IX of Sweden (r. 1604–1611). Elin Johansdotter's father and two of her uncles lost their offices and enfeoffments because of their loyalty for Sigismund. Moreover, they were incarcerated together with Tönne Eriksson for some time at Uppsala Castle.[17]

Following Tönne Eriksson's death in 1608, Elin experienced several years of widowhood until she married her second husband, Joachim von Berfeldt (d. 1619),[18] a member of an old noble family from Brandenburg. We can probably place the wedding at some point in 1616 (or later), as Berfeldt's first wife, Rebecka von Brandenstein, had died on 12 November 1615.[19] Berfeldt had two sons from his first marriage. Berfeldt served the Swedish crown for decades as an officer and artillery expert. He had the title of 'Master of Artillery of the Realm' (*rikstygmästare*), a lower official responsible for the artillery and arms production, in 1602–1610. He had received a royal manor in Fresta as enfeoffment in 1603 and purchased a stone house by Stockholm's main marketplace in 1605. However, Berfeldt passed away in 1619, leaving Elin Johansdotter widowed for a second time after few years of marriage. He was buried next to his first wife in the church of Fresta.[20] We know even less of Elin's third husband Carl von Loquin (1580–1653) except that he, too, was of German origin and outlived her. Their marriage took place sometime between 1619 and August 1625, but it is unclear when, as apparently no morning gift letter has survived (Figure 10.1).[21]

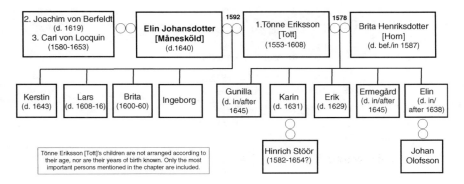

FIGURE 10.1 Simplified Family Tree of Lady Elin Johansdotter [Månesköld].

Female agency and litigation in Swedish law and practice

Lady Elin Johansdotter was involved in several cases in different courts though here we are focussing on her litigation at the Svea Court of Appeal, a popular legal venue for nobility dealing with land disputes. These comprise three different lawsuits. The first took place in 1614–1617 and revolved around Elin Johansdotter's morning gift[22] property and was against her stepchildren.[23] Indeed, Elin Johansdotter's property dispute against her stepchildren formed the opening entry of the Court's first register. It noted on 24 May 1614: 'Citation to Erik Tönnesson of Skebo to answer his stepmother, Lady[24] Elin of Berga on the distribution of the inheritance made between them.'[25] The second saw the noble Christoffer von Wernstedt (ca. 1560–1624) sue Elin for arson and slander. The Court of Appeal heard the cause in 1618, and it ended in reconciliation.[26] Finally, she was involved in litigation against Hinrich Stöör (1582–1654?),[27] the German-born husband of her stepdaughter, for allegedly not respecting the reconciliation of 1617 between her late husband's heirs and herself, and for criminal vandalism.[28]

In order to assess Elin Johansdotter's agency in her litigation in the Svea Court of Appeal, we must first investigate the framework of law and custom which defined the possibilities of women's activity in court. As law courts were largely male domains in early modern Sweden, as elsewhere in Europe, women's legal literacy tended to be weaker. Women could not hold office as judge or juror. They did not confirm land transactions as witnesses (*faste*). They did not regularly witness documents, testify in courts or act as oath-helpers in criminal cases.[29] This handicap was also evident when the court asked the parties to take an oath. This was also a problem for Elin as a woman, as will be discussed later in more detail.

While women had property rights, their rights to administer their property and conduct legal acts were curtailed by law. Moreover, in Swedish law – as elsewhere in Europe – female agency depended on marital status. According to the laws of medieval Sweden, the Town Law (ca. 1350) and Law of the Realm (1442) for the countryside,[30] a maiden's father was her marriage guardian (Sw. *giftoman*), who decided on her matrimony, betrothed the couple and presided over the wedding. If he was dead, her eldest brother replaced him, and then the closest male relative with a preference for paternal kin.[31] When a child's father died, their mother had the right to administer their inheritance with the consent of the closest relatives as long as she remained a widow. After a mother's remarriage, the children's closest kinsmen assumed guardianship unless they were unsuitable or had conflicts of interest.[32] In towns, fathers and mothers were women's marriage guardians. When they died, their nearest kin or other persons appointed by them on their deathbed assumed the duty.[33] Similarly, the legal guardians of orphaned girls and minor boys were in the first place their closest relatives, or men appointed by the town mayor and town councillors. Men reached majority at fifteen, girls only at marriage.[34] Both Swedish laws specified that the husband became his wife's legal guardian, 'having the right to sue and answer for her', after the wedding and wedding night – not before.[35] This legal guardianship ended when the husband died. Widows were free from guardianship with full legal authority to act as they wished. This reflects the law in theory, but women's guardianship practices apparently varied considerably from region to region in medieval Sweden.[36]

For both noble men and women, the appellate courts became pivotal as these were their privileged fora.[37] Between 1650 and 1690, for example, an average of 24% of all disputes adjudicated by the Svea Court of Appeal involved the nobility. As the estate formed about 1% of the population, it was markedly overrepresented.[38] Lady Elin Johansdotter was a widow when the Court of Appeal first heard the first case concerning her morning gift property. Elin was exercising her legal right in speaking for herself, but not all widows made the same choice. Maria Ågren has calculated that women formed a quarter of just over 1,400 plaintiffs at the Svea Court of Appeal in 1614–1705, and even higher in certain types of cases.[39] While this data fails to tell us much about female agency at the Swedish law courts,[40] studies confirm that they were male dominated. In the seventeenth century, women appeared in a clear minority of cases both in towns and in the countryside with considerable regional and temporal variation from under ten to slightly over 20%. Moreover, women may have become more marginalised in some regions in the course of the seventeenth century.[41]

As a widow, Lady Elin was free from the constraints of legal guardianship. Yet it can be debated whether widowhood really was a desirable estate or not. It has been suggested that the economic advantages of the married estate explain the high remarriage rates – about two-thirds – of Swedish medieval noble widows. Even if this rate dropped somewhat before the Reformation, marriage remained the preferred choice.[42] As Anu Lahtinen has pointed out, even if widows took their late husbands' place as head of the household, widowhood was not generally described in empowering terms but rather as a state of insecurity. Both widows themselves and their families described them as 'sorrowful, unprotected and pitiful'. This was partly a customary use of rhetoric but still reflects the reality that widows were occasionally forced to find powerful protectors in kinsmen, town councils, or the king against relatives or other persons harassing them and making claims on their property.[43] Lady Elin Johansdotter used similar language in her letter to Wernstedt in response to his accusations of arson. She said she would ask God to repay such untrue allegations against 'a poor defenceless woman'.[44]

Elin Johansdotter's first lawsuit: legal agency as a widow

As mentioned above, Elin Johansdotter's first cause at the Svea Court of Appeal was litigation against her stepchildren, mostly represented by Erik Tönnesson as the only son among the children of the first union, and as such, the main heir. The case involved the division of property after her first husband's death. While a widow, Elin was first represented at the Court of Appeal by an attorney but also appeared in court and later even in front of the King, in person. At the Svea

Court, both the litigating parties and their possible representatives usually had to be present in Stockholm during the court term. Elin's claims for her morning gift property were first heard at the Court of Appeal on 28 June 1614, before which she had been actively gathering testimonials together in support of her case. Her management of her own affairs related to her lawsuit and reflects her agency. While playing the 'defenceless widow' card when it suited her, the court records show her on many occasions managing her litigation. She presented claims considering a debt that Erik Tönnesson (her stepson) owed her for having organised her late husband Tönne Eriksson's funeral for which she had procured many barrels of malt for ale brewing. She also appeared as signatory to several legal pleadings, some of which had been signed in her own hand, including the division of property in 1609 after her first husband's death.[45] These all relate to the property division between her and her deceased husband's heirs.

Her opponent Erik Tönnesson appeared in person and without legal counsel, which the Swedish legal historian Jan Eric Almquist has assumed contributed to his first losing the case in the Court of Appeal.[46] Yet the next year the case was resumed and pursued energetically by Henrik and Claes Horn, Erik's maternal cousins, who had witnesses interviewed under oath. Erik made the claim that he had not had the opportunity to present the case thoroughly at the first appellate court hearings implying denial of justice. He and Lady Elin were also present at court.[47] Later, Elin, Erik and Claes Horn appeared in person in front of King Gustav II Adolf (r. 1611–1632) and were interrogated by the monarch.[48] This was unusual. King Gustav II Adolf decided to send the cause back to the Court of Appeal (*in integrum restituera*) for a more comprehensive 'search for the truth' on 26 August 1616. The Horns had successfully argued that the lawsuit had not been investigated in depth at the appellate court. Indeed, Lady Elin and her attorney Nils Bengtsson were accused of concocting false evidence and presenting 'obvious and blatant fabricated lies to the Royal Court of Appeal' on which the appellate court judges had based their first decision.[49]

Thus, the case continued at the Court of Appeal in September with another witness interrogated in the presence of Claes Horn and Lady Elin. The Court did not keep verbatim records of the discussion and statements, but we know that Lady Elin also spoke there and answered questions posed by the judges and provided them with her documents regarding the question of revenue from the children's inherited maternal estates.[50] The parties, as well as Claes Horn, attorney of Erik and his siblings as co-heirs, all attended some court sessions in October and the interlocutory sentence was given on 7 October 1616. Elin and her opponents Erik Tönnesson and Hinrich Stöör negotiated back and forth on the monetary debts, the manors Elin would have, and the financial settlement. The Court confirmed the sentence on 11 November. After all negotiations and settlements had been made, the final decision came on 30 June 1617.[51] Elin was granted her morning gift property, all debts were settled and the property division between Elin and her deceased husband's children concluded. In the process, also the inheritance lots of the heirs were determined.

Elin Johansdotter's second lawsuit: an almost invisible wife represented by her husband

The noble Christoffer von Wernstedt's cause against Elin Johansdotter regarding arson and slander was markedly different. He sued Elin for having purportedly incited a man to torch his mill and for slandering him. Wernstedt was no stranger to Elin's family as he had previously been involved in a land dispute with her stepson Erik Tönnesson. A native of Mecklenburg, Wernstedt had lived in Sweden since 1583, when he came there through the marriage of Princess Elisabet Vasa and Duke Christopher of Mecklenburg, and in the following year he had become page to King John III. Apparently in this position, he had met Lucretia Magnusdotter [Gyllenhielm, 1562–1624], the king's illegitimate niece, and they married in 1586. He was governor of Uppsala Castle for two decades and district judge in Uppland before he was appointed governor of several provinces in Northern Sweden. Thus, he had considerable administrative and judicial experience, and by the time of the case against Elin Johansdotter, his wife Lucretia was the illegitimate cousin of King Gustav II Adolf.[52]

During the time when the case reached the Court of Appeal on 4 July 1618, Elin seems a shadowy figure when compared to her previous activities in the case. Previously, she had appeared in person at a hearing organised for this case by the provincial judge (*lagman*) Count Magnus Brahe,[53] President of the Svea Court of Appeal, on 28 February 1616. At this time, she was probably still a widow, but as we do not know when her marriage to her new husband Joachim von Berfeldt took place, we cannot know for sure. What we do know is that Berfeldt appeared several times in court on her behalf in 1618, and Elin did not sign any documents or pleadings. When the case came to the Svea Court of Appeal, it had already been investigated at a lower court, where Elin had allegedly slandered her opponent's honour by calling him a thief and accusing him of harassing her family.[54] It was possibly strategically prudent to have Berfeldt manage the case as there was apparently no long-standing hostility between him and Wernstedt that may have existed between Elin and Wernstedt. At least they had cooperated in 1606 when Wernstedt was organising the coronation of Charles IX in Uppsala and Berfeldt was in charge of the fireworks.[55] This may also have been the reason why, after only few court hearings in 1618, the case between Wernstedt and Elin ended in reconciliation.[56]

For some women, the incentive to remarry may have come from a need to have a man conduct (property) litigation for them. As his wife's new legal guardian, the husband would have considerable inducements to have the disputed property judged to her.[57] Sture Petrén has claimed that several rich widows in seventeenth-century Sweden married men with legal literacy. He attributed this partly to widows tending to have property disputes with their in-laws and late husbands' heirs and partly to the procedural system that resembled a 'heated duel', which included oaths and thereby a litigant's whole personality. 'In this milieu, it was difficult for a woman to assert herself.'[58] This did not pose a problem for

Erik Tönnesson and Hinrich Stöör who offered to take oaths to confirm their claims. When the appellate court judges asked Elin whether she could take the same oath in her first lawsuit, she answered that she did not comprehend it fully, and it was read aloud to her anew. Nor was she personally allowed to take the oath, but she assured the court that one of her nearest male paternal relatives could take it for her.[59]

A widow could request the help of students or other literate persons for writing the necessary submissions and pleadings. Moreover, a widow marrying her representative would enable him to pursue the cause in person as her legal guardian and give him extra incentive to win the case in her name.[60] Indeed, wealthy Sigrid, widow of Olof Ingemarsson of the town of Gävle, who litigated in the Svea Court of Appeal, apparently married mainly for this reason around 1620. She claimed in court,

> I did not contract matrimony with him [her new husband] for the sake of lust, but so that I would have him as necessary defence against the claims on property and person that my enemies made after my late husband.[61]

Some women apparently remarried to have their husband champion their property rights and conduct litigation on their behalf. Margareta Reinholdsdotter, the former concubine and later widow of Elin's uncle Åke Carlsson, became entangled in an inheritance dispute with her in-laws after Åke's death. Margareta chose to remarry in 1629 in the middle of the litigation, and her new husband continued the case on her behalf.[62] Did Elin marry Joachim von Berfeldt for the same reason? In fact, women who appeared in person in civil cases could be in more dire straits than those with male representatives.[63]

Elin Johansdotter apparently remarried in 1616/1617 when she was deeply enmeshed in litigation against Wernstedt. She had appeared at the previous court hearing in person in this cause, and she had been involved in litigation with her stepchildren for several years (first case). The fact that Berfeldt represented her in this case represents a pattern that differed from her managing her own litigation during widowhood. Perhaps Berfeldt's personal contacts with Wernstedt, both being noble Germans in Swedish service, placed him in a good position to mediate between his wife and her offended opponent.

Elin Johansdotter's third lawsuit: legal agency first as wife, then as widow and again as wife

Lady Elin's third case, against Hinrich Stöör, her noble German-born stepson-in-law from her first marriage, was for his alleged failure to respect the reconciliation reached following the division of estate of 1617, and for criminal vandalism to servants and property. This suit went on intermittently until 1638 when the Court finally deemed it 'unnecessary and frivolous' and insisted the parties stop harassing each other by word or deed on pain of a high conditional 500-*daler* fine.[64]

Her cause against Stöör was initiated when she appeared in person at the Court of Appeal asking for a citation on 2 June 1617. She actively pursued her complaint at the first court sessions on 23 and 26 June 1617.[65] Even when the principals were represented by an attorney, they seemed to have stayed in Stockholm during the court term when the cause was being heard. Elin's undated list of court costs reveals that she had sojourned in Stockholm for four weeks, and at this point, her suit had already cost her 355 *dalers*.[66] It is unclear from the cause papers if Elin was married to Berfeldt at the beginning of the case as she was called the 'wellborn [i.e. noble] Lady Elin Johansdotter [of Berga]' throughout the proceedings.[67] However, Berfeldt was certainly involved in the wider dispute as he had tried to mediate between wife Elin and Stöör. At Elin and Berfeldt's wedding, not only Berfeldt but also many other noble men, ladies and maidens then present had pleaded on Hinrich Stöör's behalf that Elin would forgive him for attacking and battering her servants and give him her friendship again. Lady Elin provided evidence of this through the written testimonies of her own stepmother Cecilia Andersdotter [Rålamb] and stepsister Anna Eriksdotter Körning. Elin had finally agreed to a reconciliation, but only on the condition that Stöör would not wrong her in the future as 'in such a case all the crimes would be considered fresh and unatoned'.[68]

When the cause recommenced in 1627, Lady Elin appeared several times in person. Now, Elin's opponent Stöör challenged her legal agency. The records state that Stöör 'asked that her husband may come forward to answer for her'. By this point she had married her third husband, Carl von Loquin, with whom Stöör had met, and who apparently favoured a reconciliation. But Elin refused twice to have her husband represent her at court saying that she wanted to answer Stöör herself because her husband was not acquainted with the case.[69] Stöör made similar demands some months later: as Elin had a husband, let him answer in her place. She repeated her response that Loquin did not know of the matter.[70] Stöör may have thought that the case could be concluded sooner between men instead of this 'troublesome opponent',[71] and he appears to have wanted to cast Elin into the traditional mould of married women represented only by their husbands. On the other hand, Elin herself seems to have perceived her husband's guardianship simply as a possibility rather than a requirement, and she continued managing the case without her husband and without opposition from the judges. This suggests that they agreed on her legal ability to litigate independently, despite her married status.

Elin's decision was not without precedent. In Swedish practice, even married women, as joint heads of the household, could represent their husbands in court, especially if they were indisposed or away. However, occasionally the opponent or court disputed their agency, arguing that the husband was to appear in person and not be represented by his wife. Alternatively, wives could have powers of attorney to act for their husbands.[72] Anu Pylkkänen has observed that even if women (single, married and widowed) could act relatively freely in court when they were theoretically under legal guardianship, it was so limited in scope, it was not 'legally relevant, but rather a practical matter within a private household. Thus, it did not threaten the foundations of the legal system.'[73] Thus, husbands could always litigate on their wives' behalf, while the legal capacity of wives appearing for their husbands could be denied, depending on the decisions of the judges in the case. Although local courts were likely to allow married women more legal agency, Elin's case demonstrates that even appellate court judges could demonstrate flexible attitudes towards the agency of married women acting for themselves without their husbands representing them.

The cause papers of Elin's suit against Stöör contain only one document signed by Lady Elin's second husband Joachim von Berfeldt. This was an acknowledgement of debt to Elin's stepson Erik Tönnesson [Tott].[74] Similarly, there is also one single document by her third husband Carl von Loquin (or Lockwin, as he wrote his name). It seems that Elin remained very much in charge of proceedings even when she required her husband's name to expedite the case. On 17 July 1627, Elin sent a letter to the influential Gabriel Gustafsson Oxenstierna, who was a judge at the Svea Court and brother to Chancellor Axel Oxenstierna, to request that her case against Stöör proceed in court. She referred to her husband having been sent to Åland on the king's business.[75] We cannot verify whether this was true or a legal tactic. She may also have wanted to draw Oxenstierna's attention to her husband's position as a loyal servant to the King, which simultaneously made herself more vulnerable because of her husband's absence.

Then, on 9 October 1628, Elin wrote to her 'heart's dear husband' Carl von Loquin to ask that he contact Oxenstierna and request that the court case could finally be sentenced.[76] Consequently, Loquin sent a letter addressed to Oxenstierna, dated 13 October 1628 and signed in his own hand. In it, Loquin lamented the damage Stöör had done to the property and explained that he had to join the Queen, and therefore could not ask Oxenstierna personally for counsel and help. However, he expressed his humble wishes that Oxenstierna and the Court of Appeal would do their high duty and adjudicate in the case.[77] It seems that Loquin's single intervention in the cause took place because Elin requested him to do so. Perhaps this reference was to highlight his connections to the German-born Queen Maria Eleonora of Brandenburg (1599–1655) and that his wife Elin needed royal protection when he was on official business. All this suggests that despite references to her husband, she was still very much managing the case.

This was also Loquin's only intervention as he did not appear when the cause was pursued through representatives and briefs read at the Court, nor when Elin Johansdotter made several personal appearances in 1633, again showing her prominent role in the case. After that year, the case resumed its pattern of attorneys and written supplications until the final sentence.[78] Elin's active management of her court case was not common even within her wider family. When Stöör litigated on behalf of his wife Karin against his sister-in-law Elin Tönnesdotter, both married women remained almost invisible as their husbands conducted the whole case.[79] This indicates that it was not the rule that married women appeared in court in person. Naturally, women's court appearances only form the visible tip of the iceberg in litigation. The evidence from 1614 indicated that Lady Elin had actively put together the documentation she required to take her case to the Court of Appeal as mentioned above.[80] Yet Elin's many appearances at the court, especially when married, seems to represent her agency and personality as well as her strategic choices.

In some ways, her remarriages did not offer Elin such obvious legal advantages. Her second and third husbands were of German origin, and as foreigners, they lacked the traditional Swedish noble status foundation of inherited family manors. She had such property. Berfeldt had bought a town house in Stockholm, but he had also received lands from the king as enfeoffments that were revocable by the crown, and so were not as secure as inherited noble land. After many years of litigation, Elin may have felt the need of a husband supporting her legal claims, while she brought land and connections to the marriage. We know very little of Loquin, Elin's third husband, and nothing of his personal property. Probably both men lacked the extensive networks that aided people involved in lawsuits, while Elin's paternal uncles did not support her in her morning gift litigation. Berfeldt and Loquin also lacked the administrative and legal experience many Swedish noblemen had through their office-holding. Nevertheless, her decision to remarry may still have been influenced by the persisting legal troubles she was in and the need to share the burden with a husband. The timing of her remarriage certainly suggests that this could have been part of the decision. Men – even foreign-born – tended to have more extensive experience and networks than women. Moreover, in the lay-dominated Swedish legal system, many men had considerable practical legal experience through litigation and various legal and administrative tasks. Using a husband to litigate could be a strategy that gave women more options.

As has been discussed above, both married and unmarried women were to be represented in court according to law. In practice, Elin's actions suggest that married women could manage their cases in the courtroom and outside. Examples from her family circle indicate that this also applied to some extent to unmarried women. While legal guardians were to represent unmarried women, regardless of their age, in court, these women could occasionally assume greater agency by sending statements and signing briefs to be added to the cause dossier. Represented in court by their brother-in-law Hinrich Stöör when litigating against their sister Elin Tönnesdotter, Lady Elin's two unmarried stepdaughters Gunilla and Ermegård, who were around forty years old, for example, wrote statements. Wishing to deny their sister Elin Tönnesdotter her inheritance rights altogether because of her youthful sexual faux pas, some of these acrimonious statements bear their autographed signatures. Even more were written in Gunilla and Ermegård's names.[81] Similarly, a statement was given to the Court of Appeal in the name of Lady Elin Johansdotter's two unmarried teenaged daughters Brita and Kerstin Tott, referring to the time when they were 'small and minor children and had power over nothing' evidently contrasted with the current situation.[82] These examples demonstrate the scope for women to take some form of active participation even when represented by men.

Later, in the 1650s, the widowed Brita Tott authorised her two daughters (one married and unmarried) and her scribe to pursue a court case for her.[83] Moreover, Gunilla and Ermegård Tott demonstrated their own agency by initiating litigation against their brother-in-law and former ally Hinrich Stöör to partially overturn their childless sister Karin Tönnesdotter's will benefitting Stöör. At this point, they themselves – and not, for instance, their legal guardian in their place – had empowered an attorney.[84] By employing an attorney, they demonstrated some agency instead of being automatically represented by their closest male relative as their legal guardian. Apparently Gunilla and Ermegård Tott, who were around forty or fifty and had their own household(s), were considered de facto capable to largely manage their own affairs. This goes to show that Swedish single women had, in practice, wider scope for legal action after reaching majority and leaving the parental household.[85] Legal guardianship of (un)married women was obviously more nuanced and granted them more capacity to act than the law of early modern Sweden initially suggests. The same applied to Lady Elin and her agency when married.

Attorneys and representatives at the court of appeal: better success rate?

As previous research suggests, seventeenth-century Swedes, regardless of their gender, started slowly to believe that employing men of law would help in litigation. Thus, it was perceived a worthwhile investment and a good legal strategy. Yet, even if the parties were represented in court by attorneys and advocates, the parties often had to go and stay in Stockholm, or in its environs, unless an adjournment was sought in order to effectively manage their lawsuits.

The parties also participated in person at the sessions if necessary. The fact that the parties signed so many letters in their own hand demonstrates that they were present for consultation and signing the documents. In Lady Elin's three lawsuits discussed above, the parties sometimes used their relatives and in-laws as their attorneys as well as being physically present themselves. Erik Tönnesson, Elin's chief opponent in the lawsuit against her stepchildren, and his siblings were aided by their maternal cousins Henrik and Claes Horn, both important and high-ranking aristocratic officials, in the revision of the sentence of the Svea Court of Appeal.[86] This was a very successful intervention after Erik and Hinrich Stöör had first botched the case at the Court of Appeal. In their later litigation, Erik's spinster sisters Gunilla and Ermegård turned also to another maternal cousin, Klas Larsson Fleming (1592–1644), Admiral and Councillor of the Realm, whose mother was a Horn.[87]

Widows such as Lady Elin could either act for themselves in court or appoint legal representatives, such as relatives or attorneys and advocates with legal expertise.[88] In her initial court case in 1614, Lady Elin was represented by the husband of her sister Kerstin, Nils Bengtsson [Silfverbielke, d. 1640], who had long administrative experience in royal service and was governor of

Stockholm Castle at the time. He was also the legal guardian of her daughters after she had become widowed.[89] For her later litigation at the Court of Appeal, Elin used a combination of attorneys (Michil Persson in 1626 and Nils Nilsson Lindegren [1612–1681] in 1638) and relatives as her representatives.[90] After Michil Persson, she had also empowered Johan Olofsson, the vice-fiscal of the Court of Appeal and her stepdaughter Elin Tönnesdotter's husband since 12 February 1615, to act as her attorney in 1627–1628. She justified this by explaining the inconvenience of staying long away from her manor. In his elegant hand, Johan Olofsson had also penned Loquin's letter to Gabriel Gustafsson Oxenstierna.[91]

Researchers have argued that the professionalisation of the leading Swedish tribunals and an increasingly written procedure contributed to widows increasingly disappearing from town courts in the course of the seventeenth century. While, like Lady Elin, they had handled their cases in person in the 1630s, by the end of the seventeenth century, wealthy or elite widows normally only sent written pleadings or were represented by male attorneys or relatives. Yet less well-off widows continued to appear in person.[92] The seventeenth century demonstrated growing tendencies of representation in various Swedish courts, led by the courts of appeal, which first allowed advocates.[93] The predominantly written procedure at the appellate courts differed from the largely oral proceedings of the lower courts. The largely written procedure required that the parties presented their briefs labelled, for example, 'supplication' or 'replica'. These had to present the arguments of the parties clearly. Moreover, a familiarity of the proceedings of the court and the increasing professionalisation of men of law helped to formulate and argue the case.

For parties – men and women alike – who wanted to win their cases, it became increasingly sensible to make use of experienced and well-connected men to act in their stead in court. While they could still be relatives or friends, those who could afford the extra expenses employed men with knowledge of the law and litigation.[94] Elin's male opponents, for example, used some of the most noted advocates available. Although Wernstedt appeared several times in person, he had empowered Nicolaus Sabancorus to act for him. Sabancorus, one of the most learned and frequently used advocates of the late 1610s, authored the written pleadings presented that day at court (7 October 1618) in which he summarised the evidence which, he argued, proved that Elin was guilty of arson and slander. Moreover, he requested her being sentenced according to law to pay damages for the former crime and either prove the slanderous allegations to be true or be convicted for slander.[95] Similarly, in 1628 and 1631–1632, Hinrich Stöör repeatedly used Ignatius Meurer (1586–1672) as his attorney both at the *lagman*'s and appeals courts. Referring to his illness, he later gave Meurer his power of attorney on 9 October 1638.[96] The noble Åke Soop (1584–1648), judge at the Svea Court of Appeal, also presented documents written by Stöör to the Court.[97] However, Stöör occasionally wrote documents in his own hand and even appeared personally in court.[98] As this indicates, it made sense for litigants of both sexes to use experienced scribes to write documents for them as well as attorneys and advocates to represent them. Available centrally in Stockholm, such men had experience in law and they knew the practices of the Court of Appeal. Even if litigants often had to be personally at hand in Stockholm during the court sessions, they probably considered getting hired legal help worth the extra costs.

Conclusion

This chapter has investigated Lady Elin Johansdotter [Månesköld]'s litigation at the Svea Court of Appeal in the 1610s–1630s as a case study of female agency. According to Sweden's laws, single women were represented by their legal guardians and married women by their husbands, while widows were free from guardianship. However, as the case study has shown, Lady Elin's capacity to litigate did not conform strictly to the clear rules defined in the written law regarding the possibilities of single, married, and widowed women to sue and answer in court.

When widowed, Lady Elin conducted land-related litigation both at the appellate and lower level courts in person. In addition, she occasionally used relatives and attorneys as her representatives. The active role she played in her litigation at the Svea Court of Appeal corresponds with previous research demonstrating fluidity and more active female agency in practice than in law. However, her capacity to act apparently did not undergo any drastic changes when she remarried. Her second husband represented her in one cause, which might even have been the reason for a strategic remarriage, but she adamantly refused that her third husband represent her despite her opponent's repeated suggestions that he do so. At this point, the appellate court judges did not react, nor did they imply her incapacity to conduct litigation without her husband. If we compare Elin's agency to that of her unmarried stepdaughters Gunilla and Ermegård Tott, both wives and unmarried women could show more agency in litigation than the law (in theory) allowed.

Admittedly, independent agency without third-party representation cannot be automatically assumed as being tantamount to freedom of action; it could be down to a lack of powerful allies as attorneys or of funds to hire competent attorneys.[99] The Svea Court of Appeal cases analysed by Anu Lahtinen has led her to observe that '[t]hey seem to reflect a world in which women's well-being depended on the goodwill and ability of their guardians and representatives.'[100] Even in Lady Elin's case, we cannot rule out the possibility that she wanted a husband's support as her remarrying twice may have been connected to the property disputes she was involved in. The sources may not provide us with more than glimpses into Elin's personality, but they do give us some insight into her capacity to manage her affairs. Though independent-minded, on occasion, she relied on husbands and relatives as well as attorneys and scribes, suggesting she – like men – used a variety of strategies of agency or representation. Lady Elin may not have conformed to the architype of a typical married seventeenth-century

Swedish woman in every respect. Yet it is safe to conclude that in both widowhood and wifehood she made good use of the culture of flexibility within the law in Early Modern Sweden to manage her litigation.

Notes

1 I would like to the thank Teresa Phipps and Deborah Youngs warmly for their kind and useful comments on previous versions of this chapter.
2 For a discussion on the concept of women's agency, see the chapter written by Cordelia Beattie in this volume.
3 In medieval and early modern Sweden, most nobles only used their first names and patronyms. Thus, Elin was known as 'daughter of Johan' and her husband Tönne 'son of Erik'. However, in the early seventeenth century, nobles started to use surnames, often based on their coats-of-arms, probably due to foreign influences. For example Månesköld signified 'moon shield', based on the crescent moon on their escutcheon, while the Horns had a horn on their coat-of-arms. I have used family names if the persons themselves used them and added them in square brackets if they did not. Women continued to use their patronyms, coats-of-arms and possible family names after their marriage. Consequently, Elin Johansdotter kept her name through her three marriages.
4 For example, Mia Korpiola, 'A Safe Haven in the Shadow of War? The Founding and the Raison d'être of the New Court, Based on Its Early Activity', in Mia Korpiola (ed.), *The Svea Court of Appeal in the Early Modern Period: Historical Reinterpretations and New Perspectives* (Stockholm, 2014), pp. 55–108; Mia Korpiola, 'The Svea Court of Appeal: A Basis of Good Governance and Justice in the Early Modern Swedish Realm, 1614–1800', in A. M. Godfrey and C. H. van Rhee (eds.), *Central Courts in Early Modern Europe and the Americas* (Berlin 2020). pp. 305–350.
5 Maria Sjöberg, *Kvinnors jord, manlig rätt: Äktenskap, egendom och makt i äldre tid* (Hedemora, 2001), p. 10. See also Maria Ågren, *Domestic Secrets: Women & Property in Sweden 1600–1857* (Chapel Hill, 2004), p. 19.
6 The so-called Great Repossession or Reduction (Sw. *reduktion*) of 1680 revoked all counties and baronies as well as a number of major land grants and donations given to the nobility back to the Swedish crown. The Repossession was a necessity because taxable land, the Crown's main source of income, had been alienated to the nobility leaving the state close to bankruptcy.
7 Elsa Trolle Önnerfors, 'Suum Cuique Tribuere – Give to Each His Own: Court Cases Involving Swedish Nobility in the Court of Appeal 1650–1690', in Korpiola (ed.), *The Svea Court of Appeal*, pp. 163–200, here pp. 176–177, 194, 197.
8 Gustaf Elgenstierna, *Ättartavlor, 5* (Stockholm, 1930), p. 328; Elgenstierna, *Ättartavlor, 8*, p. 343.
9 Jan Eric Almquist, 'Adliga ätten Månesköld (af Seglinge) ursprung och äldsta historia', *Släkt och Hävd* 1965:3, pp. 269–298, here pp. 275–279.
10 Jan Eric Almquist, '1582 års adelsregister', *Släkt och Hävd*, 3 (1962), pp. 145–155: Johan Karlsson till Ora, Arent Karlsson till Eke, and Christer Karlsson till Seglinge. Their future in-law Tönne Eriksson was also included.
11 Almquist, 'Adliga ätten', pp. 279–280, 285, 288–289.
12 Elgenstierna, *Ättartavlor, 5*, p. 328; Gustaf Elgenstierna, *Ättartavlor, 1* (Stockholm, 1925), p. 220.
13 Hans Gillingstam and Kjell-Gunnar Lundholm, 'Tott', in Folke Wernstedt, Hans Gillingstam and Pontus Möller (eds.), *Äldre svenska frälsesläkter: Ättartavlor 1:3* (Stockholm, 1989), pp. 270–295, here pp. 270–280; Johanna Andersson Raeder, *Hellre hustru än änka: Äktenskapens ekonomiska betydelse för frälsekvinnor i senmedeltidens Sverige* (Stockholm, 2011), pp. 46–52; Tuula Hockman, *Kolmen polven perilliset. Ingeborg Aakentytär (Tott) ja hänen sukunsa (n. 1460–1507)* (Helsinki, 2006).

14 Gillingstam and Lundholm, 'Tott', pp. 280–281; Elgenstierna, *Ättartavlor*, 8, pp. 342–343. On Henrik Klasson Horn, see Eric Anthoni, 'Horn - Henrik Klasson', in *Svenskt biografiskt lexikon* [hereafter *SBL*] 19 (Stockholm, 1971–1973), pp. 353–355.
15 Gillingstam and Lundholm, 'Tott', p. 281; Elgenstierna, *Ättartavlor*, 8, p. 343; Barbro Bursell, *William Grey och Brita Tott: En berättelse om krig och kärlek i stormakttidens Sverige* (Stockholm, 2012), pp. 40–41.
16 On the main principles of Swedish early modern inheritance law, see Mia Korpiola and Elsa Trolle Önnerfors, 'Options for Post-mortem Property Planning in Medieval Sweden', in Mia Korpiola and Anu Lahtinen (eds.), *Planning for Death: Wills and Death-Related Property Arrangements in Europe, 1200–1600* (Leiden, 2018), pp. 29–65.
17 Almquist, 'Adliga ätten', pp. 285–287, 290–291; Folke Wernstedt, *Ståthållaren Christoffer Wernstedt 1542–1627: Anteckningar om Släkten Wernstedt 1* (Stockholm, 1929), pp. 47–48, 50, 113, 115.
18 He wrote his name 'Jacob Bergfelt' at least in some pleadings with his signature at the Court of Appeal, see Svea Hovrätt, Huvudarkivet, E VI a 2 aa:18.
19 The information provided by Elgenstierna (*Ättartavlor, 1*, p. 713) has been corrected by Folke Wernstedt in 'Adliga ätten "Bärfelts" nr 196 tidigare led: Ett bidrag till riddarhusstamtavlornas historia', *Personhistorisk Tidskrift*, 43 (1944–1945), pp. 62–72, esp. p. 68. See also Elgenstierna, *Ättartavlor, 5*, p. 328. Cf. Bursell, *William Grey*, pp. 12, 42.
20 Wernstedt, 'Adliga ätten', pp. 68–69.
21 Gillingstam and Lundholm, 'Tott', p. 280; Elgenstierna, *Ättartavlor 5*, p. 328.
22 Morning gifts were the most important marriage-related property transactions in medieval and early modern Sweden. The husband promised publicly in front of twelve witnesses his wife a considerable amount of property, either in land or rent, on the morning after their wedding night, 9–10, Chapter on Marriage (Sw. giftermålsbalken, hereafter G), Kuningas Kristoferin maanlaki 1442 (hereafter *KrL 1442*), ed. and trans. Martti Ulkuniemi (Helsinki, 1978), pp. 47–48. Morning gifts had become important status symbols in Sweden and they were occasionally so generous as to cause conflict in the family, Hans Petersson, *Morgongåvoinstitutet i Sverige under tiden fram till omkring 1734 års lag* (Lund, 1973); Heikki Ylikangas, 'Huomenlahja Ruotsin keskiaikaisten lakien valossa', *Historiallinen aikakauskirja*, 65 (1967), pp. 14–25; Lizzie Carlsson, *"Jag giver dig min dotter:" Trolovning och äktenskap i den svenska kvinnans äldre historia*, 1 (Lund, 1965), pp. 209–224; Mia Korpiola, *Between Betrothal and Bedding: Marriage Formation in Sweden, 1200–1600* (Leiden, 2009), pp. 78–85; Tuula Rantala, 'Monastic Donations by Widows: Morning Gifts as Assets in Planning for Old Age and Death in Fifteenth-Century Sweden', in Mia Korpiola and Anu Lahtinen (eds.), *Planning for Death: Wills and Death-Related Property Arrangements in Europe, 1200–1600* (Leiden, 2018), pp. 66–87; Anu Lahtinen, *Anpassning, förhandling, motstånd: Kvinnliga aktörer i släkten Fleming 1470–1620*, trans. Camilla Frostell (Helsinki and Stockholm, 2009), pp. 63–64.
23 RA, SH, HA, E VI a 2 aa:2 (unpaginated); Jan Eric Almquist, 'Rättstvisten om Skeboholm 1614–1616: Bidrag till släkterna Månesköds och Totts historia', *Personhistorisk Tidskrift*, 40 (1939–1940), pp. 1–22.
24 '*Fru*' was the honorary title used for married or widowed noblewomen in early modern Sweden. Its equivalent for unmarried women was '*jungfru*', 'maiden'. I have here translated '*fru*' as lady although the English term is rather problematic as the English system of gentry/nobility was quite different from the Swedish.
25 Riksarkivet (hereafter RA, Stockholm, Sweden), Svea Hovrätt (hereafter SH), Huvudarkivet (hereafter HA), B I a:1, fol. 1.
26 RA, SH, HA, E VI a 2 aa:18; Wernstedt, *Ståthållaren*, pp. 113–122.
27 On Stöör, see Gustaf Elgenstierna, *Den introducerade svenska adelns ättartavlor med tillägg och rättelser* (hereafter: *Ättartavlor*), 8 (Stockholm, 1934), p. 47. Stöör usually signed his name 'Hinrich Stör', but occasionally also 'Heinrich von Stöer', for example, RA, SH, HA, E VI a 2 aa:53, fols. 33–34.

28 RA, SH, HA, E VI a 2 aa:53, esp. fols. 123, 131, 140; RA, SH, HA, B II a:11 (1638), fol. 22.
29 For example, Anu Lahtinen, 'Gender and Continuity: Women, Men and Landed Property in Medieval Finland', in Anu Lahtinen and Kirsi Vainio-Korhonen (eds.), *History and Change* (Helsinki, 2004), pp. 32–45, here p. 38; Charlotte Cederbom, *The Legal Guardian and Married Women: Norms and Practice in the Swedish Realm 1350–1450* (Helsinki, 2017), pp. 148, 200; Andersson, *Tingets män*, pp. 87–92, 121–123. Compurgators confirmed with their oaths their belief in the oath of the principal.
30 Swedish law was written down in the Middle Ages. While King Magnus Eriksson's mid-fourteenth-century Town Law remained in force until the 1730s, King Magnus Eriksson's Law of the Realm for the countryside was replaced by King Christopher's Law of the Realm (1442) in the sixteenth century. These were supplemented by statutes and ordinances.
31 6:1, G, *KrL 1442*, ed. Ulkuniemi, p. 43.
32 15, 20–21, G, ibid., pp. 48–50; Cederbom, *The Legal Guardian*, esp. pp. 84–108; See also Mia Korpiola, 'Spousal Disputes, The Marital Property System and the Law in Later Medieval Sweden', in Cordelia Beattie and Matthew Frank Stevens (eds.), *Married Women and the Law in Premodern Northwest Europe* (Woodbridge, 2013), pp. 31–51, here pp. 33–36; Anna Hansen, *Ordnade hushåll: Genus och kontroll i Jämtland under 1600-talet* (Uppsala, 2006), pp. 129–134.
33 1–5, G, *Magnus Erikssons stadslag i nusvensk tolkning* [hereafter *MESL*], Åke Holmbäck and Elias Wessén (eds.), (Stockholm, 1966), pp. 38–40.
34 15–16, G, *MESL*, eds. Holmbäck and Wessén, p. 41. Here Swedish law differed from the English feme sole system granting single women full legal agency after majority, for example, Matthew Frank Stevens, 'London's Married Women, Debt Litigation and Coverture in the Court of Common Pleas', in Beattie and Stevens (eds.), *Married Women and the Law*, pp. 115–131, here p. 118.
35 9, G, *KrL 1442*, ed. Ulkuniemi, p. 47; 8, G, *MESL*, eds. Holmbäck and Wessén, p. 42.
36 Cederbom, *The Legal Guardian*, pp. 180–189, 269, 271–274.
37 14, 1614 Ordinance of Judicial Procedure (*Rättegångs-Ordinantie*), *Kongl. stadgar, förordningar, bref och resolutioner: Ifrån åhr 1528 in til 1701 angående justitiae och executions-ährender*, ed. Johan Schmedeman (Stockholm, 1706), pp. 138–139; Trolle Önnerfors, 'Suum Cuique Tribuere', p. 176.
38 Trolle Önnerfors, 'Suum Cuique', pp. 176–177, 194, 197.
39 Ågren, *Domestic Secrets*, p. 47. This corresponds with the 26% of female plaintiffs at the Court of Chancery (1613–1714), but was higher than the proportion of female litigants in some of the Continental imperial appellate courts, or the English Court of Common Pleas. In the Continental imperial appellate courts, female litigants were not quite as numerous. According to Irene Jung, women plaintiffs litigating alone formed about 15% of the cases at the Imperial Chamber Court (Ger. *Reichskammergericht*) in 1689–1806. Among the 108 cases from the female inhabitants of the town of Wetzlar, 60% involved widows, while married and single women formed 25 respective 15%. The approximately 46,000 cases adjudicated in the Imperial Aulic Council (Ger. *Reichshofrat*) in 1495–1806 indicate similar figures, 17% involving women. Women explicitly called single or married were among the parties. Similarly, female litigants appeared in 17% of the cases in the fifteenth-century Court of Common Pleas. Irene Jung, 'Wetzlarer Frauen vor dem Reichskammergericht', in Siegrid Westphal (ed.), *In eigener Sache: Frauen vor den höchsten Gerichten des Alten Reichs* (Cologne – Weimar – Vienna, 2005), pp. 21–28, here pp. 21, 28; Siegrid Westphal, 'Die Inanspruchnahme des Reichshofrats durch Frauen – quantitative Aspekte', in *ibid.*, pp. 29–39, here p. 32; Stevens, 'London's Married Women', p. 117.
40 In the countryside, the noble judges or their substitutes presided over local district courts with twelve peasant jurors. The court of the *lagman* or provincial judge was

the second instance in the countryside. In towns, the town councillors, elected merchants and artisans, sat at the town courts. The courts of appeal were established from 1614 on as supreme royal appellate courts while the king as the ultimate fountain of justice could exceptionally grant extraordinary legal remedies.

41 Marja Taussi Sjöberg, *Rätten och kvinnorna: Från släktmakt till statsmakt i Sverige på 1500- och 1600-talet* (Stockholm, 1996), pp. 100–101, 111–113, 220–222; Jan Sundin, *För Gud, Staten och Folket: Brott och rättskipning i Sverige 1600–1840* (Lund, 1992), pp. 103–105; Gudrun Andersson, *Tingets män och kvinnor: Genus som norm och strategi under 1600- och 1700-tal* (Uppsala, 1998), pp. 74–75, 82–85, 107–108.
42 Andersson Raeder, *Hellre hustru*, p. 46.
43 Lahtinen, *Anpassning*, pp. 62–67, 186–189; Veli Pekka Toropainen, *Päättäväiset porvarskat: Turun johtavan porvariston naisten toimijuus vuosina 1623–1670* (Turku, 2016), pp. 98, 122–124, 126–127; Bursell, *William Grey*, p. 135.
44 RA, SH, HA, E VI a 2 aa:18, fol. 348: '*fattige wärnlöse Quinna, hwilket iag skal bidia att Gudh löner*'.
45 For example, RA, SH, HA, E VI a 2 aa:2, fols. 149–51v, 263–268, 292; Almquist, 'Rättstvisten', p. 7.
46 RA, SH, HA, E VI a 2 aa:2, fols. 149–151v; Almquist, 'Rättstvisten', p. 11.
47 RA, SH, HA, E VI a 2 aa:2, fols. 152–154v.
48 Ibid., fols. 162, 165–167v, 170–171; Almquist, 'Rättstvisten', pp. 12–15.
49 RA, SH, HA, E VI a 2 aa:2, fol. 231v.
50 Ibid., fols. 157–157v.
51 Ibid., fols. 158–159v, 161–161v, 174–174v.
52 Wernstedt, *Ståthållaren*, pp. 20–79; Elgenstierna, *Ättartavlor*, 8, pp. 746–747.
53 Brahe was apparently also the legal guardian of Lady Elin's daughter Brita after her father's demise, Bursell, *William Grey*, p. 42.
54 RA, SH, HA, E VI a 2 aa:18.
55 Wernstedt, *Ståthållaren*, p. 53.
56 RA, SH, HA, E VI a 2 aa:18; Folke Wernstedt, *Ståthållaren Christoffer Wernstedt 1542–1627: Anteckningar om Släkten Wernstedt 1* (Stockholm, 1929), pp. 113–122.
57 Lahtinen, *Anpassning*, pp. 176–177, 179; Andersson Raeder, *Hellre hustru*, pp. 61, 67–71, 81, 137–138; Lahtinen, 'Prolonged', p. 137; Toropainen, *Päättäväiset*, p. 134; Stevens, 'London's Married Women', pp. 130–131.
58 Sture Petrén, 'Våra första advokater', *Svensk Juristtidning* 32 (1947), pp. 1–25, here pp. 2–3.
59 RA, SH, HA, E VI a 2 aa:2, fol. 158.
60 Petrén, 'Våra första', pp. 2–3.
61 Petrén, 'Våra första', p. 3, n. 1.
62 Almquist, 'Adliga ätten', p. 292.
63 Lahtinen, 'Gender', pp. 40–41; Toropainen, *Päättäväiset*, p. 253.
64 RA, SH, HA, E VI a 2 aa:53, esp. fols. 123, 131, 140; RA, SH, HA, B II a:11 (1638), fol. 22.
65 RA, SH, HA, E VI a 2 aa:53 nr. 1, unpag.
66 Ibid.
67 RA, SH, HA, E VI a 2 aa:53 nr. 1, unpag.
68 RA, SH, HA, E VI a 2 aa:53 nr. 1, fol. 70.
69 RA, SH, HA, E VI a 2 aa:53 nr. 1, fol. 3:

> begärte att hennes Man måtte Komma fram och sware för henne, Hon swaradhe hennes Man wedt inthe om saken Derföre will hon sware honom Stöör berettade att han hade talt medh hennes Man om de icke Kunde Komma till förlijkningh, då hadhe han swarat honom , att han gierna önskadhe, saken måtte blifwe förlijkt, Män hon swaradhe som tilförendhe, hennes Man wedt inthe af saaken vthan hon will sware honom [...].

70 Ibid., fol. 5v.
71 Ibid., fol. 4: '*orolige wedher Part*'.
72 Anu Pylkkänen, *Puoli vuodetta, lukot ja avaimet. Nainen ja maatalous oikeuskäytännön valossa 1660–1710* (Helsinki, 1990), pp. 128–130, 276–278, 305; Toropainen, *Päättäväiset*, pp. 66, 68, 112–114; Åsa Karlsson Sjögren, *Kvinnors rätt i stormaktstidens Gävle* (Umeå, 1998), pp. 107–109; Andersson, *Tingets män*, p. 298.
73 Pylkkänen, *Puoli vuodetta*, pp. 151–152, also pp. 339–342.
74 RA, SH, HA, E VI a 2 aa:53 nr. 1, fol. 48.
75 Ibid., fol. 52.
76 Ibid., fol. 102.
77 Ibid., fols. 98–8v.
78 RA, SH, HA, E VI a 2 aa:53 nr. 1.
79 RA, SH, HA, E VI a 2 aa:53 nr 2; Mia Korpiola, '"The Fall and Restoration of Elin Tönnesdotter": Land, Noble Property Strategies and the Law in Early Seventeenth-Century Sweden', *COLLeGIUM*, 2 (2007): *The Trouble with Ribs: Women, Men and Gender in Early Modern Europe*, eds. Anu Korhonen and K. P. L. Lowe, pp. 153–179. Available online (accessed 5 May, 2020) at: https://helda.helsinki.fi/bitstream/handle/10138/25757/002_09_korpiola.pdf?sequence=1.
80 Almquist, 'Rättstvisten', pp. 8–10.
81 RA, SH, HA, E VI a 2 aa:53 nr 2; Korpiola, '"The Fall"', 164–165.
82 RA, SH, HA, E VI a 2 aa:2, fols. 240–240v (*wij tå wåro små och omÿndige barn och hade macht öfwer ingen ting*).
83 Bursell, *William Grey*, pp. 152, 158.
84 For example, RA, SH, HA, E VI a 2 aa:86.
85 Pylkkänen, *Puoli vuodetta*, pp. 144–148; Andersson, *Tingets män*, pp. 92–93, 100, 280–281; Hansen, *Ordnade hushåll*, pp. 132–133.
86 Almquist, 'Rättstvisten', pp. 13–14. On the Horns, see Eric Anthoni, 'Horn', *SBL, 19* (Stockholm, 1971–1973), pp. 343–344. They were incorrectly identified as Erik Tönnesson's maternal uncles (*på deres sÿskene barns [...] wegna*) in RA, SH, HA, E VI a 2 aa:2, fol. 152.
87 For example, RA, SH, HA, E VI a 2 aa:86, fol. 24.
88 For example, Cederbom, *The Legal Guardian*, pp. 162–174; Toropainen, *Päättäväiset*, pp. 74, 115–116, 217–218, 222–224.
89 Gustaf Elgenstierna, *Ättartavlor, 7* (Stockholm, 1932), p. 155; Bursell, *William Grey*, pp. 15, 42.
90 RA, SH, HA, E VI a 2 aa:53, fols. 20–21 (Michil Persson) 133 and 140 (Lindegren). On Nils Nilsson Lindegren, see Gustaf Elgenstierna, *Ättartavlor, 5* (Stockholm, 1930), p. 13. Lindegren also represented Elin's stepdaughters Ermegård and Gunilla Tott against Hinrich Stöör, for example, RA, SH, HA, E VI a 2 aa:86, fols. 6, 8–8v.
91 RA, SH, HA, E VI a 2 aa:53, fols. 2, 29, 51–52, 80, 90: [fol. 2] '*henne faller beswärligit länge wara ifrån sitt huus*'.
92 Karlsson Sjögren, *Kvinnors rätt*, pp. 108–113; Toropainen, *Päättäväiset*, pp. 124–126, 260. See also Andersson, *Tingets män*, 106–109.
93 For example, Petrén, 'Våra första'.
94 Lahtinen, 'Prolonged', pp. 153–155, 157–158.
95 Svea Hovrätt, Huvudarkivet, E VI a 2 aa:18. On Sabancorus, see Lars Björne, Patrioter och institutionalister: Den nordiska rättsvetenskapens historia,1 (Lund, 1995), pp. 43–44, 401; Petrén, 'Våra första', pp. 10–11; Ebbe Kock, 'En svensk bokkatalog från 1500-talet', *Nordisk tidskrift för bok- och biblioteksväsen* 7 (1920), pp. 146–155, here pp. 148, 153–155; Marko Lamberg, 'The Tale of Two Courts in One Town: The Relationship between the Stockholm Town Court and the Svea Court of Appeal 1614–1624', in Korpiola (ed.), *The Svea Court of Appeal*, pp. 109–130, at pp. 114–116.
96 RA, SH, HA, E VI a 2 aa:53, fols. 75, 91, 106, 114, 118 and unpaginated. Stöör also used Meurer as his advocate in his testamentary litigation against his sisters-in-law,

for example, RA, SH, HA, E VI a 2 aa:86, fol. 7. On Meurer, see Tomas Lidman, 'Meurer, Ignatius', *SBL*, 25 (Stockholm, 1985–1987), pp. 439–441; Petrén, 'Våra första', pp. 15–19.
97 For example, RA, SH, HA, E VI a 2 aa:53, fol. 119.
98 RA, SH, HA, E VI a 2 aa:53, fol. 103.
99 For example, Toropainen, *Päättäväiset*, pp. 143–144.
100 Lahtinen, 'Prolonged', p. 157.

11
WOMEN LITIGANTS IN EARLY EIGHTEENTH-CENTURY IRELAND

Mary O'Dowd

On 30 June 1922, Irish historiography was dealt a critical blow. In the escalating violence of the Irish civil war, mines, stored in the basement of the Public Record Office of Ireland exploded. Inhabitants of Dublin watched as the city landscape was filled not only with the black smoke of fire but with the burnt remnants of the records of the Irish administration dating back to the thirteenth century: 'pieces of white paper gyrating in the upper air like seagulls'.[1] The loss of the records was devastating for Irish historiography. The impact was particularly severe for Irish legal history as most of the court records from the medieval period through to the nineteenth century were destroyed. Identifying litigants in any Irish court, regardless of gender, became a major challenge.

In recent years, historians have begun to recognise the value of uncovering transcripts, copies and edited summaries of the lost documents in order to reconstruct the history of the Irish legal infrastructure and the men and women who made use of it.[2] This process has slowly revealed the presence of women in Irish courts as executors of wills and as claimants of disputed inheritances, jointures and marriage portions. By the early seventeenth century, the Dublin administration had extended its control over the whole of the island of Ireland and English common law had gradually replaced the customary law of Gaelic society, usually referred to as Brehon law. The surviving sources provide evidence of men and women from Gaelic society engaging with the newly established legal infrastructure. The scattered documentation also suggests that in legal disputes involving property and land, women may have represented up to a quarter of the litigants in seventeenth-century Irish courts. Therefore, despite the relative paucity of legal records, Irish historiography is slowly beginning to recognise women's engagement with the early modern legal system.[3]

DOI: 10.4324/9780429278037-12

In addition to the search for copies and transcripts of lost documentation, another potential and, as yet, relatively untapped source for identifying women who appeared in Irish courts is the surviving archive of early modern English courts. Irish litigants, unhappy with a verdict in a Dublin court, could appeal the decision in a higher court in London. Tracing the appeal process of an Irish case through English court records can prove a surprisingly rewarding exercise. In the eighteenth century, many Irish litigants presented appeals to the highest court of all, the House of Lords. The printed documentation of the appellant and respondent often rehearsed the details of the case and the decisions made in the Irish courts. Dr Colman Dennehy has estimated that a woman was the sole litigant in about 10% of the Irish cases appealed in the House of Lords and this figure rises significantly when women who were named as appellants jointly with their husbands are included.[4]

A decision of an Irish ecclesiastical court could also be appealed through the English legal system. In his study of the High Court of Delegates, G. I. O. Duncan referenced a number of cases which were appeals from ecclesiastical courts in Dublin and Cork.[5] As the records of the Court are only partially catalogued, it is difficult to estimate how many Irish appeals were reviewed by the Court of Delegates but the surnames of appellants listed by The National Archives for a small section of the archive indicates that it was not inconsiderable. A random search also suggests that many involved women litigants.[6]

In this chapter, I want to demonstrate the value of pursuing such appeals through a focus on two law suits taken by women litigants which began in the Irish court system but were subsequently appealed in English courts: one, mainly, through the ecclesiastical courts and the other through the civil court system. In addition to the court records, there is information on the two cases in other contemporary sources including pamphlets and family correspondence. This documentation enables us to trace the experiences of Irish women litigants as they steered their way through a complex legal process. The two case studies also demonstrate the potential of English court records for filling in some of the gaps in our knowledge of the gender of litigants who appeared before the Irish courts in the early modern period.

First, let me introduce the two women and their individual stories. Elizabeth Leeson was a young widow of twenty-eight years of age in 1724 when she met William Fitzmaurice, the eldest son of the earl of Kerry. Leeson had married in 1720 but her husband died three years later. There were two children from the marriage.[7] The Leesons were a middle class Dublin family. Elizabeth's husband, Hugh and his father were involved in land speculation and development in the expanding city of post-Restoration Dublin. In his will, Hugh left most of his property to his son but he also arranged for his wife to have an annuity of £50 and possession of the family home in Duke Street in Dublin during her widowhood.[8]

In 1724, William Fitzmaurice was in his early thirties. He was heir to an estate estimated to be worth £5,000 per year. Despite the gap in the social standing of

Leeson and Fitzmaurice, they were immediately attracted to one another. Following their initial meeting at a social event in a fashionable house in St Stephen's Green in Dublin, Fitzmaurice began to visit Leeson at her home. Their romance flourished in the summer of 1724 but Leeson later claimed that it did not become sexual until they had made several promises of marriage to one another. The first promise in the future tense was made in June as both partners placed their hands on the Bible.[9] A couple of weeks later, they made a second promise in the present tense with their hands on the Book of Common Prayer:

> the said William takeing this Deponent [i.e. Elizabeth Leeson] by the Hand, and also takeing the Book of Common Prayer in his other Hand, sayd by the Contents of this Book I take you for my Wife, and swear I will never marry any other Woman and this Deponent having the said William by the Hand and the said Book in his other Hand, sayd I take you (meaning the said William) for my Husband, and swear I will never marry any other Man.[10]

Following the promises of marriage, Fitzmaurice placed a ring on Leeson's finger. Neither promise, however, was witnessed. Clearly concerned about this, five months after the second promise, in December 1724, Leeson asked her servant, Elizabeth Vickers to act as witness while she and Fitzmaurice read the marriage service from the Book of Common Prayer. Subsequently, Leeson said that she believed that they were married although she recognised that the union still had to be solemnised *in facie ecclesiae*, that is, in the presence of a clergyman. She said that Fitzmaurice had told her that he did not want to have a more public ceremony because he feared the disapproval of his father.[11]

Not long after the consummation of the union, Leeson became pregnant and gave birth to a son in October 1725. While she was pregnant she began to hear rumours in Dublin that Fitzmaurice had denied that he was married to her and that he had asked another woman to marry him. Despite Fitzmaurice's denials, the rumours proved to be true.[12] When Leeson learnt that the banns for the marriage were about to be proclaimed, she entered a caveat in the Dublin consistory court in November 1726 requesting a halt to the marriage arrangements on the grounds that Fitzmaurice was already contracted to her in marriage. The Irish court dismissed Leeson's suit because there was only one witness to the third promise and none to the first two. The judge in the ecclesiastical court, Thomas Trotter, followed the accepted guidelines that an espousal of marriage had to be witnessed by two people. Leeson's proctor, however, drew on the legal concept of 'half proof' to argue that she had presented sufficient evidence to enable her to take a suppletory oath to give evidence in her own defence.[13] In other words, she could testify as the second witness to the marriage promises. Trotter, however, dismissed this argument and, therefore, the existence of a contract between Leeson and Fitzmaurice. Leeson did not accept the verdict of the Dublin court and she appealed its decision to the English Chancery court. In March 1730, the latter referred the case to a Court of Delegates consisting of three bishops, four doctors of ecclesiastical law and five peers.[14] Having examined the evidence, the Delegates concluded that the judgement of the Dublin consistory court was in error and that legally, Leeson's proctor had provided sufficient evidence to entitle her to take a suppletory oath. Leeson had travelled to London to attend the court hearing and, on 10 March 1731, she 'appeared personally' before the Court of Delegates and presented a detailed written account of her relationship with Fitzmaurice.[15] Her evidence was backed up by Leeson's servant, Elizabeth Vickers who had witnessed the third promise and by her sister and sister-in-law who told of their conversations with Fitzmaurice who assured them that he would marry Leeson.[16] The totality of the evidence clearly impressed the court and despite delays by the defence questioning Leeson's right to a suppletory oath and the reliability of Vickers as a witness, on 14 March 1733, the court determined in Leeson's favour. The Court gave Fitzmaurice four months to fulfil his promise and marry Leeson. His lawyers asked for a judicial review but on 12 January 1734, the initial verdict was confirmed.[17] Despite the order of the Court, there is no evidence that the couple married. Leeson, however, continued to refer to herself as Elizabeth Fitzmaurice. In her will dated February 1736, Leeson is named as 'Elizabeth Leeson als Fitzmaurice' but written in the margin is a note that indicated that she still used the surname Fitzmaurice ('vulgarly called Fitz Maurice'). Leeson did not, however, make any reference to William Fitzmaurice in the document. She died the following year and Fitzmaurice married in 1738.[18]

In the second case, the litigant was Catherine Sarah Cunningham, a young woman who met Arthur St Leger about the same year that Elizabeth Leeson met William Fitzmaurice, that is, 1724. As in the Leeson/Fitzmaurice liaison, there was a significant social gap between Cunningham and St Leger. Cunningham's father was a captain in the army while St Leger was the son and heir of Arthur St Leger, 1st Viscount of Doneraile. Cunningham was about fifteen when she met St Leger while he was a twenty-nine-year-old widow with a son by his first marriage. The circumstance of the first meeting of Cunningham and St Leger is not clear but in 1725 a marriage was solemnised between them in Doneraile Court, the estate house of the St Leger family.[19]

The Cunningham/St Leger marriage was a private one attended only by her parents and brother. St Leger's family did not appear to know about the marriage until after the death of the first Viscount in July 1727. Like Fitzmaurice, St Leger asked that the marriage be kept secret for fear of his father's wrath if he found out about it.[20]

There was no marriage settlement agreed by St Leger with Cunningham's father which would have been expected in the marriage of an heir to an estate such as St Leger. Nor did Cunningham or her family provide St Leger with a dowry. Just over a year after the marriage, in April 1726, St Leger executed a deed 'in his own Hand-writing' agreeing to pay Cunningham £40 per annum during the lifetime of his father. The money was for her own 'separate use'. Following his father's death, Cunningham claimed that St Leger continued to recognise her as his wife. In the winter of 1727, she accompanied him to Dublin where she said she was introduced to the lord lieutenant (i.e. the head of the Irish administration) and other government dignitaries. In July 1728, St Leger executed a 'proper deed' in which he agreed to provide Cunningham with a separate annual allowance of £800.[21]

The agreement may have been prompted by the fact that Cunningham was pregnant. Towards the end of the summer of 1728, St Leger left the Cork estate to spend the winter in Dublin.[22] Cunningham remained in Doneraile but she later said that she was quite ill during her pregnancy and, as a consequence, she and her parents decided to move from Doneraile to Cork City to be closer to her physician.[23] The couple never lived together again.

Subsequently, St Leger ignored calls by Cunningham to pay the annuity agreed in the deed of 1728 and published a notice in a newspaper denying that he was married to Cunningham.[24] Cunningham who was still under age sued St Leger in the Irish Court of Chancery through her father. She asked for the annuity to be paid along with any arrears due to her.[25] In the response framed by his lawyers, St Leger pleaded his weakness for alcohol and argued that he had no memory of the wedding ceremony and he doubted that it had taken place. He admitted that he had cohabited with Cunningham but he claimed that the deed of 1728 was drawn up when he was too drunk to know what he was doing and that it was part of a conspiracy by Cunningham, her family and another male accomplice to defraud him of his inheritance.[26] The Irish court found for St Leger due to his intoxication when he signed the deed. Cunningham, (again through her father) appealed the decision to the House of Lords who accepted that the marriage had taken place and determined that St Leger should pay his wife the agreed annuity.[27] The Lords did not, however, make any decision concerning Cunningham's arrears for the payment of the annuity or the accumulated interest. By that time, St Leger had been dispatched by his family to the Isle of Man, presumably to keep him away from Cunningham and to avoid any further scandal. He was reported to be drinking heavily and may have drunk himself into an early grave.[28] He died in the Isle of Man, aged thirty-nine in 1734. Arthur St Leger was succeeded as Viscount Doneraile by his son by his first marriage, Arthur Mohan who was under age at seventeen. Cunningham was obliged to initiate a bill of revivor against Arthur Mohan's guardian, his grandmother, Elizabeth, the Dowager Viscountess of Doneraile in the Irish Chancery Court to resume her litigation. As she was now in her mid-twenties, she could do so in her own name.[29]

Arthur Mohan's guardian took a keen interest in the legal disputes involving her grandson's estate. She had formerly and unsuccessfully taken legal action to have her own jointure recognised and was, therefore, familiar with the relevant documentation in the family archive.[30] Possibly at her prompting, the legal representatives of her grandson presented a new argument. Instead of emphasising St Leger's intoxicated state when he signed the deed of 1728, they argued that his son had no legal obligation to fulfil any commitment made by his father in relation to the family estate. In a complex legal argument, the barristers pointed to a marriage settlement agreed in 1656 that, they argued, made subsequent heirs tenants in chief rather than owners of the Doneraile estate. The late Viscount's ownership was, therefore confined to his personal wealth which was very limited. He had no ownership title to the family property.[31]

After a long delay, in 1743, the Chancellor agreed that Cunningham was only entitled to claim her rights as a widow from the personal estate of her late husband. She again appealed this decision to the House of Lords but this time the law lords upheld the decision of the Irish court.[32] Despite this defeat, Cunningham continued to argue that she had, as a widow, a claim on her late husband's estate, if not through the annuity agreed in the deed of 1728, then through dower.

When Arthur Mohan died unexpectedly in 1750, Cunningham initiated a second bill of revivor against the next heir, her brother-in-law, Hayes St Leger. While the case was finally being heard in the Irish Chancery in 1763, some friends on both sides urged a settlement. The dispute had continued for over thirty years and the suggestion for a resolution was also a recognition of the persistence of Cunningham in pursuit of what she perceived to be her legal entitlement. Consequently, in 1764, Catherine Sarah, Dowager Viscountess of Doneraile and Hayes St Leger, 3rd Viscount Doneraile signed an agreement which granted Catherine Sarah an annuity of £200 for life. She was also given a cash sum of £1000 in lieu of all claims for arrears or other payments from the Doneraile estate.[33]

Both women, therefore, could be said to have had successful endings to their legal disputes but in neither case was the resolution that which they wanted when they initiated their suits. William Fitzmaurice did not marry Elizabeth Leeson and the 1728 deed in which Arthur, St Leger, 2nd Viscount agreed to give his wife Catherine Sarah an annuity of £800 was replaced by the 1764 agreement in which she was awarded a quarter of that sum.

Despite their limited success, the women litigants at the centre of both these cases are remarkable not only for initiating the legal proceedings (albeit Catherine Sarah Cunningham began her case through her father) but for persisting with them and working their way through the different courts involved. Both legal suits took a long time to come to conclusion. Elizabeth Leeson began her case against Fitzmaurice in November 1726 and did not receive a final verdict until January 1734. As we have seen, Catherine Sarah Cunningham had to wait over thirty years for her suit to be settled. Although she had married Arthur St Leger in her late teens and he had died when she was in her mid-twenties, she had to wait until her mid-fifties to receive regular payments as his widow. There were many reasons for the delays, some of which were simply the inevitable tardiness of legal disputes which involved a number of different courts in Dublin and London. The officials in the London Court of Delegates complained, in particular, of the difficulties involved in securing the relevant documentation from Irish ecclesiastical courts.[34] In Cunningham's case the deaths of her husband and his heir also, of course, added further delay.

There is, however, clear evidence that the families of both aristocratic men deliberately prevaricated and drew out the legal process for as long as possible. Initially, both defendants refused to take the cases of the women litigants seriously. William Fitzmaurice ignored the judgement of the English ecclesiastical court that he was obliged to marry Elizabeth Leeson in an ecclesiastical ceremony. He was fined and excommunicated but fled to France which made it impossible for the Court of Delegates to oversee the implementation of its decision.[35] Leeson was also of the view that Fitzmaurice deliberately requested a judicial review of the Court's decision because he knew that 'she hath spent the greatest Part of her Fortune in prosecuting her ... Cause against him and that ... [she] cannot raise any more Money to presente the same'.[36] Cunningham complained that Arthur St Leger and his son both claimed parliamentary privilege as members of the House of Lords in order to prolong her suit against them.[37] The journals of the House of Lords also indicate that the two men were reprimanded for their delay in responding to Cunningham's appeals.[38] Clearly, therefore, women who pursued litigation in their own name had to navigate not only the complexities of the court process but also the deliberate obstructions of their legal opponents.

As Leeson's comments indicate, a lengthy court case was also expensive and both women clearly struggled to find the necessary resources to continue with their suits. In 1728, Leeson sold her widow's life interest in her home in Duke Street to her brother-in-law for £100. This coincided with the period following the dismissal of her suit in the Irish Consistory Court and she may have used the money to finance her appeal to the London Court of Delegates.[39] Leeson did not have large cash reserves to fund an expensive and long court case. In 1733, when her London-based solicitor wrote to her with news of the favourable verdict in the Court of Delegates along with his bill, Leeson responded that she would pay him as soon as she could but it might be in 'small bills as I can save money', presumably from her widow's annuity.[40]

In her first appeal against the verdict of the Irish Chancery Court, Catherine Sarah Cunningham noted that she was being maintained by her father.[41] The latter was probably responsible for Cunningham's request in 1734 to the House of Lords to be permitted to sue *in forma pauperis*. In return for acknowledging that she did not have a 'worldly substance' of more than £5, she (and her father) was assigned a legal counsel free of charge.[42] It is not known when Catherine Sarah's father died but the long delays in reaching a decision on her appeals must have placed considerable financial pressure on his daughter. It may have been for this reason that in 1741 Cunningham was granted a royal pension of £100 per year for a couple of years while her second appeal was pending. The pension appears to have been withdrawn when the Irish court rejected her appeal in 1743.[43] Consequently, in order to appeal that decision in the House of Lords, Cunningham was again obliged to request to sue as a pauper.[44]

Apart from the delay and cost of the legal proceedings, the two cases have other common features. Most obvious is the class divergence between the women plaintiffs and the male defenders. Both women initiated law suits against members of well-connected aristocratic families who could use their networks and influence to denigrate and ostracise them socially. William Fitzmaurice's mother was Anne Petty, daughter of the famous economist and scientist, Sir William Petty. She was a close friend of Jonathan Swift who also took an interest in William Fitzmaurice's education at Eton and later in Oxford.[45] Anne Fitzmaurice tried to use her connections to discourage support for Leeson. In particular, she lobbied William King, the archbishop of Dublin to try to influence the judgement in favour of her son in the Dublin ecclesiastical court.[46] Fitzmaurice's sister, Arbella (later the well-known philanthropist) was married to Colonel Arthur Denny who was a Member of Parliament for County Kerry and linked the family to a wider network of parliamentarians in Dublin. Among the most active MPs in the Irish parliament while Leeson's case was being considered in the Dublin consistory court was Thomas Trotter, the judge who heard her case. It seems likely that he too was lobbied by the Fitzmaurice family for a favourable verdict.[47]

The Viscounts of Doneraile were also well connected in Dublin. Arthur St Leger had been a Member of the Irish House of Commons before he succeeded his father as Viscount Doneraile. And, as noted earlier, both he and his son, Arthur Mohun sat in the Irish House of Lords. Catherine Sarah Cunningham was not, however, without some influential support. When her appeal was due to be heard by the House of Lords in 1735, Josiah Hort, the bishop of Kilmore asked his friend and Member of the English House of Commons, George Bubb Doddington to encourage peers to attend the Lords to listen to Cunningham's appeal which he had heard in Dublin had a 'good appearance'.[48] It is not clear how effective Hort's plea was but it is striking that the two women litigants lost their initial cases in the Dublin courts but won on appeal in London where the personal connections of their opponents would have been less significant. As one contemporary noted, the Countess of Kerry's success in influencing the outcome of the legal dispute involving her son, was not 'on your side of the Water [i.e. England], answerable to the flattering Hopes which were excited in her at Home'.[49]

The defence barristers in the two cases drew on a similar rhetoric to denigrate the character and behaviour of the women. They aimed to present the women litigants and witnesses whom they summoned in support of their case as morally suspect. In an attempt to appeal the decision of the London Court of Delegates in favour of Leeson, the barrister for William Fitzmaurice submitted to the court a series of affidavits that he had collected from servants who had worked in Leeson's household.[50] They claimed that her servant and chief witness, Elizabeth Vickers, had had two children out of wedlock and that they had seen her in a settle bed with a married man in the kitchen of the house. The implication was that not only was Vickers's evidence not to be trusted but that her employer was also living in an immoral house. There was, however, a remarkable similarity in the evidence provided by the witnesses. Fitzmaurice's barristers also provided an affidavit from three of his friends who had met with Vickers's daughter, Mary, who claimed that she had some useful information for them about her mother's dishonesty. On meeting with the three men, Mary Vickers asked what would they like her to say.[51] While the men emphasised in their affidavits that they had told Vickers that they only wanted the truth, Mary Vickers's question suggests that servants viewed the law suit as an opportunity to provide either side with supporting testimony in return for a cash payment. Elizabeth Leeson wrote to her legal representative in the London court that none of the witnesses, cited in the affidavits, knew her or her servant and that she was hopeful that their evidence would be rejected as false.[52] Her hope was justified as the Court of Delegates, familiar with similar attempts to denigrate the evidence of witnesses in other cases, refused to hear the affidavits criticising the character of Leeson or her servant. They argued that Fitzmaurice had had plenty of time during the earlier court proceedings to produce that evidence and he had not done so. Similarly, when Arthur, 1st Viscount Doneraile alleged that Catherine Sarah Cunningham had committed adultery with one of his army companions that too was dismissed as unacceptable evidence by the judges in the House of Lords.[53]

The argument that the women should be perceived as sexually promiscuous resonated with the contemporary debate in England on the dangers of clandestine marriages. Both Leeson and Cunningham were portrayed as women who were endeavouring to entrap wealthy men into marriage. As the author of a pamphlet on the *FitzMaurice alias Leeson v. FitzMaurice* case, commented on the evidence presented in court:

> if such Evidence is admitted, no Man can be safe from the Artifices of an intriguing Woman, who in conjunction with her *Relations* and a *profligate Servant,* may make *Prostitution* a Step to *Matrimony,* and swear herself into what Family she pleases.[54]

There was a vibrant masculine community in eighteenth-century Dublin consisting of students attending Trinity College Dublin; soldiers temporarily stationed in the city and sons of landlords who socialised in the city, particularly during the winter months. Both William Fitzmaurice and Arthur St Leger mixed easily in this male world as they too moved with the seasons between Dublin and their families' country estates. Just over forty years after the ending of the Fitzmaurice case, Margaret Plunkett published her famous memoirs of her life as a prostitute in Dublin. She described how she began her sex work through a series of relationships with men like St Leger and Fitzmaurice who maintained her in lodgings and visited her when they were in Dublin.[55]

Despite their portrayal by the men's lawyers, however, neither Elizabeth Leeson nor Catherine Sarah Cunningham quite fitted the image of the kept woman as described by Margaret Plunkett. Leeson had her own income and when she met Fitzmaurice, she held a life interest in a house in a fashionable part of Dublin. She was not financially dependent on Fitzmaurice who, in fact, had a very limited allowance from his family and was not in a position to maintain a mistress in any significant style.[56] Leeson was also from a more socially respectable family than many of the sex workers described in Plunkett's memoir. She met William Fitzmaurice at a social event in the home of a member of one of Dublin's most respected families, the Wares.[57] It is clear too from the court documentation that members of her family were shocked when rumours began to circulate that she was Fitzmaurice's mistress. Leeson insisted to her mother, sisters and brother that she had married Fitzmaurice. When she became pregnant, she did her best to hide the changing shape of her body, almost making herself sick in the process. As she wrote to Fitzmaurice;

> At the present, the Stitches and Pains I endure, by being obliged to conceal it, can't be equall'd by any Thing but the Disorder of my Mind. It is so violent. I can hardly breathe, and I am forced for relief to send for one to bleed me.[58]

Leeson's mother and her brother urged her, however, not to leave the city as then everyone would assume that she was pregnant and that Fitzmaurice was the unmarried father.[59]

We know less about the social background of Catherine Sarah Cunningham. Her father was a soldier and soldiers were prominent among Margaret Plunkett's regular customers in her Dublin brothel. There is, however, no evidence that Catherine Sarah Cunningham worked as a prostitute. She asserted in her 1735 appeal that she had been unfairly 'injured in fame and character'.[60] As the daughter of an army captain, she was, like Leeson, of a higher social class than the women employed by Plunkett in her Dublin establishment. Her father was sufficiently well-off to maintain her when she separated from her husband. It is also unlikely that Cunningham would have been permitted to appeal the decision of the Irish Chancery court in the House of Lords or, have been granted a temporary pension from the king if it was believed that she was a sex worker eager to ensnare a wealthy man.

There is also evidence of emotional bonds and affection between both sets of partners. A central part of the evidence presented in *FitzMaurice alias Leeson v. FitzMaurice* was the correspondence between Leeson and Fitzmaurice when he was in his family home in Kerry while she remained in Dublin. The letters suggest that there was a strong sexual attraction between them and both made expressions of love. Although a widow, Leeson acknowledged that before she met Fitzmaurice, she had been a 'Stranger to [the] Passion' of love. Fitzmaurice also wrote with strong emotion to Leeson. In a letter dated 1726, he claimed that 'in Thee is my Heart; in Thee my Soul dwelleth; and without Thee I am damned'. The letter also indicated that despite his impending marriage, Fitzmaurice wanted to continue to see Leeson as a mistress: 'if you can like such a Life, find some Place for you, that we may be always within two days Journey to one another'.[61] Following the birth of their child, Leeson also expressed her willingness to contemplate a life as Fitzmaurice's mistress regardless of the strong opposition of her family: 'in spite of Mother, Sister, or all the World, I'll do whatever you think fit; even to own myself publickly to be your Mistress; for I cannot, cannot, bear the Thoughts of parting'.[62] Even at the end of the court case in 1733, Leeson forlornly held out hope that Fitzmaurice would accept the verdict of the court and have their marriage solemnised.[63]

Arthur St Leger and Catherine Sarah Cunningham lived together for at least four years before they parted. In the response to Cunningham's first appeal to the House of Lords in 1734, St Leger described a turbulent relationship. He claimed that Cunningham called him,

> the vilest and most opprobrious Names, as stupid Blockhead, a poor Animal, a poor mean-spirited Rascal, an Ideot, Eunuch, and other such like Scandalous Names; that she sung Songs in Derision of him; said she would turn him out of the House, and even laid violent Hands on him, and threw him down, for refusing to sign the pretended Deed, [i.e. the deed of 1728][64]

St Leger's response to Cunningham's appeal was intended to portray her as a woman whose bawdy and uncouth behaviour was not that of an aristocratic woman worthy of the title of Viscountess. The description implicitly suggested that Cunningham was from a lower class than St Leger and, hence, not to be trusted to tell the truth in her appeal. It is, however, worth noting that by the time of this response, Arthur St Leger, 2nd Viscount Doneraile had been banished by his family to the Isle of Man. He may not, therefore, have been actively involved in shaping the legal rejoinder to Cunningham's appeal. The latter claimed that some of St Leger's relatives had been responsible for alienating St Leger's affections from her.[65] Bishop Josiah Hort provided some support for this view when he wrote of the belief in Dublin that if St Leger had been 'sui juris' or in control of his own life that he would have been willing to cohabit with Cunningham but being 'a weak man, and a sot, his Relations have him entirely in their keeping'.[66]

Regardless of his personal preferences, Fitzmaurice too was trapped by his family expectations. For much of his life, he had a difficult relationship with his father. Educated at Eton, Fitzmaurice spent several years at Oxford but left before graduating and persuaded his uncle to fund an officer's commission despite his father's opposition. To his family's frustration, however, Fitzmaurice kept his commission for only a short period of time before he sold it and returned from France to Ireland to serve in the regiment of the Lord Lieutenant in Dublin Castle. By the time he met Elizabeth Leeson, Fitzmaurice was well aware of the possibility of his father disinheriting him completely or, at best, reducing further his revenue from the Kerry estate if he did not follow his family's wishes in relation to his marriage.[67]

The views of family and friends on the publicity generated by their law suits also had a significant impact on the women litigants. There were tensions within Leeson's family at her behaviour and the subsequent legal proceedings. Her mother and brother were particularly concerned at the social consequences of Leeson's law suit for the status of the family. When the news of the successful verdict came through from London, Leeson's mother, clearly relieved, asked that her lawyer publish a notice in the London newspapers because 'none but those who see the Papers will believe it here'.[68] Despite the positive outcome, the publicity attached to Leeson's law suit, seems to have led to a permanent fissure in the family. When she made her will in 1736, Leeson left most of her possessions to her stepsister, Katherine and stated that her executors (Katherine's husband and another unrelated man) were to give her mother, brothers, sisters and their children just one shilling each, if they made any claim to her estate. The only other principal beneficiary from Leeson's will was her servant, Elizabeth Vickers to whom she left some gowns and other clothing, possibly as a reward for her loyalty to her mistress during and after the court case.[69]

The acrimony in the extended family of Elizabeth Leeson was no doubt exacerbated by two pamphlets that were printed in the aftermath of the successful verdict. They told the story of the trial and neither flattered Leeson. The first was based on Leeson's statements to the London court and her correspondence with Fitzmaurice. The author placed the trial firmly in the context of the debate on clandestine marriages. It strongly suggested that Leeson had lied about Fitzmaurice's intentions and that he had always treated her as a mistress rather than as a wife.[70] The second pamphlet appealed to a more sensational readership presenting the correspondence of Leeson and Fitzmaurice in romantic terms. The tone was one of regret at the foolishness of a woman whose reckless behaviour led to Leeson's predicament as an unmarried mother. Such was the interest in the story that a second edition of this pamphlet was printed in 1734 when the judicial review was completed.[71] The pamphlets must have added to the sense of social shame within the extended Leeson family.

Cunningham also seems to have been socially isolated as a result of her law suit. Josiah Hort, the bishop of Kilmore noted that Cunningham had been obliged to appeal to the House of Lords as a pauper because all her friends had 'prescinded' or withdrawn from her.[72] By the time she wrote her will in 1780, Cunningham was living in Kensington. Her move to England may have been an attempt to live in a place where the details of her life were less well known. On the other hand, she remained to the end of her life proud of her status as the Dowager Viscountess Doneraile. She signed her will as 'Doneraile' and left instructions for her executor, a London based clergyman, that she be buried in a lead lined coffin in the style of a peeress of the realm. Her will suggests, however, that she had no contact with the St Leger family. The only relative noted in the document was her godson who was continuing the military tradition of the Cunningham family by serving as an ensign in the army.[73]

In conclusion, Elizabeth Leeson and Catherine Sarah Cunningham had, as women litigants, credible legal cases to defend, as their appeals in the London courts testified. They can be admired for their stamina in pursuing their suits to a successful conclusion. They withstood delays, obstruction and financial challenges as they did so. Despite their legal victories, however, the two women also experienced social denigration and isolation from family and friends.

Rather than fitting the law suits pursued by Cunningham and Leeson into the debate on clandestine marriages, it might be more accurate to note how the four principle protagonists (Cunningham, Leeson, Fitzmaurice and St Leger) were caught by the social expectations of class and economic background. The women litigants, regardless of the success of their legal proceedings, found it impossible to break through these social barriers. In the aftermath of their law suits, they may, indeed, have wondered if their legal fights had been worth the time and effort that they put into them.

From the perspective of a twenty-first-century historian, the two case studies highlight the potential of English court records for uncovering more information about the operation of the legal infrastructure of early modern Ireland and the men and women who made use of it. Despite the destruction of court records in 1922, it has proved possible to reconstruct the procedures and decisions of the Irish courts. We do not yet know if Elizabeth Leeson and Catherine Sarah St Leger (née Cunningham) were unusual as Irish women litigants in the English court system. Further research may reveal that they were not.

Notes

1 Cited in Catriona Crowe, 'Ruin of Public Record Office of Ireland Marked Loss of Great Archives', *Irish Times*, 30 June 2012.
2 The most ambitious recovery process is currently underway in the 'Beyond 1922' project based in Trinity College Dublin. The research team plan to create a 'Virtual Record Treasury' of the lost documents. See 'Beyond 1922' (https://beyond2022.ie/). See also https://www.nationalarchives.ie/article/rising-from-the-ashes/. Both accessed 10 April 2020.
3 See, for example, Mary O'Dowd, 'Women and the Irish Chancery Court in the Late Sixteenth and Early Seventeenth Centuries', *Irish Historical Studies*, vol. 31, no. 124 (Nov., 1999), pp. 470–487; Frances Nolan, '"Jacobite" Women and the Williamite Confiscation: the Role of Women and Female Minors in Reclaiming Compromised or Forfeited Property in Ireland, 1690–1703' (unpublished Ph.D. thesis, University College, Dublin, 2016); '"The Cat's Paw": Helen Arthur, the Act of Resumption and The Popish Pretenders to the Forfeited Estates in Ireland', *Irish Historical Studies*, vol. 42, no. 162 (Nov., 2018), pp. 225–243.
4 I am very grateful to Dr Dennehy for this information and for his advice on the appeal process.
5 See, for example, G. I. O. Duncan, *The High Court of Delegates* (Cambridge, 1971), pp. 109–110.
6 See https://discovery.nationalarchives.gov.uk/browse/r/h/C77. Accessed 20 October 2019. For Irish appeal cases involving women litigants in the Court of Delegate records see, for example, TNA, DEL 2/7; DEL 2/13; DEL 2/41.
7 See Hugh Leeson's will, 2 Feb. 1720 (Registry of Deeds, Dublin, Memorial, vol. 60, no. 40084). See also P. Beryl Eustace (ed.), *Registry of Deeds Dublin Abstracts of Wills* (3 vols., Dublin, 1956), vol. i, p. 170. Leeson's property deals can be traced through the index in the Registry of Deeds. Consulted online at http://familysearch.org. 2 November 2019. I am very grateful to Máire MacAonghaile for her help with the records of the Registry of Deeds and for pointing out additional references to Leeson's property in the archive.

8 *Love Without Artifice: or, the Disappointed Peer. A History of the Amour between Lord Mauritio and Emilia. Being the Case of Elizabeth Fitz-Maurice, alias Leeson and the Lord William Fitz- Maurice Relating to a Marriage-contract Between Them; Which was Confirmed by a Court of Delegates, in the Lady's Behalf, on Wednesday, March 14th 1732–3, at Serjeant's-Inn, in Chancery-Lane* (London, 1733), p. 3.
9 *Observations on the Case of the Right Honourable the Lord Fitzmaurice and Mrs. Elizabeth Leeson, Concerning a Pretended Contract of Marriage* (London, 1733), pp. 6; Statement of Elizabeth Fitzmaurice alias Leeson to the Court of Delegates, 10 March 1730 (FitzMaurice alias Leeson v. FitzMaurice (TNA, DEL 2/27)); Case of Elizabeth Fitzmaurice, Appellant against William Fitzmaurice Presented to the Court of Delegates by Francis Boycott, 1730 (TNA, DEL 2/27).
10 Ibid.
11 Ibid.
12 Ibid.
13 On the concept of 'half proof' see J. Franklin, *The Science of Conjecture: Evidence and Probability before Pascal* (Baltimore, 2001), pp. 15–63, 45, 59.
14 Not all those nominated attended all of the sessions concerning the case. See lists of attendance in TNA, DEL 2/27.
15 See statement of Elizabeth Fitzmaurice alias Leeson v. FitzMaurice to the Court of Delegates, 10 March 1730 (TNA, DEL 2/27).
16 Case of Elizabeth Fitzmaurice, Appellant against William Fitzmaurice Presented to the Court of Delegates by Francis Boycott, 1730 (TNA, DEL 2/27).
17 Petition of William Fitzmaurice, Esq commonly called Lord Fitzmaurice, no date; Petition of Elizabeth Fitzmaurice Otherwise Leeson against the Petition of William Lord Fitzmaurice, no date; Review of Case 12 June 1734 by Lord Talbot, Lord Chancellor (TNA, DEL 2/27).
18 Will of Elizabeth Leeson als Fitzmaurice, 26 Feb. 1736 (TNA, PROB 11/684/392). The will was probated on 25 August 1737. On Fitzwilliam's marriage see John Knightly, 'Lixnaw and the Earls of Kerry'. Consulted online at http://docstore.kerrycoco.ie/KCCWebsite/arts/forms/earls.pdf. Accessed 6 October 2019.
19 See *The Right Honourable Catherine-Sarah Lady Viscountess Doneraile, Wife of the Respondent Lord Doneraile in the Kingdom of Ireland by John Cunningham, Esq. her Father and Next Friend, February 1735. The Right Honourable Arthur Lord Viscount Doneraile, the Right Honourable Elizabeth. Lady Dowager Doneraile, James Barry, Esq; and others, Respondents. The Appellant's Case* and *The Respondent's Case* (London, 1735) (hereafter Appellant's Case, 1735; Respondent's Case, 1735). Copy in National Library of Ireland (hereafter NLI), Doneraile Papers, MS 34,138 (2–3).
20 Appellant's Case, 1735. See also Respondent's Case, 1735.
21 Appellant's Case, 1735; Respondent's Case, 1735. See also The *Right Honourable Catherine Sarah, Lady Viscount Dowager, Widow and Relict of the Right Honourable Arthur, late Lord Viscount Doneraile, of the Kingdom of Ireland; The Right Honourable Arthur Mohun, Lord Viscount Doneraile of the Kingdom of Ireland, Respondent. The Appellant's Case* and *The Respondent's Case* (London, 1744). Copies in NLI, Doneraile Papers, MS 34,138 (2–3). Hereafter Appellant's Case, 1744; Respondent's Case, 1744).
22 Appellant's and Respondent's Cases, 1735, 1744.
23 As there is no further reference to the child, it must be assumed that the infant did not survive the birth.
24 Appellant's Case, 1735.
25 Appellant's Case, 1735.
26 Respondent's Case, 1735.
27 Appellant's and Respondent's Cases, 1735. The verdict of the House of Lords is written on the Appellant's statement.
28 Josiah Hort, Bishop. of Kilmore to George Bubb Dodington, 10 Jan. 1734 (NLI, MS 33730/D (3).

29 There is a copy of the bill of revivor in NLI, Doneraile Papers, MS 34,138 (2–3).
30 See NLI, Doneraile Papers.
31 Respondent's case, 1744.
32 Ibid. See also Appellant's Case, 1744. The verdict of the House of Lords is written on the printed statement of the appellant.
33 A copy of the agreement is in NLI, Doneraile Papers, MS 34,138 (2–3).
34 Duncan, *The High Court of Delegates,* p. 109; TNA, DEL 2/13.
35 David Woolley (ed.), *The Correspondence of Jonathan Swift, D. D,* (4 vols, Frank am Main, 1999–2014), vol. 4, pp. 86, 87, 97–98.
36 Petition of Elizabeth Fitzmaurice als Leeson against the petition of Lord Fitzmaurice, July 1733 (Fitzmaurice alias Leeson versus Fitzmaurice (TNA, DEL 2/27)).
37 Appellant's Case, 1744.
38 *Journal of the House of Lords,* vol. XX (accessed at British History Online (https://www.british-history.ac.uk/. 20 October 2019).
39 See Registry of Deeds, Dublin, vol. 63, memorial no. 44461. Consulted at https://www.familysearch.org.
40 Elizabeth Fitzmaurice to Francis Boycott, 11 July 1733 ((Fitzmaurice alias Leeson versus Fitzmaurice (TNA, DEL 2/27)). Fitzmaurice was ordered by the Court of Delegates to pay for the court proceedings but Leeson had to pay for lawyers to present her case. See ibid.
41 Appeal, 1735.
42 *Journal of the House of Lords,* vol. 24, February 1734 (accessed at British History Online (https://www.british-history.ac.uk/. 20 October 2019).
43 'A list of all the pensions now in being on the civil establishment …' (*Journals of the House of Commons of the Kingdom of Ireland,* vol. 7, p. cxlv (accessed at https://www.hathitrust.org/, 20 October 2019)); *Calendar of Treasury Books and Papers,* vol. 5, 26 July 1742 (accessed at British History Online: https://www.british-history.ac.uk/, 20 October 2019).
44 *Journal of the House of Lords,* vol. 26, 25 January 1744 (accessed at British History Online (https://www.british-history.ac.uk/. 20 October 2019).
45 David Woolley (ed.), *The Correspondence of Jonathan Swift, D. D* (4 vols, Frank am Main, 1999–2014), vol. 2, pp. 146–147; vol. 4, pp. 86, 87, 97–98.
46 *Love Without Artifice: Or, the Disappointed Peer,* pp. 4–5.
47 Edith Mary Johnstone-Liik (ed.), *History of the Irish Parliament 1692–1800* (6 vols, Belfast, 2002), vi, pp. 443–444; D. W. Hayton, *The Anglo-Irish Experience, 1680–1730: Religion, Identity and Patriotism* (Woodbridge, 2012), pp. 129–132.
48 Josiah Hort, Bishop. of Kilmore to George Bubb Dodington, 10 Jan. 1734 (NLI, MS 33730/D (3).
49 *Love Without Artifice: Or, the Disappointed Peer,* p. 3.
50 Copies in *Fitzmaurice alias Leeson versus Fitzmaurice* (TNA, DEL 2/27).
51 The Examination of Mary Viccars of the City of Dublin, Spinster, 11 Sept. 1733 (TNA, DEL 2/27).
52 Elizabeth Leeson to Francis Boycott, 11 Sept. 1733 (TNA, DEL 2/27).
53 See handwritten verdict on Respondent's Case, 1735.
54 *Observations on the Case of the Right Honourable the Lord Fitzmaurice and Mrs. Elizabeth Leeson, Concerning a Pretended Contract of Marriage* (London, 1733), p. 58.
55 Margaret Plunkett, *The Memoirs of Mrs Leeson.* Edited and introduced by Mary Lyons (Dublin, 1995).
56 John Knightly, 'Lixnaw and the Earls of Kerry'. Consulted online at http://docstore.kerrycoco.ie/KCCWebsite/arts/forms/earls.pdf. Accessed 6 October 2019.
57 Statement of Elizabeth Fitzmaurice alias Leeson to the Court of Delegates (TNA, DEL 2/27).
58 *Observations on the Case of the Right Honourable the Lord Fitzmaurice and Mrs. Elizabeth Leeson,* p. 46.

59 Presentation of Appeal by Francis Boycott, Elizabeth Leeson's proctor in the Court of Delegates (TNA, DEL 2/27).
60 Appellant's Case, 1735.
61 *Observations on the Case of the Right Honourable the Lord Fitzmaurice and Mrs. Elizabeth Leeson, Concerning a Pretended Contract of Marriage* (London, 1733), p. 27.
62 Ibid., p. 49.
63 Elizabeth Fitzmaurice to Sir Francis Boycott, 11 July 1733 (Fitzmaurice alias Leeson versus Fitzmaurice (TNA, DEL 2/27)).
64 Respondent's Case, 1735.
65 Appellant's Case, 1735.
66 Josiah Hort, Bishop. of Kilmore to George Bubb Dodington, 10 Jan. 1734 (NLI, MS 33730/D (3).
67 John Knightly, 'Lixnaw and the Earls of Kerry'. Consulted online at http://docstore.kerrycoco.ie/KCCWebsite/arts/forms/earls.pdf. Accessed 6 October 2019.
68 Elizabeth Leeson to Francis Boycott, 11 July 173[3] (TNA, 2/27).
69 See Will of Elizabeth Leeson als Fitzmaurice, 26 February 1736 (TNA, PROB 11/684/392).
70 *Observations on the Case of the Right Honourable the Lord Fitzmaurice and Mrs. Elizabeth Leeson, Concerning a Pretended Contract of Marriage* (London, 1733; 2nd edition, 1734).
71 *Love without Artifice*. The title of the second edition was subtly changed to: *Love and Artifice: or, A Compleat History of the Amour between Lord Mauritio and Emilia. Being the Case of Elizabeth Fitz-Maurice, alias Leeson, and the Lord William Fitz-Maurice, Relating to a Marriage-contract Between Them; Which Was Confirmed by a Court of Delegates, in the Lady's Behalf, on Wednesday, March 14th 1732/3, at Serjeant's-Inn, in Chancery-Lane* (London, 1734).
72 Josiah Hort, Bishop. of Kilmore to George Bubb Dodington, 10 Jan. 1734 (NLI, MS 33730/D (3)).
73 Will of the Right Honorable Catherine Sarah Lady Viscountess Doneraile, Dowager, Widow, 28 July 1783 (TNA, PROB 11/1105/410).

12
HIDDEN IN PLAIN SIGHT

Female litigators, reproductive lives, archival practices and early modern French historiography

Julie Hardwick

In July, 1725, Justine Gantier walked along the streets in Lyon, France's second city, to the *greffe* (the building that served as the depository of legal documents and evidence) for the royal court of first instance (a *sénéchausée*) where she handed a court official a bundle of seven letters she had received from her intimate partner, Louis Delagard. She (perhaps in consultation with her lawyer or perhaps on her own initiative because seemingly women did not usually provide such evidence) deposited them as evidence in support of her paternity suit against him. Gantier was six months pregnant and Delagarde had reneged on his repeated promises to marry her.[1] Her actions transformed the kind of mundane material culture of intimacy that originally embodied the connection and commitment between intimate partners into legal evidence of betrayal to be filed and conserved, first as part of the documents generated by her case, then as an addition to the court's stored records, and finally as a part of the modern departmental archives that were first organised during the French Revolution by a series of legal acts in the 1790s.[2]

For Gantier and other women, filing a lawsuit (or threatening to and the existence of that well known threat even when not shouted during an argument) was a key way to mitigate the impact of men's unpredictability as emotional and sexual partners. Although only a few women deposited personal items as evidence, many more received and held them as concrete proof of their commitment and later in the wake of men stalling about marriage saw the same items as emblems of their deception. Apart from letters, such deposits included written promises to marry and notarised agreements between couples that laid out the terms of an out-of-court settlement. Women who filed paternity suits in this Lyon court recited their relationship history, reproductive history and sexual history as witnesses who spoke on their behalf often did too in order to secure the support of a court judgment, and indirectly the imprimatur of the state, that endorsed their

DOI: 10.4324/9780429278037-13

own behaviour as respectable and disciplined men for their failure to be reliable sexual partners.[3]

Yet the thousands of paternity suits that survive from regions across France identified in archive catalogues and by historians as *déclarations de grossesses* have become widely misinterpreted. Historians have routinely linked them to a 1556 Edict on Clandestine Pregnancy that sought to deter infanticides with the claim that it required young pregnant women to register their status with a public official. These 'mandatory' pregnancy declarations became the cornerstone of an influential historiography that highlighted the regulation of reproduction, and especially the disciplining of young women's sexuality, as one of the stand-out features of early modern state formation.[4] However, the Edict made no such requirement in 1556 or when it was subsequently re-issued multiple times.[5]

This chapter examines how these young women's assertions of legal right to repair their honour, secure financial compensation and arrange for their intimate partners to have physical custody of the babies as well as pay for their upbringing became recoded as state projects to discipline female sexuality. The history of the history of the 'pregnancy declarations' involves an archival, historiographical and methodological puzzle. 'Pregnancy declarations' have become a pivotal element in an argument that placed the regulation of gender and family as a key element in state formation. That claim has become received wisdom through a complex series of events that created and replicated an error so often that it became a truism. These factors included a debate in the eighteenth century about whether the law required a declaration that became the basis for a persistent myth, French professional archival practices, and a powerful professional confirmation bias that embraced a particular formulation of the edict and its implications as attractive because it suited a contemporary disciplinary and political impulse.

This chapter draws on thousands of pages of 'pregnancy declarations' in Lyon for the years 1660–1760. Lyon was France's second city, a major centre for textile production and printing as well as an important European crossroads. The legal actions were primarily between young workers in consensual relationships in a city where both single women and men worked most often in the silk industry and the allied textile manufacturing trades. In what were, in fact, paternity suits, young women and their witnesses narrated the course of their relationships in great detail from the early days of courtship through pressure to marry or failure to marry. They included numerous accounts of the forms of intimacy that working communities judged licit between young couples in stable relationships and many references to efforts to interrupt reproduction in the case of untimely pregnancies. Young women and their witnesses recounted relationship histories, sexual histories, and reproductive histories.[6]

The ways in which young single early modern women's litigation to manage their own sexual and reproductive lives became recast in the archives as well as in historiography is a sharp illustration of the difficulty in recovering the full range of women's uses of the legal system. This chapter demonstrates the ways in which multiple actors have braided power and intimacy in unexpected ways to reframe and elide women's efforts to mobilise legal process to manage the challenges of both predictable female fertility in a world without reliable contraception and men's unpredictability as partners in a society where premarital sex was the norm. Women litigated to control their sexual and reproductive histories and futures. No disciplinary impetus at all from the court towards women was evident. In fact, court (and community) discipline focussed on young men who were consistently held responsible for the consequences of their sexual activity: young men were often held in prison during investigations and routinely required to pay the financial costs of their intimate partners and take custody of the resulting babies.

How did these young women's accounts of their relationship and reproductive history in assertions of legal right to repair their honour, secure financial compensation and arrange for their intimate partners to have physical custody of the babies as well as pay for their upbringing become recoded as a key element of state projects to discipline female sexuality? These records are now catalogued as and routinely referred to in modern historiography as *déclarations de grossesse* and associated with the 1556 Edict on Clandestine Pregnancy. The roots of the recoding as state disciplinary projects lie in a potent combination of eighteenth-century confusions about the edict, archivists' decision making as a French national cataloguing system developed in the nineteenth and twentieth centuries, and historians' interest in questions about disciplining and gender and family as categories of analysis for other processes in the late twentieth century.

Confusion about the terms of the Edict clearly existed in the Old Regime although so did constant correction in print and court of the suggestion that it did require a declaration. Local judges – sometimes thought (or perhaps wished) that a declaration was required. Local municipalities from the late sixteenth century and especially from the early eighteenth century did make local regulations, usually requiring landlords or midwives who knew that a single woman had given birth to report the occurrence rather than seeking to impose any requirement on the expectant mothers themselves. These municipal initiatives suggest local authorities were invested in keeping track of out-of-wedlock births, but they carried no penalty for landlords or midwives who reported them, and, in fact, were mostly not enforced at all. These local regulations seem to have caused confusion among historians who sometimes conflated them with the 1556 Edict and perhaps among contemporary local lawyers and community members too.

Indeed, the *Parlement* of Paris, France's highest court, repeatedly restrained local judges and regulations, pointing out the Edict did not allow such reach and jurisprudential publications at the time also repeatedly highlighted the fact that it was an error to associate the 1556 Edict with a mandatory requirement for single women to declare their pregnancies to anyone. It annulled local decisions in Lyon and Toulouse, for example, that sought to extend regulation of young pregnant single women on the grounds that the Edict did not allow for such powers. In 1704, the court passed a ruling that required anyone who received a woman at home to have a baby to notify one of its judge or risk corporal punishment and or a fine of 250 *livres*. As with other local regulations, it focussed on the facilitators of out-of-wedlock births rather than on the young women themselves. However, when a Lyon paternity suit ruling was appealed to the *Parlement of Paris*, France's highest legal court annulled the Lyon regulation in a 1712 ruling on the grounds that its requirements went beyond the 1556 Edict. The order also forbade the Lyon court from making such regulations again.[7] By the late eighteenth century, Jean François Fournel, the leading jurisprudential scholar of the laws about out-of-wedlock pregnancy, clarified firmly in his magnum opus on seduction that the idea of a mandatory declaration tied to the 1556 Edict was an error. He pointed out that in instances when prosecutors had sought convictions of single women who had not made declarations of their pregnancy, they were unsuccessful because the Edict did not require any such action.[8]

In the nineteenth and twentieth century, professional archival practices embedded the error in multiple editions as the departmental archives were organised and re-organised, catalogued and re-catalogued. What were marked at the time of women's court actions as simple complaints (*plaintes*) were pulled into a distinctive category where archivists retitled them as *Déclarations de grossesses* and often wrote that term in pencil on the cover of the legal actions. That is, it was professional archival practitioners who generated pregnancy declarations as a separate legal category that remains easily identifiable in the guides to any French archives. Other decisions about cataloguing material similarly elided important material about women's actions and reproductive lives. Legal reports about the finding of the bodies of dead newborns around the city were catalogued in Lyon church court records under 'accidents' along with reports on deaths like drownings even though the accompanying surgeons' reports often indicated clearly that no accident was involved in a baby's death or in its body being deposited in particular locations around the city. Decisions of archivists firmly hid this eye-opening evidence about women's practices of interrupting reproduction, whether consciously or unwittingly is hard to say, while also coding women's litigation over paternity into a category whose name merged with the myth about the 1556 Edict requiring declarations.[9]

Finally, modern professional confirmation bias also seems to have shaped and continued the persistent myth that the Edict required single women to declare their pregnancies. Historians in the late 1980s and 1990s were very interested in projects of discipline and in particular in state effort to discipline subjects. The emphasis on the 1556 Edict as a way the French state sought to discipline female sexuality fitted well with that paradigm, whether the historians involved were explicitly influenced by a framework elaborated by the French theorist Michel Foucault or not. Moreover, feminist historians undertook an important project to put gender at the centre of issues/processes well beyond women's history. In this framework too, the idea of disciplining female sexuality as a critical element of state formation seemed very compelling and the *déclarations de grossesse* (along with other new legislation) seemed to provide the proof. Ironically, feminist scholarship inadvertently obscured the agency of women as legal actors.[10]

In fact, the legal actions single women filed that are now catalogued as 'pregnancy declarations' were simple complaints to the court for paternal support. Declarations were generic legal instruments used for many legal purposes both before and after 1556. They had nothing at all to do with the 1556 Edict and, in fact, the Edict did not mention declaration in any regard. Women asked for financial compensation for their costs, for the father to take custody of the child and sometimes for marriage. (Women who asked the court to compel men to marry them were also a small minority even in the seventeenth century and virtually disappeared in the eighteenth century.) Judges routinely ruled in favour of the pregnant women with very little concern for proof as men and their lawyers sometimes complained. They were one of the many ways in which women and their communities, here in court but often also out of court, sought to hold young men responsible for the reproductive consequences of their sexual activity. In doing so, single women whose pregnancies did not seem likely to lead to marriage were able to protect their reputations when witnesses and judges endorsed their claims that they had done nothing wrong.

Women who took their intimate partners to court in paternity suits were part of a specific set of relationships: couples who were publicly known, stable, monogamous, heterosexual, and marriage partners. The legal logic of paternity suits required women to be able to demonstrate that they had reasonable expectation that they would definitely be married. If they could not, the suits would be unsuccessful and the court might well not even start to entertain the case based on the initial complaint. Most of the women who brought complaints were in their mid-twenties range, that is their age made them plausible marriage candidates in a city and country where (much like the rest of Europe), couples in working communities usually married at the ages of around twenty-five to twenty-seven. They could call on neighbours, co-workers, friends, and employers who would confirm the history of their relationships and the neighbourhood expectation of marriage.

A quintessential plaintiff was twenty-five or twenty-six, working as a silk worker or in an adjacent trade like embroidery or stocking making or seamstress work. She met her intimate partner at work or through co-workers. She might well have been a migrant who came to Lyon to find work from a village in the surrounding countryside as a teenager because Lyon was a city full of young rural migrants. She was well connected in her neighbourhood with a network of community safeguarders like neighbours, friends, co-workers, kin, landlords or landladies, and employers, that is the many people who regarded themselves as invested in young couple's relationships and who watched, questioned, intervened, and regulated as necessary. She and her intimate partner had observed all the aspects of what Lyon's working communities regarded as licit for young people: they had walked out together often in the evening after work and on Sundays for an extended period of time, they had explored physical intimacy as well as emotional connections but stopped short of intercourse until marriage was firmly on the cards, they delayed intercourse until they had made explicit commitments to marry and often already received the endorsement of their neighbours and families. She was unusual only in that if pregnancy reliably followed intercourse for young couples, pregnancy had not been followed by marriage as it was in most cases, not least due to encouragement in various forms from an expanded range of community safeguarders that could grow to include clergy, social welfare officials, and lawyers.

Women with this profile who were in a position to litigate paternity suits highlighted stable heterosexual relationships as the normative, desirable form of intimacy; relationship stability was a goal communities and courts could invest in. This profile as a precondition for successful litigation over paternity, however, excluded pregnant single women who participated in the many sexual cultures that must have co-existed alongside or overlapped with this one. Young women who kissed different boys every weekend would not be successful. Women doing sex work could not find compensation via this path. (Judges consistently asked in the interrogatory stage whether payment had been involved.) Victims of coerced sex occasionally used this legal route if the perpetrator was their employer, but women who were raped by strangers or other acquaintances had no prospect of using this pathway and rape prosecutions were so rare as to be almost non-existent. Moreover, this particular form of litigation has much in common with all early modern litigation. When young couples whose communities had expected them to marry did not for many reasons, even when their sexual activity led to pregnancy, they usually settled the matter out of court, either informally or with a legal but extra judicial instrument in the form of a notarised agreement. Even when women started paternity suits, the majority did not proceed to sentencing. Explanations were very rarely given in the extant documents, but on most occasions the couple either settled out of court or in some instances did, in fact, get married. That is going to court for young pregnant women was, as always in litigation, sometimes a negotiating tactic.

The success of women who fit as this profile as litigators did not mean filing a paternity suit to help resolve the handling of their untimely pregnancies was easy for them. Even if their neighbours, co-workers, and friends knew about the pregnancies, going to court involved a different kind of going public. The legal industry was almost exclusively masculine so women plaintiffs in paternity suits encountered a sea of men as judges, lawyers, court workers like bailiffs or process servers. Women had to tell their relationship histories, sexual histories and reproductive histories to court officials who would have been unknown to them and of higher rank. They discussed the activities of their courtships, their discussions of marriage, their experiences of first intercourse, and their efforts to interrupt reproduction before or sometimes after births. Female witnesses testified alongside male deponents as to what they knew about explicit details of the couples' intimacy from holding arms as they walked out to physical intimacy short of intercourse to conversations about the course of their relationships and to the anxiety of waiting to see if marriage would follow pregnancy.

The first step to verify women's paternity claims usually came immediately after their initial petitions when they were visited at home by medico-legal experts for the court in the form of surgeons and midwives, or often before 1750 by midwives alone, who sought to ascertain whether the pregnancy was real. The timing of women's legal actions varied, from their fourth or fifth months which was almost as soon as they would have known they were pregnant until after a baby born was or sometimes after more than one baby had been born. However, the vast majority filed suits in the last three months of their pregnancies. Midwives as official medico-legal experts for the court were the exception to the otherwise all-male legal cast of actors in paternity suits. Either in the presence of surgeons or on their own, midwives observed the appearance of the women for signs of pregnancy and conducted physical examinations of at least the stomach and breasts which they must have touched firmly as they reported on whether these organs felt soft, enlarged or firm. Their assessment determined whether or not the suit would proceed because no pregnancy, meant no valid paternity suit claim. Although in most instances, midwives and or surgeons confirmed the alleged pregnancies, they sometimes reported that they could not even if women reported missing their periods for multiple months and had other symptoms like nausea and headaches.[11] For young women, these experts' inspection visits must have been fraught, high stakes affairs: strangers who relied on the physical evidence of the body based in part on feel rather than reported symptoms controlled the gateway to legal process.

In the interrogatory phase of the legal proceedings, when judges questioned plaintiffs, expectant women answered questions from the court's male officials about whether they had told their partners they were pregnant, whether their partners had given them money, whether they had had babies with other men or been familiar with other men. Male court officials asked them to explain how it had happened that they had started to have sex. Women's answers to these sets of questions were both routinised and often seemingly improvised. Women very predictably always said they had not made babies with other men (except for the handful of widows who appeared) and they virtually always said they had told their partners of their pregnancies.

Yet in response to the question of how it had happened that they began to have intercourse, they often added unprompted details about their sexual and reproductive lives that they had not mentioned in their initial petitions where women usually concentrated on relationship history summaries from meeting to conception. Young women introduced subjects like the location and often violent character of their first experience of intercourse in what had been consensual relationships or efforts to interrupt their pregnancies with a variety of potions or bleedings. These unprompted elaborations provide a rich vein of evidence about young couples' intimacy and women's reproductive health. Young women presumably expected these details to accentuate the men's errors as they attributed the termination efforts and the coerced shift from the usual forms of intimacy like kissing, caressing and touching to intercourse to men's initiative.[12]

The gendered dynamics of the legal process – and the cause of it – meant women's experiences as plaintiffs must have made them nervous, anxious and perhaps angry despite what must have been well established popular knowledge about their likely success rate. In the language of the initial petitions, they asked for judgments in their favour so that their honour would be restored and financial compensation would cover their costs. These claims both addressed the legal standard that men should provide financially for natural children as well as legitimate ones and pointed to the financial pressure single women faced from pregnancy (especially if they had to give up work) and delivery. Despite the inherently abraded nature of bringing a paternity claim in court, women and their communities saw a ruling in their favour as a public affirmation that they had not done anything wrong, so their reputations would be intact despite their status as out-of-wedlock mothers. Their honour was threatened but not lost forever by being pregnant and single, but courts and communities could ensure and accept its restoration by men being assigned responsibility for the error.[13]

On occasion, women like Gantier and her peers weaponised the material culture of intimacy when they introduced it as legal evidence. When Ysabeau Martin deposited the index card sized promise to marry that Antoine Flacheron had given her in 1680, for example, she presented his written acknowledgment of their commitment and sexual history as confirmation of his subsequent betrayal. He had promised to marry her,

> in a true and loyal marriage as soon as she or her kin asked him to in order to keep the verbal promises he had given earlier. Moreover subsequent to those I recognise that she allowed me to visit her often and to have sex with her following which she became pregnant by me.

She had kept the promise carefully for four months before she entered it as evidence in her lawsuit. Like Gantier and Martin, women and witnesses sometimes referenced material forms of affection and commitment such as gifts, letters or written promises to marry in their testimonies as part of their proof that their expectations of marriage were reasonable. Sometimes they deposited such items with the court as evidence although legally such proof was not required and its presence or absence did not seem to affect the court's decisions either way.[14] When women chose (whether at their lawyers' suggestion or because they thought they added something key) to give up these items that had embodied and confirmed their intimate connection, they reframed them as physical confirmation of the dishonourable behaviour of their partners. The deposits reflected both the way women had kept the items safely with perhaps warm feelings and the frustration and/or anger they may have felt to have found themselves unexpectedly exposed as vulnerable by men's failures to follow through with their promises. These were proof of men's perfidy in a concrete form in a way that verbal accounts from women and their witnesses were not.

Occasionally women submitted personal material that spoke directly to the emotional stakes of the contention that lay behind the delays in marriage and the step of filing a lawsuit. In 1695, Antoinette Michon deposited a letter Nicolas Alognet had written her during the course of the paternity suit. It was, she said, 'Filled with slurs and lies' that he made 'with malice and perfidy'. Philiberte de Luis, a lacemaker, deposited a letter Rene Gaultier had sent her nine weeks before she initiated a legal action. His letter showed they were arguing and he apologised for how "ardently" he spoke to her and acknowledged her tears, but also confirmed his awareness of his obligation: 'if what you say is true [i.e. she was pregnant] I know what a respectable man would do and I would not do otherwise [that is marry her]'.[15] For female plaintiffs, the filing of paternity suits had all kinds of practical implications (to have their costs covered, to secure the father's custody of the child) as well as reputational valency (they preserved their honour when courts held the father was responsible), but they must also have been high stakes emotional actions in ways that are rarely articulated in legal documents. When women said they were dishonoured by men's behaviour, their words pointed to the emotional costs of men's unpredictability as intimate partners too.

The material culture of intimacy was sometimes introduced as evidence by witnesses. Louis Paullin, for example, had shown a neighbour a letter he wrote to his father: in it he explained that Lucrece Morel was pregnant and his conscience required him to marry her. He showed it to a thirty-year-old female neighbour before sending it. Three months later, when the neighbour testified in court, she recalled that she had not only seen the letter but had shown it to their employer.[16] Witnesses' identification of the existence of such intimate artefacts even when they were not deposited in the *greffe* as official evidence likewise provided concrete confirmation of young couples' connections in different ways than recalled conversations with their promises and sweet expressions.

Women's legal actions to assert paternity posed clear risks to their intimate partners. Women almost always prevailed in their paternity suits, sometimes to the chagrin of their partners and partners' lawyers. The high success rate was due both to the inclination of court as well as community to hold men responsible for the reproductive consequences of their sexual activity and to the self-selection involved among women who brought actions against their intimate partners, that is as we have seen only those with a particular relationship profile.[17] Men faced financial costs for their partners' deliveries, were charged with custody of the infants, and found their reputations damaged by being publicly hauled into prison while investigations went on and by the airing of their failure to take responsibility for the reproductive consequences of their sexual activities. Not surprisingly, men could be angry at the prospect of a lawsuit, and sometimes issued threats to women's well-being or tried to persuade them to identify other men as fathers.[18] The alleged fathers sometimes also denied ever having had sex with the women or having ever promised marriage, claiming instead that the sex was casual and/or transactional. These defences were almost always unsuccessful, causing frustration sometimes aired in court and occasionally in pamphlets. In a 1760s pamphlet published in Lyon, for example, Monsieur Servan, a lawyer, railed against the judicial presumption that women told the truth when they made paternity complaints. He claimed that the habitual acceptance of single women's claims was 'an astonishing exception to the ordinary rules of probability and to our judgment'. Servan asserted that in "our big cities" conniving women used their fertility 'as a new kind of commerce' where false accusations of paternity against the most reputable men produced financial reward.[19] Yet these kinds of complaints seemed to have no impact on judicial practice. The court's judges were firmly on the side of women who successfully represented themselves as sexually active but only with men they were on track to marry after a publicly recognised and endorsed courtship.

Women's paternity suits reveal the way in which their legal actions worked in tandem with or parallel to their efforts to secure out-of-court settlements. The records of many suits ended before a judgment was given, perhaps due to loss of records in the intervening centuries but probably usually because the intimate partners made out-of-court settlements – that is that the use of a legal action spurred a private agreement. Even the threat of going to court could push negotiations along. Women's petitions also revealed that they had previously negotiated extrajudicial (that is legal but not via the court system) or extralegal (sometimes with the mediation of a legal official but without a formal legal instrument) settlements. Obviously, these were unsuccessful because they ended up in court anyway, but these details show that when women and their intimate partners did not marry for whatever reason, out-of-court settlements, usually on very similar terms to court decisions, were routine. These were not secret because many people usually knew but they made private agreements rather than the public nature of a legal process and record. Most women likely preferred to find an out-of-court settlement than to have to go to court. They could often reach informal agreements, often with the assistance of clergy, lawyers, social welfare institution staff, employer or family as mediators. In these ways, paternity suits as a category resembled all other forms of early litigation.

Yet when women litigated over their personal sexual and reproductive histories, they did much more too. They made public records of their private relationship, sexual and reproductive histories. These histories revealed women's – and their partners' – efforts to control their fertility during untimely pregnancies and even after the babies were born. They record the routineness of sexual violence in what had been consensual relationships and women usually continued after the violence in the ongoing expectation of marriage and no doubt fear of pregnancy. They highlight the myriad informal or extrajudicial ways in which young women with the support of community members held young men legally responsible for the reproductive consequences of premarital sexual activity if it was not followed by marriage. Unwittingly, they provided invaluable evidence for historians of what usually went undocumented.

One of the most important discoveries of the last twenty years or so is that women were ubiquitous litigators in the early modern world. Early modern women were involved in litigation in many different jurisdictions and for different purposes. In France, Spain, and many other regions, women took to courts to litigate over many subjects from insult to debt to domestic violence. A recent special issue of the *Journal of British Studies* was devoted to many aspects of women's participation in the legal system in terms of method as well as different roles like plaintiff, defendant or witness, and in search of different recourses. Women and other groups in Europe's global colonies like children, free people of colour, and indigenous or enslaved persons were also able to use European legal principles to protect their own interests in court. Even women accused of witchcraft in seventeenth-century northern Spain sometimes subsequently took their accusers to court.[20] Collectively this work has transformed our understanding of women's relationship to the state and revealed the centrality of women to the economy, to managing community norms, and to many other issues.

Young French women's litigation in paternity suits undertook legal actions defies the long-standing historiographical assumption that pregnancy declarations were the outcome of state disciplining projects. Rather the state through its legal system and legal personnel provided an important resource that women and their communities could leverage for help with the difficult situation of out-of-wedlock pregnancy. As in times of other difficulties for early modern women such as domestic violence or debt, they and their communities invited the state to help them solve their problems. Young pregnant women used the state and its courts to help them get their lives back on track. In this example as others, the state legal system was a resource for women, not a source of discipline and in particular circumstances their chance of success was high.[21] Court decisions closely followed agreements made out of court and followed a long legal standard that required the father to provide even for natural child as well as observing community expectations of what was respectable and appropriate.

The potential risks of sexual activity were of course gendered in some potent ways. Most obviously women faced the physical dangers of pregnancy, efforts to interrupt reproduction, and childbirth as well as the prospect of very difficult circumstances if their intimate partners abandoned them. Yet young expectant fathers who found themselves threatened with litigation or in prison when they refused to accept responsibility for their offspring faced very clear and sharp consequences of their sexual activity without marriage too. Women's success as litigators in these cases depended on their acceptance and appropriation of patriarchal expectations, with their emphasis on their blameless commitment to marriage and their partners' seeking to evade the obligations of fathers to support their children.[22]

Yet the ability of seventeenth and eighteenth-century French women to successfully use the legal system to mitigate the risks of out-of-wedlock pregnancy to their futures has been hidden in plain sight by contemporary confusion, by archivists' professional practices and by the confirmation biases of modern historians. In unpacking those layers and reading the copious evidence on the terms of actors at the time, it becomes clear that management of out-of-wedlock pregnancy was always local and that expectant single mothers – who had been in what were judged stable relationships where marriage was feasible – could rely on the support of their communities and courts to get their lives back on track. The patterns of secrecy and shaming often now associated with single motherhood in the past were largely creations of the nineteenth and twentieth centuries. In the Old Regime single women litigated about their pregnancies in public, with neighbourhood witnesses to support them, and in expectation that the courts would restore their honour and allow them to reset their lives by disciplining their male intimate partners.

Notes

1 Archives Départmentales du Rhône (hereafter ADR) BP3525 20 July 1725 Dossier of Gantier and Delagard.
2 French Revolutionaries first created a National Archives in 1790, a 1794 decree mandated that all pre-Revolution public and private documents seized during the Revolution should be centralised and a 1796 law created departmental archives for the newly established administrative regions that replaced the pre-Revolutionary provinces. https://francearchives.fr/fr/section/87072855.
3 Local courts across France varied in terms of whether they required this kind of relationship testimony from plaintiffs in paternity suits and this matter was determined by local jurisdictions. Cities besides Lyon that required histories included Aix, Carcassone. Grenoble, Paris, and Provins, while cities such as Châteaulaudren, Etampes, Laon, and Melun did not require them. Marie-Claude Phan, *Les Amours Illégitimes: histoires de séduction en Languedoc (1676–1786)* (Paris: Editions du Centre national de la recherche scientifique, 1986), p. 10.
4 The first reference I have found in English is in a 1978 article when Cissie Fairchilds wrote that declarations were required by French law of women about to give birth to illegitimate children. A decade later the work of Sarah Hanley elevated the importance of Edict as a pillar of state-building built in part on regulation of female sexuality through mandatory declarations of single motherhood. Many historians since, including myself, have cited Hanley to associate the Edict with mandatory declaration. Cissie Fairchilds, 'Female Sexual Attitudes and the Rise of Illegitimacy: A Case Study', *Journal of Interdisciplinary History*, 8:4 (Spring, 1978), p. 630. Sarah Hanley, 'Family and State in early modern France', in Christine Boxer and Jean Quaetaert (eds.), *Connecting Spheres* (Oxford, 1986), p. 56. See also, Sarah Hanley, 'Engendering the State: Family Formation and State Building in Early Modern France', *French Historical Studies*, 16:1 (Spring 1989), p. 11. This assertion persisted in English and French despite the fact that a number of French historians emphasised from the early 1970s that the Edict made no requirement for a declaration. See, for example, Marie-Claude Phan, '*Les déclarations de grossesse*', pp. 61–88 and Marie-Claude Phan, *Les Amours Illégitimes*, p. 5; Jacques Depauw, 'Amour Illégitime et société à Nantes au XVIII siècle', *Annales: Economies, Sociétés, Civilisations* (juillet-octobre, 1972), p. 1157; Jean-Louis Flandrin, 'A Case of Naivete in the Use of Statistics,' *Journal of Interdisciplinary History*, IX:2 (Autumn, 1978), pp. 309–315. These historians and others have used these types of documents to look at illegitimacy in a variety of ways. See also Jeremy Heyhoe 'Illegitimacy, Inter-Generational Conflict and Legal Practice in Eighteenth-Century Northern Burgundy', *Journal of Social History*, 38:3 (2005), pp. 673–684.
5 For the full text of the 1556 Edict, see François Isambert, et al. *Recueil Général des Anciennes Lois Françaises depuis l'an 420 jusqu'à la Révolution de 1789* (Paris, 1829), 13,

pp. 471–473. It was re-issued on multiple times in subsequent years, including in 1708 a requirement that priests read it from the pulpit every three months. Some cities did issue municipal regulations that required registration from the early eighteenth century. These were unrelated to the Edict and extremely unevenly enforced. See Julie Hardwick, *Sex in an Old Regime City: young workers and intimacy in France, 1660–1789* (Oxford University Press, 2020), pp. 24–32.
6   For much more on Lyon, its young workers and the patterns of intimacy in working communities, see Hardwick, *Sex in an Old Regime City*.
7   For the regulation's introduction and annulment, see Pierre Le Ridant, *Code matrimonial, ou Recueil complet de toutes les loix canoniques et civiles de France… sur les questions de mariage. Tome 2 / … Nouvelle édition par M★★★, avocat au Parlement, 1770* (Paris, 1770) p. 637. For similar restrictions on local efforts to expand regulation of reproduction in Toulouse, see Sylvie Perrier, 'La grossesse entre intimité et publicité dans les archives judiciaires de la France d'Ancien Régime', Unpublished paper, Family and Justice in the Archives: Histories of Intimacy in Transnational Perspective, Concordia University, May 2019. I thank Prof. Perrier for sharing her fascinating work in progress with me. For widespread conceptions about the Edict and legal efforts to counter them in both local and broader legal prescription, see also Véronique Demars-Sion, *Femmes séduites et abandonnées au 18e siècle: l'exemple du Cambrésis* (Hellemmens-Lille, 1991), pp. 116–120.
8   J. Fournel, *La séduction, considérée dans l'ordre judiciare* (Paris, 1781) passim and p. 86 for this error in understanding the terms of the 1556 edict.
9   The 'archival turn' has very revealing analysed the ways in which archives are layered with relations of power that highlight or elide the voices and experiences of different groups. For a range of early modern archival practices and their consequences, see the essays in 'The Social History of the Archive: Record Keeping in Early Modern Europe', *Past & Present* 230, suppl.#11 (November 2016) and Kate Peters, Alexandra Walsham, and Lisebeth Corens, (eds.), *Archives and Information in the Early Modern World* (New York, 2018).
10 Some of the key works that associated disciplining of female sexuality with state formation include Hanley, 'Engendering the State' and 'Family and State'; James R. Farr, *Authority and Sexuality in Early Modern Burgundy (1550–1730)* (Oxford, 1995); and Ulrike Strasser, *State of Virginity: Gender, Religion, and Politics in an Early Modern State* (Ann Arbor, 2004).
11 Hardwick, *Sex in an Old Regime City*.
12 By unprompted, I mean that the judges did not ask specific questions about first intercourse or, indeed, efforts to interrupt reproduction during the interrogatories. It is possible but impossible to ascertain that women's lawyers or community members might have suggested they add those details when the question of how they started to have sex came up. For these kinds of testimonies and what they reveal, see Hardwick, *Sex in an Old Regime City*.
13 For the way in which honour could be restored as well as damaged by legal action over reproduction elsewhere in early modern Europe, see for example Renato Barahona, *Sex Crimes, Honor, and the Law in Early Modern Spain: Vizcaya, 1528–1735* (Toronto, 2003).
14 ADR BP3541 14 May 1680 Dossier of Berchet and Flacheron. Relatively few such items survive as evidence in the archives today despite many references to them in depositions and it is impossible at this point to determine why. Perhaps it was unusual for women to deposit them as it was not required. Perhaps as they were not required they were lost or discarded in the *greffe* (the court's document and evidence depositary) even before professional archiving began. Many such items may have been displaced or removed during the multiple rounds of cataloguing that have been undertaken in French archives in the last two hundred years. Very rarely, a judge asked during the interrogatory if the young woman had received letters from her partner during his absence (for example, ADR BP3542 12 October 1686 Dossier of Demen and Carron), suggesting that judges may have noted such items in their considerations.

15 ADR BP3540. 12 August 1695 Dossier of Michon and Alognet; ADR BP3540 1 July 1668 Dossier of DeLuis and Gaultier.
16 ADR BP3542 13 July 1697 Dossier of Morel and Paullin. Witnesses also mentioned having seen written promises to marry, earrings, lace handkerchiefs and other small items.
17 For a fuller discussion of the opportunities and limits of women's ability to use the courts in this way if they could claim feasibly to have been in stable relationships, see Hardwick, *Sex in an Old Regime City*.
18 For the court's use of imprisonment during the investigations, a common feature of legal proceedings, see Julie Hardwick, 'Policing Paternity: historicising masculinity and sexuality in early modern France', *European Review of History* (August 2015) and Hardwick, *Sex in an Old Regime City*.
19 Joseph-Michel-Antoine Servan, *Discours de Mr. S***, ancient avocat general au parlement de ***, dans un procès sur une declaration de grossesse*. (Lyon, 17***).
20 For examples of the recent wave of work on women and litigation, see for France and Spain, Julie Hardwick, *Family Business: The Political Economies of Litigation in Early Modern France* (Oxford, 2009), Zoe Schneider, *The King's Bench: Bailliwick Magistrates and Local Governance in Normandy, 1670–1740* (Rochester, 2008), Scott Taylor, 'Credit, Debt and Honor in Castile, 1600–1650', *Journal of Early Modern History*, 7:1, pp. 8–27, Barahona, *Sex Crimes, Honor, and the Law*; for England, Laura Gowing, *Domestic Dangers: Women, Words and Sex in Early Modern London* (Oxford, 1999) and articles in the special issue, 'Women Negotiating the Boundaries of Justice in Britain, 1300–1700', *Journal of British Studies*, 58, Special Issue 4 (October, 2019); for other regions, see Bianca Premo, *Children of the Father King: Youth, Authority and Legal Minority in Colonial Lima* (Chapel Hill, 2005) and Michell McKinley, *Fractional Freedoms, Slavery, Intimacy and Legal Mobilization in Colonial Lima* (Cambridge, 2016); for accused witches litigating against their accusers, see LuAnn Homza, 'When Witches Litigate: New Sources from Early Modern Navarre', *The Journal of Modern History*, 91:2 (2019), pp. 245–275.
21 Hardwick, *Family Business*.
22 This pattern was typical of other kinds of litigation too. See for example Julie Hardwick, 'Women 'Working' The Law': Gender, Authority and Legal Process in Early Modern France', *Journal of Women's History*, 9:3 (October 1997), pp. 28–49; Hardwick, *Family Business*, pp. 188–199 and Alexandra Shepard, 'Worthless Witnesses? Marginal Voices and Women's Legal Agency in Early Modern England', *Journal of British Studies*, 58 (October, 2019), pp. 717–734.

COMBINED BIBLIOGRAPHY

For references to archival sources, see the endnotes for each chapter.

Printed primary sources

Anonymous, *Love and Artifice: or, A Compleat History of the Amour between Lord Mauritio and Emilia. Being the Case of Elizabeth Fitz-Maurice, alias Leeson, and the Lord William Fitz-Maurice, Relating to a Marriage-contract Between Them; Which Was Confirmed by a Court of Delegates, in the Lady's Behalf, on Wednesday, March 14th 1732/3, at Serjeant's-Inn, in Chancery-Lane* (London, 1734).

Anonymous, *Love without Artifice: or, the Disappointed Peer. A History of the Amour between Lord Mauritio and Emilia. Being the Case of Elizabeth Fitz-Maurice, alias Leeson and the Lord William Fitz- Maurice Relating to a Marriage-contract Between Them; Which was Confirmed by a Court of Delegates, in the Lady's Behalf, on Wednesday, March 14th 1732–3, at Serjeant's-Inn, in Chancery-Lane* (London, 1733).

Anonymous, *Observations on the Case of the Right Honourable the Lord Fitzmaurice and Mrs. Elizabeth Leeson, Concerning a Pretended Contract of Marriage* (London, 1733; 2nd edn, 1734).

Anonymous, *The Right Honourable Catherine Sarah, Lady Viscount Dowager, Widow and Relict of the Right Honourable Arthur, late Lord Viscount Doneraile, of the Kingdom of Ireland; The Right Honourable Arthur Mohun, Lord Viscount Doneraile of the Kingdom of Ireland, Respondent. The Appellant's Case* and *The Respondent's Case* (London, 1744).

Anonymous, *The Right Honourable Catherine-Sarah Lady Viscountess Doneraile, Wife of the Respondent Lord Doneraile in the Kingdom of Ireland by John Cunningham, Esq. her Father and Next Friend, February 1735. The Right Honourable Arthur Lord Viscount Doneraile, the Right Honourable Elizabeth. Lady Dowager Doneraile, James Barry, Esq; and others, Respondents. The Appellant's Case* and *The Respondent's Case* (London, 1735).

Baildon, William (ed.), *Court Rolls of the Manor of Wakefield, vol. 2: 1297 to 1309* (Leeds, 1906; reprinted Cambridge, 2013).

Bateson, Mary (ed.), *Borough Customs*, vol. 1, Selden Society, 18 (London, 1904).

Bateson, Mary (ed.), *Borough Customs*, vol. 2, Selden Society, 21 (London, 1906).

Berry, H.F. (ed.), *Register of Wills and Inventories of the Diocese of Dublin in the Time of Archbishops Tregury and Walton 1457–1483* (Dublin, 1896–1897).
Berry, H.F. (ed.), *Statute Rolls of the Parliament of Ireland, Reign of King Henry VI* (Dublin, 1910).
Bracton on the Laws and Customs of England, trans. Samuel E. Thorne, vol. 4 (Cambridge, MA, 1977).
Britnell, Richard H. (ed.), *Records of the Borough of Crossgate, Durham, 1312–1531*, Surtees Society vol. 212 (Woodbridge, 2008).
Crooks, Peter, *CIRCLE: A Calendar of Irish Chancery Letters c.1244–1509* [https://chancery.tcd.ie].
Dalrymple, Sir James, *Institutions of the Law of Scotland, Deduced from Its Originals, and Collated with the Civil, Canon, and Feudal Laws, and with the Customs of Neighbouring Nations, in Four Books* (Edinburgh, 1693).
Erskine, Sir John, *Institute of the Law of Scotland in Four Books: In the Order of Sir George Mackenzie Institutions of that Law* (Edinburgh, 1773).
Eustace, P. Beryl (ed.), *Registry of Deeds Dublin Abstracts of Wills* (3 vols, Dublin, 1956).
Flodr, Miroslav (ed.), *Právní kniha města Brna z poloviny 14. století. I. Úvod a edice* (Brno, 1990).
Flodr, Miroslav (ed.), *Pamětní kniha města Brna z let 1343–1376 (1379)* (Brno, 2005).
Flodr, Miroslav (ed.), *Nálezy brněnského městského práva, vol. I. (-1389)* (Brno, 2007).
Flodr, Miroslav (ed.), *Příručka práva městského (Manipulus vel directorium iuris civilis)* (Brno, 2008).
Flodr, Miroslav (ed.), *Pamětní kniha města Brna z let 1391–1515* (Brno, 2010).
Fraser, C.M. and Kenneth Emsley (eds.), *The Court Rolls of the Manor of Wakefield from October 1639 to September 1640* (Norwich, 1977).
Gilbert, J.T. (ed.), *Calendar of the Ancient Records of Dublin*, vol. 1 (Dublin, 1889).
Graves, James (ed.), 'Roll of the proceedings of the King's Council in Ireland, 1392–3', *Rerum Britannicarum Medii Aevi Scriptores* (London, 1877), pp. 3–252.
Hennessy, William and Mac Carthy, Brian (eds.), *Annála Uladh, Annals of Ulster*, 4 vols (Dublin 1887–1901) [edition at CELT, The Annals of Ulster (ucc.ie)]
Holmbäck, Åke and Elias Wessén (eds. and trans.), *Magnus Erikssons stadslag i nusvensk tolkning* (Stockholm, 1966).
Hope of Craighall, Sir Thomas, *Major Practicks*, ed. James Avon Clyde, 2 vols (Edinburgh: The Stair Society, 1937–1938).
Journal of the House of Commons of the Kingdom of Ireland, vol. 7, 1739–49 (Dublin, 1763). Consulted online at https://www.hathitrust.org/.
Journal of the House of Lords Vos 20–26, 1714–1746 (London, 1767–1830). Consulted online at British History Online (https://www.british-history.ac.uk/, Mills, James, *Calendar of the Justiciary rolls of Ireland*, 3 vols (Dublin, 1905–1956).
Lister, John (ed.), *Court Rolls of the Manor of Wakefield vol. 3: 1313 to 1316, and 1286* (Leeds, 1917; reprinted Cambridge, 2013).
Lister, John (ed.), *Court Rolls of the Manor of Wakefield vol. 4: 1315 to 1317* (Wakefield, 1930; reprinted Cambridge, 2013).
Lomas, R.A and A.J. Piper (eds.), *Durham Cathedral Priory Rentals, volume I: Bursars Rentals*, Surtees Society vol. 198 (Newcastle, 1989).
McCafferty, John (ed.), *The act book of the diocese of Armagh, 1518–1522* (Dublin, 2020).
McNeill, P.G. B. (ed.), *The Practicks of Sir James Balfour of Pittendriech*, 2 vols. (Edinburgh: The Stair Society, 1962–1963).
Owen, G.P. and Hugh Owen (eds.), *Caernarvon Court Rolls, 1361–1402* (Caernarvon, 1951).

Pernoud, Régine, *Les statutes municipaux de Marseille* (Paris and Monaco, 1949).
Plunkett, Margaret, *The Memoirs of Mrs Leeson*. Edited and introduced by Mary Lyons (Dublin, 1995).
Prochno, Joachim (ed.), *Zittauer Urkundenbuch I. (Regesten zur Geschichte der Stadt und des Landes Zittau 1234–1437)* (Görlitz, 1938), pp. 247–347.
Riley, Henry Thomas (ed.), *Munimenta Gildhallae Londiniensis: Liber Albus, Liber Custumarum et Liber Horn*, 3 (London, 1862).
Schmedeman, Johan (ed.), *Kongl. stadgar, förordningar, bref och resolutioner: Ifrån åhr 1528 in til 1701 angående justitiae och executions-ährender* (Stockholm, 1706).
Sellers, Maud (ed.), *York Memorandum Book*, Surtees Society, 125 (Durham, 1915).
Servan, Joseph-Michel-Antoine, *Discours de Mr. S★★★, ancient avocat general au parlement de ★★★, dans un procès sur une declaration de grossesse.* (Lyon, 17★★★).
Shaw, William A (ed.), *Calendar of Treasury Books and Papers, Volume 5, 1742–1745*, ed. (London, 1903). Consulted online at British History Online (http://www.british-history.ac.uk/cal-treasury-books-papers/vol5).
Tadra, Ferdinand (ed.), *Soudní akta konzistoře pražské (Acta Iudiciaria Consistorii Pragensis)*, tom. VII (1420–1424) (Prague, 1901).
The Good Wife's Guide: Le Ménagier de Paris, a Medieval Household Book, trans. Gina L. Greco and Christine M. Rose (Ithaca: Cornell University Press, 2009).
Ulkuniemi, Martti (ed. and trans.) *Kuningas Kristoferin maanlaki 1442* (Helsinki, 1978).
Walker, John William (ed.), *Court Rolls of the Manor of Wakefield vol. 5: 1322 to 1331* (Wakefield, 1945; reprinted Cambridge 2013).
Weikel, Ann (ed.), *The Court Rolls of the Manor of Wakefield from October 1583 to September 1585* (Leeds, 1984).
Woolley, David (ed.), *The Correspondence of Jonathan Swift, D. D* (4 vols, Frank am Main, 1999–2014).

Secondary sources

Abreu-Ferreira, Darlene, 'Women, Law and Legal Intervention in Early Modern Portugal', *Continuity and Change*, 33 (2018), pp. 293–313.
Ågren, Maria, *Domestic Secrets: Women & Property in Sweden 1600–1857* (Chapel Hill, 2004).
Alexandre-Bidon, Danièle and Didier Lett, *Les enfants au Moyen Age Ve-XVe siècles* (Paris, 1997).
Almquist, Jan Eric, 'Rättstvisten om Skeboholm 1614–16: Bidrag till släkterna Månesköds och Totts historia', *Personhistorisk Tidskrift* 40 (1939–1940), pp. 1–22.
Almquist, Jan Eric, '1582 års adelsregister', *Släkt och Hävd* (1962), pp. 145–155.
Almquist, Jan Eric, 'Adliga ätten Månesköds (af Seglinge) ursprung och äldsta historia', *Släkt och Hävd* 1 (1965), pp. 269–298.
Andersson, Gudrun, *Tingets män och kvinnor: Genus som norm och strategi under 1600- och 1700-tal* (Uppsala, 1998).
Andersson Raeder, Johanna, *Hellre hustru än änka: Äktenskapens ekonomiska betydelse för frälsekvinnor i senmedeltidens Sverige* (Stockholm, 2011), pp. 46–52.
Anthoni, Eric, 'Horn - Henrik Klasson', *Svenskt Biografiskt Lexikon*, 19 (Stockholm, 1971–1973), pp. 353–355.
Antonín, Robert et al., *Čtvrtý lateránský koncil a české země ve 13. a 14. století* (Prague, 2020).
Antonín Malaníková, Michaela, 'Poručnictví, nebo partnerství? Status manželky a majetkové poměry manželů ve středověkém Brně', *Theatrum Historiae*, 22 (2018), pp. 33–49.

Arnade, P. and Prevenier, W., *Honor, Vengeance, and Social Trouble: Pardon Letters in the Burgundian Low Countries* (Ithaca, 2015), pp. 138–172.

Arru, Angiolina 'Die nicht bezahlte Mitgift. Ambivalenzen und Vorteile des Dotalsystems im ausgehenden 19. und beginnenden 20. Jahrhundert', *L 'Homme Z.F.G.*22.1 (2011), pp. 55–69.

Baatsen, I. and De Meyer, A., 'Forging or Reflecting Multiple Identities? Analyzing Processes of Identification in a Sample of Fifteenth-Century Letters of Remission from Bruges and Mechelen', in Violet Soen, Yves Junot and Florian Mariage (eds.), *L 'identité au pluriel: jeux et enjeux des appurtenances autour des Pays-Bas, 14e-18e siècles* (Villeneuve-d 'ascq, 2014), pp. 23–38.

Bailey, Joanne, 'Voices in Court: Lawyers or Litigants?', *Historical Research*, 74 (2001), pp. 392–408.

Bailey, Merridee L., '"Most Hevynesse and Sorowe": The Presence of Emotions in the Late Medieval and Early Modern Court of Chancery', *Law and History Review*, 37:1 (2019), pp. 1–28.

Baker, John, *An Introduction to English Legal History* (Oxford, 5th edn, 2019).

Barahona, Renato, *Sex Crimes, Honor, and the Law in Early Modern Spain: Vizcaya, 1528–1735* (Toronto, 2003).

Barclay, Katie, *Love, Intimacy and Power: Marriage and Patriarchy in Scotland, 1650–1850* (Manchester, 2011).

Barclay, Katie, 'Natural Affection, Children, and Family Inheritance Practices in the Long Eighteenth Century', in Janay Nugent and Elizabeth Ewan (eds.), *Children and Youth in Premodern Scotland* (Woodbridge, 2015), pp. 136–151.

Bardsley, Sandy, *Venomous Tongues: Speech and Gender in Late Medieval England* (Philadelphia, 2006).

Bardsley, Sandy, 'Peasant Women and Inheritance of Land in Fourteenth-Century England', *Continuity and Change*, 29 (2014), pp. 297–324.

Barnes, Patricia M., 'The Chancery corpus cum causa File, 10–11 Edward IV', in R. F. Hunnisett and J. B. Post (eds.), *Medieval Legal Records Edited in Memory of C. A. F. Meekings* (London, 1978), pp. 429–476.

Barron, Caroline, 'The "Golden Age" of Women in Medieval London', *Reading Medieval Studies*, 15 (1989), pp. 35–58.

Baumann, Anette, *Die Gesellschaft der Frühen Neuzeit im Spiegel der Reichskammergerichtsprozesse: Eine sozialgeschichtliche Untersuchung zum 17. und 18. Jahrhundert* (Cologne/Weimar/Vienna, 2001).

Beard, Mary R., *Woman as Force in History: A Study in Traditions and Realities* (New York, 1986; a reprint of the 1946 book).

Beattie, Cordelia, 'Governing Bodies: Law Courts, Male Householders, and Single Women in Late Medieval England', in *idem*, Anna Maslakovic, and Sarah Rees Jones (eds.), *The Medieval Household in Christian Europe, C. 850-C. 1550: Managing Power, Wealth, and Body* (Turnhout, 2003), pp. 199–220.

Beattie, Cordelia, 'Single Women, Work, and Family: The Chancery Dispute of Jane Wynde and Margaret Clerk', in Michael Goodich (ed.), *Voices from the Bench: The Narratives of Lesser Folk in Medieval Trials* (New York, 2006), pp. 177–202.

Beattie, Cordelia, 'Your oratrice: Women's Petitions to the Late Medieval Court of Chancery', in Bronagh Kane and Fiona Williamson (eds.), *Women, Agency and the Law, 1300–1700* (London, 2013), pp. 17–30.

Beattie, Cordelia and Kirsten Fenton (eds.), *Intersections of Gender, Religion and Ethnicity in the Middle Ages* (London, 2011).

Beattie, Cordelia, and Matthew Frank Stevens (eds.), *Married Women and the Law in Pre-modern Northwest Europe* (Woodbridge, 2013).
Beimrohr, Wilfried, *Mit Brief und Siegel: die Gerichte Tirols und ihr älteres Schriftgut im Tiroler Landesarchiv* (Innsbruck, 1994).
Bellamy, J.G., *The Law of Treason in England in the Later Middle Ages* (Cambridge, 2008).
Bellomo, Mario, *The Common Legal Past of Europe, 1000–1800*, trans. Lydia Cochrane (Washington, DC, 1995).
Bender, Tovah, 'Their Father's Daughters: Women's Social Identities in Fifteenth-Century Florence', *Journal of Family History*, 38(2013), pp. 371–386.
Bennett, Judith M., *Women in the Medieval English Countryside: Gender & Household in Brigstock before the Plague* (Oxford, 1987).
Bennett, Judith M., *Ale, Beer, and Brewsters in England: Women's Work in a Changing World, 1300–1600* (Oxford, 1996).
Bennett, Judith M., *Medieval Women in Modern Perspective* (Washington, 2000).
Bennett, Judith M., 'Writing Fornication: Medieval Leyrwite and Its Historians', *Transactions of the Royal Historical Society*, 13 (2003), pp. 131–162.
Bennett, Judith M., *History Matters: Patriarchy and the Challenge of Feminism* (Philadelphia, 2006).
Bennett, Judith M. and Amy Froide (eds.), *Singlewomen in the European Past, 1250–1800* (Philadelphia, 1999).
Beres, M., 'Rethinking the Concept of Consent for Anti-Sexual Violence Activism and Education', *Feminism & Psychology*, 26 (2014), pp. 373–389.
Beresford, David, 'James Butler, 5th Earl of Ormond', 'Thomas fitzMaurice FitzGerald' and 'Richard Nugent', in James McGuire and James Quinn (eds.), *The Dictionary of Irish Biography* (Dublin and Cambridge, 2009) [online, accessed 4/11/2020]
Berry, H.F., 'History of the Religious Gild of St Anne, in St Audeon's Church, Dublin, 1430–1740', *Proceedings of the Royal Irish Academy*, 25c (1904/5), pp. 21–106.
Biancalana, Joseph, 'Widows at Common Law: The Development of Common Law Dower', *Irish Jurist*, 23 (1988), pp. 255–329.
Biancalana, Joseph, 'Testamentary Cases in Fifteenth-Century Chancery', *Tijdschrift voor Rechtsgeschiedenis*, 76:3–4 (2008), pp. 283–306.
Biniaś-Szkopek, Magdalena, *Małżonkowie przed sądem biskupiego oficjała poznańskiego w pierwszej ćwierci XV wieku* (Poznań, 2018).
Björne, Lars, *Patrioter och institutionalister: Den nordiska rättsvetenskapens historia*, 1 (Lund, 1995).
Bleeke, Marian. *Motherhood and Meaning in Medieval Sculpture: Representations from France* (Woodbridge, 2017).
Booker, Sparky, 'Moustaches, Mantles and Saffron Shirts: What motivated Sumptuary Law in Medieval English Ireland?', *Speculum*, 96 (forthcoming July 2021).
Boone, M., de Hemptinne, T., and Prevenier, W., *Fictie en historische realiteit: Colijn van Rijsseles De spiegel der minnen, ook een spiegel van sociale spanningen in de Nederlanden der late Middeleeuwen?* (Gent, 1985).
Brand, Paul, 'Ralph de Hengham and the Irish Common Law', *Irish Jurist*, 19 (1984), pp. 107–114.
Brand, Paul, 'The Birth of a Colonial Judiciary: The Judges of the Lordship of Ireland, 1210–1377', in W.N. Osborough (ed.), *Explorations in Law and History: Irish legal History Society Discourses, 1988–1994* (Blackrock, Dublin, 1995), esp. pp. 1–48.
Brand, Paul, 'Irish Law Students and Lawyers in Late Medieval England', *Irish Historical Studies*, 32 (2000), pp. 161–173.

Brand, Paul, "'Deserving' and 'Undeserving' Wives: Earning and Forfeiting Dower in Medieval England', *The Journal of Legal History*, 22 (2001), pp. 1–20.
Brasher, Sally Mayall, *Hospitals and Charity: Religious Culture and Civic Life in Medieval Northern Italy* (Manchester, 2017).
Briggs, Chris, 'Empowered or Marginalized? Rural Women and Credit in Later Thirteenth- and Fourteenth-Century England', *Continuity and Change*, 19 (2004), pp. 13–43.
Brock, Aske Laursen and Misha Ewen, 'Women's Public Lives: Navigating the East India Company, Parliament and Courts in Early Modern England', *Gender & History*, 33 (2021), pp. 3–23.
Brundage, James A. *Law, Sex, and Christian Society in Medieval Europe* (Chicago, 1987).
Brundage, James A., *Sex, Law and Marriage in the Middle Ages* (Aldershot, 1993).
Brundage, James A., *Medieval Canon Law* (London, 1995).
Brundage, James A., 'E Pluribus unum: Custom, the Professionalization of Medieval Law, and Regional Variations in Marriage Formation', in Mia Korpiola (ed.), *Regional Variations in Matrimonial Law and Custom in Europe, 1150–1600* (Boston, 2011), pp. 21–41.
Bursell, Barbro, *William Grey och Brita Tott: En berättelse om krig och kärlek i stormakttidens Sverige* (Stockholm, 2012).
Butler, Sara M., "'I Will Never Consent to Be Wedded with You!'": Coerced Marriage in the Courts of Medieval England', *Canadian Journal of History*, 39 (2004), pp. 247–270.
Butler, Sara M., 'The Law as a Weapon in Marital Disputes: Evidence from the Late Medieval Court of Chancery, 1424–1529', *Journal of British Studies*, 43 (2004), pp. 291–316.
Butler, Sara M., 'Runaway Wives: Husband Desertion in Medieval England', *Journal of Social History*, 40 (2006), pp. 337–359.
Butler, Sara M., *The Language of Abuse. Marital Violence in Later Medieval England* (Leiden, 2007).
Butler, Sara M., 'Discourse on the Nature of Coverture in the Later Medieval Courtroom', in Tim Stretton and Krista J. Kesselring (eds.), *Married Women and the Law: Coverture in England and the Common Law World* (Montreal, 2013), pp. 24–44.
Butler, Sara M., *Divorce in Medieval England: From One to Two Persons in Law* (New York, 2013).
Butler, T. Blake, 'The Barony of Dunboyne', *Irish Genealogist*, 2 (1946), pp. 107–121.
Capern, Amanda, 'Maternity and Justice in the Early Modern English Court of Chancery', *Journal of British Studies*, 58 (2019), pp. 701–716.
Carius, Hendrikje, 'Strategien vor Gericht? Die "velleianischen Freyheiten" im sächsischen Recht (1648–1806)', in Grethe Jacobsen, Helle Vogt, Inger Dübeck, and Heide Wunder (eds.), *Less Favored – More Favored: Proceedings from a Conference on Gender in European Legal History, 12th–19th Centuries, September2004*: http://www5.kb.dk/export/sites/kb_dk/da/nb/publikationer/fundogforskning-online/pdf/A07_Carius.pdf
Carius, Hendrikje, *Recht durch Eigentum. Frauen vor dem Jenaer Hofgericht 1648–1806* (Munich, 2012).
Carlier, M., *Kinderen van de minne? Bastaarden in het vijftiende-eeuwse Vlaanderen* (Brussels, 2001).
Carlin, Martha, *Medieval Southwark* (London, 1996).
Carlsson, Lizzie, *"Jag giver dig min dotter:" Trolovning och äktenskap i den svenska kvinnans äldre historia*, 1 (Lund, 1965), pp. 209–224.
Cavallo, Sandra and Lyndan Warner (eds.), *Widowhood in Medieval and Early Modern Europe* (Abington, 1999).

Cavell, Emma, 'The Measure of Her Actions: A Quantitative Assessment of Anglo-Jewish Women's Litigation at the Exchequer of the Jews, 1219–81', *Law and History Review*, 39 (2021), pp. 135–172.

Cederbom, Charlotte, *The Legal Guardian and Married Women: Norms and Practice in the Swedish Realm 1350–1450* (Helsinki, 2017).

Cesco, V., 'Female Abduction, Family Honor, and Women's Agency in Early Modern Venetian Istria', *Journal of Early Modern History*, 15 (2011), pp. 349–366.

Chabot, Isabelle, 'Family Justice and Public Justice in Dowry and Inheritance Conflicts between Florentine Families (Fourteenth to Fifteenth Centuries)', in Margareth Lanzinger, Janine Maegraith, Siglinde Clementi, Ellinor Forster, and Christian Hagen (eds.), *Negotiations of Gender and Property through Legal Regimes (14th–19th century). Stipulating, Litigating, Mediating* (Leiden, 2021), pp. 225–253.

Chatterjee, Indrani, 'Women, Monastic Commerce and Coverture in Eastern India circa 1600–1800 CE', *Modern Asian Studies*, 50 (2016), pp. 175–216.

Chaytor, M., 'Husband(Ry): Narratives of Rape in the Seventeenth Century', *Gender & History*, 7 (1995), pp. 378–407.

Cioni, Maria L., 'The Elizabethan Court of Chancery and Women's Rights', in Delloyd J. Guth and John W. McKenna (eds.), *Tudor Rule and Revolution: Essays for G. R. Elton from His American friends* (Cambridge, 1982), pp. 159–182.

Cioni, Maria L., *Women and Law in Elizabethan England with Particular Reference to the Court of Chancery* (New York, 1985).

Clementi, Siglinde, 'A Dispute over Guardianship. The Trentino-Tyrolean Noble Trapp Family between 1641 and 1656', in Margareth Lanzinger, Janine Maegraith, Siglinde Clementi, Ellinor Forster, and Christian Hagen (eds.), *Negotiations of Gender and Property through Legal Regimes (14th–19th century). Stipulating, Litigating, Mediating* (Leiden, 2021), 282–308.

Connolly, Philomena, *Medieval Record Sources* (Dublin, 2002).

Cosgrove, Art, 'Parliament and the Anglo-Irish Community: The Declaration of 1460', in Art Cosgrove and J.I. McGuire (eds.), *Parliament and Community: Historical Studies XIV* (Belfast, 1983), pp. 25–41.

Courtemanche, Andrée, *La richesse des femmes: Patrimoines et gestion à Manosque au XIVe siècle* (Montreal, 1993).

Coutts, Winifred, *The Business of the College of Justice in 1600: How It Reflects the Economic and Social Life of Scots Men and Women*, vol. 50 (Edinburgh, 2003).

Crooks, Peter, 'Factions, Feuds and Noble Power in the Lordship of Ireland, c.1356–1496', *Irish Historical Studies*, 35 (2007), pp. 425–454.

Crooks, Peter, 'The Ascent and Descent of Desmond under Lancaster and York', in Peter Crooks and Seán Duffy (eds.), *The Geraldines and medieval Ireland: The Making of a Myth* (Dublin, 2016), pp. 233–263.

D´Avray, David L. *Medieval Marriage: Symbolism and Society* (Oxford, 2005).

D´Avray, David L., 'Lateran IV and Marriage. What Lateran IV Did Not Do about Marriage?', in Gert Melville and Johannes Helmrath (eds.), *The Fourth Lateran Council: Institutional Reform and Spiritual Renewal* (Affalterbach, 2017), pp. 137–142.

Damoiseaux, S., 'L'officialité de Liège à la fin du Moyen Âge. Contribution à l'histoire de la juridiction ecclésiastique de l 'évêque de Liège (XIVe-XVIe siècles)', *Leodium*, 99 (2014), pp. 6–44.

Danneel, M., 'Orphanhood and Marriage in Fifteenth-Century Ghent', in Walter Prevenier (ed.), *Marriage and Social Mobility in the late Middle Ages* (Gent, 1989), pp. 123–139.

Davis, Natalie Zemon, *Fiction in the Archives: Pardon Tales and Their Tellers in Sixteenth-Century France* (Stanford, 1987).

de Beaumanoir, Philippe, *The Coutumes de Beauvaisis of Phillippe de Beaumanoir*, trans. F.R.P. Akehurst (Philadelphia, 1992).

De Moor, T. and Van Zanden, J., 'Girl Power: The European Marriage Pattern and Labour Markets in the North Sea Region in the Late Medieval and Early Modern Period', *The Economic History Review*, 63 (2010), pp. 1–33.

De Munck, Bert, 'Free Choice, Modern Love, and Dependence: Marriage of Minors and 'rapt de séduction' in the Austrian Netherlands', *Journal of Family History*, 29 (2004), 183–205.

DeAragon, RāGena C., 'Power and Agency in Post-Conquest England: Elite Women and the Transformations of the Twelfth Century', in Heather J. Tanner (ed.), *Medieval Elite Women and the Exercise of Power, 1100–1400: Moving Beyond the Exceptionalist Debate* (Cham, 2019), pp. 19–43.

Demars-Sion, Véronique, *Femmes séduites et abandonnées au 18e siècle: l'exemple du Cambrésis* (Hellemmes-Lille, 1991), pp. 116–120.

Dennehy, Coleman, *The Irish Parliament, 1613–1689: The Evolution of a Colonial Institution* (Manchester, 2019).

Depauw, Jacques, 'Amour Illégitime et société à Nantes au XVIII siècle', *Annales: Economies, Sociétés, Civilisations* (juillet-octobre, 1972), pp. 1155–1182.

DesBrisay, Gordon, and Karen Sander Thomson, 'Crediting Wives: Married Women and Debt Litigation in the Seventeenth Century', in Elizabeth Ewan and Janay Nugent (eds.), *Finding the Family in Medieval and Early Modern Scotland* (Aldershot, 2008), pp. 85–98.

Dodd, Gwilym, *Justice and Grace: Private Petitioning and the English Parliament in the Late Middle Ages* (Oxford, 2007).

Dodd, Gwilym, 'The Rise of English, the Decline of French: Supplications to the English Crown, c. 1420–1450', *Speculum*, 86 (2011), pp. 117–150.

Dodd, Gwilym, 'Writing Wrongs: The Drafting of Supplications to the Crown in Later Fourteenth Century England' *Medium Aevum*, 80 (2011), pp. 217–246.

Dodd, Gwilym, 'Law, Legislation and Consent in the Plantagenet Empire: Wales and Ireland, 1272–1461', *Journal of British Studies*, 56 (2017), pp. 237–246.

Dodd, Gwilym, 'Languages and Law in Late Medieval England: English, French and Latin', in Candace Barrington and Sebastian Sobecki (eds.), *The Cambridge Companion to Medieval English Law and Literature* (Cambridge, 2019), pp. 17–29.

Dodd, Gwilym, Matthew Phillips and Helen Killick, 'Multiple-clause Petitions to the English Parliament in the Later Middle Ages: Instruments of Pragmatism or Persuasion?', *Journal of Medieval History*, 40 (2014), pp. 176–194.

Dodd, Gwilym and Sophie Petit-Renaud, 'Grace and Favour: The Petition and Its Mechanisms', in Christopher Fletcher et al. (eds.), *Government and Political Life in England and France, c.1300-c.1500* (Cambridge, 2015), pp. 240–278.

Donahue, Charles, *Law, Marriage, and Society in the Later Middle Ages: Arguments about Marriage in Five Courts* (Cambridge, 2007).

Donaldson, Gordon, 'The Church Courts', in *An Introduction to Scottish Legal History* (Edinburgh: The Stair Society, 1958), pp. 363–373.

Doxiadis, Evdoxios, *The Shackles of Modernity. Women, Property, and the Transition from the Ottoman Empire to the Greek State* (Cambridge, MA/London, 2011).

Dübeck, Inger, 'Legal Status of Widows in Denmark 1500–1900', *Scandinavian Journal of History*, 29 (2004), pp. 209–223.

Duncan, G. I. O., *The High Court of Delegates* (Cambridge, 1971).

Dunn, Caroline, *Stolen Women in Medieval England: Rape, Abduction, and Adultery, 1100–1500* (Cambridge, 2013).

Dupont, G., 'Le temps des compositions: pratiques judiciaires à Bruges et à Gand du XIVe au XVIe siècle (partie I)', in Bernard Dauven and Xavier Rousseaux (eds.),

Préférent miséricorde à rigueur de justice: pratiques de la grâce (XIIIe-XVIIe siècles) (Louvain-la-Neuve, 2012), pp. 53–95.

Dupont, G., 'Le temps des compositions: pratiques judiciaires à Bruges et à Gand du XIVe au XVIe siècle (partie II)', in Marie-Amélie Bourguignon, Bernard Dauven and Xavier Rousseaux (eds.), *Amender, sanctionner et punir: Recherches sur l'histoire de la peine, du Moyen Âge au XXe siècle* (Louvain-la-Neuve, 2012), pp. 15–47.

Durand, Guillaume, *Speculum clarissimi viri Guilelmi Durandi, una cum Iohanni Andreae ac Baldi doctorum in utraque iurium* (Lyon, 1547).

Elgenstierna, Gustaf, *Den introducerade svenska adelns ättartavlor med tillägg och rättelser*, 1 (Stockholm, 1925).

Elgenstierna, Gustaf, *Den introducerade svenska adelns ättartavlor med tillägg och rättelser*, 5 (Stockholm, 1930).

Elgenstierna, Gustaf, *Den introducerade svenska adelns ättartavlor med tillägg och rättelser*, 8 (Stockholm, 1934).

Ellis, Steven, 'Parliament and Community in Yorkist and Tudor Ireland', in Art Cosgrove and J.I. McGuire (eds.), *Parliament and Community: Historical Studies XIV* (Belfast, 1983), pp. 43–68.

Ellis, Steven, 'Nationalist Historiography and the English and Gaelic worlds', *Irish Historical Studies*, 25:97 (1986), pp. 1–18.

Ellis, Steven, *Reform and Revival: English Government in Ireland, 1470–1534* (New York, 1986).

Ellis, Steven, *Ireland in the Age of the Tudors, 1447–1603: English Expansion and the End of Gaelic Rule* (London, 1998).

Ellis, Steven, *Defending English ground: War and Peace in Meath and Northumberland, 1460–1542* (Oxford, 2015).

Erickson, Amy, 'Common Law versus Common Practice: The Use of Marriage Settlements in Early Modern England', *Economic History Review*, 43 (1990), pp. 21–39.

Erickson, Amy, *Women and Property in Early Modern England* (London, 1993).

Erickson, Amy, 'Property and Widowhood in England 1660–1840', in Sandra Cavallo and Lyndan Warner (eds.), *Widowhood in Medieval and Early Modern Europe* (Abingdon, 1999), pp. 145–163.

Erickson, Amy, 'Mistresses and Marriage: or, a Short History of the Mrs', *History Workshop Journal*, 78 (2014), pp. 39–57.

Erler, Mary C. and Maryanne Kowaleski, *Women and Power in the Middle Ages* (Athens, 1988).

Erler, Mary C. and Maryanne Kowaleski, 'A New Economy of Power Relations: Female Agency in the Middle Ages', in Mary C. Erler and Maryanne Kowaleski (eds.), *Gendering the Master Narrative: Women and Power in the Middle Ages* (Ithaca, 2003), pp. 1–16.

Ernst Holthöfer, 'Die Geschlechtsvormundschaft. Ein Überblick von der Antike bis ins 19. Jahrhundert', in Ute Gerhard (ed.), *Frauen in der Geschichte des Rechts. Von der Frühen Neuzeit bis zur Gegenwart* (Munich, 1997), pp. 390–451.

Ewan, Elizabeth, 'Scottish Portias: Women in the Courts in Mediaeval Scottish Towns', *Journal of the Canadian Historical Association*, 3 (1992), pp. 27–43.

Ewan, Elizabeth, 'Impatient Griseldas: Women and the Perpetration of Violence in Sixteenth-Century Glasgow', *Florilegium*, 28 (2011), pp. 149–168.

Fairchilds, Cissie, 'Female Sexual Attitudes and the Rise of Illegitimacy: A Case Study', *Journal of Interdisciplinary History*, 8 (1978), pp. 627–667.

Fairchilds, Cissie, *Women in Early Modern Europe, 1500–1700* (Harlow, 2007).

Falzone, E., '*Poena* et *Emenda*. Les sanctions pénale et non pénale dans le droit canonique médiéval et la pratique des officialités', in Marie-Amélie, Bernard Dauven and Xavier

Rousseaux (eds.), *Amender, sanctionner et punir: recherches sur l'histoire de la peine, du Moyen Âge au XXe siècle* (Louvain-La-Neuve, 2012), pp. 113–135.

Farmer, Sharon, *Surviving Poverty in Medieval Paris: Gender, Ideology, and the Daily Lives of the Poor* (Ithaca, 2005).

Finlay, John, 'Women and Legal Representation in Early Sixteenth-Century Scotland,' in Elizabeth Ewan and Maureen M. Meikle (eds.), *Women in Scotland: 1100–1750*, (East Linton, 1999), pp. 165–175.

Flandrin, Jean-Louis, 'A Case of Naivete in the Use of Statistics', *Journal of Interdisciplinary History*, IX:2 (Autumn, 1978), pp. 309–315.

Flannigan, Laura, 'Litigants in the English Court of Poor Men's Causes, or Court of Requests, 1515–25', *Law and History Review*, 382 (2020), pp. 303–337.

Fleming, Peter, *Women in Late Medieval Bristol* (Bristol, 2001).

Flodr, Miroslav, *Brněnské městské právo. Zakladatelské období (–1359)* (Brno, 2001).

Flodr, Miroslav, 'Cesta k právu a spravedlnosti. Jan, notář města Brna', in Libor Jan and Zdeněk Drahoš (eds.), *Osobnosti moravských dějin 1* (Brno, 2006), pp. 89–102.

Fournel, J., *La séduction, considérée dans l'ordre judiciare* (Paris, 1781).

Fox, Levi, 'Some New Evidence of Leet Activity in Coventry, 1540–41', *English Historical Review*, 61 (1946), pp. 235–243.

Frame, Robin, '*Les Engleys nées en Irlande*': The English Political Identity in Medieval Ireland', *Transactions of the Royal Historical Society*, 6th series, 3 (1993), pp. 83–103.

Franziska Loetz, 'L'infrajudiciaire. Facetten und Bedeutung eines Konzepts', in Andreas Blauert and Gerd Schwerhoff (eds.), *Kriminalitätsgeschichte. Beiträge zur Sozial- und Kulturgeschichte der Vormoderne* (Konstanz, 2000), pp. 545–562.

Fregulia, Jeanette M., 'Stories Worth Telling: Women as Business Owners and Investors in Early Modern Milan', *Early Modern Women* 10:1 (2015), pp. 122–130.

French, Katherine L., 'Loving Friends: Surviving Widowhood in Late Medieval Westminster', *Gender and History* 22 (April 2010), pp. 21–37.

Froide, Amy M., *Never Married: Singlewomen in Early Modern England* (Oxford, 2005).

Garnot, Benôit (ed.), '*L'infrajudiciaire du Moyen Age à l 'époque contemporaine* (Dijon, 1996).

Garnot, Benoît. Justice, infrajustice, parajustice et extrajustice dans la France d 'Ancien Régime, *Crime, Histoire & Sociétés/Crime, History & Societies* 4 (2000), pp. 103–120.

Geary, Patrick, *Phantoms of Remembrance: Memory and Oblivion at the End of the First Millennium* (Princeton, 1994).

Gerhard, Ute (ed.), *Frauen in der Geschichte des Rechts. Von der Frühen Neuzeit bis zur Gegenwart* (Munich, 1997).

Gibson, A. J. S. and Smout, T. C. *Prices, Food, and Wages in Scotland, 1550–1780* (Cambridge, 1995).

Gillingstam, Hans and Kjell-Gunnar Lundholm, 'Tott', in Folke Wernstedt, Hans Gillingstam and Pontus Möller (eds.), *Äldre svenska frälsesläkter: Ättartavlor 1:3* (Stockholm, 1989), pp. 270–295.

Glaze, Alice, 'Women and Kirk Discipline: Prosecution, Negotiation, and the Limits of Control', *Journal of Scottish Historical Studies*, 36 (2016), pp. 125–142.

Gleixner, Ulrike, 'Das Gesamtgericht der Herrschaft Schulenberg im 18. Jahrhundert. Funktionsweise und Zugang von Frauen und Männern', in Jan Peters (ed.), *Gutsherrschaft als soziales Modell. Vergleichende Betrachtungen zur Funktionsweise frühneuzeitlicher Agrargesellschaften* (Munich, 1995), pp. 301–326.

Gleixner, Ulrike, 'Frauen, Justiznutzung und dörfliche Rechtskultur – Veränderungen nach dem Dreißigjährigen Krieg', in Klaus Garber and Jutta Held (eds.), *Der Frieden.*

Rekonstruktion einer europäischen Vision, vol. 1: Erfahrung und Deutung von Krieg und Frieden. Religion – Geschlechter – Natur und Kultur (Munich, 2001), pp. 453–461.

Godding, P., *Le droit privé dans les Pays-Bas méridionaux du 12ᵉ au 18ᵉ siècle* (Gembloux, 1987).

Goldberg, P.J.P., *Women, Work, and Life Cycle in a Medieval Economy: Women in York and Yorkshire c. 1300–1520* (Oxford, 1992).

Goldberg, Jeremy, 'Gender and Matrimonial Litigation in the Church Courts in the Latter Middle Ages: The Evidence of the Court of York', *Gender & History*, 19 (2007), pp. 49–59.

Goldberg, Jeremy, *Communal Discord, Child Abduction and Rape in the Later Middle Ages* (New York, 2008).

Goldberg, Jeremy, 'Echoes, Whispers, Ventriloquisms: On Recovering Women's Voices from the Court of York in Late Middle Ages', in Bronach Kane and Fiona Williamson (eds.), *Women, Agency and the Law, 1300–1700* (London, 2012), pp. 31–41.

Goldberg, Jeremy, 'Love and Lust in Later Medieval England: Exploring Powerful Emotions and Power Dynamics in Disputed Marriage Cases', Paper presented at *Emotions and Power c.400–1850* conference (York, 2017).

Gorman, Vincent, 'Richard, Duke of York, and the Development of an Irish Faction', *Proceedings of the Royal Irish Academy*, 85c (1985), pp. 169–179.

Gowing, Laura, *Domestic Dangers: Women, Words and Sex in Early Modern London* (Oxford, 1999).

Green, Thomas, *Consistorial Decisions of the Commissaries of Edinburgh 1564 to 1576/7* (Edinburgh: The Stair Society, 2014).

Green, Thomas, 'Romano-Canonical Procedure in Reformation Scotland: The Example of the Court of the Commissaries of Edinburgh', *The Journal of Legal History*, 36 (2015), pp. 217–235.

Greilsammer, M., 'Rapts de séduction et rapts violents en Flandre et en Brabant à la fin du Moyen-Âge', *The Legal History Review*, 56 (1988), 49–84.

Griffith, Margaret, 'The Talbot-Ormond Struggle for Control of the Anglo-Irish Government, 1414–1447', *Irish Historical Studies*, 2 (1941), pp. 376–397.

Grochowina, Nicole *Das Eigentum der Frauen. Konflikte vor dem Jenaer Schöppenstuhl im ausgehenden 18. Jahrhundert* (Cologne/Weimar/Vienna, 2009).

Habib, Imtiaz, *Black Lives in the English Archives, 1500–1677: Imprints of the Invisible* (Farnham, 2008).

Hagen, Christian, Margareth Lanzinger, and Janine Maegraith, ‚Verträge als Instrumente der Vermögensabsicherung im südlichen Tirol vom 14. bis zum 18. Jahrhundert', *Historische Anthropologie*, 25 (2017), pp. 188–212.

Hagen, Christian, Margareth Lanzinger and Janine Maegraith, 'Competing Interests in Death-related Stipulations in South Tirol ca. 1350–1600', in Mia Korpiola and Anu Lahtinen (eds.), *Planning for Death: Wills, Inheritance and Property Strategies in Medieval and Reformation Europe* (Leiden, 2018), pp. 88–118.

Haldemann, Arno, 'Prekäre Eheschliessungen: Eigensinnige Heiratsbegehren und Bevölkerungspolitik in Bern, 1742–1848' (PhD diss., University of Bern, 2019).

Hanawalt, Barbara, 'Remarriage as an Option for Urban and Rural Widows in Late Medieval England', in Barbara Hanawalt, *Wife and Widow in Medieval England* (Michigan, 1993), pp. 141–164.

Hanawalt, Barbara, *'Of Good and Ill Repute': Gender and Social Control in Medieval England* (Oxford, 1998).

Hanawalt, Barbara, *The Wealth of Wives: Women, Law, and Economy in Late Medieval London* (Oxford, 2007).

Hand, Geoffrey, *English Law in Ireland, 1290–1324* (Cambridge, 1967).
Hanley, Sarah, 'Family and State in early modern France', in Marilyn J. Boxer and Jean H. Quataert (eds.), *Connecting Spheres: Women in the Western World, 1500-Present* (New York, 1987), pp. 53–63.
Hanley, Sarah, 'Engendering the State: Family Formation and State Building in Early Modern France', *French Historical Studies* 16 (1989), pp. 4–27.
Hanley, Sarah, 'Social Sites of Political Practice in France: Lawsuits, Civil Rights, and the Separation of Powers in Domestic and State Government, 1500–1800', *American Historical Review*, 102 (1997), pp. 293–313.
Hansen, Anna, *Ordnade hushåll: Genus och kontroll i Jämtland under 1600-talet* (Uppsala, 2006).
Hardwick, Julie, *Family Business: Litigation and the Political Economies of Daily Life in Early Modern France* (Oxford, 2009).
Hardwick, Julie, *The Practice of Patriarchy* (Philadelphia, 2010).
Hardwick, Julie, 'Policing Paternity: Historicizing Masculinity and Sexuality in Early Modern France', *European Review of History*, 22 (2015), pp. 643–657.
Hardwick, Julie, 'Women 'Working' the Law: Gender, Authority, and Legal Process in Early Modern France', *Journal of Women's History*, 9 (1997), pp. 28–49, reprinted in Merry Wiesner-Hanks (ed.) *Women and Gender in the Early Modern World* (Abingdon, 2015).
Hardwick, Julie, *Sex in an Old Regime City: Young Workers and Intimacy in France, 1660–1789* (New York, 2020).
Härter, Karl, 'Konfliktregulierung im Umfeld frühneuzeitlicher Strafgerichte: Das Konzept der Infrajustiz in der historischen Kriminalitätsforschung', *Kritische Vierteljahresschrift für Gesetzgebung und Rechtswissenschaft* 95:2 (2012), pp. 130–144.
Haskett, Timothy S., 'Country Lawyers?: The Composers of English Chancery Bills', in Peter Birks (ed.), *The Life of the Law: Proceedings of the Tenth British Legal History Conference, Oxford, 1991* (London, 1993), pp. 9–23.
Haskett, Timothy S., 'The Medieval English Court of Chancery', *Law and History Review*, 14 (1996), pp. 245–313.
Hawkes, Emma, '"[S]he Will... Protect and Defend Her Rights Boldly by Law and Reason..."': Women's Knowledge of Common Law and Equity Courts in Late-Medieval England', in Noël James Menuge (ed.), *Medieval Women and the Law* (Woodbridge, 2000), pp. 145–161.
Helmholz, Richard H., *Marriage Litigation in Medieval England* (Cambridge, 1974).
Helmholz, Richard H., 'Bankruptcy and Probate Jurisdiction before 1571', *Missouri Law Review*, 48 (1983), pp. 415–429.
Hicks, Michael, *Wars of the Roses* (Yale, 2010).
Hillman, Richard and Pauline Ruberry-Blanc, 'Introduction', in Richard Hillman and Pauline Ruberry-Blanc (eds.), *Female Transgression in Early Modern Britain: Literary and Historical Approaches* (Ashgate, Farnham, 2014), pp. 1–14.
Hledíková, Zdeňka, '*Zápisy manželských sporů – nepovšimnutý pramen 15. století*', in Zdeněk Beneš and Eduard Maur and Jaroslav Pánek (eds.), *Pocta Josefu Petráňovi* (Prague, 1991), pp. 79–93.
Hledíková, Zdeňka, 'Soudní akta generálních vikářů', *Sborník archivních prací*, 1/XVI (1996), pp. 157–171.
Hledíková, Zdeňka and Jan Janák, *Dějiny správy v českých zemích: Od počátků státu po současnost* (Prague, 2005), pp. 179–188.
Hockman, Tuula, *Kolmen polven perilliset. Ingeborg Aakentytär (Tott) ja hänen sukunsa (n. 1460–1507)* (Helsinki, 2006).
Hoffmann, František, *Středověké město v Čechách a na Moravě* (Prague, 2009).

Homza, Lu Ann, 'When Witches Litigate: New Sources from Early Modern Navarre', *Journal of Modern History*, 19 (2019), pp. 245–275.
Houstoun, R. A., 'Women in the Economy and Society of Scotland', in R. A. Houston and I. D. Whyte (eds.), *Scottish Society 1500–1800* (Cambridge, 1989), pp. 118–147.
Houstoun, R. A., *The Population History of Britain and Ireland, 1500–1750* (Cambridge, 1995).
Howell, Martha, 'The Problem of Women's Agency in Late Medieval and Early Modern Europe', in Sarah Joan Moran and Amanda Pipkin (eds.), *Women and Gender in the Early Modern Low Countries* (Leiden, 2019), pp. 21–31.
Howlin, Niamh and Kevin Costello (eds.), *Law and the Family in Ireland 1800–1950* (London, 2017).
Hubbard, Eleanor, *City Women: Money, Sex and the Social Order in Early Modern London* (Oxford, 2012).
Hutton, Shennan, '"On Herself and All Her Property": Women's Economic Activities in Late Medieval Ghent', *Continuity and Change*, 20 (2005), pp. 325–349.
Hutton, Shennan, *Women and Economic Activities in Late Medieval Ghent* (New York, 2011).
Ingendahl, Gesa, *Witwen in der frühen Neuzeit: Eine kulturhistorische Studie* (Frankfurt a. M., 2006).
Ingendahl, Gesa, 'Verträgliche Allianzen. Verwandtschaftsbeziehungen in Heiratsverträgen der Freien Reichsstadt Ravensburg', *Geschichte und Region / Storia e regione* 27:2 (2018), pp. 102–122.
Jacobsen, Grethe 'Women and Men in Legal Proceedings: A European Historical Perspective', *NAVEIÑ REET: Nordic Journal of Law and Social Research*, 3 (2012) (published 2015), pp. 97–111.
Jan, Libor (ed.), *Dějiny Brna 2. Středověké město* (Brno, 2013).
Janišová, Jana and Dalibor Janiš, 'Manželství v historických souvislostech', in Renáta Šínová and Ondřej Šmíd (eds.), *Manželství* (Praha, 2014), pp. 21–34.
Johnson, Tom, *Law in Common: Legal Cultures in Late-Medieval England* (Oxford, 2020).
Joye, S., *La femme ravie: le mariage par rapt dans les sociétés occidentales du Haut Moyen Âge* (Turnhout, 2012).
Jung, Irene, *'Ihrem Herzen Und Charakter Ehre Machen': Frauen wenden sich an das Reichskammergericht* (Wetzlar, 1998).
Jung, Irene, 'Wetzlarer Frauen vor dem Reichskammergericht', in Siegrid Westphal (ed.), *In eigener Sache: Frauen vor den höchsten Gerichten des Alten Reichs* (Cologne – Weimar – Vienna, 2005), pp. 21–28.
Kane, Bronach C., *Popular Memory and Gender in Medieval England: Men, Women and Testimony in the Church Courts, c.1200–1500* (Woodbridge, 2019).
Kane, Bronach C., and Fiona Williamson (eds.), *Women, Agency and the Law, 1300–1700* (London, 2013).
Karras, Ruth Mazo, *Unmarriages: Women, Men, and Sexual Unions in the Middle Ages* (Philadelphia, 2012).
Kaufmann, Miranda, *Black Tudors: The Untold Story* (London, 2017).
Kelleher, Marie, *The Measure of Women: Law and Female Identity in the Crown of Aragon* (Philadelphia, 2010).
Kenny, Gillian, *Anglo-Irish and Gaelic Women in Ireland, c.1170–1540* (Dublin, 2007).
Kermode, Jennifer (ed.), *Enterprise and Individuals in Fifteenth-Century England* (Stroud, 1991).
Killick, Helen, 'The Scribes of Petitions in Late Medieval England', in Helen Killick and Thomas W. Smith (eds.), *Petitions and Strategies of Persuasion in the Middle Ages: The English Crown and the Church, c.1200–c.1550* (Woodbridge, 2018), pp. 64–87.

Kittel, Ellen and Kurt Queller, 'Wives and Widows in Medieval Flanders', *Social History*, 41 (2016), pp. 436–454.
Klassen, John Martin, 'Marriage and Family in Medieval Bohemia', *East European Quarterly*, 19 (1985), pp. 257–274.
Klassen, John Martin, 'The Development of the Conjugal Bond in Late Medieval Bohemia', *Journal of Medieval History*, 13 (1987), pp. 161–178.
Klassen, John Martin, 'Household Composition in Medieval Bohemia', *Journal of Medieval History*, 16 (1990), pp. 55–75.
Klinck, Dennis R., *Conscience, Equity and the Court of Chancery in Early Modern England* (Farnham, 2010).
Kock, Ebbe, 'En svensk bokkatalog från 1500-talet', *Nordisk tidskrift för bok- och biblioteksväsen* 7 (1920), pp. 146–155.
Kopičková, Božena, 'Manželské spory žen pozdního středověku v protokolech ústředních církevních úřadů v Praze', *Documenta Pragensia*, 13 (1996), pp. 57–65.
Korpiola, Mia, '"The Fall and Restoration of Elin Tönnesdotter": Land, Noble Property Strategies and the Law in Early Seventeenth-Century Sweden', *COLLeGIUM*, 2 (2007): *The Trouble with Ribs: Women, Men and Gender in Early Modern Europe*, eds. Anu Korhonen and K. P. L. Lowe, pp. 153–179. Available at: https://helda.helsinki.fi/bitstream/handle/10138/25757/002_09_korpiola.pdf?sequence=1
Korpiola, Mia, *Between Betrothal and Bedding: Marriage Formation in Sweden, 1200–1600* (Leiden, 2009).
Korpiola, Mia (ed.), *Regional Variations in Matrimonial Law and Custom in Europe 1150–1600* (Leiden, 2011).
Korpiola, Mia, 'Spousal Disputes, The Marital Property System and the Law in Later Medieval Sweden', in Cordelia Beattie and Matthew Frank Stevens (eds.), *Married Women and the Law in Premodern Northwest Europe* (Woodbridge, 2013), pp. 31–51.
Korpiola, Mia, 'A Safe Haven in the Shadow of War? The Founding and the Raison d'être of the New Court, Based on Its Early Activity', in Mia Korpiola (ed.), *The Svea Court of Appeal in the Early Modern Period: Historical Reinterpretations and New Perspectives* (Stockholm, 2014), pp. 55–108.
Korpiola, Mia, 'The Svea Court of Appeal: A Basis of Good Governance and Justice in the Early Modern Swedish Realm, 1614–1800', in A. M. Godfrey and C. H. van Rhee (eds.), *Central Courts in Early Modern Europe and the Americas* (Berlin, 2020). pp. 305–350.
Korpiola, Mia, and Elsa Trolle Önnerfors, 'Options for Post-mortem Property Planning in Medieval Sweden', in Mia Korpiola and Anu Lahtinen (eds.), *Planning for Death: Wills and Death-Related Property Arrangements in Europe, 1200–1600* (Leiden, 2018), pp. 29–65.
Kowaleski, Maryanne, 'Town Courts in Medieval England: An Introduction', in Richard Goddard and Teresa Phipps (eds.), *Town Courts and Urban Society in Late Medieval England, 1250–1500* (Woodbridge, 2019), pp. 17–42.
Kuehn, Thomas, *Emancipation in Late Medieval Florence* (New Brunswick, 1982).
Kuehn, Thomas, *Law, Family, and Women: Towards a Legal Anthropology of Renaissance Italy* (Chicago, 1991).
Kuehn, Thomas, 'Person and Gender in the Laws', in Judith Brown and Robert C Davis (eds.) *Gender and Society in Renaissance Italy*, (New York, 1998), pp. 87–106.
Kuehn, Thomas, *Heirs, Kin, and Creditors in Renaissance Florence* (Cambridge, 2008).
Lahtinen, Anu, 'Gender and Continuity: Women, Men and Landed Property in Medieval Finland', in Anu Lahtinen and Kirsi Vainio-Korhonen (eds.), *History and Change* (Helsinki, 2004), pp. 32–45.

Lahtinen, Anu, *Anpassning, förhandling, motstånd: Kvinnliga aktörer i släkten Fleming 1470–1620*, trans. Camilla Frostell (Helsinki and Stockholm, 2009), pp. 63–64.

Lamberg, Marko, 'The Tale of Two Courts in One Town: The Relationship between the Stockholm Town Court and the Svea Court of Appeal 1614–1624', in Mia Korpiola (ed.), *The Svea Court of Appeal in the Early Modern Period: Historical Reinterpretations and New Perspectives* (Stockholm, 2014), pp. 109–130.

Lanza, Janine M., *From Wives to Widows in Early Modern Paris* (Aldershot, 2007).

Lanzinger, Margareth, *Das gesicherte Erbe. Heirat in lokalen und familialen Kontexten, Innichen 1700–1900* (Vienna/Cologne/Weimar, 2003).

Lanzinger, Margareth, 'Aushandeln von Ehe – Heiratsverträge in europäischen Rechtsräumen. Einleitung', in Margareth Lanzinger, Gunda Barth-Scalmani, Ellinor Forster, and Gertrude Langer-Ostrawsky (eds.), *Aushandeln von Ehe: Heiratsverträge der Neuzeit im europäischen Vergleich* (Cologne/Weimar/Vienna, 2015, 2nd edn), pp. 11–25.

Lanzinger, Margaret, 'Von der Macht der Linie zur Gegenseitigkeit. Heiratskontrakte in den Südtiroler Gerichten Welsberg und Innichen 1750–1850', in Margareth Lanzinger, Gunda Barth-Scalmani, Ellinor Forster, and Gertrude Langer-Ostrawsky (eds.), *Aushandeln von Ehe: Heiratsverträge der Neuzeit im europäischen Vergleich* (Cologne/Weimar/Vienna, 2015, 2nd edn), pp. 205–367.

Lanzinger, Margareth, 'Emotional Bonds and the Everyday Logic of Living Arrangements: Stepfamilies in Dispensation Records of Late Eighteenth-Century Austria', in Lyndan Warner (ed.), *Stepfamilies in Europe, 1400–1800* (Abingdon/New York, 2018), pp. 168–186.

Lanzinger, Margareth, Ellinor Forster, Janine Maegraith, Siglinde Clementi, and Christian Hagen, 'Konfliktpotenzial und Streitgegenstände im Kontext ehelicher Vermögensregime', *Frühneuzeit-Info*, 26 (2015), pp. 104–115.

Lanzinger, Margareth and Janine Maegraith, 'Konkurrenz um Vermögen im südlichen Tirol des 16. Jahrhunderts', *L 'Homme. Z.F.G.*, 27.1 (2016), pp. 15–31.

Lanzinger, Margareth and Janine Maegraith, 'Houses and the Range of Wealth in Early Modern Gender- and Intergenerational Relationships', *Jahrbuch für Europäische Geschichte / European History Yearbook*, 18 (2017), pp. 14–34, pp. 17–18 (open access https://doi.org/10.1515/9783110532241-002)

Lanzinger, Margareth, Janine Maegraith, Siglinde Clementi, Ellinor Forster, and Christian Hagen (eds.), *Negotiations of Gender and Property through Legal Regimes (14th–19th century). Stipulating, Litigating, Mediating* (Leiden, 2021).

Larson, Peter L., *Conflict & Compromise in the Late Medieval Countryside: Lords and Peasants in Durham, 1349–1400* (New York, 2006), p. 187.

Larson, Peter L., 'Widow-Right in Durham, England (1349–1660)', *Continuity and Change*, 33 (2017), pp. 173–201.

Laumonier, Lucie, 'Meanings of Fatherhood in late Medieval Montpellier: Love, Care, and the Exercise of *Patria potestas*', in Raffaella Sarti (ed.), Men at Home, *Gender & History*, 27 (2015), pp. 651–668.

Le Ridant, Pierre, *Code matrimonial, ou Recueil complet de toutes les loix canoniques et civiles de France... sur les questions de mariage. Tome 2 /... Nouvelle édition par M***, avocat au Parlement, 1770* (Paris, 1770).

Leneman, Leah, *Alienated Affections: The Scottish Experience of Divorce and Separation 1684–1830* (Edinburgh, 1998).

Leneman, Leah, *Promises, Promises: Marriage Litigation in Scotland 1698–1830* (Edinburgh, 2003).

Levack, Brian P. 'Law, Sovereignty and the Union', in Roger A. Mason (ed.) *Scots and Britons: Scottish Political Thought and the Union of 1603* (Cambridge, 1994), pp. 213–237.

Lidman, Tomas, 'Meurer, Ignatius', *Svenskt biografiskt lexikon,* 25 (Stockholm, 1985–1987), pp. 439–434.

Lightfoot, Dana Wessell, *Women, Dowries and Agency: Marriage in Fifteenth-Century Valencia* (Manchester, 2016).

Loengard, Janet Senderowitz, 'Legal History and the Medieval Englishwoman: A Fragmented View', *Law and History* Review, 4 (1986), pp. 161–178.

Lowe, Kate, 'Visible Lives: Black Gondoliers and Other Black Africans in Renaissance Venice', *Renaissance Quarterly,* 66 (2013), pp. 412–452.

Luddy, Maria and Mary O'Dowd, *Marriage in Ireland, 1660–1925* (Cambridge, 2020).

Lydon, James, 'The Middle Nation', in James Lydon (ed.), *The English in Medieval Ireland* (Dublin, 1984), pp. 1–26.

Lyons, Mary Ann, 'The Kildare Ascendancy', in Patrick Cosgrove et al. (eds.), *Aspects of Irish Aristocratic Life: Essays on the Fitzgeralds and Carton House* (Dublin, 2014), pp. 47–59.

Maegraith, Janine, 'Gender Imbalance in the Use, Ownership, and Transmission of Property in Early Modern Southern Tyrolean Urban and Rural Contexts', in Margareth Lanzinger, Janine Maegraith, Siglinde Clementi, Ellinor Forster, and Christian Hagen (eds.), *Negotiations of Gender and Property through Legal Regimes (14th–19th century). Stipulating, Litigating, Mediating* (Leiden, 2021), pp. 193–222.

Maegraith, Janine, 'Selling, Buying and Exchanging Peasant Land in Early Modern Southern Tyrol', in Thomas Ertl, Thomas Frank, and Samuel Nussbaum (eds.), *Busy Tenants. Peasant Land Markets in Central Europe (15th to 16th centuries)* (Stuttgart, 2021), 193–229.

Mahmood, Saba, *Politics of Piety: the Islamic Revival and the Feminist Subject* (Princeton, rev. edn 2012).

Makowski, Elizabeth, '"*Deus est procurator fatuorum*": Cloistered Nuns and Equitable Decision-Making in the Court of Chancery', in Kenneth Pennington and Melodie Harris Eichbauer (eds.), *Law as Profession and Practice in Medieval Europe: Essays in Honor of James A. Brundage* (London, 2011), pp. 205–217.

Martin, F.X., 'The Crowning of a King at Dublin, 24 May 1487', *Hermanthena,* 144 (1988), pp. 7–34.

Mason, Rebecca, 'Women, Marital Status and Law: The Marital Spectrum in Seventeenth-Century Glasgow', *Journal of British Studies,* 58 (2019), pp. 787–804.

Matthew, Elizabeth, 'James Butler the 4th Earl of Ormond', *Oxford Dictionary of National Biography* (online edition, www.oxforddnb.com, Oxford, 2008).

McCavitt, John, '"Good Planets in Their Several Spheares": The Establishment of the Assize Circuits in Early Seventeenth Century Ireland', *Irish Jurist,* new series, 24 (Winter, 1989), pp. 248–278.

McDonough, Susan, *Witnesses, Neighbors, and Community in Late Medieval Marseille* (New York, 2013).

McDougall, Sara, *Bigamy and Christian Identity in Late Medieval Champagne* (Philadelphia, 2012).

McDougall, Sara, 'Women and Gender in Canon Law', in Judith M. Bennett and Ruth Mazo Karras (eds.), *Women and Gender in Medieval Europe* (Oxford, 2013), pp. 163–178.

McIntosh, Marjorie Keniston, *Controlling Misbehavior in England, 1370–1600* (Cambridge, 1998).

McKee, Sally, 'Domestic Slavery in Renaissance Italy', *Slavery & Abolition,* 29 (2008), pp. 305–326.

McKinley, Michelle, *Fractional Freedoms, Slavery, Intimacy and Legal Mobilization in Colonial Lima* (Cambridge, 2016).

McNabb, Jennifer, '"She Is But a Girl": Perceptions of Young Women as Daughters, Wives, and Mothers in the English Courts, 1550–1650', in Elizabeth S. Cohen and Margaret Reeves (eds.), *The Youth of Early Modern Women* (Amsterdam, 2018), pp. 77–96.

McSheffrey, Shannon, *Gender and Heresy: Women and Men in Lollard Communities, 1420–1530* (Philadelphia, 1995).

McSheffrey, Shannon, 'Sanctuary and the Legal Topography of Pre-Reformation London', *Law and History Review*, 27 (2009), pp. 483–513.

McSheffrey, Shannon, 'A Remarrying Widow: Law and Legal Records in Late Medieval London', in Kim Kipeen and Lori Woods (eds.), *Worth and Repute: Valuing Gender in Late Medieval and Early Modern Europe: Essays in Honour of Barbara Todd* (Toronto, 2011), pp. 231–252.

McSheffrey, Shannon and Julia Pope, 'Ravishment, Legal Narratives, and Chivalric Culture in Fifteenth-Century England', *The Journal of British Studies*, 48 (2009), pp. 818–836.

Menuge, Noel, 'Female Wards and Marriage in Romance and Law: A Question of Consent', in Katherine J. Lewis, Noël James Menuge, and Kim M. Phillips (eds.), *Young Medieval Women* (Sutton, 1999), pp. 152–171.

Mercer, Malcolm, 'Select Document: Exchequer Malpractice in Late Medieval Ireland: A Petition from Christopher Fleming, Lord Slane, 1438', *Irish Historical Studies*, 36 (2009), pp. 407–417.

Michaud, Francine. *Un signe des temps: Accroissements des cries familiales autor du patrimoine à Marseille à la fin du XIIIe siècle* (Toronto: Pontifical Institute of Mediaeval Studies, 1994).

Mielke, Christopher and Andrea-Bianka Znorovsky (eds.), *Same Bodies, Different Women: 'Other' Women in the Middle Ages and the Early Modern Period* (Budapest, 2019).

Milsom, S.F.C., *Historical Foundations of the Common Law* (London, 1981).

Möhle, Sylvia, *Ehekonflikte und sozialer Wandel. Göttingen 1740–1840* (Frankfurt a. M./New York, 1997), pp. 189–191.

Montenach, Anne and Deborah Simonton, 'Introduction: Gender, Agency and Economy: Shaping the Eighteenth-Century European Town', in Deborah Simonton and Anne Montenach (eds.), *Female Agency in the Urban Economy: Gender in European Towns, 1640–1830* (New York, 2013), pp. 1–14.

Moore, Lindsay R., *Women before the Court: Law and Patriarchy in the Anglo-American World, 1600–1800* (Manchester, 2019).

Muldrew, Craig, *The Economy of Obligation: the Culture of Credit and Social Relations in Early Modern England* (Basingstoke, 1998).

Müller, Miriam, 'Peasant Women, Agency and Status in Mid-Thirteenth to Late Fourteenth-Century England: Some Reconsiderations', in Cordelia Beattie and Matthew Frank Stevens (eds.), *Married Women and the Law in Premodern Northwest Europe* (Woodbridge, 2013), pp. 91–113.

Musson, Anthony, *Medieval Law in Context: The Growth of Legal Consciousness from Magna Carta to the Peasants' Revolt* (Manchester, 2001).

Musson, Anthony (ed.), *Boundaries of the Law: Geography, Gender and Jurisdiction in Medieval and Early Modern Europe* (Aldershot, 2005).

Neville, Cynthia J., 'The Law of Treason in the English Border Counties in the Middles Ages', *Law and History Review*, 9 (1991), pp. 1–30.

Neville, Cynthia J., 'Common Knowledge of the Common Law in Later Medieval England', *Canadian Journal of History/Annales Canadiennes d'Histoire*, 29 (1994), pp. 461–478.

Nodl, Martin, 'Pronikání kanonického práva do českého prostředí, jeho recepce nařízeními církve a rezistence laického prostředí vůči kanonickým předpisům',

in Pavel Krafl (ed.), *Sacri canones servandi sunt. Ius canonicum et status ecclesiae saeculis XIII-XV* (Prague, 2008), pp. 650–658.
Nodl, Martin, 'In facie ecclesiae', in Martin Nodl and Paweł Kras (eds.), *Manželství v pozdním středověku: rituály a obyčeje* (Prague, 2014), pp. 53–61.
Nolan, Frances, '"Jacobite" Women and the Williamite Confiscation: The Role of Women and Female Minors in Reclaiming Compromised or Forfeited Property in Ireland, 1690–1703' (unpublished PhD Thesis, University College, Dublin, 2016).
Nolan, Frances, '"The Cat's Paw": Helen Arthur, the Act of Resumption and The Popish Pretenders to the Forfeited Estates in Ireland', *Irish Historical Studies*, 42 (2018), pp. 225–243.
Nubia, Onyeka, *Blackamoores: Africans in Tudor England, Their Presence, Status and Origins* (London, 2013).
Nugent, Janay, 'Reformed Masculinity: Ministers, Fathers and Male Heads of Households, 1560–1660', in Lynn Abrams and Elizabeth Ewan (eds.), *Nine Centuries of Man: Manhood and Masculinities in Scottish History* (Edinburgh, 2017), pp. 39–57.
Ó Cléirigh, Cormac 'The O'Connor Faly Lordship of Offaly, 1395–1513', *Proceedings of the Royal Irish Academy*, 96c (1996), pp. 87–102.
O'Dowd, Mary, 'Women and the Irish Chancery Court in the Late Sixteenth and Early Seventeenth Centuries', *Irish Historical Studies*, 31 (1999), pp. 470–487.
O'Dowd, Mary, 'Women and the Law in Early Modern Ireland', in Christine Meek (ed.) *Women in Renaissance and Early Modern Europe* (Dublin, 2000), pp. 95–108.
O'Dowd, Mary, *A History of Women in Ireland, 1500–1800* (Harlow, 2005).
O'Dowd, Mary, 'Marriage Breakdown in Ireland, c. 1660–1857', in Kevin Costello and Niamh Howlin (eds.), *Law and the Family in Ireland 1800–1950* (London, 2015), pp. 14–20.
O'Hara, Diana, *Courtship and Constraint: Rethinking the Making of Marriage in Tudor England* (Manchester, 2000).
O'Malley, John W., *Trent: What Happened at the Council* (Cambridge, MA, 2013).
Ogilvie, Sheilagh, *A Bitter Living: Women, Markets, and Social Capital in Early Modern Germany* (Oxford, 2003).
Ormrod, W. Mark, *Women and Parliament in Later Medieval England* (Cham, 2020).
Ormrod, W. Mark, Bart Lambert and Jonathan Mackman, *Immigrant England, 1300–1550* (Manchester, 2019).
Ozment, Steven, *The Bürgermeister's Daughter: Scandal in a Sixteenth-Century German Town* (New York, 1998).
Pedersen, Frederik, 'Did the Medieval Laity Know the Canon Law Rules on Marriage? Some Evidence from Fourteenth-Century York Cause Papers', *Mediaeval Studies*, 56 (1994), pp. 111–152.
Perrier, Sylvie, 'La grossesse entre intimité et publicité dans les archives judiciaries de la France d 'Ancien Régime', Unpublished paper, Family and Justice in the Archives: Histories of Intimacy in Transnational Perspective, Concordia University, May 2019.
Peters, Kate, Alexandra Walsham and Lisebeth Corens (eds.), *Archives and Information in the Early Modern World* (New York, 2018).
Petersson, Hans, *Morgongåvoinstitutet i Sverige under tiden fram till omkring 1734 års lag* (Lund, 1973).
Petrén, Sture, 'Våra första advokater', *Svensk Juristtidning*, 32 (1947), pp. 1–25.
Phan, Marie-Claude, 'Les déclarations de grossesse en France (XVIe-XVIIIe siècles): essai institutionnel', *Revue d'histoire moderne et contemporaine* 22:1 (January-March 1975), pp. 61–88.

Phan, Marie-Claude, *Les Amours Illégitimes: histoires de séduction en Languedoc (1676–1786)* (Paris, 1986).
Phillips Jr., William D., *Slavery from Roman Times to the Early Transatlantic Trade* (Manchester, 1985).
Phipps, Teresa, 'Misbehaving Women: Trespass and Honor in Late Medieval English Towns', *Historical Reflections/Reflexions Historiques*, 43 (2017), pp. 62–76.
Phipps, Teresa, 'Female Litigants and the Borough Court: Status and Strategy in the Case of Agnes Halum of Nottingham', in Richard Goddard and Teresa Phipps (eds.), *Town Courts and Urban Society in Late Medieval England, 1250–1500* (Woodbridge, 2019), pp. 77–92.
Phipps, Teresa, *Medieval Women and Urban Justice: Commerce, Crime and Community in England, 1300–1500* (Manchester, 2020).
Phythian-Adams, Charles, *Desolation of a City: Coventry and the Urban Crisis of the Late Middle Ages* (Cambridge, 1979).
Pommeray, Léon, *L'Officialité Archidiaconale de Paris Aux XVe-XVIe Siècle: Sa Composition Et Sa Compétence Criminelle* (Paris, 1933).
Pope, J., 'Abduction: An Alternative Form of Courtship?', Paper presented at IMC Kalamazoo (Kalamazoo, 2003).
Poska, Allyson. 'The Case for Agentic Gender Norms for Women in Early Modern Europe', *Gender and History*, 30 (2018), pp. 354–365.
Power, Eileen, *Medieval Women*, ed. Michael M. Postan (Cambridge: Cambridge University Press, 1975).
Premo, Bianca, *Children of the Father King: Youth, Authority and Legal Minority in Colonial Lima* (Chapel Hill, 2005).
Prior, Mary (ed.), *Women in English Society 1500–1800* (Methuen, 1985).
Pronay, Nicholas, 'The Chancellor, the Chancery, and the Council at the End of the Fifteenth Century', in H. Hearder and H. R. Loyn (eds.), *British Government and Administration: Studies Presented to S. B. Chrimes* (Cardiff, 1974), pp. 87–103.
Pryde, George Smith, 'Burgh Courts and Allied Jurisdictions', in *Introduction to Scottish Legal History* (Edinburgh: The Stair Society, 1958), pp. 384–395.
Pylkkänen, Anu, *Puoli vuodetta, lukot ja avaimet. Nainen ja maatalous oikeuskäytännön valossa 1660–1710* (Helsinki, 1990).
Rantala, Tuula, 'Monastic Donations by Widows: Morning Gifts as Assets in Planning for Old Age and Death in Fifteenth-Century Sweden', in Mia Korpiola and Anu Lahtinen (eds.), *Planning for Death: Wills and Death-Related Property Arrangements in Europe, 1200–1600* (Leiden, 2018), pp. 66–87.
Reyerson, Kathryn, *Mothers and Sons, Inc. Martha de Cabanis in Medieval Marseille* (Philadelphia, 2018).
Reynolds, P., *How Marriage Became one of the Sacraments: The Sacramental Theology of Marriage from Its Medieval Origins to the Council of Trent* (Cambridge, 2016).
Rich Abad, Anna, 'Able and Available: Jewish Women in Medieval Barcelona and their Economic Activities', *Journal of Medieval Iberian Studies*, 6 (2014), pp. 71–86.
Richardson, H.G. and G.O. Sayles, *The Irish Parliament in the Middle Ages* (Philadelphia, 1952).
Rigby, Steven, *English Society in the Later Middle Ages* (New York, 1995).
Rigby, Steven, 'Gendering the Black Death: Women in Later Medieval England', *Gender and History*, 12 (2000), pp. 745–754.
Romney, Susanah Shaw, '"With & Alongside His Housewife": Claiming Ground in New Netherland and the Early Modern Dutch Empire', *The William and Mary Quarterly*, 73 (2016), pp. 187–224.

Rose, Jonathan, 'Medieval Attitudes toward the Legal Profession: The Past as Prologue', *Stetson Law Review*, 28 (1999), pp. 345–368.
Rosenthal, Joel, 'Other Victims: Peeresses as War Widows, 1450–1500', *History*, 72 (1987), pp. 213–230.
Ruddock, Alwyn A., 'Alien Merchants in Southampton in the Later Middle Ages', *English Historical Review*, 61 (1946), pp. 1–17.
Salonen, Kirsi, Marriage Disputes in the Consistorial Court of Freising in the Late Middle Ages', in Mia Korpiola (ed.), *Regional Variations in Matrimonial Law and Custom in Europe, 1150–1600* (Leiden, 2011), pp. 189–209.
Sanderson, Margaret, *A Kindly Place? Living in Sixteenth-Century Scotland* (East Linton, 2002).
Schäfer, Regina, 'Inheritance Disputes from Ingelheim Court Records on the Threshold of the Early Modern Period (Fourteenth to Fifteenth Centuries)', in Margareth Lanzinger, Janine Maegraith, Siglinde Clementi, Ellinor Forster, and Christian Hagen (eds.), *Negotiations of Gender and Property through Legal Regimes (14th–19th century). Stipulating, Litigating, Mediating* (Leiden, 2021), pp. 52–83.
Schmidt, Heinrich Richard, 'Hausväter vor Gericht. Der Patriarchalismus als zweischneidiges Schwert', in Martin Dinges (ed.), *Hausväter, Priester, Kastraten. Zur Konstruktion von Männlichkeit im Spätmittelalter und Früher Neuzeit* (Göttingen, 1998), pp. 214–236.
Schmidt-Voges, Inken, *Mikropolitiken des Friedens. Semantiken und Praktiken des Hausfriedens im 18. Jahrhundert* (Berlin, 2015).
Schmidt-Voges, Inken, 'Instrumente und Strategien zur Regulierung familialer Konflikte in der Frühen Neuzeit', in Wim Decock (ed.), *Konfliktlösung in der Frühen Neuzeit* (Berlin/Heidelberg, 2021), ch. 30 [forthcoming].
Schmidt-Voges, Inken and Katharina Simon, 'Managing Conflict and Making Peace', in Joachim Eibach and Margareth Lanzinger (eds.), *The Routledge History of the Domestic Sphere in Europe, 16th to 19th Century* (London, 2020), pp. 254–268.
Schneider, Zoe, *The King's Bench: Bailliwick Magistrates and Local Governance in Normandy, 1670–1740* (Rochester, 2008).
Schubart-Fikentscher, Gertrud, *Das Eherecht in Brünner Schöffenbuch* (Stuttgart, 1935).
Seabourne, Gwen, *Imprisoning Medieval Women: The Non-Judicial Confinement and Abduction of Women in England, ca. 1170–1509* (Farnham, 2011).
Seabourne, Gwen, 'Coke, the Statute, Wives and Lovers: Routes to a Harsher Interpretation of the Statute of Westminster II c.34 on Dower and Adultery', *Legal Studies*, 34 (2014), pp. 123–142.
Seabourne, Gwen, 'It Is Necessary That the Issue Be Heard to Cry or Squall within the Four [Walls]': Qualifying for Tenancy by the Curtesy of England in the Reign of Edward I', *The Journal of Legal History*, 40 (2019), pp. 44–68.
Seabourne, Gwen, *Women in the Medieval Common Law* (Abingdon, 2021).
Shahar, Shulamith, *The Fourth Estate: A History of Women in the Middle Ages*, second edn, trans. Chaya Galai (London, 2003).
Shaw, William Arthur, *The Knights of England: A Complete Record from the Earliest Time*, vol. 1 (London, 1906).
Sheehan, Michael M., 'The Formation and Stability of Marriage in Fourteen-Century England: Evidence of an Ely Register', *Medieval Studies*, 33 (1971), pp. 228–263.
Shepard, Alexandra, 'Manhood, Credit and Patriarchy in Early Modern England c. 1580–1640', *Past & Present*, 167 (2000), pp. 75–106.
Shepard, Alexandra, 'From Anxious Patriarchs to Refined Gentlemen? Manhood in Britain, circa 1500–1700', *Journal of British Studies*, 44 (2005), pp. 281–295.

Shepard, Alexandra, *Accounting for Oneself: Worth, Status and the Social Order in Early Modern England* (Oxford, 2015).
Shepard, Alexandra, 'Worthless Witnesses? Marginal Voices and Women's Legal Agency in Early Modern England', *Journal of British Studies*, 58 (2019), pp. 717–734.
Shepard, Alexandra and Tim Stretton, 'Women Negotiating the Boundaries of Justice, 1300–1700: An Introduction', *Journal of British Studies*, 58 (2019), pp. 677–683.
Signori, Gabriela, *Von der Paradiesehe zur Gütergemeinschaft. Ehe in der mittelalterlichen Lebens- und Vorstellungswelt* (Frankfurt a. M./New York, 2011).
Simon-Muscheid, Katharina, 'Frauen vor Gericht. Erfahrungen, Strategien und Wissen', *Historische Zeitschrift*, Beihefte 31 (2001): pp. 389–399.
Sjöberg, Maria, *Kvinnors jord, manlig rätt: Äktenskap, egendom och makt i äldre tid* (Hedemora, 2001).
Smail, Daniel Lord, 'Démanteler le patrimoine: les femmes et les biens dans la Marseille mediévale', *Annales. Histoire, Sciences Sociales*, 52:2 (1997), pp. 343–368.
Smail, Daniel Lord, *The Consumption of Justice: Emotions, Publicity and Legal Culture in Marseille, 1264–1423* (Ithaca, 2003).
Smail, Daniel Lord, 'Witness Programs in Medieval Marseille', in Michael Goodich (ed.), *Voices from the Bench: The Narratives of Lesser Folk in Medieval Trials* (New York, 2006), pp. 227–250.
Smail, Daniel Lord, *Legal Plunder: Household and Debt Collection in Late Medieval Europe* (Cambridge, 2016).
Smith, Erin McGibbon, 'The Participation of Women in the Fourteenth-Century Manor Court of Sutton-in-the-Isle', *Marginalia* 1 (2005), II, http://merg.soc.srcf.net/journal/05margins/smith.php.
Smith, Jamie, 'Women as Legal Agents in Late Medieval Genoa', in Charlotte Newman Goldy and Amy Livingstone (eds.), *Writing Medieval Women's Lives* (Basingstoke, 2012), pp. 113–129.
Smith, R.M. 'Women's Property Rights under Customary Law: Some Developments in the Thirteenth and Fourteenth Centuries', *Transactions of the Royal Historical Society*, 36 (1986), pp. 165–194.
Smith, R.M. 'Coping with Uncertainty: Women's Tenure of Customary Land in England c. 1370–1430', in Jennifer Kermode (ed.), *Enterprise and Individuals in Fifteenth-Century England* (Stroud, 1991), pp. 43–67.
Spence, Cathryn, '"For His Interest?" Women, Debt and Coverture in Early Modern Scotland', in Cordelia Beattie and Matthew Frank Stevens (eds.), *Married Women and the Law in Premodern Northwest Europe* (Woodbridge, 2013), pp. 173–190.
Spence, Cathryn, *Women, Credit and Debt in Early Modern Scotland* (Manchester, 2016).
Sperling, Jutta Gisela and Shona Kelly Wray (eds.), *Across the Religious Divide: Women Property and Law in the Wider Mediterranean (ca. 1300–1800)* (London, 2010).
Sprague, William C., *Blackstone's Commentaries, Abridged* (Chicago, 9th edn, 1915).
Spring, Eileen, *Law, Land, & Family: Aristocratic Inheritance in England, 1300 to 1800* (Chapel Hill, 1993).
Stevens, Matthew Frank, 'London Women, the Courts and the "Golden Age": A Quantitative Analysis of Female Litigants in the Fourteenth and Fifteenth Centuries', *The London Journal*, 37 (2012), pp. 67–88.
Stevens, Matthew Frank, 'London's Married Women, Debt Litigation and Coverture in the Court of Common Pleas', in Cordelia Beattie and Matthew Frank Stevens (eds.), *Married Women and the Law in Premodern Northwest Europe* (Woodbridge, 2013), pp. 115–131.

Stone, R., 'The Invention of a Theology of Abduction: Hincmar of Rheims on Raptus', *The Journal of Ecclesiastical History*, 60 (2009), pp. 433–448.

Stretton, Tim, *Women Waging Law in Elizabethan England* (Cambridge, 1998).

Stretton, Tim, 'Coverture and Unity of Person in Blackstone's *Commentaries*', in Wilfrid Prest (ed.), *Blackstone and his Commentaries: Biography, Law, History* (Oxford, 2009), pp. 111–128.

Stretton, Tim, 'Stepmothers at Law in Early Modern England', in Lyndan Warner (ed.), *Stepfamilies in Europe, 1400–1800* (Abington, 2018), pp. 91–107.

Stretton, Tim, 'Women, Legal Records, and the Problem of the Lawyer's Hand', *Journal of British Studies*, 58 (2019), pp. 684–700.

Stretton, Tim, and Krista J. Kesselring, 'Introduction: Coverture and Continuity', in Tim Stretton and Krista J. Kesselring (eds.), *Married Women and the Law: Coverture in England and the Common Law World* (Montreal, 2013), pp. 3–23.

Sundin, Jan, *För Gud, Staten och Folket: Brott och rättskipning i Sverige 1600–1840* (Lund, 1992).

Tallon, Geraldine (ed.), *Court of Claims, Submissions and Evidence, 1663* (Dublin, 2006).

Tanner, Norman P. (ed.), "Trent: 1545–1563," in *Decrees of the Ecumenical Councils, Volume II (Trent – Vatican II)* (Washington, DC, 1990), pp. 657–799.

Taussi Sjöberg, Maria, *Rätten och kvinnorna: Från släktmakt till statsmakt i Sverige på 1500- och 1600-talet* (Stockholm, 1996).

Taylor, Scott, 'Credit, Debt and Honor in Castile, 1600–1650', *Journal of Early Modern History*, 7 (2003), pp. 8–27.

Teich, Mikuláš (ed.), *Bohemia in History* (Cambridge, 1998).

Titone, Fabrizio, 'The Right to Consent and Disciplined Dissent: Betrothals and Marriages in the Diocese of Catania in the Later Medieval Period', in Fabrizio Titone (ed.), *Disciplined Dissent. Strategies of Non-Confrontational Protest in Europe from the Twelfth to the Early Sixteenth Century* (Rome, 2016), 139–168.

Todd, Barbara J., 'The Remarrying Widow: A Stereotype Reconsidered', in Mary Prior (ed.) *Women in English Society 1500–1800* (London, 1985), pp. 54–92.

Todd, Barbara J., 'Demographic Determinism and Female Agency: The Remarrying Widow Reconsidered…Again', *Continuity and Change*, 9 (1994), pp. 421–450.

Tolloi, Philipp, *Das Bürger- und Inwohnerbuch der Stadt Brixen von 1500–1593. Edition und Kommentar* (Magisterarbeit, Wien, 2012).

Toropainen, Veli Pekka, *Päättäväiset porvarskat: Turun johtavan porvariston naisten toimijuus vuosina 1623–1670* (Turku, 2016).

Trolle Önnerfors, Elsa, 'Suum Cuique Tribuere – Give to Each His Own: Court Cases Involving Swedish Nobility in the Court of Appeal 1650–1690', in Mia Korpiola (ed.), *The Svea Court of Appeal in the Early Modern Period: Historical Reinterpretations and New Perspectives* (Stockholm, 2014), pp. 163–200.

Tucker, Penny, 'The Early History of the Court of Chancery: A Comparative Study', *English Historical Review*, 115 (2000), pp. 791–811.

Tucker, Penny, *Law Courts and Lawyers in the City of London, 1300–1550* (Cambridge, 2007).

van Caenegem, Raoul Charles, *Geschiedenis van het strafrecht in Vlaanderen van de XIe tot de XIVe eeuw* (Brussels, 1954).

Van Dussen, Michael and Pavel Soukup (eds.), *A Companion to the Hussites* (Leiden–Boston, 2020).

van Houts, Elisabeth, *Medieval Memories: Men, Women, and the Past, 700–1300* (New York, 2001).

Vann Sprecher, Tiffany, 'Power in the Parish: Community Regulation of Priests in the Late Medieval Archdeaconry of Paris, 1483–1505' (unpublished doctoral thesis, The University of Minnesota, 2013).
Verini, Alexandra, 'Medieval Models of Female Friendship in Christine de Pizan's *The Book of the City of Ladies* and Margery Kempe's *The Book of Margery Kempe*', *Feminist Studies* 42 (2016), pp. 365–391.
Vleeschouwers-van Melkebeek, Monique, 'Aspects du lien matrimonial dans le Liber Sentenciarum de Bruxelles (1448–1459)', *The Legal History Review*, 53 (1985), pp. 43–97.
Vleeschouwers-Van Melkebeek, Monique, 'Mortificata est: het onterven of doodmaken van het geschaakte meisje in het laatmiddeleeuws Gent', *Handelingen: Koninklijke Commissie Voor de Uitgave Der Oude Wetten En Verordeningen van België*, 51–52 (2011), pp. 357–435.
Walker, Garthine, '"Strange Kind of Stealing": Abduction in Early Modern Wales', in Michael Roberts and Simone Clarke (eds.), *Women and Gender in Early Modern Wales* (Cardiff, 2000), pp. 50–74.
Walker, Garthine, *Crime, Gender, and Social Order in Early Modern England* (Cambridge, 2003).
Walker, Garthine, 'Just Stories: Telling Tales of Infant Death in Early Modern England', in Margaret Mikesell and Adele Seeff (eds.), *Culture and Change: Attending to Early Modern Women* (London, 2003), pp. 98–115.
Walker, Sue Sheridan, 'Litigation as Personal Quest: Suing for Dower in the Royal Courts, circa 1271–1350', in Sheridan Walker (ed.), *Wife and Widow in Medieval England* (Ann Arbor, 1993), pp. 81–108.
Walker, Sue Sheridan (ed.), *Wife and Widow in Medieval England* (Ann Arbor, 1993).
Walsham, Alexandra, 'The Social History of the Archive: Record Keeping in Early Modern Europe', *Past & Present*, 230 (November 2016), pp. 9–48.
Warner, Lyndan. 'Before the Law', in Jane Couchman, Allyson M. Poska, and Katherine A. McIver (eds.), *The Ashgate Research Companion to Women and Gender in Early Modern Europe* (Farnham, 2013), pp. 234–254.
Watts, John, 'Richard of York, Third Duke of York', *Oxford Dictionary of National Biography* (online edition, www.oxforddnb.com, Oxford, 2011).
Wernstedt, Folke, *Ståthållaren Christoffer Wernstedt 1542–1627: Anteckningar om Släkten Wernstedt 1* (Stockholm, 1929).
Wernstedt, Folke, 'Adliga ätten "Bärfelts" nr 196 tidigare led: Ett bidrag till riddarhusstamtavlornas historia', *Personhistorisk Tidskrift*, 43 (1944–1945), pp. 62–72.
Westphal, Siegrid, 'Die Inanspruchnahme des Reichhofrats durch Frauen – quantitative Aspekte', in Siegrid Westphal (ed.), *In eigener Sache: Frauen vor den höchsten Gerichten des Alten Reichs* (Cologne/Weimar/Vienna, 2005), pp. 29–39.
Westphal, Siegrid, 'Frauen in den höchsten Gerichten des Alten Reiches: Eine Einführung', in Siegrid Westphal (ed.), *In Eigener Sache: Frauen vor den Höchsten Gerichten des Alten Reiches* (Cologne/Weimar/Vienna, 2005), pp. 1–17.
Whittle, Jane, 'Inheritance, Marriage, Widowhood, and Remarriage: A Comparative Perspective on Women and Landholding in North-East Norfolk, 1440–1580', *Continuity and Change*, 13 (1998), pp. 33–72.
Wieben, Corinne, 'Unwilling Grooms in Fourteenth-Century Lucca', *Journal of Family History*, 40 (2015), pp. 263–76.
Wiesner-Hanks, Merry, *Women and Gender in Early Modern Europe* (Cambridge, 3rd edn, 2008).

Wiesner-Hanks, Merry, *Challenging Women's Agency and Activism in Early Modernity* (University of Amsterdam Press: Amsterdam, 2021).
Winer, Rebecca, 'Conscripting the Breast: Lactation, Slavery, and Salvation in the Realms of Aragon and Kingdom of Majorca', *Journal of Medieval History*, 34 (2008), pp. 164–168.
Winer, Rebecca, *Women, Wealth, and Community in Perpignan, 1250–1300: Christians, Jews, and Enslaved Muslims in a Medieval Mediterranean Town* (Aldershot, 2006).
Wiślicz, Tomasz, *Love in the Fields: Relationships and Marriage in Rural Poland in the Early Modern Age: Social Imagery and personal Experience*, trans. George Szenderowicz (Warsaw, 2018).
Wormald, Jenny, 'Bloodfeud, Kindred and Government in Early Modern Scotland', *Past & Present*, 87 (1980), pp. 54–97.
Worthen, Hannah, 'Supplicants and Guardians: The Petitions of Royalist Widows during the Civil Wars and Interregnum, 1642–1660', *Women's History Review*, 26 (2017), pp. 528–540.
Ylikangas, Heikki, 'Huomenlahja Ruotsin keskiaikaisten lakien valossa', *Historiallinen aikakauskirja*, 65 (1967), pp. 14–25.
Youngs, Deborah, '"She Hym Fresshely Folowed and Pursued": Women and Star Chamber in Early Tudor Wales', in Bronach Kane and Fiona Williamson (eds.), *Women, Agency and the Law, 1300–1700* (London, 2013), pp. 73–85.
Youngs, Deborah, '"A Vice Common in Wales": Abduction, Prejudice and the Search for Justice in the Regional and Central Courts of early Tudor society', in Patricia Skinner (ed.), *The Welsh and the Medieval World: Travel, Migration and Exile* (Cardiff, 2018), pp. 131–153.

Online sources

A Dictionary of the Scottish Language, https://dsl.ac.uk/.
Dictionary of the Older Scottish Tongue, https://dsl.ac.uk
England's Immigrants 1330–1550, www.englandsimmigrants.com
English Pounds: Scots Pounds, http://www.pierre-marteau.com/currency/converter/eng-sco.html
Histoire des archives publiques en France, https://francearchives.fr/fr/section/87072855
Oxford English Dictionary, https://www.oed.com
Palmer, Robert C., Elspeth K. Palmer, and Susanne Jenks, 'The Anglo-American Legal Tradition', http://aalt.law.uh.edu/aalt.html
Scotland's People, https://www.scotlandspeople.gov.uk/

INDEX

abduction 7, 49–62
  abduction and consent 49–58
  violence 48, 49, 50, 51, 52, 54–55, 56, 57
adultery 34, 66, 90, 91, 93, 201
agency 5, 7
  of abducted women 48, 53, 58, 59
  and female litigants 63, 99, 101–102, 110, 173–174, 176, 177, 178, 180, 181–184, 186, 212
aldermen 48, 51, 52, 53, 54, 57, 58, 59
alimony 18–20, 70, 71, 75, 138, 140, 141, 147
Annals of Ulster 86
annuities 194, 197–198
arbitration 8, 17, 23, 35, 109, 152, 154, 155, 218
archival practices 210, 212, 221
arson 177, 179, 185
attachias writ *see* Chancery
attainder 6, 81, 82, 86–88, 91, 93

Balfour, Sir James: *Practicks* 137
Billingham (Co. Durham, England) 118, 120, 121, 122, 124
Bishop Middleham (Co. Durham, England) 118, 123, 124
Black Death 117, 126, 128
Blackstone, William: *Commentaries on the Laws of England* 100
Bohemia 4, 7, 63–75
Bolam (Co. Durham) 118, 120, 127
Book of Common Prayer 195
borough courts *see* courts

burgh courts (Scotland) *see* courts
Brabant, duchy of 48, 51
Bridgnorth (Shropshire), bailiffs of 108
Bristol 109
Brixen (South Tyrol) 153, 159, 162, 164, 165
Brno 63–67; Book of Law 54–67
Butler (family)
  earls of Ormond 82, 86, 87
  Edmund 91
  James, 4th earl of Ormond 86
  William, 7th baron of Dunboyne 81, 86–89, 90, 92

Caernarfon 1, 10
causae suspiconis/'cases of suspicion' 16
Chancellor of England 107, 108, 217, 218
Chancery *see* courts
Charles IV, Holy Roman Emperor 64
Charles IX of Sweden 175, 179
children
  legal guardians of 18, 21, 145, 146, 147
  legitimacy of 69, 70, 71, 138, 211, 212, 216
  maintenance of 8, 20, 146–147, 159, 162–163, 210, 211, 213, 216
  orphans 19, 34, 65, 176
  from previous marriages 143
  property and personal rights of 65
  and remarried widows 144–145
  stepchildren 146, 147, 174, 176, 177, 180, 184
church courts *see* courts

civil prosecution 139
clergy 36, 214, 218
Commentaries on the Laws of England (Blackstone) 100
Commissar judge (Scotland) 133, 138, 144, 147
community 155, 157, 159; *see also* neighbours; neighbourhood
Conisbrough (Yorkshire): manor court 118, 119, 121
consent 36–44, 59
  abductees and 56–58
  abduction and 49–51
  marriage and 32, 36–44, 49–56, 65, 68, 69, 73, 75
  in legal narratives 53–56
  legal value of 51–53
consistory courts *see* church courts
Council of Trent 44, 49
courts
  amercements 122, 123, 124, 127
  borough courts 116, 120, 122, 124 (*see also* town courts)
    of Crossgate 118, 119, 120, 122, 123, 124
  burgh courts (Scotland) 135, 138, 141
  Chancery, English court of 6, 7, 18, 99–115, 195
    bills 102–103
    certiorari writs 103, 107–108
    corpus cum causa writs 103, 104–107
    procedendo writs 103, 109–110
    sub pena writs 103–104
  Chancery, Irish court of 198–199, 202
  church courts 81, 103–104, 199, 200 (*see also* canon law; marriage)
    consistory courts (Ireland) 81, 195, 196, 199, 200
    commissary court: of Glasgow 133, 135, 137–148
    of Liège 51, 52, 53, 54, 58, 59
    of Paris 32–36, 37–44
    of Prague 63, 64, 67–74
  civil courts of South Tyrol 159–168
  Court of Common Pleas 100, 101
  Court of Delegates 196, 198, 199, 201
  Court of King's Bench (England) 100, 101
  Court of King's Bench (Ireland) 86
  Court of Requests 100, 101
  Court of Session (Scotland) 136
  equity courts 99, 100
  fees/cost of going to court 20, 25, 33–34, 84, 181, 199

  avoiding court fees 154, 162, 164
  fines 19, 33–34, 41, 49, 51, 91, 122, 124, 125, 180, 199, 212
  halmote courts 118, 119
  Imperial Chamber Court 156, 158
  leet courts 105, 108, 118, 119
  manorial courts (England) 107, 111, 116–119, 123, 127
  Palace Court (Marseille) 14, 15–16, 17, 18, 20
  Parlement (of Paris) 211–212
  sénéchausée (royal court of first instance, Lyon), 209, 211–220
  Svea Court of Appeal 173, 176–178
  town courts 1, 64, 104, 106, 109, 116, 120, 122, 124, 135, 138, 141, 162, 164, 165, 185
Coventry 105, 106
coverture 3, 100, 106, 107, 110, 116, 119, 120, 121, 122, 135, 173
Crossgate (Durham) *see* Durham
Cunningham (St Leger), Catherine Sarah 4, 196–205
Czech lands 63–75

Daletown (Yorkshire) 118
debt 19, 65, 91, 104, 106, 107, 108, 109, 110, 119–122, 123, 127, 138, 140, 143, 152, 153, 158, 178, 182, 219
déclarations de grossesse 211, 212
defamation 1, 90, 105, 140, 161, 179, 185
  denigration of character 200, 201, 203
  name-calling 90, 203
  slander 90, 176, 179, 185
Denny, Arabella 200
Denny, Arthur 200
detinue 108, 120
divorce/separation 6, 34, 66, 67, 68, 74, 75, 81, 90, 93, 108, 157
domestic/spousal violence 66–67, 69, 72, 75, 169, 203, 219
dower 3, 15, 22, 25, 82, 84, 87–89, 93, 198
  dower lands 6, 9, 81, 82, 86–93
dowry 14, 17, 18–22, 24–27, 35, 67; *see also* marriage portion
Dublin 193, 194, 195, 197, 198, 200, 201, 202
Dunboyne (co. Meath) 91
Durham 9
  bishopric estate 118, 121, 123, 124, 126, 127, 128
  borough of Crossgate 118, 119, 120, 122, 123, 124

priory estate 118, 119, 120, 121, 123, 124, 125, 127, 128

Edict on Clandestine Pregnancy (1556) 210–213
Edinburgh 138, 143
Edward II of England 82
Edward VI of England 83
elopement 48, 49, 50, 56, 58–59; *see also* abduction
equity
 courts 99, 100
 jurisdiction 81, 83, 92 (*see also* Chancery)
Eriksson [Tott], Tönne 174, 175
Erskine, Sir John: *Institutes of the Law of Scotland* 144, 145
executors/executrices 65, 85, 103, 104, 109, 120, 121, 142, 193

family; *see also* children; stepfamilies; stepchildren
 connections and influence in litigation 9, 82, 83, 85, 86. 93, 199, 203–204
 legal conflicts 22, 140, 158–167, 177–178, 180–183
 relationships 136, 137, 174–175
FitzGerald, Thomas, earl of Kildare 81, 83
FitzMaurice, William 194, 195, 198, 199, 200, 201, 202, 203, 204
Fournel, Jean François 212
France 4, 14–31, 32–47, 199, 209–222
 cataloguing of archives 211

Gävle (Sweden) 180
gender guardians 5, 154, 155, 156, 159, 160, 161, 162, 164, 165, 167, 168
George, Duke of Clarence 83
Ghent 53, 142
gifts *see* marriage
Glasgow 8, 9, 138, 139
 commissary court 133, 135, 137–148.
Great Repossession of 1680 (Sweden) 173
guardianship (legal); *see also* gender guardian
 of women 66, 100, 133 173, 176, 177, 186
 of children 18, 21
 marriage (giftoman) 176
Gustavus Adolphus, king of Sweden 178, 179

Henry VII of England 83
Henry VI of England 82–83, 86, 94
Hereford, bishop of 108
House of Lords (English) 194, 197, 198, 199, 202, 203, 204

House of Lords (Irish) 200
husbands; *see also* marriage; remarriage; widows
 authority of 3, 157, 158
 as co-litigant 142, 143, 147, 194
 violence by 69–72, 74
 as guardians 66, 173, 176–177
 wives represented by 179–180, 182, 186
 wives litigating without husbands 181–182, 186
 'negligence' 162
 'weakness' 163
Hussite Wars (1420–1436) 64

Imperial Chamber Court *see* courts
Ingelheim (Rhineland) 154
Ingleby Arncliffe (Yorkshire) 118
inheritance
 laws and practices 14, 21, 22, 65, 136, 140, 143, 145, 157, 158, 160
 partible 175
Ireland 3, 4; 81–98; 193–208
 court system 194
 ecclesiastical courts 194; 193
 legal infrastructure 83–85, 193
 parliament 83–85, 89, 91, 200
 Public Record Office of 193
 Wars of the Roses 82–83

Johansdotter, Elin 6, 9, 173–192
jointure 194, 197
jus mariti 137

Kastelruth (South Tyrol) 153
Kempe, Margery 42

law
 Brehon law 193
 canon law 49, 50, 53, 56, 59, 65–67, 73, 74 (*see also* church courts; marriage)
 civil law 153, 155, 159
 common law (England) 3, 84, 85, 88, 91, 92, 99–101, 106, 110, 116, 193
 customary law 57, 99, 118, 153, 193
 Gaelic law 193
 knowledge of, 7, 33, 36, 38, 40, 42, 44, 59, 110, 156, 164, 185, 216
 Roman law 15, 16, 17, 66, 154
 Saxon Code of Procedure (1622) 155–156
 town/municipal law 63, 65, 66, 67 (*see also* town courts)
  Brno 64
  Sweden 176

Tyrol Law Code (1532) 154
lawyers *see* legal counsel
Landesordnung 153
Leeson (FitzMaurice), Elizabeth 9, 194, 195, 198, 202–205
leet courts *see* courts
legal counsel 16, 27, 53, 56, 58, 59, 100, 102, 105, 121, 135, 139, 154, 174, 177, 178, 181, 182, 184–186, 196, 197, 198, 199, 200, 201, 204, 209, 211, 213, 214, 216, 218
legal records 1, 2, 4, 10, 48–50, 54, 63, 138, 193; *see also* scribes
  in archives 4, 16, 103, 194, 209, 210, 212
  format 102–103
  formulae and framing devices 5, 15, 35, 37, 84, 102, 105, 138–139
  historiography 50, 138, 193
  reliability of 5, 48, 50, 58, 138
  signatories to 178, 182–183
  study of 105
  written language of 17, 23, 35, 55
  Verfachbücher 153, 159
Leuven 48, 49, 51
  bailiff of 51, 52
leyrwite 123, 127
libel precept 139
litigants, proportion of female 2, 16, 34, 70, 8, 101, 119, 141–142, 16, 177
London 99, 104, 106–107, 108, 109, 124, 194, 196, 198, 199, 200, 201, 204
Loon, county of 51
love 53–56, 202
loveday 109; *see also* arbitration
Low Countries 7, 48–62
Lyon 209, 210, 211, 213

majority, age of 50, 176
manorial courts *see* courts
Maria Eleonora of Brandenburg 182
marriage; *see also* abduction; divorce/separation
  abandonment of 70, 72, 108
  age of, 213
  banns 195
  bigamy 44, 69–70, 73–74
  clandestine 43, 49, 65, 73, 74–75, 196, 201, 204, 205
  coerced marriage 7, 33, 36, 41, 45, 48
  consent 36–44, 49–56
  consummation 35–37, 39, 43
  contract disputes 33–35, 37–44, 63, 69–72, 72–73, 195–196, 196–198
  courtship 72; dowry 14, 17–20, 21–22, 24, 26, 35, 67, 196
  gifts, 38, 39, 68, 71, 90, 216
  guardian (giftoman) 176
  hand-clasping ritual 39, 40, 68
  morning gift 175, 176, 177, 178, 183
  portion 157, 159, 160, 162–165, 193
  pre-contract 72, 73
  pregnancy and 213, 214
  promises/expectations of 195, 209, 214, 216, 217, 218
  rings 73, 195
  spousal relations 65–67
  spousal disputes 66–69
  unsatisfactory marriages 73–74
marital property 133–135, 143, 152–153, 157, 159, 162, 163, 168; *see also* jointure
marital status (of women) 6, 8, 9, 67, 69, 81, 116, 120, 121, 127, 135, 136, 141–142, 143, 147, 148, 154, 155; *see also* coverture; married women
  and agency 176
  importance of 9
  recording of 120, 122, 127, 136–137, 143
married women
  as category 135, 136, 145, 147
  in court 3, 16, 66, 85, 100, 106, 116, 120, 121, 135–136, 137, 141–142, 143
  and husbands in court 16, 85, 100, 106, 107, 121, 181–182, 183, 186
  and natal families 22
  surnames 135 (*see also* coverture; marital status)
marital violence 69–72
martial service 91, 93
Marseille 6, 14–31, 35; legal structure in 15–17
Meath (Co. Westmeath) 86
  Bishop of 81, 90
  Sheriff of 91, 92
Mecklenburg 179
mediation *see* arbitration
midwives 211, 215
minors; *see also* children
  abduction of 50, 53, 56, 57
  guardianship of children 18, 173, 197
  marriages of 57
Much Wenlock (Shropshire) 108

narratives (legal) 6, 8, 48, 49, 57, 59
  consent in 53–56
neighbours
  as arbiters 168
  conflict between 152, 168

as witnesses 213, 214, 217
neighbourhood
  connections 42, 152, 155, 213, 220
  expectations of marriage 213
notaries 16, 17, 26, 27, 35, 37, 38, 39, 40, 42, 48, 102, 104, 137, 157
Nottingham 106, 116, 122
Nugent, Margaret 6, 9, 82–93
Nugent, Richard, Lord of Devlin 85–86, 88, 90–91

oaths 176, 178, 179, 180
oath-helper 121, 176

Paris 7, 32–47
  Officialité of 33–34
  Parlement of 211, 212
Parliament
  English parliament 85
  Irish 81–87, 89, 91, 92, 200
  prerogative court of 82
  private petitions in 81
  record 84, 85, 87, 88, 91, 92
  rolls 89
paternity suits 8, 209–222
petitions 15, 20, 82, 83–85, 88, 90, 92, 93, 103, 110–111
de Pizan, Christine 42
Plunkett, Margaret
  Memoirs 201, 202
poverty 6, 19, 84, 105, 106, 153, 177
  in forma pauperis 199
Prague
  diocese of 64
  marital disputes in ecclesiastical courts 67–74
pregnancy 7, 195, 197, 202, 210–220
  Edict on Clandestine Pregnancy 210, 211
  out-of-wedlock pregnancy 7, 212, 219–220
  'pregnancy declarations' 7, 210, 212, 213
prison 32, 103, 104, 105, 106, 107, 211, 217, 219
property; *see also* inheritance; marital property
  disputes 1, 134, 136, 141, 151, 154, 157, 176, 178, 179, 186
prostitution *see* sex work
Puster Valley (South Tyrol) 153

rape 51, 54, 214; *see also* abduction; sexual violence
ravishment 108; *see also* abduction

recognizances 107
remarriage/remarried widows 8, 9, 25, 26, 134–137, 139, 140, 142, 147, 164, 175, 180, 183, 186
  and children 144–145
  and husbands 139, 142, 143, 145, 146, 180
  property and status 125, 135–137, 144–147 176, 177, 179, 180, 183, 186
Richard, Duke of York 81, 83, 86
Richard II of England 82
Richard III of England 83

St. Helens Auckland (Co. Durham) 118, 120, 125, 127
St Leger, Arthur, 1st Viscount Doneraile 196
St Leger, Arthur, 2nd Viscount Doneraile 196, 198–199, 201, 203
sanctuary 107
scolds/scolding 119, 123, 124, 125
Scotland 3, 123, 134, 136, 139
  legal handbooks 134
  Scottish Reformation 137 (see also Glasgow; Edinburgh)
scribes 5, 50, 51, 102, 184, 186
  scribal conventions 120, 127, 128, 135, 142
seduction 53, 71
Senatus Consultum Velleianum 153
separation 6, 34, 66, 67, 68, 74, 81, 90, 93, 97; *see also* divorce
servants 85, 104–105, 123, 124, 126, 127, 140, 145, 146, 156, 162, 180, 181, 195, 196, 200, 201, 204
sexual activity 210, 214 215
  potential risks of 219
  premarital 218
  reproductive consequences of 211, 213, 217, 218
sex work 201, 202, 214
sexual violence 55, 215, 218; *see also* rape
Sigismund III Vasa, king of Sweden 175
singlewomen (unmarried women) 3, 9, 42, 104, 116, 121, 122, 137, 142, 156, 158, 173, 181, 183, 184, 186, 210, 211, 212, 213, 214, 215, 216, 218, 219, 220
slavery 23, 105, 219
Sonnenburg, abbey of 153, 159
southern Tyrol 6, 8, 152–172
  Tyrol Law Code of 1526 153–154, 158, 161, 165
Southwark 107, 108
Spain 4, 219

stepchildren/stepfamilies 73, 133, 134, 145, 146, 147, 157, 167, 174, 176, 177, 178, 179, 180, 181, 183, 184, 185, 186, 204
Stockholm 181, 183–186
Stöör, Hinrich 176, 178, 180, 181, 183, 184, 185
surgeons 215
Sweden: law 176–177
    Svea Court of Appeal 173, 176–178

Tametsi 44–45
tenants 8, 116, 117, 118, 119, 123–127, 128, 140
theft 86, 104, 106, 122, 156
Thomas FitzGerald, Earl of Kildare 81
Tönnesson [Tott], Eric 175, 176, 178, 180, 182
Toulouse 211
town courts *see* courts
trespass 1, 91, 101, 105, 106, 107, 109, 119–123, 125, 127

Upper Lusatia 69
Uppland, province of 174
Uppsala Castle 175, 179

violence 66–67, 124, 161
    abduction 48, 49, 50, 51, 52, 54–55, 56, 57
    coerced marriage 32, 33, 41
    domestic/spousal 66–67, 69–72, 75, 169, 203, 219
    physical 32, 66–67
    sexual 55, 215, 218
virginity 70, 71, 75
von Berfeldt, Joachim 175, 179, 181, 182, 183

von Loquin, Carl 175, 181, 182
von Wernstedt, Christoffer 176, 179, 180, 185

Wakefield (Yorkshire) 120, 121–122, 125
Wars of the Roses 82, 92
Westminster 42
    abbot of 107
    archdeacon of 107
Wexford, county of 87
widows 6, 14, 18–22, 24–27, 41, 69, 81–83, 85, 88, 89, 94, 104, 108, 109–110, 117, 158–159, 174, 175, 180, 184–185, 186, 194, 196
    agency 177–178
    and children 145–147, 159, 166–167
    identification of 126–127
    legal guardianship 173, 176, 177, 186
    remarriage 133–148, 180, 183, 186
    widowhood rights 134, 136, 144–147, 159, 163–166, 174, 198, 199
wills (testaments) 18, 25, 103, 104, 140, 166, 204
Winchester, bishop of 107
witnesses 9, 16, 17, 33, 34, 37, 38, 39, 40, 41, 42, 43, 44, 45, 52, 53, 65, 68, 70, 139, 155, 156, 178, 195, 196, 200, 201, 209, 210, 214, 216, 217, 220
    depositions 138
    interrogation 178
    lack of 37, 38, 39, 45, 63
    testimony 17, 23, 25, 35, 36, 41–42, 68, 214

York, Cause Papers 42, 43

Zittau 63, 64, 68, 69, 71–73
Zittauer Urkundenbuch 68, 70

Printed in the United States
by Baker & Taylor Publisher Services